Keggie Carew has lived in London, West Cork, Barcelona, Texas and New Zealand. Before writing, her career was in contemporary art. More recently, she has studied English Literature at Goldsmiths, run an alternative art space called JAGO, and opened a pop-up shop in the East End of London called theworldthewayiwantit. She lives near Salisbury.

DADLAND

Keggie Carew grew up in the gravitational field of an unorthodox father who lived on his wits and dazzling charm. As his memory begins to fail, she embarks on a quest to unravel his story, and soon finds herself in a far more consuming place than she had bargained for. Tom Carew was a maverick, a left-handed stutterer, a law unto himself. As a member of an elite SOE unit, he was parachuted behind enemy lines to raise guerrilla resistance in France, then Burma, in the Second World War. But his wartime exploits are only the start of it . . . Through her rackety English childhood, the poignant breakdown of her family, the corridors of dementia and beyond, Keggie pieces herself — and Tom — back together again, and celebrates the life of an impossible, irresistible, unstoppable man.

KEGGIE CAREW

◆

DADLAND

Complete and Unabridged

CHARNWOOD
Leicester

First published in Great Britain in 2016 by
Chatto & Windus
an imprint of Vintage
London

First Charnwood Edition
published 2018
by arrangement with
Vintage
Pengion Random House
London

This book is a work of non-fiction based on the life,
experiences and recollections of the author and her
father. In some limited cases the names of people
and the details of events have been changed solely to
protect the privacy of others.

A catalogue record for this book is available
from the British Library.

ISBN 978–1–4448–3640–0

Published by
F. A. Thorpe (Publishing)
Anstey, Leicestershire

Set by Words & Graphics Ltd.
Anstey, Leicestershire
Printed and bound in Great Britain by
T. J. International Ltd., Padstow, Cornwall

This book is printed on acid-free paper

For Patrick, Nicky and Tim,
who each have their own versions;
this is only mine.

'Birds prefer trees with dead branches,' said Caravaggio. 'They have complete vistas from where they perch. They can take off in any direction.'

Michael Ondaatje, *The English Patient*

Contents

FAMILY TREE

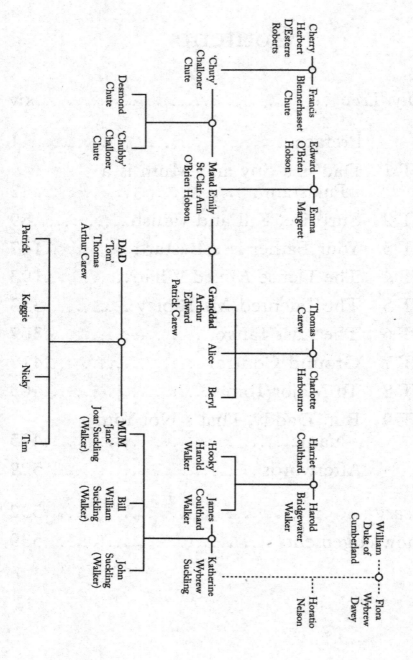

Preface

It is 1964. I am seven, and barely eye level with the counter of the hardware shop in Fareham High Street. Dad is buying paint. We have been in the shop a while and I'm getting bored. He is joking with the shop assistant. He hasn't enough cash to pay for everything so he gets his chequebook out. I smile inwardly, because I have just thought up a trick. On tiptoe I look over the counter as Dad signs the cheque, my eyes following his pen as it glides across the bottom right-hand corner. I squint a little, manage to hold my excitement in, then say, 'But Daddy, that's not your name.'

Dad looks down at me. The shop assistant looks down at me, then straight at Dad. I look up at them. Oh, delicious freeze-frame moment for I have got the world to stop. I stretch it out with my round child's eyes. Power. A tiny taste of it. I have trounced him at his own game, the bluff, the double bluff, which is it? Dad laughs uncomfortably. They are the minutest flickering seconds when he doesn't know what to do, but they are enough. The shop assistant looks back and forth.

'You rotter!' Dad says in his foghorn voice. 'You sod!'

This is obviously quite new for the shop assistant. Who, even as he takes the cheque and rings the till, is not a hundred per cent sure. We

1

leave the shop. I am prancing with victory because behind the bluster I know Dad is tickled pink. Because I had him on the hop — which is normally *his* mischief. I was not to know it then, but I had taken my first unwitting step into his world. A place where you never quite knew where you were. Where even this ruse of mine about his name turned out to be, in a way, right on the money.

PART 1

DAD IS A SPY
AND MUM IS A PAKISTANI

1

My dad is cutting a hole in a two-litre plastic milk bottle. The hole is opposite the handle so he can pee into it and hold it at the same time. It's his favourite invention. For now. He's making one for me and won't be persuaded otherwise. He has them all over the house in case he gets caught short. Still very practical, then. Going through his pockets for a penknife I find a note. It says, *My name is Tom Carew, but I have forgotten yours.* He has been giving this note to everyone.

* * *

I'm showing Dad a picture of Mum. I often do this when he comes to stay. The photograph of Mum sits on the windowsill in a silver frame next to a photograph of him. A posthumous needle at my stepmother.

'What relationship with that woman?' Dad asks.

'Your wife,' I tell him. 'My mother. Jane.'

'Really?'

'Yes.'

'Incredible!'

'Yes.'

'I can see it now.' His voice is a little wistful.

'Good.'

'Incredible . . . ' His voice trails off; he is

5

holding the photograph. 'Is that my wife?'

'Yes. She was,' I tell him. 'Your first wife.' Actually she was his second but we won't go back that far. Nor do we mention the third.

'Incredible,' he says. 'Is it really? What's her name?'

'Jane,' I say.

'I've drifted,' he says. 'Haven't I?'

'Yes, Dad,' I laugh, 'you certainly have.'

The photograph is a black-and-white picture he took in 1953, just after they were married and went to live in Gibraltar, where he was stationed, and where my elder brother, Patrick, and I were born. Mum, her salty loose curls, smiling, a ripple of sea behind.

'What's her name?' he asks again.

'Jane.'

'She's very attractive,' he says.

'Yes, she is.'

A glint ignites both eyes, 'So how can that be your mother?'

Touché. He's in a good mood. But what he far prefers is photos of himself.

'You're an egomaniac, Dad.'

'A *what?*'

'E-go-ma-ni-ac,' I enunciate slowly.

Jonathan, my husband, looks askance. Tries to clip me with his eye.

'Hego-nami-hat?' Dad says.

I deal out a photograph of him in dashing army uniform.

'Who's that?' he asks.

'Who do you think?'

'Is that me?'

'Yup.'

'GO ON!' he chides. He's enjoying himself. Centre of attention again. 'How old am I there?'

'Twenty. Twenty-one.'

'No! How old am I now?'

'Ninety-seven,' I lie.

'I'm not.'

'You are.'

'Really?'

'Really.'

'I can't be.'

'Eighty-seven then.'

'Eighty-seven?'

'I promise.'

He looks at me as if I've gone mad.

★   ★   ★

Dad loves it here. Which has its problems. He doesn't want to go home. He won't sleep in a room but stays in a shed in the garden with his two dogs who sleep with him, and who are allowed *to do anything they want*. Jonathan calls the little one Psycho Dog. It guards things. When Dad tries to get into bed it sits bang in the centre of his pillow then growls and spits if you try to move him off. In the morning I invariably find Dad at the bottom of the bed, no bedclothes, foetally curled, trying to keep warm, with the dogs stretched out slap in the middle. Yet he won't have it any other way. Dad is an easy guest, and, at the same time, a very high-maintenance one. He thinks we are always

7

in the garden in the sun. Having drinks. Picking veg. Talking about him. He feels useful here. And all he wants is jobs. Seven a.m.: 'Give me a job.' From dawn till dusk every day: 'What's my next job?' They are getting harder to find. Something he'll succeed at, something that doesn't bore him, something that will give him a sense of achievement at the end. If possible, something where he can invent *a better way of doing it* — with a piece of string, a bungy-clip, or No More Nails, which he applies with his hands straight from the nozzle and then wipes all over *my* fleece, which he is wearing because, just before he came, he unpacked all his clothes and brought three Mars bars and two rolls of kitchen towel instead. Any job with his penknife is popular, such as cleaning lichen off the garden chairs. That lasts an hour. But penknife jobs are high risk, however much he likes them, because he gets carried away: scrape, scrape, cut, cut, gouge, gouge. Washing seed trays is safe, if dull, but he can put them all over the lawn to dry, and this, pleasurably, looks like a lot of work. There should be *A Book of Jobs* for the demented, for I am running low. Mentally, Dad is shot; physically, he's indestructible. Nothing tires him. He can touch his toes. Pain doesn't affect him. He has *never* had anaesthetic at the dentist, and still does his own first aid. Apart from yesterday, when he came back from trimming the hedge and was compelled to ask for a plaster. I reeled back in horror at the saucer-sized wound in the palm of his hand where a length of old Sellotape had worn away revealing a shiny scarlet swathe of no-skin.

'You *can't* use secateurs with a wound like that! Why didn't you tell me?'

'Don't be ridiculous!'

★ ★ ★

Dad has lost the word for an *orange* (the soft 'o'), and for me, but not *fastidious* or *scrumptious*, and other slightly old-fashioned words. While I don't seem to have a gender, I do have an 'industry' — which he wants to join (run, more like). His business and my business could work together.

'But I don't have a business, Dad.'

'Not business. You know. Your thing. Your . . . your industry. Your . . . I could be in production for you.'

He is looking at me hopefully.

But all I can give him is a sigh.

I place another photograph in his hand.

'Who's that?' he asks.

'Who do you think?'

It was taken in 1963. I know this because of the snowman — the infamous freeze of '63. I point to the tall man in the brick-red canvas sailing smock, smoking a pipe.

'You,' I say.

'No!'

'Yes, it is.'

'What, the man with the pipe?'

'Yes,' I point. 'There's Mum with Nicky, there's Patrick in the middle, and that's me.'

9

'No!' Then his voice goes nostalgic. 'You were sweet once.'

In five minutes he will have forgotten and we can do it all again.

* * *

'How old am I?' he asks.

'You're eighty-seven, Dad.'

He looks downcast.

'I never thought I'd go bonkers,' he says.

'You've only lost your memory, but you've got everything else. Look at you. You can still touch your toes. You're not an old crock!'

'Lucky to have no memory,' he says.

I look at him quizzically.

'I'm happy to have my mind totally on those dogs. And I don't mind you either!'

* * *

At school I told my teachers Dad was a spy, and Mum (who was born in Quetta) was a Pakistani. They didn't believe me on either count. So, next day I took in the yellowing 1945 newspaper cuttings from the *Statesman*, and the *Times of India*, and the *Daily Sketch*. They referred to Dad, thrillingly, as 'Lawrence of Burma', or 'Colonel X'.

Times of India
'Lawrence of Burma'
Irishman's Exploits As
Secret Service Agent

Known among his colleagues as 'the mad
Irishman', a 25-year-old professional soldier who was formerly a gunner, today has
the reputation of being 'the Lawrence of
Burma'. A Secret Service agent who has
organised guerrilla bands of natives to
harass Jap lines of communications and
send intelligence reports to British military
commanders, his name cannot yet be
revealed, but a partial story of the work he
and other British officers have done can
now be told.

The Irishman, who is now a lieut-
colonel, hails from Dublin. He joined the
army when he was 17. His wife was formerly an ATS ack-ack gunner stationed
with a battery in Hyde Park, London. He
married her after he returned from the
French-Swiss border where he had helped
to organise the Maquis. After a honeymoon
of three short days he was flown to Burma
and dropped into Arakan by parachute.
His Colonel and Commanding officer of
this Secret Service intelligence outfit is a
tall stout-built Scotsman with a profound
knowledge of Burma . . . 'The mad Irishman,' said the Colonel to me, 'admits
himself that he has never been any further
east than Regent Street, London. When he
was told he would have to jump into the

11

jungle in Burma he just gave us one of his blarney Irish smiles and said: 'So I am to jump into the dense mixed what?''

The article goes on to describe the nature of these missions — how agents risked their lives organising the native Burmese into guerrilla bands to sabotage the enemy. How some were caught and tortured or beheaded by the Japanese, but most outwitted them. It said the guerrilla forces 'killed as many as 1,500 Japs'.

★   ★   ★

'Did *you* ever kill anyone, Dad?' I recall asking as a child.

'Um. Well,' he hesitated.

I could see him thinking about it, which was a little chilling.

'No, I don't think I *personally* killed anyone,' he said.

Maybe he thought I meant with his bare hands . . .

★   ★   ★

As Dad slowly leaves us, I try to haul him back — from the bottom of cardboard boxes and forgotten trunks; from letters buried in desks; from books I previously had not known about; from photographs I am unfamiliar with; from diaries never meant for my eyes. I am the manic charity-shop rummager rifling through old clothes. I don't know why I have taken on this

12

task; as it is, I've been under the gravitational pull of his influence far too long. Except that suddenly I need to make some sense of it all. It's not just Dad I want to stick back together again. This is an exorcism. And a ghost hunt. Rebuild him. Rebuild me.

2

Aside from the newspaper cuttings I paraded at school, and the few anecdotes Dad told, I knew little about the real story of his secret war. He rarely talked about it, and we, his children, at the centre of our own universes, rarely asked. When I came to think about it, I knew embarrassingly little about his life, *before us*, at all. Born in Dublin in 1919, brought up in Cambridge; he met Mum in Trieste; my brother, Patrick, and I were born in Gibraltar (1955, 1957); we came back to England; they bought a house in Fareham in Hampshire in 1958, where my sister Nicky and younger brother Tim were born (1959, 1961); that was about it. Dad *always* rooted himself in the present, and since he'd remarried in 1976, any reminiscences pre-Stepmother, in the omnipresence of her earshot, were in one way or another shut down. Unless she took them over . . . for I came to learn Dad's past was under ownership and there were laws of trespass — of which I had better be mindful. In discombobulated half-sentences and (to my ear) ostentatious tone, Stepmother commandeered the telling of Dad's story of being in the 'You know, you know, SOE! Secret Operations Executives.' It would have been wise to judge my words carefully, but tact was never my best game and I would correct her: 'SPECIAL, SOE was for *Special* Operations Executive.' For I knew that much; and that SOE was set up during the Second World War by Churchill to conduct irregular warfare; its mission to orchestrate and aid resistance against the enemy from inside France and the other occupied territories. Special Operations Executive, with an emphasis, as insiders liked to put it, on the O. Clever little teenage shit. It was also known as Churchill's Secret Army; the Baker Street Irregulars (the HQ was in Baker Street); and sometimes the Ministry of Ungentlemanly Warfare. Stepmother's shoulder pads might puff up a millimetre or two, but solely to re-oxygenate those magnificent lungs. 'You know your father was, was, a secret agent, and er, doing all sorts of things, parachuting and what-have-you, and er, er . . . ' There was a correlation: the less information, the more commanding the voice. 'He, you know, got the Croix de Guerre!' she'd brag loudly. While Dad would only laugh.

I also knew that Dad was a Jedburgh, which I accepted without understanding what it actually meant. I could hear the bray of Stepmother's voice, 'Jedbraaaaagh . . . ' An instinct for self-preservation guided me: better not to ask. I might have intercepted Dad on his own, but for some reason I did not. Conversations of this kind had a peculiar way of doubling back to Stepmother, leading to competition, one-upmanship, jealousy: not Dad's of course, but hers, and mine.

Stepmother never failed to let us know when they had been to an SOE reception at the Club (Special Forces Club), or a memorial service at Westminster Abbey, or the American Embassy,

15

or the French Embassy, or a Jedburgh reunion at Peterborough Cathedral, or 'a marquee luncheon [yes, she said, luncheon] courtesy of the Countess Fitzwilliam'. After a Jedburgh reunion in France Stepmother remembered the Countess of Paris 'and what-have-you', while Dad, on the back of their itinerary, had scrawled: *It's a pantomime*. Neither would she pass over the opportunity to lavishly recount the occasions of meeting the charming daughter or son of a fellow Jedburgh accompanying their parent to these functions, secure in the knowledge that, with her as gatekeeper, no such invitation would be afforded to us. We knew better than to ask; the rules were unspoken and understood. Not by Dad, blithely oblivious of any eye-daggers shot in our direction if we ever got ahead of ourselves. For years I believed he knew exactly what the score was, but I was wrong. The strictures laid down by our stepmother would never have been believed by Dad because they were simply inconceivable to him. Things that did not exist in his own make-up found little space in his imagination. He could be curiously naive for such a worldly man. Sadly I was not so guileless. For me — in Stepmother Territory — as the least compliant yet possibly least robust of Dad's children, the safest distance from the subject was well away. Until in the autumn of 2003, long before I, or my siblings, (or anyone) would have dared anticipate, Stepmother died and Dad's door was wide open once again.

Dad needed help. At eighty-four he was shattered by grief and utter exhaustion and (unknown to us) had begun to suffer tiny strokes in his brain. However hard he tried to hide his memory gaps we began to notice — not that he was forgetting things, he had always forgotten things. It was the *type* of things he was forgetting: our names; his address. And less easy for me to accept, his comprehension of everyday stuff was sliding too: how his bedside light switched on; where the voices on the radio were coming from; why he had to *wait* for the kettle to boil. We put it down to stress and bereavement until finally my sister took him to the doctor who sent him for a scan.

★   ★   ★

I keenly and selfishly felt the irony of the timing: the first time in thirty years I was able to spontaneously pick up the phone, without the mental preparation, without Stepmother hurdles to navigate, without the anxious dread, was the moment Dad began to disappear. Small clusters of brain cells dying. Minute infarcts. Obstruction of the blood supply to the cerebral tissue. Oxygen not getting as far as it should. Everything floating in suspension, but just out of reach: his past, his life, his world. Him. Dad was bewildered, frustrated and confused. We showed him photographs to try to jog his memory, but nothing coherent seemed to click. 'What?' 'Who?' 'Where?' I felt like a stranger gaping in. And I was fuming with Stepmother. I had glumly accepted my lot, but here was a last unexpected chance to spend the slimmest slice of time with

17

him *out* of the Restriction Zone, and it was too late. I spat futilely down the phone to my sister, 'She sucked every last drop out of him, and now when *he* needs help for once, she's not even bloody here!' As far as I could see she couldn't have organised it better if she'd tried.

One minor satisfaction was that with Stepmother gone I could at least rummage around in the attic. Which was how I began this journey: casual, unwary, cross-legged in front of two metal trunks, the musty smell of old letters pulling me into a world I had no idea about. The first foray produced an exciting haul. I stacked up letters, photographs, all Granddad's pocket diaries: *Letts, Collins, Farmer and Stockbreeder, The Universal*, every year since 1923; there were two cassette tapes in their plastic boxes labelled in Dad's handwriting: *Tom talking to Dr Robert Taylor on Burma, 1978*; two A4 bound manuscripts; and the 1945 Indian newspaper cuttings I hadn't seen since I was a child.

I took a bundle downstairs to show Dad. 'Look at this! 'Colonel X, an Irish agent who can't be named . . . ''

The first manuscript was a slim spiral-bound document with the Special Forces insignia (a wing either side of the initials SF in a red circle) on the cover: *The Jedburghs: A Short History*, by Arthur Brown. The second manuscript was fatter and glued to a cloth spine with Japanese calligraphy across its pale lemon cover. Dad had written across the top: *JEDS — Tom Carew, see yellow tabs*. Inside, its title: *A Postscript to Arthur Brown's The Jedburghs: A Short*

18

History, compiled by Glyn Loosmore. I let the pages fan into my hand. Dad's handwriting in different-coloured pens, annotated up and down the margins in blocks and leaning towers, skimming in and out of paragraphs, exclamation and question marks sandwiched between the text.

Dad was thrilled by my finds; with fat felt-tip coloured markers he labelled a cardboard box for me to carry home: **KEGGIE IS THE CUSTODIAN OF TOM'S WAR — STORAGE JOB**.

Two months later, in early February 2004, a smart embossed invitation arrived in the post for Dad to attend 'The 60th Jedburgh Anniversary': a weekend-long reunion to be held in Peterborough. My sister wanted to know, Would I go with him?

Yes, I certainly would.

3

It is 11 June. High summer. Hot sun, blue sky. I am on the train from Salisbury to London to meet Dad and take him on to Peterborough. I have bagged a table and made a stack of everything I've brought about the Jedburghs in front of me. Some letters, maps, photocopied pages from books, and the two A4 manuscripts — each, it turns out, the devoted labour of a Jed (as they like to be called). I am chiding myself for leaving it until now to begin my reading in earnest. *The Postscript* follows the Jedburgh story beyond France into the Far East, which explains the Japanese calligraphy — a haiku by the seventeenth-century poet, Basho: 'Summer grasses, all that is left of the dreams of soldiers.' These two manuscripts are to become my introduction to what the Jedburghs were about.

Ten minutes into my journey I become increasingly aware of the attention of a distinguished-looking man sitting diagonally opposite me. His eyes flicker back and forth from map to upside-down page. I can tell he *knows* something. He clears his throat and introduces himself. He is Michael Tillotson, military obituarist to *The Times*, and he is intrigued by my reading matter. Astonishing how quickly, once you've begun to rub the lamp a little, how odd coincidences, which so often feel propitious, begin to occur. I explain I'm on my

20

way to meet my father to go to the sixtieth anniversary of a special unit of SOE. What special unit? my travelling companion wants to know. The Jedburghs, I tell him. He sits up a little straighter. Yes, he knows about the Jeds. I explain I am trying to read up as much as I can, for *I* know very little. We talk about wartime resistance in France and later in Burma, and the coming reunion; I bite my lip with instant regret as a boast slips out when I mention Dad's Distinguished Service Order, one of the highest decorations for gallantry. He smiles politely, he would like to write the reunion up in *The Times* he tells me; he gives me his card and I promise to send him some information.

Statesman of India, Friday 18 May 1945
'Lawrence of Arabia' methods in Railway Demolition

By Stuart Gelder

British officers and men with Burma volunteers have parachuted among and behind Japanese positions during the past few months to assist guerrilla resistance, gather intelligence and do demolition work. Some of them came straight from France, where they had been fighting with the Maquis . . . Within a week or two of landing in India some of them, knowing the geography of the country only from books and not a word of the language, were falling through the moonlight into jungle clearings with radio sets, light arms and as much ammunition as they could carry . . . They blew up railway lines, organised scouts to report Japanese movements and were able to signal useful information about targets to the RAF . . . One of the most daring of these officers is a young Irish lieutenant colonel who parachuted into Arakan in December.

The sixtieth reunion is in Peterborough because of its proximity to Milton Hall, the requisitioned stately home where the Jedburghs were trained in 1944. We are staying at the Bull. Everyone is milling in a scrum of greetings in the hotel foyer. 'Hello, Tom!' 'Hello!' Dad pats a shoulder. He can't remember anybody's name. The direction of flow is jostling towards the bar where, luckily, as well as a drink, we are handed name tags. There are twenty-two out of the original 300 Jedburghs here, including the American and French Jeds who have come to England especially for the occasion, accompanied by wives, daughters and sons; there are widows too, and the children of Jeds killed in action or no longer with us. I look about me. A bobbing sea of whitecaps, an eyepatch, a shiny pate, a black beret, pressed shirts, ties, blazers, name tags pinned to lapels; sprightly eighty-five-year-olds, a stoop here and there, but hardly a paunch in the room. They have been meeting up like this only in the last fifteen years. I shake hands, introducing myself. Ron Brierley; Dick Rubinstein; John Sharp — Dad's radio operator

22

in Burma — and his wife, Ivy. From the outside we might seem like a Darby & Joan Club, charity volunteers or an *Antiques Roadshow* do. No outward sign that I am in a room of firebrands, mettlesome kittle cattle, mischief-makers and mavericks.

★ ★ ★

Roll back sixty years. The men were in their early twenties and Britain had been at war with Germany for four years. France was shot through with the creeping poison of Nazi occupation and ravaged psychologically, geographically, economically. The climate was one of fear and betrayal. There were pockets of underground resistance known as 'the Maquis' — a Corsican word used to describe the scrubby underbrush and mountain thickets claimed by outlaws, adopted by the partisans, or *maquisards*, who had taken to the hills. But the Maquis were lacking in arms, supplies, manpower and expertise, and by 1944 many had been caught and shot. The Gestapo meted out appalling reprisals to their families and any person who might have supported them. Thousands were deported to labour camps; hangings and public executions by firing squad were rife in partisan areas, and in extreme cases whole villages were burned to the ground. Not surprising, then, were the increasing instances of collaboration with the enemy, or at least, compliance; the choice most made was to save their skin. Since 1942, SOE's F Section had been inserting French-speaking agents into France to lay down the foundations for a resistance and build up sabotage circuits, but the work was extremely high risk and many had been detected, their networks infiltrated or disbanded. By 1944, the Allies had all sorts of misgivings about what kind of help might be relied upon from inside France. There were reports of poor security, infighting and power struggles between local Maquis leaders, besides all the other problems that went with leading a clandestine life in the forest. Most French men of fighting age had been transported to German labour camps under the Service du Travail Obligatoire,[1] which meant in 1944 the majority of Maquis recruits were hot-headed boys of sixteen or middle-aged men, untrained, undisciplined and inexperienced, driven by anger, revenge, or simply the need to escape being sent to Germany. So it is easy to see where the confidence deficit came from. Come the invasion the Allies would need a viable resistance that was disciplined and co-ordinated. Which was where the Jedburghs came in. Their job would be to turn these resistance cells into an armed guerrilla network able to sabotage the Germans, and rise — when required — to support the Allied invasion. Discreet, highly trained, guerrilla warfare experts.

The story goes that when the director of SOE was trying to think of a code name for his new special unit, the train he was travelling on paused at the Scottish Borders town of Jedburgh (a

---

[1] The 1942 scheme, introduced by Germany, triggered the inception of many Maquis bands who fled to the hills to escape the labour camps.

place associated with bandit raids on English settlements in the sixteenth century and for what was known as Jedburgh Justice: execution first, trial afterwards). Others hold the name was merely a blind finger landing on a page of meaningless words. Either way, Jedburghs they became.

Three hundred volunteers recruited from the armed forces of Britain, America and France (the French contingent coming from regiments stationed in NW Africa when Germany invaded France). Three men to a team; one hundred teams. In each team: two officers and a radio operator. One officer would be British or American, the other had to be French.[1] The teams would be parachuted into enemy-occupied territory at night where there was known to be resistance activity or potential — they would attach themselves to the local Maquis, establish direct short-wave wireless communication with London, arrange arms drops, train the partisans; then plan and carry out tactical operations. No more random acts of sabotage that only irritated the Germans, but specific targeting: blowing key transport lines; cutting enemy communications, laying ambushes. First of all, to stop Hitler getting reinforcements to Normandy after D-Day once the Allies had landed; and then, do everything possible, right across France, to thwart their retreat.

---

[1] Or the nationality of the enemy-occupied country where the team would operate — eight teams were dropped in Holland.

25

The Jedburghs were the first direct collaboration between the American and British Secret Services: British SOE and American OSS (Office of Strategic Services — precursor of the CIA), combining as SFHQ (Special Forces Headquarters) which would come under General Dwight D. Eisenhower's jurisdiction in the combined British and American force: SHAEF (Supreme Headquarters of the Allied Expeditionary Force). It wasn't quite as cosy as far as the French were concerned. Personal relations between Charles de Gaulle, the querulous French leader in exile, and his principal allies, Churchill and Roosevelt, were frosty and suspicious, still smarting from the swift and shocking French capitulation of 1940. While there were diplomatic consultations with the French, French channels had the reputation of being notoriously lax on security, so as far as specific details of the planned invasion were concerned, de Gaulle was excluded.

Someone is tapping a glass with a spoon.

Dad and I have both drained our glasses of wine. A man consulting a sheaf of papers is telling us what time the coaches are coming, what time supper is, going through the itinerary. It's a humbling experience meeting this handful of surviving Jeds. They're a lawless rackety bunch, and I am beginning, quite quickly, to get an idea of what the SOE recruiters were looking for. Even now, in their eighties, they mutter irreverently and heckle during the welcome speeches. Someone shouts something from the back, and they all shout in unison, 'Some shit!' A roar of laughter. I am bewildered. Ten minutes

26

later it happens again. Someone shouts, 'Forty-eight!' Then half the room responds: 'Forty-nine! Fifty!' And everyone bellows, 'SOME SHIT!' They dissolve into laughter. This, I discover, is the Jedburgh tradition reserved for any speaker who dares to go on too long. It came from one of the American trainees who, when ordered to do fifty push-ups, counted the last few out loud: 'Forty-eight. Forty-nine. Fifty!' then jumped to attention with a very audible, 'Some shit!' The British Jeds parodied it and it quickly caught on as a tactic to sabotage boring lectures from visiting officials, and now pops up at the merest provocation — as a Jed hallmark.

4

Milton Hall. The Jedburgh nursery. Our first outing by coach is a visit to the house, long since back in private ownership. Seat of the Fitzwilliams when the first stone was laid in 1594. It's a massive pile set in a 600-acre park with thirty acres of gardens and a large ornamental lake with an island, all looking very idyllic, surrounded by sheep. Hard to imagine the wartime scene sixty years ago: the accommodation huts, the rows of khaki-coloured tents, the obstacle courses, the demolition pits and firing ranges, every type of German and French vehicle lined up to practise on; the truck ruts scribbled across the great lawns.

Milton Hall, it transpires, is the house where Margaret Thatcher received the phone call in 1982 telling her Argentina had invaded the Falkland Islands; it is also the house that kindled the imagination of Daphne du Maurier when she visited as a child — her impressions of Milton sowed the first seeds of inspiration for Manderley, the setting for *Rebecca*. I learnt of Milton Hall's connection to *Rebecca* whilst watching a repeat of a 1971 BBC documentary on du Maurier presented by young Oxford posh-boy, Wilfred De'ath. Candy-striped laundered shirt, big fat tie, clever bordering on cocky; De'ath *also* turns out to be not what he seems. Feted as a bright new TV presenter, he chucked it all in and spent a decade swanning from fancy hotel to fancy hotel to the nick, without ever paying a bill. The type of *neck* required to enable this brand of swindling would, I can't help thinking, be second nature to a good Jed, and reminds me of the deportment Dad deployed when he lived in London in his van and required the use of the Ritz's bathrooms. Chest out, head up, striding in, greeting everyone, as if he owned the place.

Disgorged from the coach at the back of the house we are shown about. We visit the walled vegetable garden where you can still see the bullet holes from the Jeds' shooting practice pockmarking the old brick. Harry Verlander, a Jed wireless operator, remembers there were thirty rounds of ammunition available for practice every day. He says it was not unusual for shots to be taken at any promising target. Some of the livestock escaped, but the clock and weathervane were not so lucky. In one room of the house a display of Jedburgh memorabilia has been set up: Sten guns, pistols, American carbines, knives, maps, parachute jumpsuits, grenades, fuses, detonators, black-and-white photographs of blown-up bridges and trains, and a rather heavy-looking wireless transmitter built into a suitcase. It's a B2 short-wave radio set, the kind used at the time by most SOE agents in the field. It was too cumbersome for the Jeds and needed a power source — which made the chance of detection higher, so a modified version called the Jed Set was developed which could be carried in a canvas backpack and operated in the open, powered by a hand-crank generator. The Jed Set was their most vital equipment, it had a 600-mile range, and weighed thirty pounds, including a spare battery.

★ ★ ★

We meet Tommy MacPherson of team Quinine, and his radio operator, Arthur Brown — author of *The Jedburghs* manuscript. Guest of honour is Daphne Park, the Jedburghs' cypher instructor, now Baroness Park of Monmouth. Daphne became an unlikely legend as a Cold War spy, famous (among the initiated) for burning top-secret documents and hiding the ashes in her knickers.

Her face lights up, 'Hello, Tom!'

Dad stretches his arms towards her and gives her a whopping kiss.

Daphne was recruited into *the secret side of things* after her over-elaborate answer on cyphers failed her an examination in encryption for the FANYs (First Aid Nursing Yeomanry). Her paper found its way into the hands of the head of coding at the Special Operations unit, who recognised a unique brilliance and employed her straight away. Daphne taught coding in the dairy barn at Milton Hall until she called a senior officer 'incompetent' and was sacked for insubordination. After the war she became a controller for MI6. She is a warm but formidable presence and it doesn't surprise me to learn she lists 'Difficult places' as a recreation in *Who's Who*. In the Belgian Congo coup of 1960 she smuggled Prime Minister Lumumba's private secretary to safety in the boot of her 2CV. An excellent cover, she assures us, because nobody took a 2CV seriously; the secretary was to become head of intelligence in the new government and one of Daphne's most useful sources. The cypher system Daphne taught the Jedburghs is called the One-Time Pad — mathematically unbreakable and still used today. Each radio operator was given a unique pad of randomly generated cypher tables — each sheet could be used only once to encrypt a message then had to be destroyed; to decipher the message an identical twin pad was kept at the receiving station.

The radio operators not only had to be proficient at high Morse speeds (at least twenty-five words per minute instead of the usual army speed of ten to twelve), but know their radio sets inside out and the intricacies of running repairs under very primitive conditions. In case anything happened to the radio operator everyone had to be competent in cyphers; if the pad was lost, each agent had a special poem that only he and his home station knew. Dad said he forgot his poem the moment he got on the plane.

We walk about, they joke and reminisce. The Jeds began their day at 6.00 a.m. and finished at 9.00 p.m., if there weren't night exercises. By the end of the training there would be nothing about guerrilla warfare they wouldn't know: how to blow up a train, a tree, a railway line, a road, a canal, a factory, a power station, a dam, a reservoir, high-tension pylons; they had to be able to set a mine, attach a clam, lay tyre-bursters, throw a grenade by instinct, neutralise a booby trap, prepare an ambush. There was observation and memory training; intelligence-gathering; how to conduct surveillance; how to know if you were being followed; reception techniques for receiving air-dropped supplies; night parachuting; there were lessons in unarmed combat, silent killing and survival; they would have to be able to swim with a limpet mine and pitch a lump of plastic explosive into a moving train.

I look at Dad quizzically. 'Silent killing?'

He shrugs his shoulders.

★　★　★

Someone mentions their self-defence instructor, William Fairbairn, schooled in the oriental arts having spent thirty years as a policeman in Shanghai. He taught them joint manipulation, pressure points, nerve centres, and how to dispatch a sentry silently. After a few sessions with Fairbairn they knew exactly how to use their fists, elbows and knees to inflict serious damage to the body's delicate areas; they learnt chin-jabs, headbutts, fingertip jabs; how to kick; how to escape from wrist holds, throat holds (one hand/two hands), body holds (front/ rear), and what they called 'Come with me' holds (being held by the collar with one arm forced up the back). Fairbairn's usual advice was to follow each manoeuvre with a good kick in the groin.

```
Never fail to carry the sentry out of
the  way  when  killed  or  captured.
```

32

Impress on students the necessity for speed, silence and practised co-operation. Point out the circumstances under which it would be foolish to attack a sentry at all. Practise all of the above in the dark. Aim at tying up and gagging a sentry in under 2.5 mins.

Not surprising they enjoyed themselves. Knife fighting at speed — where to aim, which arteries to cut; how to shoot a .45 calibre pistol instinctively — going straight into a semi-crouch firing two shots in rapid succession, something they were told to practise continually as they walked around the camp. That must have been a sight: 300 men randomly dropping to their knees like cowboys quick-drawing their guns. Drills in reloading, over and over, until they could change a magazine at lightning speed — something they would have to be able to do blindfolded as if they were fighting from a cellar, or a ditch, or on a dark night. Never freeze. Do something. Shoot in short bursts. Make sure you can see your target.

It's a laugh being at Milton Hall with this unruly lot. We've eaten all the sandwiches and someone has gone to the kitchen to beg some more. Not chosen for their manners, they managed to get rid of their first commanding officer within a week for trying to pull them together by foot-drill and shouting 'Par-ade . . . shun!' Their parting gift was to demonstrate their new demolition skills by booby-trapping his lavatory which exploded when he pulled the chain. His replacement, Colonel Musgrave, was more accommodating; an ex-big-game hunter who taught them how to cook hedgehogs, rats and mice, and survival techniques far grislier than Ray Mears's. Musgrave's lecture notes for living off the land advise that animals provide more wholesome and digestible food when eaten raw; that horses killed in action or dead dogs should still be warm to ensure their freshness; and that all birds are edible, although coots are tough and unpalatable. Musgrave was determined that all food prejudice should be banished and the right frame of mind created from the outset. Raw snails were just as tasty as oysters, and cleaner feeders because they live on wholesome foliage; while dogs and cats provided substantial amounts of excellent protein and could be captured by friendly advances. 'All objections to wholesome food are hysteria,' Musgrave banged home. 'Be sure to include the livers!'

Granddad's diary, 1944
2 February: *TC arr. home looking tired. Likes his new job.*

5

By early February 1944, 300 volunteers who had no idea what they were volunteering for converged from various preliminary training centres on ME65, the code name for Milton Hall. Fifty American officers, fifty British, a hundred French and a hundred sergeant wireless operators (forty British, forty American, twenty French); all thrown in together. There were university lecturers, taxi drivers, Foreign Legionnaires, American college football giants; there was a stunt man, a poacher, a policeman. What they all had in common was getting through the intensive selection process: a gamut of physical and psychological aptitude tests; followed by perplexing interviews with confounding *non-military* questions; followed by intelligence tests, word-association tests, even the Rorschach inkblot was used for personality assessments. Each man was put through exercises designed to test his ability to think fast, improvise, invent, adapt, and to check his tolerance for frustration: a task set with faulty equipment, for example, or a hindering assistant. All proceedings were scrutinised by Military Testing officers with clipboards taking notes, measuring even a moment of hesitation. The point, of course, was to see how each person might react in stressful or dangerous situations in enemy territory. Would he go to ground and hide, or would he get on with it? For once, many of the high-flyers accustomed to whistling past the finishing line got stuck, while those used to being disciplined for some minor offence or passed over, found themselves going on to the next stage. What SOE was looking for was the unconventional, unsubmissive types, the spirited individualist, men not afraid to stick their neck out or, as the Jeds put it, the troublemakers. But it was a complicated list of requirements because they would also need self-discipline, confidence, nerve, courage, self-reliance, diplomacy; to be perceptive, persuasive, assertive, imaginative. Someone who could work in a team but survive completely on his own in hostile territory — if he had to.

Everyone here has a different story of their recruitment. Aubrey Trofimov ('Trof'), remembers being locked in a cellar with instructions to try to get out. He loosened some bricks, climbed along a duct, escaped through a grate, then sneaked up on a guard and frogmarched him to the commanding officer's desk where he announced, 'I'm here and could technically shoot you.' Dick Rubinstein remembers them being divided into groups of eight and after some exercises having to rank in order of merit the men he would be prepared to take into enemy-occupied territory — what the Americans called a 'fuck your buddy test'. One of the American Jeds answered each word-association question with the same answer: Girls, Girls, Girls. The Americans livened things up at Milton Hall, yet the British rejected a third of the officers preselected by the American Secret Service and sent them home.

When war broke out in 1939 Dad had been in the last class of officer cadets at the Royal Military Academy in Woolwich. He passed out bottom, or so he claims.

'I had more punishments built up by half-term than they had punishing parades to attend, and was only commissioned because of the circumstances. I didn't *cause* any trouble,' Dad tries to explain, 'I just questioned everything. I wanted to know why. When I was given an order to polish boots, I asked why? 'TO SEE IF YOU CAN DO IT!'' he roars, then begins to laugh. 'So I polished one. Oh, they could get a lot of distaste into the word, 'CAREW!''

By 1943 Dad was an anti-aircraft gunner in Gibraltar, bored stiff with only the odd Vichy plane to fire at, when he picked up on a request from the War Office on the noticeboard wanting volunteers to operate in small units overseas. 'In the back of my mind, I knew one day a colonel was going to tell me to do something and I was going to tell him to get lost and end up court-martialled. Far better if I'm going to get killed, I get killed because I've made a balls of it, not because some idiot colonel made a hash of it.' So Dad applied with his friend, Alistair. The account of his selection is in the Imperial War Museum sound archives:

We had to climb up a tree — I hate heights — to ropes between two trees and then you had to go along these ropes. It really wasn't my scene. And I got across one and then the other one, and then a higher one, and I looked down below and the instructor said, 'You can do the top one if you want.' I called him a shit or something worse that that. 'That's the only fucking one I've got to do, isn't it? If I don't do that one I don't pass. You can't con me.' So I climbed up there, got stuck halfway through, but had to take the risk and got to the other side. When we got down I said to Alistair, 'Did you do the top level?' He said, 'No, I didn't, the instructor said it was voluntary.' Well, it was the only one you *had* to do and they never took him. I never heard of him again, and he was much more suitable than I was. He was much more active, strong, intelligent; he was a really bright guy. And he wanted that job, but of course he didn't realise that the top one was the only one he had to do.

Milton Hall was unusual in that the men were never separated by rank. All Jedburghs were quartered together, messed together, trained together, and in all matters of food, equipment and privilege, were treated identically. The Americans were popular not least for the superior rations that came with them. Breakfasts were feasts of fruit juices, peanut butter, kippers, marmalade, maple syrup, waffles, warm rolls and coffee; delights the British were not accustomed to, let alone as wartime fare. Where America provided food, equipment and weaponry, it was left to the British to provide the training.

'From the British we learned all the dark arts,' wrote Bill Colby, the American Jed who would later become head of the CIA.

★ ★ ★

Everyone at the reunion remembers the parachute training and their first jump. The white-knuckle wait for their turn, the green light, the sudden blast of air, the slight jerk of the harness and the glance upwards for the opening chute, then the feeling of elation as they floated gently down, until the instructor's voice shouting orders from the ground cut through: 'Keep your legs together, knees bent, face the front, use your guide ropes . . . ' Then down, the bump, a roll, a swivel round to face the chute as the wind filled it, pulling each man to his feet. There were mistakes: parachutes not opening, static lines attached to the plane which purled the canopy out not being fastened correctly, with dire consequences — on one of the first training sessions a young paratrooper was killed in front of them, the Jeds on the ground had to watch him fall like a stone. Everyone needed to complete a certain number of jumps, one of which was from a 600-foot-high tethered balloon. It was the jump nobody forgot. When you jump from a plane the parachute opens quickly because the slipstream from the speed of the plane yanks out the static line which inflates the canopy; whereas jumping out of a balloon means a straight fall of about 200 feet before your parachute opens. Which the instructors failed to mention . . . and which, if you are in the harness counting down, is a *very* significant delay. Everyone mid-drop thought their number was up. Instead of prayers, fear or circumspection, Dad's reaction was that when he got down he was bloody well going back to the parachute packing shed to give those girls hell for not packing his chute properly. He just had no concept of his own mortality.

Every day at Milton was crammed full. Classes in French: customs, mannerisms, culture, geography, politics; there were even lessons on how the French held a knife and fork, something the Americans were advised to take note of. Lectures on the Nazi Party and its organisation; the Gestapo; the German Army, uniforms, ranks; Vichy uniforms and ranks; they could not afford to mistake identity. They had to know how every type of gun, pistol, rifle, shotgun, sub-machine gun — British, American, French, German — was stripped, reassembled, cleaned; or if it had to be left behind, rendered ineffective for enemy use. The syllabus was mind-boggling. Explosives: how to make up charges in the dark, and then link them. Railway sabotage: derailments, line-blowing, signals, locomotives, rolling stock. Destruction of food/ammunition/petrol dumps by incendiarism. Grenades: live throwing; house fighting, crowd fighting, street fighting — by day, by night. There was the desk stuff, the practical outdoor stuff, and the physical stuff. They had to be super-fit and capable of covering great distances on foot in difficult conditions. And there were plenty of what they called Nerve Tests. Physical and mental strength could make all the difference in saving their skin.

What distinguished the Jedburghs from SOE's F Section agents was this intensive paramilitary training. Yet neither were they crack teams like the Special Airborne Service (SAS) whose missions were specific: in and out fast, with limited objectives. The Jeds could be working with the partisans for months so an essential criterion in selection had been 'political adaptability and tact' as well as leadership. Jedburgh teams would need to gain the trust of the different Resistance factions in the area so they could co-operate and work together. They had to become soldier-diplomats.

At the end of each day after dinner they drank Algerian wine, smoked American Chesterfield or Camel cigarettes, then settled down to the more serious business of poker and chess. It was every young man's perfect timetable.

CONFIDENTIAL
WEEKLY REPORT: 12 MARCH 44
Record of Individual Student: Carew, Thomas Arthur.

LANGUAGE QUALIFICATIONS
Quite good.

PHYSICAL TRAINING
Quite fit, works hard when inclined.

SIGNALLING
A. SENDING.
B. RECEIVING.
C. CODES.
D. PROCEDURE.
Good.

LEADERSHIP
Does not impress.

ENEMY UNITS
A. KNOWLEDGE.
B. ACCURACY.
Is attentive.

RECEPTION COMMITTEE
REPORT ON PRACTICAL WORK.
Did well in recent test.

SECTION LEADER'S REPORT
This officer takes classes very easily, is inclined to clown too much.

GENERAL
Is not a fool, but gives a good impression of one.

6

'How old am I?'

'Ancient.'

'No, really.'

'A hundred and twenty-seven.'

'No, I'm not.'

'You're eighty-seven, Dad.'

'I don't feel eighty-seven.'

'You don't look it, either.'

A devilish grin. 'I might be old, but I'm not dead.'

'You've had a good life,' I tell him.

'Well, I don't remember it,' he says, then concludes happily, 'so I don't forget it either.'

⋆ ⋆ ⋆

We are getting more and more non sequiturs like this. They make me laugh. And I can see how much he likes it when he makes me laugh. Yet he also infuriates me. And I blame him for a lot. I blame him for Mum. I blame him for what happened to the family. And sometimes I blame him for me. I wonder what will happen when he gets worse. I know I couldn't live with him. But it is getting worse. He is getting harder and harder to keep occupied. He doesn't watch telly any more because he can't untangle the different voices, they roll together with the background music and all he hears is sound-mush. Radio

43

likewise. 'What's going on?' 'Who's that?' 'Bloody ridiculous!' Thankfully it is never *his* failing; always theirs. Neither does he read any more; and he is spending less and less time in his shed. What he does do, is go up the road to the shops to buy torches, or batteries, or Sellotape, or string, where each item curiously seems to cost twenty quid. He certainly doesn't hang about for the change. After one particularly exasperating day I suggest to my sister we could simply drop him off somewhere, in some town, 'Just wait there, Dad.'

Not that long ago I did lose him. Jonathan and I had moved to Salisbury and a few years had passed since Dad had visited us in the East End. Then, he'd hop on a train from Battle, get off at London Bridge, catch a cab, and arrive at our place in Redchurch Street and we'd go for a curry, or a bagel, then wander around the back streets of Brick Lane. Dad marvelled at it. He'd sweep hand-twirling bows to the Asian women in their bright saris; applaud in admiration at the street-vendors' pat; poke around the vast dark garages full of junk; have a yarn with everyone, look at this, look at that. These were *our* days when we could do what we liked. But now he was on his own; he had been diagnosed with dementia and was visibly depressed. I thought if we could meet at Waterloo and have the day in London together, it would take him out of himself. Cheer him up.

My sister thought it was a bridge too far.

'He's too old,' she said. 'He panics.'

'Dad? Panic?'

'Yes. He does.'

Nevertheless I pushed for it, and with the help of Marissa, Dad's cleaner, to make sure he got on the right train, we arranged to meet.

I rang the night before to remind him.

'Meet me under the big clock at Waterloo, Dad. Do you remember the big clock?' I shouted down the telephone.

'Glok?'

'Clock.'

'GLOG?'

'C-L-O-C-K. You know. You remember, Waterloo station. WATERLOO.'

'Walter Carew?'

'Oh God . . . Wa-ter-loo East, Dad,' I enunciated slowly.

'What?'

'WATERLOO EAST. Don't stay on till Charing Cross.'

Silence. Oh dear.

'Are you there?'

'Yes, yes.'

'Have you got my number in your wallet? Get your wallet out, Dad.'

I heard a rustling down the line. He dropped the receiver. I waited. *Kerfuffle, kerfuffle.* He picked it up again. He read a number.

'Yes! Good! Put it back in your wallet, Dad. Have you put it back?'

'Yes.'

'If anything happens, ask someone to ring that number. Okay?'

'Yes, yes.'

I don't know if it was nervousness that made

45

me laugh out loud when I put down the phone, or my warped nature.

★ ★ ★

My train arrived (into the main station) fifteen minutes before his, enough time for me to leg it over to Waterloo East. I told the guard at the top of the stairs I was meeting my ninety-year-old-unaccompanied-Dad, and he let me onto the platform. The train from Battle pulled in. People got off. I scanned left, right, left, right. I couldn't see him. I couldn't see him and he was easy to spot. He had a good thick head of silver hair and a bristly white beard; he looked like Ben Gunn. And he would be carrying a dirty old bag. But no silver hair, no beard, no old man anywhere. I began to panic. Everyone had got off. But not Dad. So I jumped on the train and charged through the carriages calling his name, 'Tom, Tom! Tom Carew!' Everyone was looking at me. But not Tom. They were slamming the doors. I looked out of the window to check he wasn't on the platform. He wasn't. The train started to move and I was on my way to Charing Cross.

'I'm looking for my ninety-year-old father, Tom Carew,' I broadcast loudly as I covered the entire length of the train. 'Tom Carew? Tom Carew?'

But Tom Carew was definitely not on it.

Then it dawned on me. He'd got off at London Bridge. When we lived in the East End he *always* got off at London Bridge and caught a cab. Something would have triggered in his brain

46

when the train stopped there. I must have had
Genuine Disaster stamped all over my face
because when I got to Charing Cross another
astonishingly kind guard ignored my no-ticket-
status, lifted the barrier without a second
thought, and put me on a train straight back to
London Bridge (I love you train-station-guard,
you rare free-willed, precious thing); but now it
was nearly FORTY minutes since the Battle
train would have stopped at London Bridge, and
God knows where Dad would be. I knew at least
one thing: I knew he wouldn't be sitting sensibly,
waiting at London Bridge. He could never sit
still for a moment. He'd be off. Looking for a big
clock, or a cab, or God knows what.

I rang my sister.

'I've lost him.'

'Shit,' she said.

I explained: 'He never got off the train.'

'Oh no,' she said.

We both laughed nervously. I was grateful she
wasn't cross.

Then she laughed again, a bit louder.

'What?' I asked.

'I'm on a bus,' she told me, 'we're just going
round Trafalgar Square and I caught myself
looking out of the window for him.'

We both laughed. A slightly mad laugh.

'I'd better get off the phone,' I said, 'in case he
rings.'

Every millimetre to London Bridge the train
squeaked and shunted and shuddered; the
journey was interminable. 'Come on, come on.'
Clunk, clunk. A red-brick building, another. A

buddleia bush growing in the grey flint chips. Another. Eeeeek. Clunk. Slower. Slower. Creaking to a halt. Easing off again. I was sweating. 'COME ON. COME ON!'

At last the train slowly pulled into London Bridge. My face was squashed against the window. My carriage inched to the end of the platform. Of course, no Dad. I'd lost him. My sister was right. His memory was too far gone, and it was too much to ask, and I should have known better. I had let him down. He was on the loose. And it wasn't funny. Even though it was.

I got off the train and sighed loudly. I was sick with the thought of where he might have got to, what he might be doing, and how on earth I would ever find him.

I walked slowly up the platform.

Then my phone rang.

It was PC Groom.

★　★　★

Dad was in the police tea room at Waterloo station having a cup of tea. By the time I got there he was surrounded by half a dozen constables or more. He was the centre of attention and he was putting on a show. He had always enjoyed adversity, a problem to solve. The adrenalin had kicked in and he was having a ball, even his memory seemed to have come back, because, as PC Groom told me, he had been describing to his rapt young audience how to blow up a railway line. Which was something he knew a bit about.

48

I walked over to him, smiling, shaking my head. 'Sorry, Dad.'

But he couldn't have been more pleased. Because he *had* been waiting under the clock all along. In the right place. At the right time. As directed. I had rushed onto the train that he had already got off. In my panic I'd missed him. He had slipped by me under his new yellow corduroy hat (which I had bought him!), concentrating on his mission to get to the clock. Which was where he waited, minute after long minute, for no daughter to turn up. And where, half an hour later, he collared PC Groom.

'Aaaaaaah,' his deep voice rolled out as he stood up to greet me.

Then he slapped my bum. And all the policemen laughed.

7

The Jeds were kept in the dark about their mission until 24 February 1944 when everyone was called into the main ballroom: the speaker was Eric Mockler-Ferryman, SOE's director of operations. Unusually for a Jedburgh lecture you could hear a pin drop as Mockler-Ferryman described how they would be parachuted behind enemy lines at night in teams of three to train, supply and organise the Resistance. He divided their duties under three headings: Liaison, Organisation, and Leadership, and explained they would be representing the Allied high command and passing on orders received from London. As compatibility was essential each team would self-select: so a French officer would pair off with a British or American officer, and between them they would pick their radio operator. These officer pairings jokily became known as *getting married* and so, during the following weeks the *courting* began. A trial period of working together was known as *the engagement*, then if successful, the marriage was recognised and the team was assigned a code name.

```
NOTES ON THE USE OF JEDBURGHS
[by Colonel Musgrave]
1. Development of Resistance potential.
2. Leadership as and when required.
```

3. Individual acts of sabotage on specified targets.
4. Provision of Intelligence.
5. The preparation and laying out of landing fields for aircraft.
6. Organisation of reception committees.
7. Instruction in guerrilla warfare and the use of all weapons appertaining thereto.
8. Flank protection for an advancing army.

AREAS OF OPERATION
Tactical
1. Destruction of railways, roads, and bridges in order to interfere or completely stop the flow of enemy reinforcements towards the front line.
2. Ambushing enemy convoys.
3. Destruction of intercommunications such as telegraph lines and cables etc.
4. Destruction of forward petrol dumps.
5. The preservation of all the above in order to facilitate a breakthrough by our own troops.
6. The protection of our own flanks immediately after a breakthrough.
7. The provision of guides and intelligence for our forward troops.

So. Now they knew what they were supposed to do. Dad teamed up with Robert Rivière — a Frenchman ten years older than himself, and a young American radio operator, John Stoyka.

Their team was code-named Basil. Most Jedburgh teams were allocated male Christian names: Godfrey, Jim, Norman, Alan, Cedric, etc.; a few were given the names of spices or medicine: Cinnamon, Chloroform, Novocaine; and a few got cars: Chrysler, Bugatti. From then on each team would train together and go on 'schemes' designed to test them in as realistic a situation as possible. These schemes might last anything from forty-eight hours to ten days. They could be parachuted into a remote part of Scotland and have to live off the land; hijack an American base; or escape from the Home Guard who would obligingly step in as the Gestapo. They were quite resourceful, if occasionally over-eager, terrorising the British countryside in the process, raiding hen houses, shouting in German accents, shooting off the odd round. On one occasion they were dropped on the moors with a live sheep for supper — I know Dad let his go, he couldn't see the need to kill it if he didn't have to. But Harry Verlander made a sheepskin rug from the leftovers of his dinner, and has still got it. In another exercise they were dropped 'blind' miles away from Milton Hall with no idea where they were, no papers or money, and instructed to make their way back within twenty-four hours without being picked up by the police or the Home Guard. A task they all accomplished — only to find one team back in record time, already shaved, washed, dressed, and drinking rum and ginger wine by the Elizabethan window in the Great Hall. They had simply walked onto the railway line with their carbines and hijacked a train.

These are the stories the men tell. That night, lying in bed in the Bull, I wonder about the ones they don't.

Revision and practice of killing or capturing and gagging a sentry.
Do it under varying circumstances.
Vary the manner in which the sentry carries his rifle.

A daily period of a quarter of an hour to help train the student's memory and impress on him the value of attention to detail. All his senses are to be trained, and some problems must be set which make him use several senses at the same time.

As the Jeds team up, SOE agents already behind the lines are organising their circuits of spies and Maquis saboteurs, collecting intelligence to aid attacks on railways, canals, factories, aircraft production, hydroelectric plants, and anything else to help reduce Germany's war strength in preparation for the Allied invasion. Factory slow-downs and stops become a common occurrence, rolling stock and train tracks are sabotaged, oil dumps set on fire, water reservoirs contaminated, power supplies constantly interrupted. At a Michelin factory in Clermont-Ferrand 300 tons of tyres go up in smoke; at a Bronzavia firm an explosion causes a two-week halt of wireless-equipment production; at a Renault factory tank production is down twenty per cent; at Montluçon anti-tank guns are destroyed.[1]

From 1941 to 1944 there were more than ninety SOE circuits in operation across France; mostly code-named after occupations: Wheelwright, Salesman, Stockbroker, Donkeyman, Acrobat, Ventriloquist, Wrestler, Silversmith, etc., and run by undercover bilingual British or French agents from F Section; but as D-Day approaches, de Gaulle claims the exclusive right to control *all* subversive activity in France — with the aim of unifying it. As much as President Roosevelt might dislike it, General Eisenhower knows that the person most able to rally support in France is de Gaulle, so it is agreed that French and British SOE agents will come under the jurisdiction of de Gaulle's umbrella organisation, the Forces Françaises de l'Intérieur (FFI). But French lack of security and experience causes the transfer of command to be delayed. So for now SOE maintains its circuits alongside those controlled by the Free French.

★ ★ ★

The Jeds train and practise their schemes, the days stretch out longer, the tension builds, and British and American chiefs and their military strategists do everything possible to keep preparations for the Normandy invasion, code-named Overlord,

---

[1] The Maquis leader who carried out this sabotage learnt his skills from a booklet picked up from an Allied propaganda drop.

under wraps. Eisenhower asks Churchill to revoke all foreign diplomatic privileges. Then comes a coastal ban: a ten-mile-wide strip from the Wash to Land's End is closed to all non-resident incomers — to ensure any unwanted visitor (i.e. spy) would easily stand out. Double agents, meanwhile, are busily drip-feeding misleading intelligence back to German high command; the most successful of these is Juan Pujol, a Spanish double agent code-named Garbo, who has created a complex network of fictional pro-Nazi spies based in England who have been supplying subtle snips of information carefully engineered to convince the Germans that the main invasion would take place at the Pas de Calais, hundreds of miles north-east of Normandy. The Allied deception plan, Operation Fortitude, includes an entire fake army of dummy trucks and inflatable tanks stationed in the south-east, accompanied, most convincingly, by General Patton, and looking (from above) as if it were gearing up to head for Calais.

But not everything has been going to plan. The Gestapo's shortwave signal direction-finding has been working overtime and a number of circuits have been infiltrated. Archdeacon, Bargee, Bricklayer, Delegate, Liontamer, Priest and Surveyor are all under enemy control; Monk is down; Parson, Acrobat and Inventor are broken; Prosper naively did a deal with the Gestapo with the result that now their cache of weapons is in German hands and they've all been executed.

On 2 March, SOE agent Jean Millet and a female radio operator are parachuted into France on Mission Eclaireur: to organise safe houses, landing sites, reception committees and dropping grounds for the Jedburgh teams.

★ ★ ★

We have had our tea, eaten the cakes, and now Dad is chatting up Sophie, a French general's daughter. The three of us wander off happily into the more formal gardens by the lake, which is how, astoundingly in my view, we miss the coach back to the hotel. But this, I am quick to learn, is typical of the Jeds who *bloody well go on without you*. The problem of how we will get back to the hotel — no car, no bus service, no mobile phone — is grist to the mill for Dad who spins on his heel and speeds nimbly towards the house. Just before he reaches the entrance, and without breaking stride, I notice he has developed a terrible limp; he hobbles inside and disappears. We wait, Sophie and I, and just as we are wondering what has become of him, Dad reappears, limpless with a nonchalant grin on his face. He has blagged us a lift back to the Bull with Milton Hall's estate manager. There is a photograph of Dad and me (courtesy Sophie), name-tagged, standing in front of the house waiting for our ride; Dad wearing his Special Forces tie, his thick white hair groomed for a change, beard cropped, with that knowing look of his, so *very* pleased with himself.

In my room that evening as I read about the Jeds in Glyn Loosmore's manuscript, my eye strays from the text to Dad's handwriting in the margin:

56

the Jeds had to undergo great trials requiring inhuman efforts. Often assigned to missions not previously fore-casted, they owed their survival to their per-fect and even exceptional physical condition, confirmed by many of them to be the out-come of the training received at Milton Hall.

Nonsense we were Excellent Poker Players and did hardly any exercise. Mostly we played with explosives during the day . . . At night we did some exercises but never too strenuous.

* * *

As a child I suffered from chronic car sickness. Having to sit sideways on the bench seat in the back of our Dormobile camper van on our summer holiday, squashed between my siblings in the heat, didn't help, so Dad built a narrow wooden stool over the handbrake, between the driver and passenger seat in the front. There was no seat belt of course, but there I perched, between Mum and Dad, much more happily facing forwards with a widescreen view all the way to Spain; brothers and sister in the back (green for a different reason). Invariably, after we'd got a few miles under our belt and the sun had come out and the road had become a winding ribbon ahead of us (no motorways in those days), Dad would wedge his knees under the steering wheel, spread both hands wide apart, and begin to clap. Great joyful claps, cracking the air in his open palms. It infected us all; not even Mum could resist it. Something had freed itself, and the clapping was its signal. It felt as if we were a band of ragamuffins on the open road under the bright blue sky and all our problems could trail back into the grey we'd left behind. Sometimes I worked the gears. Dad would put his foot on the clutch and shout, 'Second!' or 'Third!' or whatever gear he wanted, and I would oblige. On a downhill stretch we would try to go as fast as we could: 'Third!' he boomed, 'Fourth!' and I would slot the gears in and egg him on: 'Faster, Dad!' and faster we went. Once, down a very long hill, the road whizzing beneath the wheels, everything shuddering, the dashboard creaking, the plates in the cupboards rattling, the drawers sliding open, the roof-rack tarpaulin flapping, the needle hit ONE HUNDRED. Which was when Dad turned to me, his face completely deadpan, and shouted, 'BRAKE! BRAKE!'

8

The wider sweep of the Jedburgh plan involved a mind-numbing amount of organisation in a very limited amount of time. Aside from the Jeds, their instructors and extended staff at Milton Hall, there were hundreds of personnel (all signed up to the Official Secrets Act) who would be required to join up the dots: in signals, supply, planning and liaison with all the different commands. Their training had to run in parallel. And then there were logistics: the planes, crews, provisions, supplies, and the enormous tonnage of arms — manufacturing them, transporting them, packing and then delivering them — at night by parachute behind enemy lines. To enable the weapons and explosives to survive the 600-foot drop, thousands of metal cylinders known as Type C containers had to be fabricated: each stamped from sheet metal with reinforced ribs, a parachute compartment at one end, three latches and four carrying handles (they could weigh over a ton when full and needed four men to lift them). Packing lists stretched across pages: Sten guns, Bren guns, rifles, carbines, pistols, smoke pistols, silencers, bullets, knives, grenades, Cordex, plastic explosives, limpets, clams, radio sets, tear gas, primers, detonators, safety fuses, igniters, charges, switches, pencil time fuses, binoculars, torches, toolkits, bicycle repair kits, first-aid kits, crimpers, nails, string, cable, matches, striker boards,

Vaseline, Bostik, wire, wire-cutters, adhesive tape, infrared homing devices, night glasses, corned beef, chocolate, blankets, biscuits, cigarettes, sugar, soap, coffee, socks, boots, batteries, battery-chargers, generators, incendiaries . . . SOE even designed a small motor scooter (the Welbike) specifically to fit in these containers.

As the D-Day invasion approached, availability of aircraft became critical; to supply the operational requirements of the Jedburghs, the Americans would provide their B24 Liberator bombers and specially trained crews from their secret base at RAF Harrington, Northamptonshire. The code name given to these covert flights was Carpetbagger. Carpetbagger pilots were trained to fly low, at night, without lights, in poor weather, and over mountainous terrain; so missions could only fly when there was enough moonlight to follow their route. They kept to low altitudes (around 2,000 feet) to avoid detection by enemy radar (less time to focus on low-flying aeroplanes), and for better visibility so they could navigate using distinctive landmarks — rivers, lakes, roads, etc. — only climbing to 7,000 feet if they had to avoid enemy fire. These planes were specially modified with their nose, waist and belly guns removed, leaving just the rear guns for protection; bomb racks were stripped out and replaced with racks to hold the containers; a ply trapdoor was fitted to make the 'Joe hole' for the agents (known as 'Joes') to jump out of; the oxygen was removed (not needed for low-flying missions); and then the whole exterior was painted with non-reflective black paint to make it hard to be picked out by searchlights.

Each Jedburgh team parachuted in would be met by a reception committee (RC), normally prearranged by a message transmitted by the BBC in their *messages personnels* broadcasts to France which went out after the evening news bulletin. Surreal disembodied sentences were disgorged in a stream — which the Germans knew perfectly well contained orders for the Resistance: 'La Tour Eiffel penche à droite'; 'La girafe a une laryngite'; 'Le coucou est cocu'; but without a code they could crack, they rarely knew who they were for or what they meant. Each Maquis group had been allocated a sentence which, if heard in the broadcast, they recognised as their particular cue, with the second part of the phrase conveying the specific message, possibly for a pre-planned act of sabotage to go ahead, or to prepare for a parachute drop.[1]

It was the RC's task to mark out the drop zone (DZ) with a triangle of bonfires, wait for the planes, light the fires when they could hear them approaching, then flash an agreed Morse-code letter to the incoming aircraft to confirm the landing site was secure. After the drop they would collect the supplies, then disappear. The local

---

[1] The BBC *messages personnels* not only helped reduce radio traffic — a dangerous activity for a radio operator behind enemy lines — but the system was also used to flood the airwaves with false messages to fox the Germans into thinking something else was up.

people who made up the RCs broke curfew and risked their lives hiding in the dark, waiting in the woods with their carts, trucks, wagons, horses or bicycles. To disguise their mission the planes making these drops would often jettison bundles of propaganda leaflets away from the DZ on the flight home to make it look like that was their only intention.

★   ★   ★

Jedburgh casualty rates were expected to be between fifty and seventy-five per cent. They could jump in, but not out again. SOE radio operators behind the lines had been averaging four to six weeks of transmission before detection. So to many it was a surprise, to put it mildly, when SOE decided the Jedburghs would be dropped behind enemy lines in uniform: safer, it was argued, because if caught, men in uniform were protected by the Geneva Convention. This failed to take into account Hitler's order to immediately execute any Allied personnel captured behind the lines. A more convincing justification was the boost to morale the arrival of uniformed specialist troops could give the partisans — as envoys heralding liberation; that, and the air of authority the uniforms would lend.

The wearing of uniform behind enemy lines while affording a measure of protection in the event of capture, undoubtedly adds somewhat to the chances of it. JEDBURGHS who find the wearing of uniform interferes with the performance of their task in the field, may, therefore, choose to change into plain clothes.

Curiously, Dad's French civilian clothes were issued to him from a sealed gallery just off the main dinosaur hall at the Natural History Museum in London.[1] The suggestion was to get used to them by wearing them about town. As Dad was standing nonchalantly in Piccadilly Circus in his French clobber a passing stranger did a double take, winked at him, then asked when he would be off to France.

★ ★ ★

By spring, with most of the training covered, the Jeds began to get the odd day's leave. For Dad, whose parents lived in Cambridge, it was easy to get home so naturally he took a bunch of Americans with him. I have a slightly surreal picture in my head, Dad punting on the River Cam, gliding through water meadows, past the hallowed spires, by Byron's pool, tour guide for his American chums, going over 'throat holds' in his head, with the trace of explosives on his fingers.

---

[1] SOE station XVB, known as the Demonstration Room, occupied three sealed galleries in the Natural History Museum, used to store field equipment.

Granddad's diary, 1944

26 March: *TC cheered us up and helped so much. TC on river with AMERICANS.*

30 April: *TC left a little sad we thought. So were we.*

9

May 1944. D-Day getting closer. The enormous influx of American troops heading to the south of England increases daily. At Milton Hall a hundred Jedburgh teams, trained, eager and restless, are waiting to be deployed. But wait they must; nothing can be risked to jeopardise the top-secret plans for invasion. They play football, cards, poker, carry on with their exercises and schemes. For Overlord to succeed — and many experts give its chances only fifty-fifty — the Allied landings must rapidly build up strength in numbers to withstand a counter-attack. The first three days will be critical. They are desperately relying on the element of surprise: that small window when the enemy, hopefully, will be off balance and caught unawares.

1 June. The BBC transmits the first lines from Verlaine's 'Autumn Song': *Les sanglots longs des violons de l'automne*'. Throughout France the words are instantly recognised by *maquisards* sitting around their wireless sets as 'the attention phrase' to alert *all* Resistance groups to listen nightly.

In southern England, 5,000 ships and 11,000 aircraft prepare for battle.

Deep in the woods of Charnwood Forest in Leicestershire, the Jedburghs are in the middle of an eight-day scheme called Exercise Lash, rehearsing with the Home Guard as surrogate partisans.

3 June. Eric Mockler-Ferryman travels to Portsmouth to meet Eisenhower's chief of staff. He explains in detail the scope and ubiquity of SOE's circuits and how much damage they could achieve. Eisenhower sends Mockler-Ferryman back to London with an order for the Resistance to make *maximum effort* on the night of the invasion, instead of the phased activity originally planned.

The first Jedburgh team, Hugh, arrives at 46 Devonshire Close, London W1, the SOE briefing house, to receive their operational orders.

4 June. The weather is bad. Eisenhower is on a hill nine miles north of Portsmouth, looking out to sea. Storms are forecast over the Channel. The chief meteorologist, John Stagg, is brought in. Stagg predicts a break in the storm on the morning of 6 June.

Team Hugh are given maps printed on silk, their codes, their contacts, their cover stories, their radio crystals.[1] They are to be dropped near Poitiers with instructions to stop the two main lines of traffic through the region. They are told to get their affairs in order, write final letters home, collect their weapons and pack. In addition to each man's personal code name, the two Frenchmen in the team are given pseudonyms and false papers — to spare their families in case they are caught.

5 June. The BBC transmits the second stanza

---

[1] Stamp-sized slices of quartz in Bakelite housing. The thickness of the quartz determined the signal wavelength.

of Autumn Song': '*Blessent mon coeur d'une langueur monotone.*' It is what all Resistance groups have been waiting for: the call to arms, the start of the invasion's sabotage operations. At 9.15 p.m. a stream of D-Day action-phrases rolls thick and fast: '*Odille porte un pyjama jaune*'; '*Les taxis arriveront à neuf heures*'; '*La girafe est dans le lac*' . . . 306 of them, the programme lasting far longer than the normal six-minute broadcast. Road, rail and cable-cutting teams across France rally into action, each with a particular task. Bursts of explosions punctuate the night. Axle oil is syphoned from German tank-transporter cars and replaced with ground carborundum (parachuted in especially) which gums up the parts that the oil usually lubricates. Railway lines are severed; roads are blocked; petrol dumps are blown; electric pylons come down; communication wires are cut. At 11.00 p.m. a black bomber takes off with eight crew, twenty canisters of weapons, and Jedburgh team Hugh. Churchill goes to bed telling his wife, Clemmie, that 20,000 men might be dead by the morning. Over Milton Hall the skies are filled with lights and the continuous drone of aircraft flying south.

6 June. 2.00 a.m. Two SAS teams are dropped south of the Normandy beaches, north of Saint-Lô. They carry flare guns and recordings of men shouting, mortars and gunfire. They will be followed by 500 dummy hessian parachutists and a planeload of pintail bombs. The pintail bombs fall faster than the dummies and discharge light flares to illuminate the phantom force. The dummies are nick-named Ruperts and

fitted with firecrackers to simulate gunshot and designed to blow up on impact so the Germans won't find them. It is part of the deception plan to lure the enemy away from the beach-heads and the genuine drop zones before the real landings begin.

Just becoming visible on the horizon off the Normandy coast, an armada of ships slides through a grey dawn. At first light, three battalions of British sappers wade ashore to begin to clear the mine-strewn beaches. Three-quarters of them will have perished before the day is done.

The German regiment dispatched to eliminate the elusive paratroopers wastes the entire morning in the woods searching for them, as American seaborne forces begin to lodge themselves ashore.

Meanwhile, the RAF has taken out eighteen of twenty-four bridges across the Seine, while 23,000 *real* Allied paratroopers and glider troops are being scattered over the fields of Normandy. Operation Overlord, the invasion to liberate France, has begun.

★ ★ ★

As Allied forces pile in, Resistance groups at work on the road and rail networks are upsetting German transport more effectively than they could have hoped. In twenty-four hours 950 lines have been cut with rail traffic down to just thirty per cent of its normal capacity. All traffic has been halted between Toulouse and Montauban. Diplomat teams have cut the rails around Troyes; Farmer have cut the rails at Lille;

while Wrestler and Shipwright have sabotaged lines in Indre, which is keeping a formidable SS armoured division[1] held up in Toulouse instead of steaming up to join the battle in Normandy.

The Germans depend heavily on rail — out of the fifty-nine divisions in the west only ten are Panzer divisions (an all-arms motorised division), the majority are on foot, or on horse with horse-drawn artillery. Three and a half million horses in service with all those equine bellies to feed. Let alone 14,000,000 hooves to shoe! Tens of thousands of tons of iron a year that could have been going into tanks, aircraft . . . But then you have to feed motorised transport too, and the Nazis, with only Romania to supply them, are chronically short of fuel, whereas the Allies, with America as the largest oil producer in the world, can slosh around in the stuff. After four years of occupation the Germans have siphoned France's assets dry and crippled the economy, not just by not paying for anything, but adding insult to injury by billing the French treasury 'Occupation Costs and Reparation Charges' of 20 million choking Reichsmarks a day.

Team Hugh (who will get only six hours' sleep in the next five days) estimate there are 3,000 would-be *maquisards* in their region, but they need to be armed and trained. Eisenhower and Churchill are impressed; the Resistance is pulling its weight and doing as well as the air-force bombing raids. What SOE had been striving for, what so many agents and patriots

---

[1] A division is about 15,000 men.

had given their lives for, has blossomed overnight into a French national uprising. A show of rebellion big enough for de Gaulle to say, France will liberate herself.

10

The summer of 1966 was the Holiday of the Drowned Bodies. We were camping on the dunes at Berria, on the Atlantic coast near Santander in Spain. Dad, out sailing his tiny mini-sail dinghy with Patrick, found two bodies floating in the sea. A man and a woman. Dad stripped off, dived in, and managed to haul them on board (which was quite a feat considering the size of the boat and its kit-set flimsy construction), then sailed back to the beach and got them ashore. Patrick's job (at ten years old) was to hold the boat in the water. I remember the terrible commotion. Mum running down the beach; Dad, still naked, running up the beach carrying first one body, then the other, and laying them on the sand. A crowd beginning to gather. Dad shouting something and someone racing off. My sister and I standing, watching, dumbstruck at the sidelines. Then Dad knelt over the man, and with his big freckled hands crossed over like angels' wings, he began to push up and down on the man's chest, his hands flying and pumping, all the time cursing him to breathe. Nicky and I were sure Dad would fix this. But he didn't. Then he went over to the woman. Same thing: his hands flying like wings as he pushed up and down. Mum, I remember, had tied a towel round Dad's waist to cover him. Patrick, out of sight, was standing in the sea with the boat. While

Nicky and I, with frogspawn eyes, caught images of things that would haunt us. The legs of the woman, her skin white and cold as bacon fat, lifting slightly with each thrust. Again and again. But Dad didn't fix her either. The ambulance didn't come for ages, it was too late, and Mum and Dad were upset, and Patrick (still holding the boat) was worried, and Nicky and I were completely spooked, and God knows where Tim was.

'Always swim with the current,' Dad lectured us that night. 'Never fight it. If the current is against you, don't try to get back to land however close you are. Go with the current. Swim out to sea if you have to.'

We listened, not arguing for once. Swim out to sea, like some metaphor for life. I tried to imagine it. But I could not. Just me and the sea. Far out on the horizon. My pale stick legs kicking just below the surface, enough to catch the upward glance of the hungry sharks below. The endless volumes of darkening water beneath me. The inky depths marking me out, breathing at me, saying, Swim with me and I will take you out. I knew if it came to it, I would struggle for land. I knew I would reach out for the rocks, snatch at the slippery bladderwrack; I would gasp and swallow and fight. I would fix my mind on getting to the shore. I would hear Dad's words knowing he was right. Yet I would fight and fight.

It was a moment that formed me. I carried my prescient failure like a dark secret. The lesson, ferocious in its urgency, became a moment for introspection, not the lifebelt it was meant to be. Thrown by a man who so often threw physics at his airy children. Dad's favourite lessons were always the least believable. What to believe, what not to believe. But when he gave us the lesson of the drowned bodies, we all knew, this time, what to believe.

★　★　★

6 June 1944. Midday. The Germans, lulled by the bad weather, and expecting the Allies at Calais, have been caught unawares. Indeed, the deception plan has been so successful they remain convinced the main invasion will come ashore between Boulogne and the Somme, and the landings at Normandy are merely a diversionary tactic. Instead of rushing everything available to Normandy, the bulk of the German forces stay where they are, waiting, looking through their binoculars to an empty horizon.

Nevertheless, there are terrible losses on the beaches. There are places where the water is dyed crimson by the British, American and Canadian troops who will never step out of the sea. The Normandy fields become graveyards and by mid-morning Allied airborne units are missing 4,000 men. The fighting is hellish. But by nightfall, along a sixty-mile stretch of coast, 155,000 men are ashore.

As the reality of the situation begins to strike home the Germans start to mobilise. In Caen eighty *maquisards* in captivity are executed. Panzer divisions and reserves set off from Brittany, the

Atlantic coast, northern Europe, Germany and the Med. German troops in Normandy need to hold the Allied advance until they arrive. It's a race. Who can slow down who. And an intensely vulnerable time when the Germans will try to push Overlord back into the sea.

Eisenhower orders SFHQ to obstruct German reinforcements pouring towards Normandy, and in other areas to tie German forces down. Jedburgh teams begin to be parachuted to Resistance groups at strategic locations across France. Team Frederick is dropped into Brittany, followed by Felix and Giles, then Francis, Gilbert, Hilary and Horace; there are more than 60,000 German troops stationed in Brittany who need to be cut off. Team Hamish joins Hugh in western France; Quinine jumps into the Lot; Ammonia into the Dordogne; Bugatti is dropped further south; team Harry lands west of Dijon; Chloroform to the south-east; and team Veganin is parachuted into the Rhône Valley — with the first Jedburgh loss: Veganin's wireless operator is killed in the jump after a parachute malfunction.

On SFHQ's war-room walls giant maps are speckled with coloured pins that identify key rail, road and telecommunication targets, and the nearby Resistance groups. Where Churchill, Roosevelt and SOE had designs on *controlling* the French Resistance, Eisenhower understands the necessity of having a French military commander lead them. To boost the morale of the French, while maintaining influence, Eisenhower brings General Pierre Koenig, de Gaulle's military advisor and commander of the FFI, into the allied command staff of SHAEF; and by so doing, integrates the Resistance into the Allied strategy.

The Maquis keep the Germans busy repairing rails, clearing roads, rebuilding bridges. Jedburgh team Quinine have laid a mine a little way beyond where they have felled some trees which lie across the road, and which will blow up the tank brought in to clear them. Beyond the mine is a further barricade covered by hidden snipers in the wood. Above this barricade, grenades hang delicately from over-hanging branches with their pins out. An ambush like this could hold a convoy up for a day. Repeat the process all the way to Normandy and it could add weeks to the journey. Seventy thousand tyre bursters are parachuted in. One SS division runs out of tyre-repair kits and takes six days to travel sixty-seven miles. The 2nd SS Panzer Division 'Das Reich' ordered to Normandy from Toulouse takes seventeen days to get there when it should have taken three. Petrol dumps are blown. Bridges destroyed. The Maquis have made sure no trains are going north, so they begin to march and have team Quinine on their back. Incessant sniper bullets buzz like wasps round German ears. Hold-ups, ambushes; a bunched-up division delayed on a main road makes a good target for the RAF. By the time the Panzer division gets to Normandy it will be a shadow of its former fighting self. Shredded, demoralised, its nerves on edge and with a bitter pill to swallow — had it been on time it *might* have made a difference in pushing back the Allies' very tenuous grip on the Normandy bridgehead. Across France the attacks continue. In Brittany, fourteen Jedburgh teams are organising 20,000 partisans. South-west of Dijon a 10,000-ton ammunition dump is destroyed by fire; the explosions last for three days. The SS begin to hunt their enemies down. Nazi reprisals are ruthless. Resistance fighters are shot; anybody found helping them is shot. If a house is used by the Resistance, the house is burnt to the ground. And the neighbours' houses for good measure. For every German killed, ten *maquisards* are executed. As a deterrent against ambushes Germans are arriving in towns with live Frenchmen strapped to the front of their armoured cars. In the Jura, in eastern France, civilians are forced to walk ahead of troop columns to clear away obstacles.

Dad and the other waiting Jeds at Milton Hall smoke more cigarettes and keep sorting their kit.

★　★　★

On 8 June in Tulle, south of Limoges, there is a rumour (unsubstantiated) the Germans have discovered forty dead officers with their genitals sliced off and stuffed in their mouths.

On 9 June Das Reich, the same SS division tormented by Quinine, round up 120 local men for execution: dirty shoes are enough evidence to convict a *maquisard* of hiding in the hills. Ninety-nine men between the ages of sixteen and sixty are hanged from lamp posts and balconies across Tulle, and it only stops there because the rope runs out. The remainder will be shipped to Dachau. Later the same day, a popular German commander is captured. There is known to be Maquis activity around the nearby village of Oradour-sur-Vayres.

★　★　★

On 10 June Das Reich arrive in Oradour-sur-Glane. Their German commander has not returned. It is market day. Everyone is ordered into the main square, men, women, children. The men are split from the women and children and locked in barns which are surrounded by armed SS. At two o'clock the barns are torched. Anyone who attempts to escape is machine-gunned down. Then the houses are set on fire. At five o'clock, the church is set alight. In all 642 men, women and children are killed in a monstrous act of terror, to set an example to other resistors; or possibly a mistake, because they were in a town that shared another's name, but not its river.

At Vannes the Germans castrate captured *maquisards* and leave their corpses on the roadside with their mutilated groins exposed; in Kerhoaden they hammer the flesh of partisans into rags on an anvil.

12 June. Some 35,000 German troops and two SS armoured divisions are en route to Normandy from the Russian front.

13 June. The British are unable to exploit a gap in the German defences and the chance to take Caen passes.

The first V-1 doodlebug flying bomb falls in London.[1]

★ ★ ★

As far as the Jeds are concerned, they should be going in faster. But SFHQ cannot spend their force too quickly because no one knows how the battle will play out. Pressure on the Germans will need to be turned up at different times and different places right across France; they must be elastic to changing conditions. So teams are held back. The Jedburghs must be patient. There are plenty of collaborators ready to betray anything suspicious and much to be lost by taking action before the time is right. And timing is crucial. Guerrilla warfare is most effective when the enemy is occupied — engaged in fighting or about to go into battle. To go in too early is normally disastrous — it gives the game and too much information away; by its nature a guerrilla force can never match the power of its enemy. But the value of a small number of well-trained, well-placed men could be magnificently disproportionate. Better to make stealthy strikes with minimal heroics then dissolve back into the landscape. At all costs avoid providing targets for the enemy to attack. The Jeds put it plainer: surprise, kill and vanish.

---

[1] Which prompts political pressure from Churchill for General Montgomery to wrap up in Normandy and overrun the doodlebug launch sites in northern France. Caen doesn't fall until the end of July.

Back in Normandy, Overlord is not progressing as planned. Bad weather causes delay and the Germans are not reacting as expected. Instead of pulling back to let their enemy overstretch itself then counter-attack, they dig in. They will not give up a foot. Normandy is of too much strategic importance. They have deep-water ports in Brittany with army, navy and air bases which they cannot afford to lose. The Normandy battle becomes one of terrible attrition. Inch by inch British soldiers must slog it out — and it looks to the world as if they are not getting very far, but inch by inch they grind one Panzer division after another into the ground.

Meanwhile the Americans are bogged down in a maze of ancient hedgerows that tower over them every hundred yards, twenty-foot high, ten-foot thick and bristling with German guns rendering the tanks they've brought ashore virtually useless. Week after week. A field at a time. The toll is appalling: 6,774 casualties in Normandy, on average, every day. And this will continue for seventy-seven days.

18 June. Jedburgh team George, together with a large group of FFI partisans and an SAS team, are under attack. Too much activity has brought too much attention. George has to blow their supply dump and flee their farmhouse base. In the battle 300 Germans are killed against seventy *maquisards* and six SAS.

★ ★ ★

Dad writes a letter home: 'I got the 'low-down' up in London on Friday . . . we had the Radio planes[1] coming over. They were certainly rather frightening. Two or three times we had to dive for cover. On one occasion it came so close that everyone was under the table — we even had the classic occurrence of a clash of heads of two colonels . . . It was really funny and everyone forgot the raid for at least ten minutes.' He tells his parents he won't be able to get home because 'we spend our whole time, Sundays included, working fairly hard'. What he doesn't say is that he and the other Jeds still waiting are climbing up the wall.

20 June. Churchill urges SFHQ to up the supply of arms to the Maquis. The first Jedburgh teams have set up command posts and are busy training recruits, trying to instil good guerrilla doctrine. They dish out weapons and explosives, plan ambushes; signposts are taken down, trees felled across roads, sugar slipped into petrol tanks. Near Dinan team Felix has supplied arms to 3,000 men. And German troops are wasting more and more time dealing with them.

★ ★ ★

On 1 July, all clandestine SOB operations in France, including F Section circuits and the dispatch and control of Jedburgh teams, are formally passed over to the French to be

----

[1] Doodlebugs, V-1s.

co-ordinated by General Koenig's FFI London headquarters, the EMFFI.[1] The transfer results in bureaucratic headaches, confusion and dispatch delays.

Nevertheless. In the Indre, traffic is virtually out of action. Rails have been cut in the Rhône Valley, the Tours-Poitiers line, the Bourges-Vierson line, the Toulouse-Bordeaux-Angoulême line, lines east of Nancy and south-east of Brussels — all cut. Telephone and cable lines have been cut including the Paris-Bordeaux underground cable, the Paris-Limoges cable and all telephone lines leading into Normandy. Hitler diverts Panzer divisions to squash the Resistance. Thousands of Germans who might be on their way to Normandy are otherwise engaged.

One gamble does not pay off: 1,200 containers of arms are dropped to 3,200 partisans on the Vercors Massif, a mountain plateau twenty-five miles long, south of Grenoble. The SS bomb the area continuously for four days then send in more than 10,000 combat troops. The resistants don't stand a chance: 650 *maquisards* and 200 civilians are killed; villages are razed to the ground; partisans are shot, hanged and tortured and left with their tongues and eyes cut out. Two *maquisards* are crucified. The uprising had broken every rule of guerrilla warfare, it was premature, unplanned and unorganised, and they weren't trained or armed sufficiently. The perverse upshot is that 10,000 enemy troops have been considerably tied up doing it.

---

[1] État-major des Forces Françaises de l'Intérieur.

20 July. The Allied invasion is five weeks behind schedule with troops in Normandy barely ten miles inland. Nearly fifty days after D-Day the Allies have gained as much ground as they had hoped to gain in a week. Even though they are being considerably weakened in the process, the thing about the Germans is that they will never throw in the towel.

Jedburgh teams have suffered injuries in the jump and lost supplies, with too many occasions when Jed Sets didn't survive the drop. Things on the ground with the Maquis are very different from practice with the Home Guard at Milton Hall. Lack of discipline, carelessness and infighting between local groups are cutting the Jeds' work out. Rival groups are ambushing drop zones and stealing supplies with French communists hoarding arms to fight the Gaullists later. The Maquis are not what the Jeds expected. Wild trigger-happy youths; a farmer who needs to get back to his cows; a cantankerous butcher; a fifty-year-old miller with a paunch and a taste for red wine. One fourteen-year-old boy wearing his trophy German helmet nearly gets his head blown off; another does when he rests his chin on his rifle and momentarily nods off. These boys and men need to be drilled over and over again.

Meanwhile, Dad and the remaining Jeds at Milton Hall just want to get going. Dad writes home: 'I'm still in the same position as I was two months ago — waiting — no news whatsoever, I wish something would move — it's getting very monotonous here. Morale is going down and down — in spite of it all morale needs just one small fillip and it'll be right up again. I wish it would come soon.'

★　★　★

In the first days of August US forces break out of Normandy; the Allies establish a foothold, and begin to push the Germans east. On 15 August, the Allied invasion of southern France, Operation Dragoon, lands near Toulon, from the sea and the sky. Allied Command orders the redoubling of efforts by the Resistance. Things move faster in the south. By 28 August, US commander General Alexander Patch and his 7th Army have taken control of Marseilles and are moving north up the Rhône. The object is to meet up with General Patton near Dijon to prevent German Panzer divisions forming a line of defence along the Rhine. As they are pushed from the south and west, the Germans will be heading for a natural mountain pass, fifteen miles wide, in the high country of eastern France near the Swiss border, called the Belfort Gap. The pass falls between the southern rim of the Vosges mountains and the northern rim of the Jura. A huge concentration of enemy movement is expected to funnel through this narrow corridor — the perfect opportunity for guerrilla warfare.

Three days before the Operation Dragoon landings, SFHQ call Basil down to London to receive their orders.

83

11

Dad, Robert Rivière and John Stoyka arrive at 46 Devonshire Close, the Jedburgh briefing house. There are people running up and down the stairs, desks overflowing with paperwork, telephones ringing. It is so busy everywhere they have to wait twenty minutes in the corridor for a room.

Basil will be parachuted into eastern France, just south of Besançon, to the forested uplands of the Jura, close to the Swiss border in the region known as Franche-Comté. It is in the expected line of the German retreat where enemy numbers will be swelling and dangerous. Intelligence coming in from Jedburgh teams south of the Loire have reported tens of thousands of enemy troops on the move.

Maps are rolled out across the table, large scale, small scale, regional maps, town maps, road maps, aerial photographs, long shots, detail shots. The topography of the area, with its steep gorges and turbulent rivers, its wooded valleys of oak, beech and pine, and its narrow winding roads is ideal ambush and sabotage country — with plenty of cover for hideouts and thick forests to disappear into after a raid. The team is fed with as much information as it is possible to digest: where German garrisons are located; enemy formations; terrain; local conditions, curfews, numbers of *maquisards* in the area, their state of readiness, activity; leaders: names, addresses, personal details; SOE agents: code names and contacts; safe houses, not-so-safe houses; landing grounds, reception committees.

★ ★ ★

Basil are briefed to contact the French agent, Ligne; set up a wireless link with London, then arrange parachute drops to supply arms, train recruits, then plan and facilitate operations. Ligne is the code name for Pierre Hanneton, recently inserted as de Gaulle's representative to take overall charge of resistance in the region. The area has proved dangerous territory for SOE's F Section, with Gestapo arrests and the breaking up of the Acrobat and Stockbroker circuits.

There is a knock at the door. Harry Rée walks in.

Harry is the British agent César, who ran Stockbroker and who recently had a fight with the Gestapo and escaped to Switzerland with a couple of bullets in his leg. After a spell in hospital he escaped across the Pyrenees into Spain and arrived back in Britain a month ago. He has come in to talk to Basil and two other Jedburgh teams, Cedric and Brian, who will also be going into the region. Rée enjoys a certain claim to fame in SOE for his innovative methods of 'blackmail sabotage'. His most celebrated coup was to persuade Monsieur Rudolphe Peugeot — at the time manufacturing tank parts and Focke-Wulf engines for the German air force — to assist in subtle sabotage interventions in his own factory: spanners jamming up the works, little breakdowns, one problem after another, enough to stop production but far less damaging to his valuable property than letting RAF Bomber Command have a go.

Rée has the young Jeds' full attention. He gives them information on the locals and specific dangers of the area; the smallest detail could make all the difference. He describes the atmosphere in the Jura: the lack of stability, the feelings shared by many that France is being *shot to pieces* from the inside by Frenchmen in acts of revenge and banditry upon other Frenchmen; the sense of guilt, responsibility and frustration; that once it had been easy to point the finger at the Germans, but now the Allies are coming in for a share of the blame. He describes how the population lives from news bulletin to news bulletin, becoming over-elated by good news, and excessively depressed with the bad news. '*À fleur de peau*,'[1] he says in impeccable French. They are informed that the agent sent in to replace Rée to rebuild Stockbroker was killed two days after his arrival. What has survived and is still operating with active Maquis groups is the sub-circuit, Treasurer.

'Any questions?'

What hasn't been mentioned, and what Basil will soon find out, is that the agent running Treasurer is notorious for being impossibly difficult to work with.

---

[1] Everything is on the surface of the skin.

86

A thick pall of cigarette smoke hangs in the air. The Jeds are allocated their BBC Action Messages, given personal codes, and escape maps printed on silk. To protect his family in France in case he is caught, Rivière is issued forged ID papers in the name of Roger Raincourt. From now, wherever they are, whoever they are with, whatever the circumstances, Dad and Stoyka will only refer to him as Raincourt. Each man memorises the danger codes to be sent in case they are caught and transmitting under duress. And each man receives a letter signed by General Koenig appointing the bearer as his representative. And money. Plenty of it. Dad and Raincourt are given 100,000 francs each; Stoyka, 50,000. The forged notes need to look as if they have been long in circulation. So they must spend hours crumpling them, dirtying them, folding and unfolding them, rubbing them in the earth. Full briefing over, it's a night out on the town before going back to Peterborough to collect their kit. Then it starts to rain.

PART 2

SURPRISE, KILL AND VANISH

1

Dad pees all over the garden. I have not seen him visit the loo in the house in a week. We have an outside privy but God knows if he's been using it, because lately, he doesn't seem to be able to find his way from the house to the shed, fifty feet away, where he sleeps with his dogs. These days he seems to sail rather than walk. I watch him, tacking precariously across the lawn, hands in pockets, each change of direction impelled by *going about* with a slight lean.

There are some things better not to know; others would be a shame to miss out on. Peeing tales have been a theme with Dad. In the early 1970s, when he worked in London during the week, a two-hour drive from where we lived in Hampshire, he lived in his van. It was an old blue Bedford he'd fitted out himself. For peeing he drilled a hole through the metal floor into which he slotted a funnel. This delighted him. His favourite inventions were always the simplest ones. And so, like an old dog cocking his leg, he was able to relieve himself anywhere, anytime, any place; and most importantly, without having to ask permission. Thus, merrily he sprinkled the highways, until something began to pong. The smell got worse and worse. He couldn't fathom it. And soon he couldn't go near it. He swore it couldn't possibly be connected to the set-up with his funnel. How could it be? Until eventually he discovered it was. Unknown to Dad, the floor of the van had a double skin and his drill had only perforated one of them. He'd been filling the vast cavity under the floor and transporting his pee up to London and back again until it was well and truly stewed. His van was a vast mobile chamberpot.

Dad never got to the end of this story without tears of laughter streaming down his face. But now, if I repeat it back to him, he looks at me blankly.

★ ★ ★

The latest peeing adventure put a smart lunchtime bar in Salisbury on the map. We had been on an outing, it was after three in the afternoon and I was waiting outside while Dad went in to use the Gents. I waited and I waited. Which was unusual because Dad was normally in and out in a flash. Eventually he reappeared, acting a bit sheepish.

'What happened, Dad?'

'Couldn't find it.'

'Why didn't you ask?'

'Couldn't find anyone.'

'What do you mean?'

'No one there.'

I looked at him oddly. 'So what did you do?'

He looked sly. 'Oh, I found somewhere.'

I was between dreading-to-think and dying-to-know. 'Where?'

'In there,' he shrugged, looking over his shoulder.

I peered around the door. He was right, there was no one about.

'Show me,' I asked with foreboding, but at the same time egging him on.

Dad led me towards the bar, a river of polished walnut that bisected the centre of the room; upside-down glasses glinting from the wooden racks overhead. Then he pointed over the bar. I paled. Gingerly I looked over. He was pointing to a very small circular beaten-copper sink. A slice of lemon and a sprig of mint rested on a small chopping-board beside it. I felt like a pillar of salt with my mouth open. Dad shrugged again.

Then a young barmaid came in. Oh, so sorry, she said, they were just closing. Flustered, I thanked her. Dad did a sweeping bow, twirled his hand even. I linked my arm firmly through his to remove him; I hardly dared breathe, cheeks straining, inflating to explode. Now it's on my city tour. The copper sink Dad peed in.

★　★　★

Dad, Raincourt and John Stoyka are back at Milton, kit packed, ready to go. But it is still raining. It rains and it rains. And it rains. No Carpetbagger flights in this weather. They miss the moon phase. They wait and play poker and look up at the sky. A whole week goes by. They pace the room, scrutinise the maps, go over the details in their heads. Nerves give way to impatience. Until at last, there is a break in the clouds. They get the call. They're on.

26 August. 2000 hours, Basil are driven out to the secret airfield at Harrington where a black Liberator bomber is waiting on the runway. A team of dressers help them strap on their equipment: compass, torch, water canteen, commando knife, binoculars, canvas money-belt, Colt .45 pistol in holster with extra clips of ammo, two grenades, a carbine across their chest, maps, some basic first aid, morphine, water-purifying tablets, whistle, spare socks, matches; their pockets bulge with their radio crystals, French chocolate and cigarettes. The American Colt is a tremendous status symbol amongst the Maquis; the British, used to a Webley or an Enfield, are also impressed. 'A real hairy beast,' said one Jed, Stanley Cannicott. 'It had double the muzzle energy and could really knock down an elephant.' Over the top goes the jump-smock to stop anything catching on the Joe hole, then their parachute is strapped on.

★ ★ ★

The last thing they are handed is a phial of pills: Benzedrine to keep them awake; some knockout pills 'to drop in Jerry's coffee'; and a cyanide suicide pill encased in rubber, which can be held in the mouth safely until you need to crack it with your teeth. Stoyka's radio and the rest of their kit has been packed separately in one of the twelve canisters to be dropped with them. After all the delays everyone is on edge. They are driven out to the aircraft. They meet Arnold Stamler, their American pilot, and his Carpet-bagger crew. Dad wants to check that their radio and personal kit are on board. He is assured everything is on board and there is no time anyway. The bomber's four engines are already turning and the noise is deafening. They waddle over to the fuselage and the unwieldy bulks of Dad, Stoyka and Raincourt are hauled inside.

2050 hours. Operation Bob 188A takes off, according to the records 'in a less than calm atmosphere'. On board: eight crew, three Joes, twelve Type C containers of weapons and explosives, eight packages of kit, propaganda leaflets and supplies.

For five hours they fly without lights, south-east across France with only their navigator, a map and the moonlight to guide them. Twice, they come under anti-aircraft fire. Stamler has delivered supplies on these special missions before, but this is the first time he has dropped Joes. Five cold long noisy hours. Mouths soured by tobacco. The sound of the engines rattling their eardrums, the fuselage acting like a steel drum. By the time they get to the Jura they are almost in a trance. They approach the target: 47°00'N-06°10'E, north-west of Pontarlier, and just north-east of Granges-Maillot. Stamler drops height to 600 feet. He levels the aircraft, slows to 125 mph, a speed barely above a stall. Gerry Dray, the dispatcher, checks the static lines, which pull the parachutes open, are hooked up correctly to the floor. Three small lights marking out a triangle at the drop zone are just visible below. All eyes skinned for the flashing Morse letter from the reception committee. They need the letter B. At the edge of the clearing a light begins to flash. Dash-dot-dot, dot. It's hard to make out. They circle the ground. Dash, dot-dot-dash, dash, dot, dot. They need to verify the correct letter. They circle again. And again. Back over the pinpoint of flashing light. Dash, dot, dash, dot-dot. Stamler assures them they are in the right place. They make another circuit of the ground. Dash, dot-dot, was that a dash or a dot? *Come on. Come on.* Another circuit. Dad looks at his watch. 0150 hours. Twenty minutes! *Jesus.* It would have been far safer to get in and out as quickly as possible and not be flying about like this. The flashing continues but the order remains unclear. The tension is palpable. They make a sixth circuit of the ground and still the letter is unidentifiable. They really don't want to abort, not now. Unanimously they decide to jump anyway. 'Running in,' comes the American drawl from the cockpit as the three Jeds shuffle up to the Joe hole. Dad checks his knife is easy to get at in case he has to cut himself free. 'Action stations.' The exit flaps open, a cold inrush of air. Below their feet, the moonlit fields and tops of trees. The containers go first. The men are silent. Gerry Dray's eyes fixed on the dial — waiting for the cue. Dad edges closer, feet together, hands to his side, *Don't look down.* The light goes green. 'GO!' shouts Dray. Dad tips himself forwards. A safe gap, then 'GO!' Raincourt. 'GO!' Stoyka.

Aliens falling. A gun in their pocket and a poem in their heads. The wind rushes upwards, then relief as the harness tugs. The silk rustles then blooms as each parachute fills with air. But at the back of their minds, as the earth speeds towards them, is the fear that the drop zone might have been compromised and uncertainty about the reception waiting for them. Dad reaches up to grab his shroud lines; a gentle sway, but barely a moment, straight into landing position . . . knees up, crouch. Now! He hits the ground harder and faster than he expected. The canopy collapses behind him. A roll to the right; head in. The pull of the chute drags him along the ground. Instead of being dropped a safe 600 feet, it can't have been more than 300. Stoyka is stunned. Raincourt has broken a finger. Dad looks around. The field is moving with figures, black silhouettes are running towards him. Then a flood of relief: the voices surrounding him are French. Before he can gather himself someone is briskly shaking his hand. Dad hauls in his chute, unclips his harness, and allows himself a deep draught of the balmy French night. Men are running back and forth collecting the scattered canisters. The three Jeds make their way to the wooded corner of the field. They are struck by how the reception committee is comprised of boys under eighteen and men over fifty. There is an alarming reckless bravado in the Maquis as they shout to each other, lighting cigarettes with great flaming branches, disregarding basic security. 'Where are the Germans?' Dad wants to know. 'Pff! At least two miles away!' The containers are loaded into the waiting wagons and carts, which is when they discover Stoyka's radio is missing, as is *all* their personal kit. Instead they find a consignment of cocoa and the packages of propaganda leaflets. They can only assume their Jed Set will end up where the leaflets should have, in Paris.

'We had only what we stood up in, and our pistols,' Dad writes in Basil's report. 'We were taken to Granges-Maillot, a nearby chateau and suffered from excessive hospitality.'

Sounds to me like they got blind drunk.

★ ★ ★

Dad and I are in the garden watching the tiny dot of an aeroplane write its contrail across the sky. I tell him the dot is full of people, and tea trolleys.

'Don't be ridiculous,' he says.

2

I make a pilgrimage to Granges-Maillot. It is midsummer; a camping holiday with Jonathan and dogs. I have no idea what to expect. I imagine we will buy a ticket from a booth to look round the chateau of Granges-Maillot with a few other tourists and I will be eager (and unable) to tell anyone why we are there, and the surrounding area will be overlaid with sixty-nine years of development with new roads, housing estates and shopping centres and enormous signs for the Intermarché and Carrefour. I feel apprehensive as we exit the motorway near Dole and cross the River Doubs. Jonathan is driving. We pass through the small towns of Vaudrey and Mouchard. We drive through Salins-les-Bains, past the grey stone clock tower and the market square. I try to picture the town as it would have been in 1944, German soldiers marching, staff cars with swastikas, roadblocks, checkpoints, queues for bread, bicycles; austere, grimy, poor. Out of Salins we climb steadily, through buttercup dairy pastures and mixed forests of beech, ash, spruce and pine. I am alert and pitched slightly forward in my seat. Looking, looking. Craggy limestone outcrops break through the trees. Fast cold rivers gouge their way through the plunging valleys. No supermarkets, no commercial zones. Astonishingly it feels like very little might have changed in these interim years, tidier surely, more prosperous certainly, but no new conurbations, no new roads carving through the landscape. Jonathan describes it as *Mary Poppins* country; he is a New Zealander, I think he means *The Sound of Music*. At Levier we need to turn off and find the D356, barely a threadworm on the map. There is no sign for the D356, but one to Maillot leads us to a minor road that winds through the forest. Every tree, every field, every bridge, each bend in the road feels significant; foolish I know, but everything suddenly seems to pulsate with meaning. A small sign to an FFI memorial, so hidden we almost miss it, points to a narrow lane on our left. We follow it until we arrive at a clearing where we park. I feel an overwhelming sense of anticipation, and poignancy too, that I am here and Dad is not here with me, and I wonder why, in all the camping holidays when we were young he never brought us here. We get out, look around. Just beyond where we've parked is a high stone wall, above which, framed beneath the beech canopy, is our first glimpse of the chateau of Granges-Maillot, a banded exoskeleton of white stone ribs, standing alone in the middle of the forest. There is no one here. No ticket office. No booth. No tourists. Nobody at all.

A more formal sign, commemorating the Maquis de Maillot who died during the German occupation, points us onwards, 700 metres more. We follow the track. Into some woods. Out. Across a field. Back into the woods again. We climb steadily, picking our way around boulders and roots, along the narrow path, deeper into the forest. It is easy to imagine the Maquis here, moving like deer, fleet-footed through the understorey. Another arrow urges us on.

The path continues to climb until we enter a tiny clearing and see the double cross of the Croix de Lorraine, symbol of the French Resistance. And my heart sinks a little, for instead of being on our own in the forest, undisturbed with our imaginations, there is someone here: a man with a trowel in his hands, weeding around the base of the monument. We walk slowly up. He greets us cordially and steps back to allow us to read the inscription.

We smile and nod politely, bow our heads to read the eleven names of the Maquis who died. I turn to the man and in pitiful schoolgirl French blurt out, '*Dans le guerre mon père travaille avec le Résistance ici, avec le Maquis, et quand il arrivé dans le nuit, il resté dans le château ici.*'

Miraculously the man appears to understand, tips his head gently to one side and nods. He tells us during the war the chateau was the home of his grandmother, it was she who gave safe shelter and support to the Maquis. He is doing a little maintenance on the memorial before he returns to Paris in the morning.

We nod and smile. '*Votre grandmère, ah.*' I stagger on and try to explain that Dad came by '*avion par le parachutage . . .*' I mime floating by parachute pointing to the sky. '*Il venu avec deux autres hommes . . . un Français, et un Américain. Ils arrivent dans un place caché près d'ici avec beaucoup d'équipage pour aider le Résistance — le Maquis, contra les Allemandes.'* Oh dear. There might have been some Spanish in there; my accent isn't bad but I'm sure the grammar is dreadful. He inclines his head again like a bird listening, then tells us the terrain where the parachutes landed is nearby, at a place called something beginning with, I think it is R . . . followed by '*rghrnghnee*', something that sounds like a revving lawnmower.

'*Vous connais la place où les parachutes arrivée?*' I ask incredulously as I mime the parachutes landing again.

'*Oui, oui. Rgneueouon-eoueee,*' he repeats the name.

We still cannot untangle it. It is commemorated, he says, and not far away. Not for a moment had I considered the actual site of Basil's drop zone would be traceable, or remembered by anyone after all this time.

'*Où est là, exactement?*' I ask.

He explains again.

We look at him blankly. And that is when he kindly offers to take us there; he could drive us but it's easier to walk he suggests, maybe half an hour through the forest. And so we very gratefully and very excitedly and very politely follow our guide back along the path to pick up a wider forest track behind the chateau which takes us higher up into the forest. Our companion explains the road was constructed by his grandfather for transporting logs to Besançon. We pause at the iron gates at the rear of the chateau. He tells us on a clear day between the two central chimneys you can see Mont Blanc, a hundred miles away.

The track winds gently upwards. There is an airy scooped-out sensation in the pit of my stomach. This doesn't feel quite real, like walking without touching the ground. The forest shade brings coolness to the warm day, everything seems fluttery feathery, weightless, our words, our steps. Then the trees begin to thin out and glints of sun pool together, and the stripes of daylight that flash between the trunks begin to broaden across the path until a golden haze fuzzes ahead of us, as if at the end of a tunnel, and we emerge from the forest at the brow of a hill into blue sky and a large clearing of open pasture. We are 1,000 metres above sea level. The Doubs Valley, the Jura mountains, the whole region of the Franche-Comté pours out before us, with only Switzerland to the east, its Alps obscured by clouds. It is exactly how one might imagine a drop zone to be. A gently rolling green plateau necklaced by dense woods where the Maquis and reception committee could hide; gathering kindling to light the signal fires, waiting to hear the particular drone of the American bombers, flashing out Morse letters with a torch, tracking the trajectory of the parachutes descending like thistledown.

We stand together silently. The landscape falls away into the ruffle of a hazy blue horizon. It slides in my mind's eye from day to night, from full colour to monochrome as I try to cross the portal of Time and see this ground as if for the first time, from the air, under a starry night. I crease up my eyes to conjure dark silhouettes, a moonlit face, a flare of fire. I try to imagine it. The flapping of silk, the thud of a metal canister as it hits the ground, a curse beneath a breath, the receding drone of a plane accelerating away, running steps across grass, an urgent whisper, an ox restless in its traces pawing at the ground. And I am thinking: Dad, I am here.

The track traverses the pasture leading us to the crown of the hill where a group of polished granite blocks mark the Aire de la Résistance. Black parachutes are etched into the stone with a gold inscription, commemorating this landing ground, code-named Gibier. The place name we could not catch earlier is Reugney. Our friend will leave us now. We thank him profusely. I bitterly regret my failing tongue. He suffers me to take a photograph of him. It is only as we shake hands farewell that I ask his name, which is Philippe de la Rochefoucauld. I notice in my photograph that he is still carrying his gardening gloves.

★ ★ ★

The walk back to our van, down the logging road, through the forest to the chateau, is the same journey Dad would have made with the Maquis de Maillot and their commandant, Bernard, on that August night in 1944 almost exactly sixty-nine years ago. Attentiveness all-animal, eye acute, ear acute, his, and mine as I try to alchemise the past, to walk into that one particular night, slip into his twenty-four-year-old skin. I scan for a

104

tree that might be more than seventy years old as a witness; there are majestic trees here but this forest is harvested and I cannot be sure. Was he walking, sharing a swig from a flask, in a scrum of men and boys jostling and backslapping? Or bumping along, his feet dangling out of the back of a cart? Out here, the Maquis had begun to think they'd been forgotten, the arrival of a *parachutage* was an occasion for excitement, and this one had been long in the waiting. There is a sense of wild intoxication then. The arrival of the Jedburghs in uniforms a harbinger of liberation. And the containers of weapons a massive boost for this group who had been without arms, without expertise, without direct communication. The atmosphere is contagious. The Jeds share out their chocolate and cigarettes.

The road is charged with resonance. Hooves, boots crunching, cartwheels rolling, matches striking, a bicycle being pushed, the click-click of ammunition clips slotting into Sten guns, the wind in the higher branches, low voices, laughter. Dad spoke what he called *gutter French* — not so many words, but he could deliver them convincingly among a lot of guttural noises from the back of his throat. The smell is of fresh pine needles, ox sweat, hessian, canvas, garlic and tobacco. The red disembodied glows of lit cigarettes move in the darkness; the moon splinters through the canopy, a glitter of stars; a pistol butt caught in the flash of a lamp, the blue gleam of gun metal; dark shadows sliding across the track. Like an old photograph, the colour is drained out. And everything that had up to now been in their imagination is in front of their eyes. This is it. They are down. The adrenalin still surging, each nerve ending razor-wired. Relief. Excitement. Fear. Worry. That their kit is not here. That their radio is not here; the radio that is their lifeline and the link with London so crucial to their role. We *had only what we stood up in, and our pistols.* In these first hours they must trust their lives into the care of strangers. As they make their way down this forest road in the darkness Dad must have wondered if anything could ever be the same again. It is a marked moment; a rite of passage. Adrenalin, heightened awareness, and a sense of freedom. His heartbeat and life force all bountiful. Because from now on it's serious. No more clowning. No one over his shoulder with a clipboard. One wrong step and they are a tear in their mother's eye.

3

Basil wake, if they went to sleep at all, to a view of the Alps and miles of forest stretching out in front of them. They have a visitor. A tall Frenchman in his late thirties walks into the room talking; lean, sunburnt, receding hairline, a distinct strut in his stride, his face animated as his blue eyes flicker over each young visitor. He is dressed as a commercial traveller, scruffily suited in a blue jacket, skew-whiff spotty tie, threadbare trousers pinned at the ankle — having arrived by bicycle. It is Joseph Barthelet, code-named Boulaya, chief of the Resistance in the Besançon area. His English is better than Dad's French; they are shaking hands when another man arrives, younger, slick in a brown leather jacket: Orcla, who is Colonel Lagarde, the commandant of the FFI's Groupement Frontière du Doubs. The two most influential Maquis leaders in the area have come to take Basil on a tour of the region's various Maquis groups.

Out of the 2,000 recruits only 300 are armed, and then with what Dad reports as 'a collection of which the British Museum would have been proud'.

While there is plenty of rivalry within the Maquis, what makes co-operation with the Jedburghs comparatively easy is what is on offer by way of arms and expertise; these groups who

107

up to now had been fighting with scant supplies, won or stolen, suddenly have, as they see it, their own Allied HQ with direct radio access to the storeroom. Which makes it all the more imperative for Basil to replace their lost radio. Somehow they manage to get hold of a short-wave B2 agent's radio set in working order, and with their unbroken radio crystals Stoyka is able to send his first message back to SFHQ:

Arrived safely. Radio and all personal equipment had not arrived. Please
replace. Position of Maquis — 3-4,000
ready in 6 days. 1,000 men already
instructed and organised but less
than 300 armed. Extremely urgent to
have arms and equipment for another
500 men. Maquis well trained, led and
disciplined. Possibilities in area
enormous.

Things move astonishingly fast, for later that day Basil join a cadre of *maquisards* with some Cossacks from the Ukraine in an ambush on a German convoy transporting a consignment of arms, supplies, vehicles and horses. The Cossacks were POWs and volunteers brought by the Wehrmacht to this part of France for anti-partisan duties: to *neutralise* the FFI and protect the Belfort Gap. However, they had no argument with the French and were tired of their shoddy treatment. They sensed which way the war was going, and after one too many days' rail-track mending, were in secret talks with the Maquis.

On the day of Basil's arrival, an entire Cossack battalion encircles their German barracks and in a barrage of machine-gun fire kills all their German officers. Eight hours later, another Cossack battalion north of Besançon does the same.

It's a timely coup. In addition to their fearsome reputation the Cossacks bring captured horses, wagons, supplies, ammunition and a huge cache of arms. I find a photograph of these short, stocky, battle-hardy men just after their defection, lining up in front of the leather-jacketed figure of Colonel Lagarde and Albert, the notorious SOE agent and organiser of the Treasurer circuit, whom Dad is just about to meet . . .

The ambush of the German convoy is fast and ferocious. Machine guns rattle through their ammunition, bullets spraying across the road, gunfire pipping off boulders. They dash from tree to tree. *Keep your posture straight and thin.* A grenade tears up the undergrowth; a Cossack drags a German mounted officer off his horse, another is shot out of the saddle. The element of surprise pays off. They take eleven prisoners, along with the weapons, vehicles, horses and supplies. But the local German garrison quickly gets wind of the attack and sends out an infantry unit. Basil and their new comrades are surrounded and under fire.

'We refused to 'accept battle', and retired well into the woods in great haste with our booty,' Dad's report coolly informs.

They take cover in the steep wooded valley

outside Ornans, a medieval town on the banks of the River Loue. Germans swarm through the forest, but awkward terrain is an advantage for the Jeds and partisans who are faster and fleeter than their enemy; they scuttle along gullies and skid down ravines until they eventually disappear deep into the woods with their prisoners and captured supplies. Their first test. They have been blooded.

They have escaped. But then the German commander sends an ultimatum that he will raze Ornans and shoot 200 hostages unless the eleven prisoners and supplies are returned. It is decided the Maquis leader, Bernard, with a captain and a prisoner (to prove they are still alive and being well treated), will talk to the German commander. What is said must have been more than a little menacing, because the Maquis get to keep both supplies and prisoners without reprisal; helped in no small measure, according to Dad, by the graffiti he made some boys paint on the garrison walls that read: 'WHICHEVER German gives the order WILL BE assassinated WHATEVER it costs.'

The overall situation was not looking good for the Germans, and luckily this commander understood it was not an idle threat. Nevertheless, it was a daring gamble and Ornans was fortunate for the risk of reprisal was real: in a fortnight's time, only a few miles up the road, the Gestapo will shoot twenty-two men hiding in a cellar.

★ ★ ★

Each day the atmosphere becomes more desperate and dangerous. Anyone caught helping the Resistance is shot. There is not a rail yard in France which does not display the sign: 'AVERTISSEMENT: peine de mort contre les saboteurs. Pour le pays, pour ta famille, pour ton ravitaillement, pour toi.' Notices with thick bold type, barking 'APPEL' 'To the French Population!' are slapped on doors along the main streets boasting the latest threats and atrocities and signed personally by the German garrison commander: 'It is also my duty to hold the ENTIRE POPULATION responsible for the fact that up till now we have been unsuccessful in our attempts to lay hands on these cowardly murderers and give them the punishment they deserve.' Night raids by the Gestapo regularly drag boys of fourteen and fifteen off to be shot. In Besançon, Vital Deray, a nineteen-year-old Resistance fighter, is permitted to write a last letter to his family just a few minutes before he is put in front of a firing squad. There are hundreds of these last letters from teenage boys to their mothers and fathers.

Parents, maman . . . take courage . . . Here's my modest last will: I leave my camera to my brother Michel whom I loved very much, my watch to my dear, kind Daddy who wasn't always strict enough with me, my bicycle to my brother Julien who is such a loving son to our mother, the watch I have here with me to dear Mother along with everything I possess including my heart

111

. . . I must hurry to write these last lines. Be strong. My hand's trembling a bit . . . A big kiss to you, Mummy: my love to all, Daddy, brothers; I love you. Your son, your brother, who's sending you hugs and kisses for the last time.

Be strong. Vital Deray

Letters telling tales on fellow citizens pile high on German desks, naming this grocer, that restaurant, the son of a neighbour, the nephew of a friend. The pro-Nazi French Vichy government have their own secret police, the Milice, who, being French, can far more easily infiltrate the Resistance.

Dad learns to trust communists, nuns, priests and schoolteachers, because they have less to lose; whereas 'respectable' French with money or position tend to value that more than their country's freedom. His assessment sounds harsh to me as certain death was the punishment for hiding an agent. But the Jedburghs have to be feral, follow their instincts and make quick decisions on who they can rely on. As Allied troops approach, the Maquis begin their own bush-trials for collaborators with swift executions; the Jeds have little option but to look the other way.

Dad has enough problems to deal with: it's not proving easy to get the Maquis to clean their guns; keep their mouths shut; follow safety procedures; stop holding up the tobacconist's; indeed, stop taking potshots at any opportunity. Sometimes it's just fear, terrified young boys spooked into shooting a moving cow and giving their position away; but more often than not, they simply can't resist bagging a German helmet. Now they must learn how to wait, and silence is unnerving; if someone lets loose, it blows everything. There is no rest, no relaxation, no down time. Take a piss against a tree and you get shot in the back. Clean guns, still tongues and smart timing save lives, and success depends on the Maquis following orders. The Jeds try tact, persuasion, the promise of arms, they sing French anthems, raise toasts and even listen to interminable patriotic speeches. But sometimes stronger measures are necessary. One trouble-maker can put everyone's life in danger. The Jeds call them Napoleons. And will shoot them if they have to.

4

I wanted to be an Elf. I didn't want to be a Brownie or a Girl Guide, I wanted to be an Elf. I went on and on, relentlessly, about it. Threw sulks and begging fits.

'I want to be an elf. I want to be an elf. Why can't I be?'

But I never got either Mum or Dad to budge. Patrick tells me he had wanted to be a Scout, but he wasn't allowed to be one of those either. I thought it was because it was a nuisance, because Mum couldn't be bothered to take me up the road to wherever the Elves hung out. But Patrick tells me it was because Dad saw it as one step away from Hitler Youth.

* * *

Dad is whittling down the end of a long dowelling rod.

'What are you making, Dad?' I enquire.

'Oh, you know, a, a . . . a . . . a stick.'

He's always liked cylindrical lengths of wood. They are light and strong at the same time. In his London home in Kennington he barred the basement windows with dowelling rods, from the inside. It saved him a fortune. From the street it looked very convincing. Each length cut to size and painted iron grey, then spaced two inches apart and held in place by a small wad of

114

Blu-Tack top and bottom. Dad countered any jeering with, 'Well, they're not going to break the window to find out they're *not* iron bars, are they?'

'What kind of stick?' I ask.

'Oh, you know . . . ' He carries on whittling.

Half an hour later I see him at the front gate.

He is saying to my neighbour, 'I don't remember you, but I do remember your teeth. They're very distinctive.'

★ ★ ★

After the ambush Basil move to a safe house at Clucy, near Salins-les-Bains, where they send a message to Théodule, the SOE agent running the Treasurer circuit. Théodule, who is Albert, who *was* Captain A. P. Townsend, who *was* Pat, who *is* the very tall, very young, French aristocrat, Alain Jean René Maze-Sencier le Comte de Brouville. Who is haughty, superior, quick-tempered, implacable, arrogant, driven, brilliant, tempestuous, obstinate, fastidious, bullish, highly strung, eager, and *very* possessive. Albert has tremendous knowledge and influence in the region but he resents Basil coming. And Basil are expecting two more Jed teams, Maurice and Norman, to be dropped into the area that night, along with a *parachutage* of supplies. The reception committee has been organised, but to deploy the teams, plan operations and ensure the weapons are distributed successfully, they need Albert's co-operation. They arrange to rendezvous after the drop.

28 August. Midnight. Basil wait with the

reception committee in the cover of the forest perimeter. They hear the distant drone of the Liberator bombers and see four black silhouettes appear over the horizon. Three boys run out to light the small bonfires that mark out the triangle. The planes fly over. They flash the Morse letter: K. Count one, two, three, cut the light; one, cut; one, two, three, cut. They flash it again. The night sky fills with parachutes as metal canisters come thudding down. One plane circles and flies over again dropping three dark silhouettes. With Norman down safely, the reception committee sweeps through the area. Sixty containers of arms and numerous packages are loaded onto waiting carts.

Still no sign of Maurice. Basil elect to wait. But no other plane arrives. Eventually they abandon the site and make their way, very late, to a farmhouse — to meet Albert.

Dad's entrance is recounted in a magazine article published after the war by Ronnie Noble, a war correspondent and news cameraman for Universal News, who had escaped from a POW camp in Italy, crossed the border from Switzerland and joined the Resistance in hope of getting an inside story. 'Rendezvous at Midnight' reads like a camped-up story out of *Boy's Own* (although by the time Noble published his article the detail had become muddled):

> we sat around the radio listening for the *messages personnel* . . . At last our own message came through. '*Le canard est sur le lac.*'

We cheered . . . we were to receive our biggest ever arms drop and a special agent was coming to advise us on the operation. A convoy of cars set off to the dropping-ground and guards were placed on the perimeter . . . The fires were built and we stood, waiting for midnight, when we should hear the drone of our aircraft approaching.

Small groups of men stood silent, ears strained . . . It was a risky situation, for if we lit the guiding fires too soon, German patrols might see them and attack . . .

Yes, there it was, a quiet droning in the distance.

Albert, our commandant, stood by with his torch to flash the code letter which would open the planes' bellies and shower arms and equipment down to us.

'Light the fires!' Albert yelled . . .

The aircraft swished above us, a light blinked and Albert replied. In a flash the chutes were out and dropping all around us . . . The area, so quiet a few minutes ago, was now a scene of intense activity. Parachutes were buried, canisters opened, arms distributed, ox-drawn carts loaded with equipment . . . But there was no sign of our special agent . . . Three hours later, tired but jubilant, we went back to our HQ.

'But where the hell is our expert?' grumbled Albert . . . There was a knock at the door. Everybody scrambled for a weapon. '*Entrez!*' growled Albert.

I'll never forget the next moment. The

door opened slowly and there facing us stood a young man, in Harris tweed jacket, corduroy trousers, smoking a pipe. 'Excuse me, gentlemen,' he said. 'My name's Carew . . . Got lost somehow.'

When the laughter died down he gave us the plan. 'In three days we shall be relieved,' he said. 'In the meantime, we must attack the Germans in Besançon.'[1]

I can imagine Dad saying something like that. For pleasure, effect, to defuse a tense atmosphere, tongue firmly in cheek. He loved his pipe; amazingly (to me) it seems there was always something to put in it. The plane carrying Maurice, it turns out, failed to locate the DZ and set off the air defences at Dole, so had to abort the mission.

Albert has had command of the area for months and it has become a way of life, an outlaw existence he has developed a taste for. He passes himself off as an English agent *pretending* to be French, speaking in heavily English-accented French to his Maquis comrades, only

---

[1] This article was cut out and kept by Dad's parents with no indication what paper it came from. In *Shoot First*, Noble describes asking the Jedburghs to drop a cine-camera to him, but the War Office would not oblige. No camera meant no story, so the Jeds gave him a big bundle of francs from the stack of forged notes in one of the canisters so he could make his way back to England.

becoming natively fluent when unobserved. The disguise gives him authority with the French, for he is preposterously young for his role; and if he is caught by the Gestapo, being able to *prove* he is French and not a British agent (who as far as Hitler was concerned was outside the protection of the Geneva Convention) could save his life. Because the area is now so thick with Germans, he and his American radio operator, Paul (who every girl falls in love with), are constantly on the move. He smokes continuously, doesn't eat, doesn't sleep. He has gone almost feral living under the wing of an armed gang, with plenty of wine and plenty of deference. The Jedburghs dropping in on his patch like this with all their kit and promises of arms and guerrilla know-how rankles. He'd prefer the weapons without the experts. He is suspicious they will undermine his authority and doesn't like the intrusion one bit. The tension caused by his pique is so bad it almost jeopardises the whole operation. Ligne, the head of the FFI of the region, is forced to intervene. They agree to a division of labour: the Jedburghs will plan attacks and train volunteers; Albert will concentrate on his intelligence work — getting agents into German-held towns and garrisons for information. Dad is in charge of ambushes, explosives and small-arms instructions. They set straight to, and blow up a railway line.

What camaraderie they must have felt, these rugged Robin-Hooders, dirt blending in with their suntans, torn shirts, torn neckerchiefs, nicotine-stained fingers. Regrouping back in the forest after they've derailed a train. A warren of hiding places, lookouts, river crossings; navigating a network of intersecting paths, remembering glades, boulders, landmarks — the pine that leans at an angle after a storm, a shoulder of limestone which juts above the canopy, a pylon, a precipice. They move at night, learn the sky; sleep in a shepherd's shelter, a haystack, a convent, a barn, a tent in the trees made of parachute silk. Early-morning mist is good cover. A bike is hidden in a cave; a car in a haystack — the Germans are now commandeering any form of transport. There is milk, butter if you are lucky, honey, eggs, bread, the semi-liquid *cancoillotte* cheese, red wine, Calvados, acorn coffee, a rabbit barbecued over the fire. This is when Dad gets his taste for rough red wine. They hack off a slice of cured meat with a knife, tear a thick hunk of bread, knock back a slug of brandy fermented from last year's dregs; the Maquis laugh as they wipe their mouths with their sleeves, they call it *limonade des parachutistes*. Dad teaches them how to unscrew sections of rail on one side of the track so that the whole train, in one sleek motion, will gracefully subside. They are eager, dirty and *alive*. This was where it started. What Dad called *being his own man*. How would anything measure up to this? At night, above the clearing of their camp in the forest, there is a bowl of stars.

5

Dad's getting worse. He's beginning not to recognise his own face.

'I'm amazed at what goes on,' he says.

'What do you mean?'

'This,' he says, pointing to his beard and whiskers, 'I didn't put any of this on.'

'Maybe it just grew by itself,' I suggest.

He thinks that's funny. '*Someone* put it on.'

'Who?'

'Those people. The ones that come in.'

'You mean Alison, or Vanessa?' I ask, referring to his carers.

He pouts. His face is still very expressive.

'When did they do that?' I ask.

'I don't know.'

He looks at himself in the mirror, 'If it's not me, then it's someone else,' he says mysteriously.

★ ★ ★

What is to become of him? Every day we give him a handful of pills. They arrive packed, dated: Monday, Tuesday, Wednesday . . . each sealed pocket containing his prescribed confection: irbesartan, furosemide, citalopram, quetiapine, clopidogrel, bisoprolol, verapamil (no grapefruit), bumetanide. What if we don't give him these any more? What if we *do* give him grapefruit with verapamil? What are we really doing for Dad in our First

World with our rich resources, our complex pharmaceuticals, our humane ways, our ethical behaviour, our warped cruelty? I am getting in a bind about Dad. One minute he thinks he is going mad, the next he thinks we are trying to rob him. He was always proud of his clear, unencumbered thinking. I hope my memory of him won't be of this demented old man. I wonder how the old Tom would deal with the new one. He could never bear this *type of thing*; he would have shuddered and shrugged; or just said, 'Sad.' Or, 'There we are,' and clap his hands, and move on. Once, he said he'd sail away if he had to, for whatever reason, when the time came, he'd get in his boat and head out to sea. He loved the sea and the wind, pitching himself against the elements. It brought him alive. Which is why he liked sailing small boats. If I was able to describe the new Tom to the old one, he'd laugh and say, 'Shoot me, for Christ's sake.' And he would mean it. I don't know how to shoot my dad, or when to.

* * *

There is one of life's pleasures he still enjoys. Chocolate. Anything sweet, in fact. He pushes his chicken around, but makes very quick work of the chocolate ice cream over which I've drizzled two large spoons of golden syrup.

'Scrumptious. Hmmm . . . Terribly good!' He ponders on this, 'How absurd to say *terribly* good.'

I can see him searching for a better word. I wait.

'Sexually good!' he says, looking triumphant.

122

★ ★ ★

A sudden crack of gunfire whistles past the trees. The Jeds and partisans scatter deep into the forest. German soldiers fan out to scour the terrain. Dad gets separated. He manages to hide in some dense undergrowth. When the heat dies down he makes his way to a safe house, the home of a local schoolteacher. That night, as he sits around their kitchen table, wireless on in the background, he hears, to his utter astonishment, a message for *him* from the BBC. '*Ici Londres! Les Français parlent aux Français,*' and then, '*Un message pour Basil.*' It repeats, '*Un message pour Basil.*'

I vividly remember Dad's recollection of this from my childhood: the story of him hiding in a French schoolteacher's house when he gets a message from the BBC. The surreal gravitas of his situation — on his own, a young man hiding in a French house in enemy-occupied territory hot with Germans all around, and the BBC transmitting a personal message. It struck him powerfully. The message tells Dad another radio has been dropped for them and to go to the 'friend in the north'. The friend in the north is the SOB agent Émile, George Millar.

As Dad sleeps on a rough cot in the cellar of the schoolteacher's house, the Jedburgh team Augustus, dropped in Picardy, take advantage of a rainy night for cover on their journey towards the German lines near Laon, in a horse-drawn cart. At 2215 hours the heavens open and they are in the middle of a torrential downpour with

123

lightning, thunder and driving rain. It is impossible to hear or see anything. At a cross-roads outside the village of Barenton-sur-Serre they run into a German roadblock. They are surrounded and searched. Their radio is discovered in the back of the cart. Half an hour later three Jedburghs are lying side by side on the road; each man shot in the head.

★ ★ ★

At the Jedburgh reunion I'd asked Dad what it was *really* like in France.

'I was a nobody,' he'd replied. 'We lived in the forest . . . that kind of thing . . . ' he sounded wistful. 'It was a splendid life. You know. Fundamental. I liked it. I am inventive — it suited me. If we were chased we were faster than the Germans . . . ' His voice trailed off. 'I was wandering around, I did my best to see if I could help. I was a nobody really . . . '

'What about your Croix de Guerre? You got one of those, that must have been for something.'

Dad guffawed, 'Those? They came down with the rations!'

'Were you ever frightened?' I had asked him.

'I don't know. I suppose I must have been.'

There were vehicles but precious little fuel, unless it was stolen; bicycles were the mainstay, but the Maquis usually had a car hidden away in a barn somewhere. Dad's favourite was the Citroën Traction Avant, which, with tyres filled with hay, could be driven in the forest. Many vehicles had been converted to run on burning charcoal with jerry-built contraptions welded behind the boot or with large balloon-bags strapped on top. They were called *gazogénes* and worked by generating water-gas from injecting steam over the charcoal.

Dad once told me he had a car powered from a balloon of gas on the roof, but I was a teenager and he had that look in his eye and I didn't believe him.

'Good try, Dad. Too dangerous,' I scoffed, 'you can't con me. It would blow up.'

He let it go with his ubiquitous shrug and it was long forgotten.

Years later, I was watching an episode of *Dad's Army*, in which Jones pulls a ruse to get free petrol coupons for his butcher's van only to be scuppered by Captain Mainwaring, who converts it to run on gas from a bag on the roof. I could feel my vanquished grin spread.

Dad must have guessed I would find out about *gazogènes* one day, and that when I did, the moment would transport me back to our conversation. He had got one over me even if he couldn't chalk it up at the time. There, for him, was the pleasure in it: he could and would enjoy the future whether he was there or not. I rang him straight up.

'You bastard,' I said.

* * *

August plays out. Enemy numbers are flooding into the area daily; the air corridor is busy with a stream of transport planes — German Junkers

52, lumbering overhead towards Germany. Stoyka radios SFHQ for more arms *and boots!* A request Basil complain is ignored. Not so surprising considering the tonnage of rifles, machine guns, rocket launchers, grenades, mortars and rounds of ammunition being dropped to the Resistance all over France at the time — more than 6,000 tons of it in 4,000 Carpetbagger sorties between July and September. Jedburgh missions are gaining a reputation with Allied command, as countless acts of sabotage on German troop movement makes life easier. With each success more volunteers pour in; demand is overwhelming supply with 30,000 *maquisards* waiting for weapons and potential recruits estimated at 100,000 or more. But while Eisenhower wants 120,000 partisans armed, he also fears arming them *too* lavishly in case of serious problems after liberation between the different factional groups. Everywhere in France the Germans are under pressure and troops in retreat are swelling numbers on all roads heading towards the Belfort Gap. Persistent movement of heavy Wehrmacht traffic makes security for airdrops more and more difficult to guarantee, which is why the Jeds and the Maquis are forced to rely on captured weapons and whatever deserters like the Cossacks bring with them.

As Eisenhower pushes east, American and French North African troops from the Operation Dragoon landings, led by General Patch, are pursuing Panzer divisions at speed north up the Rhône Valley. The Germans requisition food, livestock, petrol, bicycles, all vehicles. SHAEF want the enemy kept on the roads where they can be got at, not to let them stray into the hills and forests. A German troop train is derailed on the Besançon-Belfort line. Basil receive orders to shut off escape routes and control the border with Switzerland.

While the FFI wrests command of some areas, Besançon and the route to Belfort is still under German control. The enemy is jumpy. The Jedburghs must keep their focus: the bad bullet is the one you aren't waiting for. North of Besançon, on the DZ where team Cedric is expecting an arms drop, they encounter 800 Germans camping in the field.

SFHQ in London is receiving a hundred transmissions a day giving the positions of German troops and requesting airstrikes. Ambushes and roadblocks funnel convoys onto secondary roads in narrow valleys where they can be picked off. It is where the terrain of the Jura is accommodating. Road signs are swivelled round and the routes controlled by the Maquis are guarded by sentries armed with passwords. There is a smell of death in the forests, German soldiers rot in ditches and by the side of the road. Crows circle. In a wood outside Besançon, a fourteen-year-old *maquisard* is shot dead when he mistakes some Germans for partisans when they wave the French flag.

2 September. Basil to SFHQ:
Information received from good source
— concentration of 40 tanks in Dijon,
Gray and Vesoul area. 40,000 men

marching from Dole to Besançon yesterday 1 September. Enemy seen to be
forming lines of resistance.

2 September. SFHQ to Basil:
For all the chiefs of the region. The
Germans are proceeding with all means
of transport to the departments of
Jura and Cote d'Or in order to evacuate their men. Do everything possible
to hinder them.

For the Jedburghs, as the Allies approach the
danger increases. The constant enemy movement
and speeding armoured vehicles of retreating
Germans are at their most menacing, reoccupy-
ing villages and towns which a day or two before
had been liberated. The situation is confused. It
is a perilous time for guerrilla fighters who have
no means of direct communication with
oncoming troops — who have no idea where the
Jeds are. They are between a rock and a safe
place with lots of fireworks in between. At any
moment they could find themselves in the midst
of a heavy assault of shelling or artillery barrage.
While they don't have contact with forward
troops they do have contact with London. Stoyka
has to use his emergency 'skeds' instead of his
allocated time slots for contacting London
because the Germans are jamming the airwaves;
without his Jed Set (the replacement Jed Set
broke on landing) he is dependent on power for
the B2 transceiver which the Germans keep
cutting off without warning. But when three

enemy planes keep circling over the house where he is transmitting he knows he has been detected. He stops sending, and coolly waits till they leave.

An American intelligence officer sent by General Patch turns up with a message for Basil to preserve the bridges for Patch's troops and ensure they are not blown by the enemy in their departure.

★ ★ ★

4 September. Basil have planned an assault on the German garrison at Mouthe, and are ready to go. All roads are cut and the Swiss frontier securely guarded. At noon, with three companies of FFI and a company of Tirailleurs Algériens, the siege begins.

> Basil to SFHQ:
> The attack went in at about 1600 hours.
> German resistance was strong, and only
> after 2 hours' hard fighting was the
> garrison taken. Over 120 prisoners and
> many killed, our losses were slight . . .

The next day they attack the larger garrison at Pontarlier, twenty-four kilometres north.

> Basil to SFHQ:
> The attack went in at 0800 hours.
> PONTARLIER was ours by midday, after the
> usual incidents that go with every
> fight . . .

The area is in a state of flux. Thousands of Germans in trucks, tanks, cars, on foot, on horses, on bicycles, Germans arriving, Germans leaving, all streaming east into the bottleneck of the Belfort Gap. Hitler is nursing visions of launching an armoured counter-attack. The Germans set up delaying positions south of the Doubs and establish a defensive line halfway from Besançon to Belfort.

Team Norman is in the middle of a firefight until dawn with Germans retaking the village of Nods. Norman's radio operator, the American 'Lou' Lajeunesse, watches a young Maquis boy drop a grenade into a passing tank turret. The Germans disembowel the boy with a bayonet, gouge out his eyes, then cut his nipples off. Two weeks before, Lajeunesse had witnessed the execution of the fourteen-year-old boy who cranked his radio generator. In a week's time he will be transmitting from a farmhouse when some Germans will barge in and kill the farmer and his wife. Lou will swiftly tap out the co-ordinates of the house before he climbs out the window. From the woods nearby he will watch an American bomber blow the house to pieces with the Germans inside. Retribution isn't usually as sweet.

6

I am at the National Archives in Kew. The release of SOE's classified files inundates me with names, code names, towns, places, *groupements* and *sous groupements*, bureaus, operations, colonels, captains, half-captains, commandants, regiments; just the acronyms for the patriot organisations grind to standstill traffic across the page. George Millar called it the Alphabetical Resistance: there is the FTP, the FFI, the APA, the AS, the BCRA, BOE, ETA, CAD, CAS, CE, CFC, CNR, FANA, FN, GF, JAC, JIC, LSGD, MCF, SAP, OCM, TSI, and that is only the start of them. I am swallowing dates, places, facts: this ambush, that town liberated; but this doesn't convey the red-blooded teeth of it, the youth of it, these *very* young black sheep dropped (literally) into the danger zone; and yet, in so many instances, thriving there. A danger zone that becomes a passport to self-discovery. There is exhilaration in the fear, fear in the exhilaration, the thrill of not just life-on-the-tightrope but everything that goes with it. Hunger. Courage. Loyalty . . . Love. Humour and passion too. The darkest jokes. Fundamental, Dad called it. And this is uncomfortable for a daughter: to report her father brave seems so plainly partisan. Fight was fuelled by adrenalin so in the moment fear was put aside, but the minutes leading up to action could be very different, and a failure of nerve could be fatal for everyone: containing fear was crucial for it easily became contagious. At Kew I stare out of the window at the ornamental pond below where a moorhen guards its nest.

★ ★ ★

8 September. To supply the increasing number of guerrilla forces Basil receive an arms drop of 1,200 containers of weapons from fifty-six planes to a DZ eight kilometres long. It is a spectacular *parachutage* and a massive logistical exercise that takes thirty-six hours to collect. The same day, after forty-eight hours of heavy fighting, the Allies take Besançon. More than 2,000 Germans have been captured or killed. But the surrounding villages in the front line are still overrun.

9 September. The first German V-2 rocket lands in London. Fragments are found in Chiswick so hot they are untouchable while others are coated with ice. Before it hit London, the rocket is believed to have reached a height of thirty-eight miles.

```
Basil to SFHQ:
Maquis leaders playing politics. Our
team has become separated and we are
out of touch with one another. Send
instructions as to steps to be taken.
This message is from Sergeant Stoyka.
```

Raincourt has set up his HQ in Pontarlier, but the last time Stoyka heard from Dad was in Salins with Colonel Lagarde, training his *maquisards* into the 1st Battalion of the Regiment Franche-Compté. In one of the last areas to be liberated, Dad's cobbled-together regiment of young guerrillas has been fighting at the heels of the German retreat and been in nearly every action up to Pont-de-Roide. They have no greatcoats or blankets and are hungry, wet and cold. Dad writes, 'the doctor (whose name escapes me) and his nurse, Christine, were always working, and it seems never tired'.

They are right in the thick of it, crawling around the German lines; mortars rumbling all night in the distance; flashes lighting up the whole sky from mines, bombs, artillery. There are German guns dotted on the hillside, a sniper on the ridge, and the house behind them is being shelled by American guns. The Germans are desperate, battle-hardened and everywhere — stealing food, stealing anything. Corpses lie all over the road, bootless, weaponless. Then things take a turn for the worse.

Dad thought the Americans were coming up either side of them, only to discover they are now a small island surrounded by Germans with no means of communication with the Allies who don't know they're there. They have to get back across the lines and make a break for it. The route ahead is mined. A wave of machine-gun fire rattles out. The Americans attack. The Germans counter-attack. Dad and his men are in the middle. Which is the moment Dad learns *never* to mix guerrilla forces with regular forces. 'I thought that's enough of that game. We had to split up and infiltrate back. I was rescued by some nuns. Nasty situation.' I'm not sure Dad was *rescued* by the nuns. Patrick remembers Dad telling him they had to escape through a sewer system, but it was definitely a convent where he and his FFI unit received refuge. Once safely behind the convent gates they are able to rest for a couple of days. In Basil's report, Dad writes drolly, 'The hospitality of the nuns was of the very best.'

I can hear his voice. The mischief in it. But it is hard to know what was written for his superiors, what boxes had to be ticked, how much artful glossing over or skating round the less orthodox . . . his eyebrow raised imperceptibly as he wrote. His praise of the Maquis responds to qualities he enjoyed in himself: 'in spite of the youth of the officers of the FFI they did their job well, although unorthodoxly. They were quick, and willing to take advice, and learned the lessons of experience quickly. What they lacked in training they made up in versatility.' That deadpan expression of his, impossible to read. He was excellent at poker, and excellent at chess.

Not every Jedburgh is as lucky. In the Vosges, north of Basil, team Jacob, dispatched alongside an operation mounted by the SAS, are also surrounded and outnumbered. In the shoot-out, of thirty-three men captured only the Jed radio operator will survive. The one officer who escapes operates briefly on his own but is eventually captured, beaten, put under prolonged interrogation then sent to a concentration camp. Although the Red Cross is notified he is a

POW two months later on 25 November, Dad's twenty-fifth birthday as it happens, the Nazis execute him in a bomb crater at Gaggenau.

Arthur Brown wrote that by late summer France 'was a disgusting place to be'. The FFI was becoming chaotic with local leaders vying for power, making wide sweeping arrests and executing collaborators without trial. Lou Lajeunesse assigns a fourteen-year-old to guard some prisoners for half an hour, only to come back and discover the boy has shot them all. 'They tried to escape,' the boy says smiling. Head shaving; branding; killing; parading; stoning; mutilating: 30,000 French die in *the purification of France*, the same number shot and executed by the Nazis during occupation. It was a dark time for the Resistance. And time to leave.

As France becomes liberated and German troops pour back as fast as they can across the Belfort Gap with Allied armies chasing them, instructions from London come in for Jed teams to exfiltrate. But it is de Gaulle who wants them out.

* * *

In the *Weekend* section of the *Telegraph*, 1 January 1994, splashed across a double-page spread, is an article about George Millar returning to the village of Vieilley for a reunion with his French comrades after fifty years. Under the heading 'The Old Unbeatables', the photograph shows George standing in front of

135

the entrance to some sewers where he hid from the Germans half a century ago. Could this be the same sewer Dad remembered? They were in the same region at the same time and knew each other, but I don't know if they were ever in the same scrapes. I do know Dad swapped his Jedburghs' officer uniform with George for a car. Or that was how Dad told it. All the Jedburghs had a uniform in their kit to be worn if the Germans were closing in on them, but George Millar, attached to SOE's F Section, did not, and as a wanted spy he was in a far more dangerous position. A deal was struck. Dad expected to be given an old banger with flat tyres stuffed with straw, but to his delight the car turned out to be one of the most wonderful convertible French motors of the day. Over time this car took on a mythic status — Dad described the chrome, the paintwork, how the hood went into the boot on a cantilever. Many years later, a friend sent him a picture of a Peugeot 402 Convertible with the note, 'Hope, this is 'the car'!' Dad of course was convinced it was. Maybe. Although, I think it was far more likely to have been a Citroën Familial, or at a stretch a Cabriolet.

Either way, on 26 September, Dad conveniently dodges the plane sent to pick him up, and drives the car to the house of the schoolteacher who sheltered him near Clucy, and he says his farewells: to Lagarde, to Boulaya, to Bernard, to Albert, to Captain Patoar, and Captain Voirin, his lieutenants Devik and de Camp, and, no doubt, to the nurse, Christine; he collects Stoyka and they leave Besançon. With the taste of marc on his lips Dad drives all the way from the Jura to Paris, across newly liberated France, and up the Champs-Élysées.

Alas, Dad's plans to continue celebrating after the 350-kilometre journey are short-lived. De Gaulle orders all British SOE agents out of France within forty-eight hours. After his triumphant return from exile he is in no mood for sharing victory. He wants his hands firmly on the reins; he suspects the British and Americans might undermine his political strength, or, worse, try to keep their armies in France and take over her overseas possessions.

It was Clementine Churchill who, just before de Gaulle's return, said to him, 'General, you must not hate your friends more than you hate your enemies.' To which he famously replied, 'France has no friends, only interests.' As for the Maquis, de Gaulle is forced to acknowledge their role, but considers many of its leaders a dangerous revolutionary threat with communist leanings, and is both alarmed and irritated at the public support they are getting. He moves swiftly to break up their liberation committees which includes, petulantly, sending their British comrades home. From a lay point of view I am surprised de Gaulle enjoyed the bargaining position he did, considering how many lives, limbs, resources and expertise Britain and America gave for France's liberation, but that is politics for you, and there was a very real fear France could descend into civil war.

So barely a day after his arrival in Paris Dad is

recalled to London. A day that will become etched in his memory, because at the end of it he parks his *glorious* car outside a Parisian fruit and veg shop, runs his finger over the shiny chrome, along the gleaming paint, then walks into the shop nonchalantly, and in his inimitable Dad-way, tosses the stunned shopkeeper his keys.

7

The historian James Holland lives at the end of our lane. He knows about Dad. He would have liked to have interviewed him about SOE, but it's too late now. Even so he rings me to say he has been lent some Sten guns, and wonders if seeing the guns might jog Dad's memory a bit. He also has a helmet, a grenade and an old radio set. Things Dad should be familiar with. He invites us down to have a look. There are heavy boxes of rifles with telescopic sights.

Dad picks up each object and smiles. He dutifully inspects the guns. Rolls a grenade in his palm as if it were an overripe mango. Turns the German helmet, politely, a full 360 degrees.

I point to the radio set. 'Look, Dad. Do you remember these?'

'Oh, yes,' he says.

'And this? Did you have one of these?' I ask, showing him the Sten gun.

'Oh, yes,' he says knowingly.

I meanly pick up a biro off Jamie's desk. 'And this?'

'Oh, yes.'

We are driving back up the lane when he turns to me and says, 'He's a bit younger than me, I think.'

'Who?'

'That man.'

'The man we've just seen?' I splutter, incredulous.

'All those guns,' Dad muses.

A laugh explodes out of me. Jamie, fresh-faced, irrepressibly youthful, is more than fifty years Dad's junior. I shake my head; no matter what the company, Dad has always seen himself as the brightest and freshest, and consequently, I suppose, by some curious deduction, the youngest in the room.

★ ★ ★

Dad is listening to the wood pigeons in the ash tree.

'What's that bird say?' he asks.

'What do you mean, Dad?'

'Listen.'

I listen. *Cooo-coo-roo, coo-c-cooo-roooo.*

He repeats, mimicking the pigeon, '*Tom Carooo Tom Carooo Tom Carooo.*'

I nod. 'You're everywhere, Dad.'

We sit together at the end of the garden and watch the sun set across the pasture. Insects rise, the day's last rays snagging their gossamer wings, tracking each indecipherable flight. He is completely immersed in it. I watch him watching. He is far away. We sit together, floating in and out of each other's consciousness, aware and unaware, silent with our private thoughts. His world is fading. Coming and going in front of his own eyes; each name hazy, each face a blur of memory. Every house he lived in, every girl he loved, slip-sliding away. Night is beginning to surround him. He stands helplessly, ears ringing with noises he cannot understand, words that don't make sentences, sounds that don't make words, faces that are completely new to him, places that he knew so well until yesterday. The hourglass has slowed and quickened simultaneously. And yet. The idea of one day him not being in the world seems an impossibility.

★ ★ ★

In the post-mortems after France, the Jedburghs' commonest complaint was Timing. They all believed they could have achieved more had they gone in earlier. This was most keenly felt by the nineteen teams dropped into high densities of battle-experienced enemy troops in eastern France with little time to get to know their partisans. Apart from the early Brittany teams, the main stream of Jed missions were deployed after the Allied breakout in the north, and the Dragoon invasion in the south. The reasoning behind not deploying teams before the invasion was the risk of jeopardising security in the intense secrecy surrounding Overlord, and that too many teams inserted too early could leave no reserve. And of course before D-Day it was unknown if the Resistance would have any meaningful effect. Nevertheless many Jeds believed if they'd had more time and all the arms they'd asked for, they would have been able to sort out the German Army entirely and prevent *any* of their troops getting home. The other Jedburgh gripe was Supply. Team Alastair, after not receiving their requested drop, sent a tart message in capitals back to base: 'IF YOU DID

NOT INTEND TO GIVE US ANY SUPPORT WHY DID YOU SEND US?' Basil's report also lamented SFHQ's failure to respond adequately to their messages: 'London instead expressed verbose sympathy for casualties which only wasted our time deciphering.' Basil also complained about their briefing, particularly in regard to being unprepared for Albert, 'considering the information London must have had. His character was such that we found it difficult at first to see eye to eye with him. Luckily it worked out all right, but he could easily, and nearly did cause the complete failure of our mission.'

Yet, plenty of arms did make it in and thousands of acts of sabotage accumulatively took their toll on the German military machine. One Allied commander estimated the FFI reduced Germany's efficiency in southern France to forty per cent. I don't know how you can measure these things. But without the Jedburgh missions, primed by the SOE circuits operating in France in 1943 and 1944, it's hard to imagine how an inexperienced, undisciplined and poorly armed Maquis, however passionate and courageous, could have slowed the Wehrmacht down. Even in retreat the Germans were a formidable enemy, some angry, some vengeful, some brainwashed into believing in their eventual victory. Yet the French Resistance came together at a crucial time, in numbers large enough to take the Germans on. And things might have gone a different way had German troops got to battle faster when the Allies were struggling to secure a bridgehead in the first few days of the invasion.

The Jedburghs were given unfailing support by the Maquis. What irked, for the Maquis and Jedburghs alike, were the thousands of 'October *maquisards*', or *naphtalines* (mothballs) as they were called, who rapidly donned FFI armbands at the last minute. While not wanting to take anything away from their brave French comrades, more irksome still for the Jeds has been the gaping omission in French history of SOE's role in their Resistance. Some dedicated museums barely give a mention to SOE circuits or Jedburgh agents, or credit the extent of the Allied arms drops which made resistance feasible.

Out of 278 Jedburghs dropped into France, eighteen lost their lives and twenty-four were wounded. Two died when their parachutes failed to open, one was killed by accident by the unintended discharge of a *maquisard*'s gun, and four were captured then executed. An astonishingly low casualty rate for such a high-risk venture.

For years after the war the Jedburghs were virtually unheard of, their secret guarded by the Official Secrets Act; they had, after all, volunteered knowing any success would be kept classified, or if caught, they would be shot. It is only since archive files have recently become accessible that the name Jedburgh has emerged. Now there are Jedburgh re-enactment groups where you can dress up as a Jed in all the gear, send radio messages and bivvy down for the night; there are websites and books and SOE chatrooms with threads trying to authenticate

143

Jedburgh Special Forces wings on eBay. Dad would be amazed. For the Jeds themselves, memories remained within. I don't know if Dad ever told Mum that much about what he got up to, but even if he did, as a codist who had signed the Official Secret Act herself, she would never have dreamed of telling us. But I think more the reason why he, or the other Jeds, did not talk about it was simply, How Does One Begin?

* * *

Dad might be on his way home, and France liberated, but his *irregular* war is only just beginning. Soon after he returns to England he will be packing his kit again. But right now there is something else on his mind. In less than two weeks, to his parents' absolute horror, he is going to get married . . .

Granddad's diary, 1944
2 October: *Telegram by phone TC hopes to be home in two days. Good news.*
3 October: *8.30 p.m. TC arrive home look-ing well and fine and a MAJOR. Enjoyed his job with the MARKEE [sic].*
6 October: *TC left for town 3.30. VERY SAD all of us as he's going to marry that awful woman.*

* * *

It is Sunday, the last day of the Jedburgh reunion. We are in the coach again, on our way to a memorial service for the Jeds at Peterborough Cathedral. Dad and I are sitting at the back. The Jeds have all been told to wear their medals. Dad whispers to me how embarrassed he is.

'Why? Don't be embarrassed. Be proud. I'm proud. I'm *really* proud of you, Dad.'

'Yes, but . . . you know . . . ' he flusters.

'What?' I ask confused.

'My medals . . . ' he grimaces.

'What about them?'

He glances up the coach, a wicked glint flashing from his eye, he tips his shoulder slightly for his mouth to move closer to my ear, 'Mine are so much . . . ' he hesitates dramatically, '*heavier* than theirs.'

★ ★ ★

But in the service when we recite 'They shall grow not old, as we that are left grow old', we both cry. For different reasons. I have become swept up in this. These wiry old lions. Their properness. Their improperness. Their tidy jackets. Their name tags. Their risky humour. Their imagination. Their *no shit*. I am ashamed of what we haven't done with our freedom and their victories. Living off the fat of the land. With our central heating and our power steering and our fast food and our leaf-blowers and our shopping malls. My tears are self-indulgent: about loss, the world; and about me probably. While Dad is just having a cry.

PART 3

YOUR FATHER IS A BASTARD

1

Dad was married three times. To Margot in 1944, just after he'd returned from France; to Mum, who was christened Joan but called Jane, in 1953; and from 1976 until she died in 2003, to Stepmother. As children we knew Dad had been married to someone before Mum — or, rather, that he'd been divorced, which with a child's logic doesn't quite register as the same thing, because Dad being divorced had meant that Mum couldn't have a normal wedding in a church, and we certainly knew about that. She felt hard done by. 'Margot!' Mum jeered when she was having a row with Dad. 'Margot,' she taunted, 'Margot, Margot!' Dad, unsurprisingly, never mentioned her. It was, we could only assume, a *nothing*, a banana skin, a wartime romance that hardly lasted a day. And that is what I had always believed; until amongst Dad's papers I came across a decree nisi absolute and discovered Dad's marriage to Margot lasted more than six years, from October 1944 until January 1951. My sister, who knew more than the rest of us, said Margot went off with a well-known sports commentator called Max who was sometimes on the telly. In 1974, Margot was killed in a road accident. I don't know how Dad found out, but he did; and he wept. I remember this, because it was at the height of our own family troubles, and Margot's name entered our house once more: 'Margot! MARGOT!' Mum spat out in ridicule at Dad's tears. Margot was just another trigger to her endless rage.

Something nags at me enough to check the divorce certificate again: 'Certificate of making Decree Nisi Absolute (Divorce) No. 604. In the High Court of Justice. PROBATE, DIVORCE AND ADMIRALTY DIVISION (DIVORCE). Between Thomas Arthur Carew, Petitioner, and Edna Margaret Carew, Respondent.' The marriage is dissolved, it says, because the respondent has 'deserted the Petitioner without cause'. It tells me they were married in the parish church of White Waltham, in the county of Berks. And then my eye whips back to the date. Which is horribly familiar. Because 10 October is the day Dad was married to Mum. It was *Mum and Dad's* wedding anniversary. I check again because it's hardly believable. What on earth possessed Dad to marry for the second time on the *same* day? Did he think that way he'd remember it? Or had he just forgotten? It might have been funny if it hadn't been tragic — for Mum, that is. Did he never think to mention it? Why in a million years . . . ? My bet is he just hoped the unfortunate coincidence would go away. For him it would have been a small thing. Until, of course, Mum found out.

I am interested in Margot. I imagine a dark-haired beauty with very red lips. I go back to Granddad's diaries but the information is minimal; invariably the weather: *overcast*, or the ill health of Dad's mother, Maud. Granddad refers to Maud as *MC* for Maud Carew, while he is *self*, and Dad, a bit more confusingly, is either *TC* (his initials) or *Arthur*, his middle name — the name his family called him. The 1944–5 diaries are home-made (wartime), stitched together by Granddad himself. I go straight to 10 October 1944. Nothing. Back to Granddad's note on 6 October: *VERY SAD all of us as he's going to marry that awful woman.* I flick back and forward. No mention of Margot. It is as if the marriage never happened and she ceased to exist.

Granddad's diary, 1944–5
22 October: *TC home 5 p.m. with dogs.*
24 October: *TC 3 p.m. left for London?*
27 October: *TC telephoned to say going 'out again'.*
29 October: *TC home for few hours before going out to Burma. TC left 4.30 p.m. SAD & yet HAPPY.*

Then I notice in the margin in tiny letters written vertically, *TC married on 10th Oct.* That's it. Obviously nobody went. I trawl back, a year, two years, to see if I can find Margot. There are quite a few mentions of a Babs who *calls TC*, and *comes to tea* . . . And then I find her.

20 December 1942: *TC gone on that awful girl.*
8 July 1943: *TC out with awful M.*
26 December 1943: *TC out all day with woman, looks worn out and old.*
17 March 1944: *TC arr. with usual cold.*

MC & self had unpleasant time with him re his woman.

But there's no mention of Margot's crime, or why she did not find favour with Granddad and Maud. She is the nameless *woman* or *awful girl*. In the following years, when Granddad does mention Margot by name, he spells it MAGGOT, with capitals.

Granddad's diary, 1946
23 June: *TC and MAGGOT arr. 5.30 p.m. Now some acting will commence between Maggot and self to be nice.*
25 June: *TC & MAGGOT here for tea and dinner. MC acting too. All 4 acting to be nice. Glad when all over.*
26 June: *TC and M here for luncheon and dinner. Self tired of them. Now TC and M got everything they can get out of MC, goodbye and b— you all.*

Granddad's voice interjects across time, his few words revealing things I never knew: the home mood, and a very different background perspective. Granddad's diaries, for all their brevity, set the atmosphere of Dad's youth, a curtain-twitching lookout, which, in a sort of Greek or Shakespearean sense, have begun to take on the role of the Chorus.

★ ★ ★

For years I believed there were no photographs of us when we were young because Mum or Dad hadn't taken any. Maybe I thought developing film was too expensive then. Yet I do remember Dad's camera well, in its square leather case. Just nothing that came out of it, certainly nothing that ended up on the mantelpiece. As far as I knew there was virtually no record of us growing up at all, except the awful Max Carding studio portraits of four decapitated heads, scrubbed up and floating two above two in ghostly ellipses. There were no baby pictures, certainly, or family snapshots from the early years. So it was quite momentous for me when, after Mum died in 2001, I found boxes and boxes of slides shoved right at the back of her bureau. Hidden away, but not *thrown* away. Of Dad. Of Mum. Of us! There was an old Bakelite electric slide-viewer too.

I plugged in the old cord flex, it whirred and miraculously a grubby square of yellowy light illuminated the wall. I worked my way through the boxes, and through every small cardboard window frame. I slotted them in. Mum, a fag between her pouting lips. Holding the silver cup she won sailing. In a beautiful red coat. In her Dame Edna glasses. Patrick, as a baby. And me! In Gibraltar. In the garden of the house in Fareham. Up a tree. On the beach at Perranporth. At Wickham fair. Patrick wearing a plastic Viking hat. Patrick with a milk carton on his head! Me in my Spanish dress. Patrick and I on a merry-go-round horse together. Impossible!

Patrick and I stand under 'the arch' in our school uniforms; I don't know why he is holding his gumboots. We both have a bunch of Mum's chrysanthemums to take to school (I hated their bitter smell and plasticky petals). The arch that didn't arch, that led onto Union Street, the arch where one day Patrick and I hid in the alcove where the dustbin lived with our battery of stolen eggs, five enormous trays of them, to pelt every passer-by. A policeman paid us a visit afterwards. Dad thought it was funny; Mum was enraged. One hundred and fifty eggs! I have no idea what she'd planned to do with them.

One by one the slides lit up, and I stared. The honeyed sun; the soft red bricks of our old garden wall; my duffel coat. The Dormobile, and the caravan, and the old army tent. Mum's yellow psychedelic dress, her Dolly dress we called it. My younger blonde sister, Nicky; and even younger blonder Tim. My Beatles cake! And the ancient-me child: me. My intake of breath punctured the air as each new rectangle of light pinned our past to the wall. Through scratched acetate and bits of fluff came Berria beach in Spain and our gypsy camp in the dunes; 1964, 1965, 1966 . . . Here was the back door where a robber broke in and stole our lunch money from our coat pockets. Mum chased him up the street. Everyone marvelled at how brave she was! And here we are all together. I want to dive back in. Make it all right. I want to snuff up the earth-brick smell. I want to touch the garden wall. I want to start again. Bring back to life a hope in their come-to-nothing dreams.

Our house at 75 High Street in Fareham, Hampshire, had a long narrow passage down the middle, tiled in black-and-white lino squares,

154

which we used to roller-skate down. At the end of the passage was the telly room for *The Man from U.N.C.L.E.* (me, Nicky *and* Mum drooling over Illya Kuryakin). In 1964 we bought a record player and two records: 'She Loves You' and 'I Want to Hold Your Hand' which we played over and over until Mum bought 'I'm into Something Good' by Herman's Hermits. Then we got 'Downtown' and, much to my disgust, something by Peter, Paul and Mary. Later, by the time of Flower Power, the favourite was 'Time of the Season' by the Zombies — which I particularly liked for the breathy *Hhhh-ah!* bits where we joined in and wriggled about like charmed snakes. Mum had some much heavier records that were 78s, but I can't remember ever hearing them. We were all conscious there was *very little money* in the house, but we did have drawers and drawers of Green Shield stamps which Mum stuck into books and then took somewhere in exchange for roasting pans. Mum's cooking speciality was Smash, frozen peas, tinned mince, and for pudding, tinned peaches; once a week we had a roast with spectacular roast potatoes, which Mum parboiled then smothered with fawn-coloured fat from the fawn-coloured bowl in which she collected dripping. I don't think of her as a cook, but every now and again she would pull something out of the hat, like a gooseberry fool, or, memorably, her Graveyard pudding, which was butterscotch Instant Whip in which she positioned blanched almonds upright like tombstones. Other people's mums made roly-poly jammy-tarts and cakey things, but our mum made Graveyard pudding. If Dad cooked it was always what he called 'a muckage', which was anything in the fridge mixed up with a can of bully beef, a handful of currants and a massive dose of yellow curry powder.

Ours was not a house of books, or music, or art, but Mum did read to us at night: *The Scarlet Pimpernel, Coral Island*, poems from *Palgrave's Golden Treasury*; my favourites were *The Forsaken Merman*, and *The Highwayman* which I would make her read again and again. I loved them for the pictures they put in my head, the purple moors and windswept shores with bells ringing in deserted fishing villages. We were snobbishly forbidden Enid Blyton, but Patrick had the *Swallows and Amazons* series, and I had the *Arabian Nights* with the mesmerising and otherworldly illustrations by Edmund Dulac whose blues were deeper and more beguiling, seas wilder, nights somehow darker yet fuller with stars, horizons farther, silks more sumptuous, velvet dresses more encrusted with jewels, than anything I could have imagined. There were goblins, ghosts and pale death-faces; caverns glittering with mist and mystery; villainous expressions of trickery and deceit. 'Everything about her was white,' it said beneath the ice-white princess gliding across a glacial landscape with two polar bears in *The Dreamer of Dreams*. I did not do much reading, for the pictures with their captions alone were enough to send me into reverie; I was bewitched.

There were very few pictures on our walls: a framed bullfighting poster on grey silk advertising Mum's favourite bullfighter, El Cordobés; a picture of a mermaid (Dad's?) with preposterously large breasts which hung in the dining-room alcove above the Gluggle jug; two small oil paintings of Andalusia; and two large (drab I thought) flower embroideries by Mum's mother. Downstairs our house smelt of molasses from Dad's home-made black stout, burnt pans and my rabbit hutch; upstairs it smelt of Airfix glue, balsa wood and Matey bubble-bath, and once a year at Christmas, there was the smell of Bronnley lemon soap which was strictly Mum's. Our narrow bathroom, with the 'Please Remember, Don't Forget' poem, overlooked the neighbours' bathroom below, which Dad discovered one evening when they left their light on with the curtains open and we all watched a naked lady having a bath. This excitement was soon followed by a man in a mackintosh behind Nicky and me in the queue for the Embassy cinema in Fareham coaxing us into the doorway alcove of the telly shop next door to show us the new tellies, but instead letting a pink droopy sausage flop out of his flies.

The best bit of our house was up a ladder through a hatch in the ceiling of Patrick's bedroom. The attic stretched the length of the house, it was musty and full of cobwebs and cross-beams, but fantastic for feasts; although you had to be very careful where you trod or you might go through the ceiling: as Mum did when Patrick took up the floorboards in his bedroom then put the carpet back. We were in the sitting room below when her whole leg burst through the light fitting in a tangle of wires.

My bedroom was on its own at the end of the corridor with The Huge Wardrobe full of noises and heavy coats. The wardrobe terrified me. At night I lay in my cold bed, rigid for hours, ears straining, waiting for The Man to come out. I could hear him breathing, but I could hardly go and get Dad. What would he think of me? 'Don't be wet,' he would chide if we ever baulked at anything. I could never be wet, it was unthinkable. Until one night the rustling noises became so loud and the breathing so distinct that fear overtook my imagination; I weighed up my pride against my untimely death and timidly crept downstairs. Dad, thankfully without any reproach, came back with me and searched diligently through every coat, but the man had already gone.

Dad's domain was the garage with the pitch-black dirt floor which smelt of sacks, damp canvas, gun grease, pipe smoke and more brewing. It remains in my memory an endless dark space where he kept the huge Union Jacks he had pinched from the army, and huge pulleys which he sometimes hooked us up to, and tents which weighed a ton with separate sacks for the poles (scaffolding more like) and large (useless) wooden pegs, and the army camp beds which, with the slightest movement, flipped over. I knew this to my peril, having tipped out of one in Spain once while still fast asleep. Somehow I made my way under the tent flap, and rolled to the bottom of a very long, very steep hill (still fast asleep), where I met a hedge which turned out to be the only thing between me and a railway line, where I remained until I woke the next morning, furious with whoever had played this trick on me. I marched back to find an empty tent, not because I was being searched for, but because they had all gone off to play crazy golf.

In the early days, around 1961 when Tim was born, Dad used to ferry us about one at a time on his Lambretta (while smoking his pipe); until in 1964 we got the Dormobile, which had a pop-up roof hinged on one side that yawned open to reveal two bunks. Patrick recently enlightened me on the Dormobile's sleeping arrangements: me and Nicky in the bunks in the pop-up roof; Mum and Tim on the bed; while Patrick and Dad slept *under* the van in plastic bags with their heads sticking out.

We were Spock children. Dr Benjamin Spock's message — that you know more than you think you do — resonated with Dad who was already certain he knew more than anyone else. Spock promoted the ideology that children were individual and should be encouraged, unhampered by petty rules and society's niceties, to become themselves in a more easy-going environment. At least, this was how Dad interpreted it. But the longer the reins he gave us, the more Mum tried to haul them in. It must have been such drudgery for her, washing clothes (by hand), making beds (no duvets) and frying up fish fingers; her children either singing 'One Wheel on my Wagon' in a tuneless loop, or exterminating each other. Games always ended in a scrap, a tangle of eight arms flaying around

159

like egg-beaters. Until the door slammed; a flip of the switch. All eagerness and delight when Dad came home.

2

'Your father is a bastard.' Mum's exact words.

What she technically meant was *illegitimate*. It was something exotic, a bit scandalous and a little outré. Being conceived out of wedlock was no small matter in 1919; and this was in Ireland. We saw it purely as an occasion for another boast: 'Our father is a bastard! A *real* one!' Mum had loathed Dad's mother, Maud, and didn't try to hide it; if she mentioned her at all it was rarely without a sneer, or the prefix 'That bitch, Maud', while Dad held his tongue. Maud died in 1958, very inconveniently, as it was barely a month after Dad, Mum, Patrick and I had arrived back in England from Gibraltar to begin our new life. Which induced Dad to ask Granddad to come and live with us . . . wherever that was going to be. And Granddad accepted. And Mum's heart sank, and there was nothing she could do.

Maud is my middle name. A sop, apparently, to my ailing grandmother — and another black mark against her as far as Mum was concerned. It was always a curse: 'Maud! Maud!' 'MAUDY!' my brother Patrick jeered. '*Come into the garden, Maud!*' he cocked a snook and minced his hips. 'Maud!' Mum taunted when she was angry with me, 'You're just like Maud.' More than forty years later I discovered I was. The first photograph I was ever to see of my grandmother

161

materialised mysteriously one day when Dad produced it with no explanation, a rabbit out of a hat. It was a shock. Not just because I had never seen a photograph of my grandmother, and so assumed (without thinking much about it) there weren't any, but because it was the first time I had ever seen myself in anyone before. There was something utterly familiar, the way she lowered her eyes, the shape of her nose. It was almost as if I could tell what she was thinking. I cannot find myself at all in my blonde mother, my blond brothers and sister, or even my father (though I have his skin); but when I look at her I know I am connected. The photograph of Maud was taken at her wedding to her first husband, Challoner Chute, in 1911, when she was twenty-seven years old. And at this age I can scarcely squeeze a ghost between us. Dad gave us all a copy of the photograph, blown up. I don't know why I had never questioned the previous absence of pictures of his mother, but it was puzzling; Maud just popped up, like the other bubbles of Dad's memory that were coming to the surface; and then disappeared.

I have asked Dad on a few occasions what his mother was like. He could never find a single word to describe her. 'She was . . . er . . . ' and then he got stuck. It was as if he had hardly met her at all. If I pressed further he said she was always ill. And then he used the word 'fey'. Fey. I once asked Dad what she died of, but he couldn't tell me. He floundered and listed some organs: liver, heart, kidneys, lungs — like a terrible stew. I am curious about Maud. When I rang Terence Miller, Dad's friend from the Perse School in Cambridge, he described Dad's mother as 'gypsyish, with long scarfs. Always seeming to be in a permanent 'fit of the vapours', but for what reason, unknown.' It is Granddad, in his inconsequential diaries, who reveals how things were. Year after year, day after day, as far back as 1923, relentless and dismal, is the account of Maud's woe: the Harley Street specialists, the doctors, the moods, the *MC bed days*, the *bilious* days, the *heart* days, the *off-the-deep-end* days. On the rare occasions when she is not unwell, another Maud emerges: *MC new house shoes; MC new hat; MC cardigan; MC dress fitted* — every item recorded by Granddad with its price. *Cape* — £17. Seventeen pounds for a cape in 1950 sounds an awful lot to me, but MC is happy with it for a few days; then it's back to *MC bed all day; MC feeling rotten; MC bilious; MC griping; MC little walk*; so-and-so *brought flowers for MC*. Day after day after day. And if she's not in bed, it's *MC up and a nuisance; MC indigestion; MC grumbling as usual; Overcast cold E wind. MC horrid woman, her self, self all the time*.

Granddad met Maud in 1918 at the end of the Great War, at Ballyseedy Castle, in County Kerry, just outside Tralee. She was ten years his senior, and a widow with two small boys. Her husband, Challoner Francis Chute of Chute Hall, known as Chuty, had been an officer in the Royal Munster Fusiliers. He had been killed four years earlier in the Battle of Mons in 1914, when Maud was three months pregnant with their second son. Maud was a frequent visitor to Ballyseedy, the seat of the Blennerhassett family, who were close relatives of Chuty. And twenty-five-year-old Granddad was employed there, to look after the horses. He had returned to his native Ireland having been discharged from the navy following a year in hospital after his submarine was sunk by a torpedo in the Dardanelles.

From one of Dad's trunks I have unearthed an enigmatic and rather curiously typed letter to Granddad from Nesta Blennerhassett on Ballyseedy headed notepaper, dated 3 November 1918, summoning him to arrive on Tuesday by train. She thanks him for agreeing to help her, 'I assure you I want it badly,' she writes, promising him 'a pleasant little financial surprise'; yet in the same breath cannot be troubled to have him collected from the station or even find out the time of the train. Whatever Nesta wanted badly, the upshot is that Granddad remained at Ballyseedy, poached from his position as farm manager at another grand house, Warren's Court, Lissarda, County Cork. And so it is thanks to Nesta that Granddad met Maud; from which it follows, now I think about it, that it is entirely due to Nesta, that Dad, and I for that matter, are even here.

Three months later, Granddad received another beseeching letter, marked 'Private', this time from Nesta's daughter, Hilda Blennerhassett, who wants 'a man who we trusted' to get on a ship and sort something out in Portuguese East Africa. She suspects the family 'has been swindled and the sooner it is cleared up the better'. Hilda says her mother 'does not much like' the idea of Granddad leaving Ballyseedy, but they need someone who understands the value of land and cattle. Furthermore, if he does go, her mother would like all the crops and necessary spring work done before he leaves.

Hilda's response to Granddad's refusal more than a month later — 'So you are going to be married . . . Who is the lady? You did not mention her name . . . ' — has about it all the innocent calm before the storm, and belies what must have been an inconceivable notion for them. Working for the landed gentry was one thing, marrying them, quite another. Their darling Maud — from lord of the manor to groom of the yard? Little wonder Granddad did not mention her name. For Maud Emily St Clair had married well and came from a respectable family herself — the O'Briens and Hobsons of Lanahrone House in Limerick. Now she was a widow, Chute Hall would be going to her dead husband's younger brother, and after a roll in the hay with Granddad, she was pregnant with her third child. Or suspected she was. Her eldest son, Desmond, was five, her second son, Challoner, known as Chubby, had just turned four.

1918 might have been the end of the Great War, but it was the beginning of the Irish War of Independence and there was unrest in the air. Everything in Ireland was uncertain; in the general election held in December (in which women could cast their first vote), out of 105

Irish seats, Sinn Féin took an unprecedented seventy-three. It was a landslide victory for the Irish nationalists who refused to go to Westminster (or were unable to — thirty-three of the elected were in jail for republican activity), and instead held an Irish Assembly in Dublin to declare independence from British rule. Of course Westminster was not going to go along with that, and it didn't take long for tensions to escalate. Young Irish nationalists, who would become the Irish Republican Army, started acting on their own initiative.

★　★　★

I decide to contact my half-cousin, my half-uncle Desmond's son. We have not seen each other for years. He lives in a large country house in Scotland where he and his wife run, by all accounts, a gloriously bountiful, attractively madcap, benevolently Basil Fawlty B&B. It transpires, when I speak to him, that he has inherited 'an attic full of stuff' from Desmond, who acquired the lion's share of his mother's possessions. All sorts of things, he says, and he is certain there are some old letters from Dad. I am hungry to see. He promises to search them out for me. Jonathan announces the All Blacks are playing Scotland at Murrayfield, which apparently decides it; we book our plane tickets and hire a car.

I recognise my cousin immediately. Thin as Jack Sprat in threadbare Jermyn Street suit, Viyella shirt and narrow tie; his neck doesn't quite touch the collar's edges. I warm to him straight away; robin-eyed, quick to please, he hops about, picks up our luggage, whooshes it into the house, quite a grand three-storey home with 1643 over the door. Each room is full to the gunwales with armchairs, paintings, antique side tables, dressing tables, chaises longues, Persian carpets on top of other carpets, more chairs, corner cupboards of porcelain, knick-knacks, crystal, silver, enamelware . . . We are shown around. Alarmingly, on the floor in the hall there is a tiger-skin with its head on. Oliver Cromwell stayed here; Bonnie Prince Charlie dropped in, apparently. My cousin leads us up a grand staircase to the drawing room, halfway up on a landing he opens a cupboard door, but quickly has to shut it again as another world pours out. The drawing room is furnished with gilt mirrors, sofas, chintz draperies, occasional chairs and occasional tables, and flooded with light from a large bay window at the far end where a grand piano sits, reminiscent of a stage-set for a Jane Austen music recital. On top of the grand piano, the mountain of letters, papers and photographs that he has dug out for me, await. My eyes rub their hands.

Diaries, letters, wills, bills, and God knows what. There is a lot of Chute family stuff. There is the letter to Maud from Captain Jervis (as a prisoner of war) written on 29 August 1914, describing the moment Maud's husband Chuty was killed, at the end of a very long day, in the pouring rain, at Étreux, as he covered the withdrawal of his company. Jervis relates the scene in detail:

My dear Mrs Chute,

I am most deeply grieved to have to write and give you a few little details of the death of your most gallant husband, as I am unfortunately the senior officer who survived the action.

The Regiment was left in a somewhat exposed position, and the orders for a withdrawal seemed to have gone astray. Chuty with his guns which he handled during the day with really wonderful skill, covered the withdrawal of my Company at midday. It was pouring with rain, and with an entire disregard to personal comfort characteristic of him, he lay down in six inches of water to manipulate his guns the better.

. . . Owing to the help of your husband's guns, the Company got safely through and rejoined the Battalion. The enemy now was on three sides of us, and the Artillery opened fire. Chuty brought his machine guns back at the gallop along the road under a positive hail of lead. It was a splendid feat and successfully accomplished and once again the guns were placed in position.

We were now completely surrounded, and your husband crossed the road to try and find a target to aim at. As he crossed he was shot in the right side and thigh, and fell dead.

Up to the last he was cheery and full of spirits as ever; in fact he was the life and soul of the Mess. It is impossible to realise that we'll never hear his voice again. He will leave a large gap, not only in the Regiment, but in each and all his brother officers' hearts. It may be some small consolation to you to know that before the action he was looked upon as the best Machine Gun Officer of the Brigade.

Jervis tells Maud how the Germans allowed them to send out a burial party the following day, 'and they found Chuty and buried him with the eight other officers of the Regiment who were killed, in a grave separate from the men. He was buried with all his personal effects on him.' No doubt a photograph of Maud in his breast pocket, with his two-year-old son, Desmond, as well.

May I, on behalf of the surviving officers and men of the Regiment, now prisoners in the German hands, tender our most sincere sympathy for a loss which we know only too well is one which can never be replaced. Dear Mrs Chute if there is anything else that I can do or tell, write to me • General Stab, Berlin, via Denmark, and I shall be only too happy to try and carry out your wishes . . . I feel as though I had lost my best friend, I can say no more.
 Believe me,
 Yours very sincerely, H. S. Jervis.

I am struck by this letter from a brother-in-arms to the fallen soldier's wife: his understanding of what she needs to know. There is care and thought and love in it. How does one begin, yet Jervis seems to know exactly. Chuty, dashing lieutenant, immortalised hero, dead at twenty-nine. When the news arrives from France, his mother Cherry is inconsolable. Her notebooks are here too. From a warm Irish summer's day of carefully inscribing a recipe for cucumber sandwiches (I swear: peeling, slicing, spreading butter) she is plunged into a profound darkness which she expresses explicitly, page after page.

Here in front of me too, a copy of the *Limerick Chronicle*, Saturday 1 July 1911, reporting the wedding of Mr Challoner Francis Trevor Chute to Miss Maud Emily St Clair Anne Hobson at St Mary's Cathedral in Limerick on 29 June. Thirty column inches. Every detail: the ivory thread of Maud's gown, the silver cords, the jewelled net, the lover's knot of Honiton lace, the veil, the satin train lined with silver tissue draped with orange blossoms and white heather. Of the five bridesmaids bearing lilies, lavender and sweet peas, one is called Miss Ruggles Brise. The presents are listed by each named giver alphabetically, inch after inch after inch; the rose bowls and silver sugar sifters, the nutcrackers and candlesticks and sauceboats and travelling clocks and shoe-buckles; there are Limerick lace collars, silver pincushions, bon-bon baskets, 'a brass palm stand', 'a glass grape stand', 'a case of pine apples'. Under B: 'Dr Blood, mother of pearl ink stand'. Under F: 'Mr and Mrs C. H. Fitt, purse bag'. Under G: 'The Knight of Glin, heather [*sic*] writing case'. Oh, for a heather writing case! Under L: 'Lanahrone Servants, silver-mounted bread plate'. Miss Little gives 'a sachet'. A sachet? Under M: 'Mr and Mrs MacGillicuddy case of serviette rings'. Would that be MacGillicuddy from MacGillicuddy Reeks, that wild craggy peat-soaked mountain bog of Kerry I have walked, with its tantalising glimpses of sea? Under S: 'Miss Shine, necklace'. Under V: 'The misses Vincent, Thermos flask'. It reads like a board game that hasn't been invented yet.

Maud's in-laws boast a knickerbocker glory of names: the Westropps, the Massy-Westropps, the Blennerhassetts, the D'Esterre Roberts, the baronets of Blennerville, the knights of Glin! There are sirs, ladies, reverends, 'onourables, colonels, captains, a chancellor and a Lady Inchiquin. Yet no mention of the bride's mother or father; it is her uncle, Frederick, Mr F. St Clair Hobson, who gives her away and entertains the guests at his residence, Lanahrone, afterwards. Amongst Dad's papers I'd found a note in his handwriting saying his mother's father had committed suicide. Here he is on the piano; his death notice in the *Limerick Chronicle*, 1886: 'Edward O'Brien Hobson, Lanahrone House, 10 October, age 34 years' — that unlucky 10 October again. Maud was only three. And twenty-three when her mother and aunt died in 1907. On that June day in 1911, exchanging vows with Challoner, son of Francis Blennerhassett Chute, Justice of the Peace, of Chute Hall, Tullygaron, a whopping great Proddie pile if ever there was one, Maud must have believed all her struggles were behind her.

I google Lanahrone House, and up comes a paragraph in the *Old Limerick Journal*: 'The St Clair Hobsons' residence, Lanahrone House, stood well back from the road and commanded a splendid view of the river . . . Hobson is reputed to have been the first man in Limerick to drive a motor car.' I google Maud's uncle Frederick. He too is in the Limerick County death notices, dead by February 1912, less than a year after he gave Maud away. Frederick was the county sub-sheriff of Limerick, an unpopular man I can only suppose from the smattering of dubious deeds I am able to uncover: the evictions 'of four more tenants put out of their holdings' (in total 20–30 families) on the Glensharrold Estate (for which he was accompanied by a force of fifty police); the 'seizure of nine cows' for non-payment of rent; the 'seizure of plants and flowering shrubs & etc.' from a plant nursery after a Mr Abraham refused to pay what he considered excessive rent. The sale of these items was forced to adjourn, however; for the reason: 'Not a single purchaser from either county or city of Limerick attended.' Yes! Memories in Ireland run deep. For Granddad's sake I am glad he never had to hobnob with Frederick.

No father, no mother, and within three years no husband either, and now she has two sons. Life for Maud spirals upwards then downwards very fast indeed. And then . . . in easy riding distance, just a few miles down the road from Chute Hall, at Ballyseedy a new young man is in charge of the horses. But something else happens to Maud before we arrive at this. Another husband crops up. My cousin points it out: an insurance certificate, addressed: 'Mrs Maud St Claire Moore' dated 12 November 1918. So insignificant-looking one could have passed it by. Maud married again, and one can only assume was widowed again — for the toll was heavy on young men in the First World War. In Maud's young life there seems to be an awful lot of death and dying. Another rustle through the letters from banks and solicitors brings up a note from the Bank of England, also addressed to Maud as Mrs M. E. St C. A. Moore in Dublin, dated 11 December 1919. I really don't know what this means, because by now, two-week-old baby Dad, born on 25 November, is squawking in the background. Had Granddad not yet made an honest woman of her? Could baby Tom have been a Moore? Or is this (more likely) just the slow wheels of bureaucracy? Secrets of these kinds get buried deep. Yet in all these papers there is no official record of Granddad's marriage to Maud at all. No certificate. No newspaper clipping. No wedding photographs. No lists of gifts: one bale of straw? Not a scrap. Whenever it was — there was no celebration for Arthur and Maud. Maud *had* to get married, but life with Granddad would be a far cry from the one she'd been expecting, and I don't think she ever forgave him. By 1920 Maud is being addressed as Mrs Carew, and Granddad, at twenty-six, with his wife and three boys, is moving from job to job with little money of his own, if the down-at-heel photographs are anything to go by.

There might not be a wedding certificate, but there is a Permit to Carry Arms in Defence of the Realm. These are nervous times, hostilities in Ireland have worsened and Granddad has a revolver and forty rounds (its details noted carefully in the flyleaf of his diary: 5 Chambers Cal S. W Harrington & Richardson).

Employed by the gentry, having served in the Royal Navy, there would have been no ambiguity about which side Granddad was perceived to be on. Attacks on the British administration have increased, particularly against the Royal Irish Constabulary (who are mainly Catholic), not just for their supplies of arms, but to demoralise and ostracise them. This violence, at first unpopular with the Irish people, begins to gain support after brutal retaliation from the British in the shape of a heavy-handed, undisciplined force of trigger-happy ex-servicemen, known as the Black and Tans,[1] brought in to bolster the RIC in January 1920. Boots, breeches, Webley revolvers strapped to their thighs, they quickly gain their reputation. It is an RIC squad, allegedly, who shoot dead the republican lord mayor of Cork, Tomás Mac Curtain, on 20 March 1920 at his home in front of his wife. Reprisals on both sides escalate with indiscriminate killings, house burnings and midnight raids. In fear, or sympathy, some of the RIC begin to abandon their rural posts and co-operate with

---

[1] From their improvised mix of dark police uniforms and khaki army attire — and the name of the famous Limerick hunt.

174

the Irish Republican Army. Abandoned rural police stations across the country are burnt to the ground. In August the British give themselves sweeping military powers to intern on suspicion without trial and use the death penalty. Thousands of republicans are forced to go on the run. They group together in camps and safe houses, and organise themselves into 'flying columns', squads of about thirty to forty men. On 25 October, the next lord mayor of Cork dies — in Brixton prison after seventy-four days on hunger strike. In Dublin, on the morning of 21 November, the IRA kills fourteen suspected British agents. That afternoon government forces open fire indiscriminately into a Gaelic football match at Croke Park in Dublin, killing twelve in the crowd. It will be called Bloody Sunday. In four days, Dad will have his first birthday.

Granddad and Maud's position, with little protection, is becoming ever more perilous. One revolver is not going to save them. Kerry is a stronghold for deep republican sympathies; and Cork hardly less so. Yet it is to Cork that Granddad returns to his old job as farm manager at Warren's Court, Lissarda — another Big House, as they were known. But Big Houses are not safe places to be. Chute Hall for one has been burnt to the ground, and farm labourers are hard to find — or count on to cross picket lines. Hay is destroyed in the field, fences are broken, livestock scattered, and empty graves are dug outside landowners' doors. Three days after Dad's birthday seventeen Auxiliaries (elite Crown forces) are killed just a few miles away in an IRA ambush; two weeks after that, Crown forces set Cork city on fire.

In June 1921 it is Warren's Court's turn to become the next Big House pyre, and Granddad and Maud are forced to flee to England. Dad is not yet two years old, Chubby is six, and Desmond is eight — and old enough to remember.

Uncle Desmond gave me a vivid picture once, of the day they left: he said all the sheep on the farm were slung around the perimeter fence of the house with their throats slit.

I am being called for tea. On my way downstairs I can't help keeping my eyes peeled out for 'a brass palm stand'.

★ ★ ★

As Granddad and Maud began their new life in Cambridge, Ireland descended into civil war. The Anglo-Irish treaty of December 1921 split the republicans, brother against brother. Those 'pro-treaty' accepted a self-governing 'Irish Free State' (of twenty-six counties) *within* the British Commonwealth with an oath of allegiance to the Crown; those against stuck out for an all-island Independent Republic. 'Free State' government troops started executing anti-treaty republicans and Ballyseedy became the site of an infamous massacre.

In the early hours of 7 March 1923, in a tit-for-tat retaliation for an IRA bomb-trap, nine IRA men were taken by army lorry from Ballymullen barracks, Tralee, to the Ballyseedy crossroads and tied to a mined log. The log was detonated, but one of the nine, Stephen Fuller, was blown clear by the force of the blast, and in the confusion managed to escape into the Ballyseedy woods. As he ran for his life he could hear the rattle of the Free State troops' machine guns making sure the eight remaining bodies were dead. The official version — that the prisoners were killed while clearing a booby-trapped road — was never swallowed by the local population. In 1997, RTE made an in-depth television documentary, *The Ballyseedy Massacre, 1923*, which has since been portioned out on YouTube. Amongst the dramatic reconstructions, maps, photographs, official documents, letters and historical narrative, there is archive footage of Fuller describing his escape. He remembers his last cigarette, his hands being tied behind his back, being chained with the eight others to the mined log, and the blast that blew him free. Old eyes and ears tell their story: Kitty Curran, a girl at the house where Fuller was given shelter; Rita O'Donnell, who heard the second and third blasts; Margaret Hickey, who describes the body parts scattering in all directions: 'It was a shocking sight. For days afterwards the birds were eating the flesh off the trees at Ballyseedy Cross.' These were the last bloody and bitter months of the Irish Civil War, and the Ballyseedy massacre remains frozen in Irish memory as the time when childhood friends became bitter adult enemies.

I have watched the documentary more than once. Peered closely at the filmed shots of the road, the bridge, the crossroads, the scraggy gorse, the collapsed stone walls, the bloated grey watercolour sky. And wondered how many hundred times my grandfather, young Arthur Edward Patrick Carew, must have driven a pony and trap past the very spot, trotted along that naked road, thinking of what crops he must bring in, what horses needed a visit from the smithy; and once that business was done with, his mind sliding sideways, to that dark-eyed, dark-haired visitor to the castle. The young widow, Maud.

If Granddad and Maud didn't like Margot, I don't think they liked Chubby's wealthy American heiress wife Jeanne either. Jeanne's family turn out to be very deeply committed (or as far as Granddad and Maud are concerned, nutcase) Baha'is,[1] and very rapidly Chubby falls into their consecrated grip. 'Bien chère Maud, beloved dearest,' is how Jeanne addresses her mother-in-law, 'I lift mine eyes up to the hill . . . '; 'Tarry no longer for He has come!' 'How proud you must be of Arthur to guard his Queen so well!' Jeanne's letters from America pile on the 'Glory to God's and endless preachings, and how precious Maud is in their prayers. By 1968 Jeanne has become a Baha'i

---

[1] Baha'i faith teaches all humanity is equal and part of one family. The Baha'is have been persecuted in Iran (where the faith originated) and other Muslim countries because their teachings challenge long-held traditional Islamic belief.

missionary in South America. On 20 April, the *Morning Record*, a local Connecticut rag, reports her return from a visit to 'the primitive people of the jungle and the Altiplano', where she has been 'Bringing Proclamation of Baha'u'llah to All Peoples'. Jeanne, referring to herself as 'beloved handmaid', explains to Maud that every woman who wants security cannot but be a Baha'i, for the Baha'i faith is synonymous with world peace and women's rights. I am sure Maud was thrilled with that. 'Bien chère Maud: How fortunate that spring comes early in England and you both can be in the sun — the life-giving sun! But more important is the Spiritual Sun, the prophet, and above all the new Manifestation!' She finishes up with a good old gloat: 'Blessed is your son Challoner that he is occupied much with things spiritual and a follower of the 'new Revelation', which is probably when the scissors came out.

Of her three sons, Chubby (who I remember as a big kind man) seems to be the one who upset Maud most. Amongst the correspondence on the piano is a letter he wrote to his mother on 16 March 1939, after a massive fight they'd obviously had over his choice of company. He asks her not to lose her dignity in the way she addresses him: 'I know there is a certain amount of ill feeling at home. I do not want to be patronising but I feel very sorry for you who came into this world in a far better position than you are now.' No one would be allowed to forget it. Maud's resentment and anger with Granddad for not being her dashing lieutenant from Chute

Hall. For not being . . . anything. Or having anything. Or really *doing* anything. No work to speak of, certainly; except for tending to her. God knows what they lived on — Granddad's naval disability pension; Maud's allowance as widow of Lieutenant Chute; trust money from the O'Briens or Hobson family in Ireland? And every day her two elder boys, dark-eyed, dark-haired, reminding her. From Chute Hall, to Ballyseedy to a dump of a cottage in Cork to rented accommodation in Cambridge: 3 Howes Place, owned by the Housing Association for Officers' Families which will shelter her for the rest of her life. Maud is in exile. Never to go home. All her Honiton-lace dreams will suffocate in this little house in windy Cambridge. Three sons at war. Menopausal when there was barely a word for it. Blackouts, sirens and Spam, and the East wind whipping over the fens, and every day Granddad scribbling in his diary: *MC out of sorts*; *MC bad mood*; *MC in devil of a state*; *NE wind, MC in bed all day*; *Dr K came to vet MC*. On 17 November 1929, Granddad's own father, Captain Thomas Carew, pops up to mention the matter in a letter from the Hotel de Liège, in Nice, where he has been playing skittles: 'If your wife is not improving, I should take her to London to see a specialist before it is too late.' He signs himself Affectionate Father' and sounds anything but. I think it *was* too late. But Maud digs in. For another thirty years with everyone fretting: 'Sorry that precious Maud is so frail and cannot seem to build herself up on a generous diet, alas!' writes Jeanne; 'We are so

180

sorry [and thank Baha'u'llah miles away] that dear Maud does not improve more quickly.' Depression? ME? Hypochondria? *MC nag horrible as usual selfish; MC rotten because self played cards last night; MC continued her old game again*. Year after year. I'm beginning to agree with Mum. Throttle her. Maud could never rally herself. Not even for her sons' weddings. Desmond has to actually leave his own wedding reception at the Savoy to visit her: *DC annoyed having to come all the way to see his mother for a few hours and leaving the Savoy with its atmosphere, certainly not very pleasant here.*

So it goes, until 17 April 1958: *Rain. Doctor came. Gave MC injection. 1.15 p.m. MC died. How I'll miss Maud, God knows.*

★ ★ ★

There is a hitch. I can feel it coming in my cousin's sudden awkward demeanour. He is sitting down next to the piano beside me staring at his feet. He looks embarrassed and uncomfortable. He has come to tell me I won't be able to have Dad's letters after all, because his wife feels they must stay in 'the collection'. Sidetracked by gun licences, Irish troubles, brass palm stands, scissored beheadings and Maud's misfortune, I have not even started on the letters from Dad — assuming naturally I would be taking them home. I am speechless. I want to say, But they are *my* father's letters. But I nod, tight-lipped. Possession is nine-tenths of the law.

And I am a well-looked-after guest in this house. My cousin tells me I am welcome, however, to use the photocopier. While the house is huge, the kitchen is tiny, but apparently there is a table in there somewhere, beneath the twenty teapots, the forty plates, the jam, the cornflakes, the newspapers, the bills, the letters, the phone, the butter, the pound of bacon, the bowl of sugar, under which there is a photocopier. So, for more than an hour I stand over it, laying face down newspaper cuttings from the *Limerick Chronicle*, condolence letters to Maud on Chuty's death; letters from Chubby and Jeanne, from Desmond to Dad, from Maud's father, Edward O'Brien, written in 1866, pushing the lid down firmly as the photocopying light sweeps beneath.

That night, with everyone in bed, I creep down the corridor. Across the tiger, into the drawing room. Through a narrow slit where the pulled chintz curtains don't quite meet, a slice of moonlight rules a bright line across the vast polished lid of the grand piano. I tiptoe across the room, heart thumping. Beneath the stacks of Desmond's and Chubby's letters, the diaries, and wills and insurance certificates, I slip out the bundle of Dad's letters that I had separated earlier. As fast and as quietly as I can, I tiptoe back to our room.

3

Murder is in my head. Didn't someone kill their wife with poisoned gloves? Dad is driving me crazy. I get up. He gets up. I go outside. He is following me. Precariously. Everywhere I go he is right behind me. I am the opposite of Peter Pan; I have two shadows hobbling after me. I double back to fetch him. We sit together in the shed. He nods off. I start to prune a bush nearby. But he wakes. He is there, helping. Holding the rose, getting a thorn in his hand. He is a mobile baby. A mobile baby who doesn't sleep during the day. Who needs constant attention. Who doesn't understand anything you say to him. But he understands what *he* says. My sister said this. She said, 'It sounds silly, but . . . ' No, I know exactly what she means: you cannot say to him, 'Are you okay?' He doesn't understand. Yet he can tell you that he wants the radio off when he wants it off. Not before, or after. Only during. He only exists during. There is no past any more. Except a very distant past. Mostly it is now. He is a mobile baby who instead of screaming to be fed, demands jobs. But now he can't do any jobs. He can't even tear up newspaper for the compost heap. He gets confused. Where to put the paper. How big. Which way. How many. How. He is a mobile baby with two psycho-dogs. Growling, snarling, moulting; sharp-clawed, cushion-sucking, plate-licking psycho-dogs. His babies. Who are wary of me. I sweep them away with my foot when he isn't looking. And if they snarl I grab them by the neck so they can't bite, and hurl them out, snapping as they fly into the garden. He is bored, but cannot follow anything; 'Water these plants, Dad,' I say, holding the watering can out to him. He points to everything: 'This?' 'This?' To everything apart from the plants.

Which doesn't matter now because it is raining again. But, guess what, we have no electricity for the day because they are mending the fallen power lines, and our day trip is scuppered because I left the *frigging* ignition key in the ignition, because the car window was left down (by guess who) and I had to put it up, because it was raining, and you can't put the windows up without the key in the ignition. These modern cars. But just as I was doing so, guess who started cleaning the leaves off the bonnet with his penknife, so I leapt out, grabbed penknife and then forgot to take the frigging fff-ing key out of the frigging fff-ing FFFF-ing! ignition, so overnight the battery's gone flat; which I only discover when we are dressed neatly and sitting in the car to go on our planned day trip; because if we stay at home I know the power supply is going to be *interrupted from 9.00 a.m. to 5.00 p.m. for repair works.* We get out of the car and Dad thinks we're there, thankfully I suppose. So we sit in the shed and watch the monsoon summer rain, with no lights on, and the psycho-dogs growl and scratch and get under my feet, and very quickly Dad gets bored, and starts thinking of his Organisation which he has left at home. He huffs and puffs.

'How far are we?' he wants to know.

'From what?'

'My, my, my you know, Organisation.'

And I start thinking of the poisoned gloves.

★ ★ ★

I am sitting on the floor in my shed, surrounded by the various piles I have collected of Dad's letters to his parents: pre-war, post-war, from India, Norway, Gibraltar, Ceylon, Finland, Trieste, Palestine. All addressed to 'My dear Mummy & Daddy', and signed 'your loving son, Arthur'. There is a box of photographs, another of manuscripts, reports, army documents; files of marriage certificates, divorce certificates, death certificates. My desk is stacked high with books on guerrilla warfare, the Jedburghs, Burma, SOE; I have a couple of CDs of three hours of interviews with Dad from the Imperial War Museum; and I have the two ninety-minute tape cassettes labelled *Tom talking to Dr Robert Taylor on Burma, 1978*. I have tried to listen to these tapes, this historian's interview with Dad, but in she comes. The Interruption. The slicing Margaret Thatcher voice. My stepmother. Every few minutes she pipes up with a comment that pitches the moment into her lap. She was master of it, and I am transported back to the well-spring of all my impotent rage: this is what happened, this is what *always* happened. And each time I reach out to press PLAY, I feel that fire ignite in my chest, my jaw tensing, my palms beginning to sweat. I know I must persevere, I must overcome it. I insert cassette A. I don't bother to rewind, pot luck, I will just dive in. I press PLAY.

TC: I was one of the first good terrorists. I understand these terrorists. Totally. I understand the PLO. I understand everything they do. I daren't say so. To friends, society. I know *exactly* how they're feeling. They have been deprived of their homeland and everything else. How else can they get it? They are never going to be given it back. Terrorism is [inaudible]. What right has one got to torture? What right has one to be a terrorist? I hope I'll never have to be again, but when the chips are down I don't mind being one.

SM: You won't be one again, because you won't be allowed to be!

I hit STOP.

★ ★ ★

Defy age. Defy pain. Defy authority. For the sake of it. Helped, not inconsiderably, by that big voice of his. What an instrument. But in 1988 Dad's voice all but disappeared into a gravelly whisper after an aneurism, and the consequent slackening of his vocal cords. How often what is taken is what we have most relied on, or what defines us, as if it were a test . . . It could almost

186

make one believe in a god. The loss of Dad's voice was not helped by his increasing deafness which in turn was exasperated by the auditory chaos of our modern world, yet a shrug was all it got. His booming percussion was hushed into a rush of air that learnt to blow out windy words which eventually our ears got used to. Yet, the problem and its solution was not something entirely new to him. It was easy to think of Dad as a supremely confident man, but it wasn't always so. He had been born left-handed and forced at school, as was common at the time, to write with his right, which effected some kind of cross-wiring that caused a terrible stammer. It was an enormous handicap as a young man so he came up with various techniques for disguising it, stretching out vowels and connecting them with long sing-song ooohs or aaahs which he'd snap off with the word he wanted as if he'd bagged it with a net. Tellingly, after the war his stammer virtually disappeared, although he kept his party trick of being ambidextrous. 'My dad is anti-Texas,' I bragged knowingly to a friend at school.

★ ★ ★

I find myself doing sums, counting back the years. You are fifty-four when your father dies, old as I am now, and you might say (you would) the happiest time in your life had not yet begun. And just after Granddad dies (so, free to leave), you leave Mum. She was forty-nine. When it started to all go wrong, you were, I don't know

187

any more . . . When you met the woman who would become your third wife, I don't know that either. Fifty fifty-two? I thought she came after, or at the same time, but I was naive. You are sixty-five when you can 'suddenly stop *worrying* about money!' Almost sixty-nine when your heart, as you put it, 'blows out' the aneurism which almost does for you, but in the event becomes the reason you win the fight with your wife to allow you to finally stop working. 'By God she was determined,' you laughed admiringly, your new pacemaker crouching like a small toad beneath your freckled skin, 'The first serious fight we've ever had!' If she'd known how good the pacemaker would be, you might have lost that battle too.

You are seventy-three when you come, on the spur of the moment, to look for me, I am not at home so you take a punt and walk down Brick Lane. I am in the bagel shop and see you through the window, a great white froth of hair striding down the street.

'That's my dad!' I say, astonished, to my friend Mary. I bounce out of the door. 'Dad! Dad!' And you turn; with your broad-beam smile, arms open holding a thousand cubic metres of air. 'There you are!' Miraculously (your luck) we have met up without prior arrangement, and off we go, like three truants: Mary, me and you. We love the hub and rub of the East End, the yak and tease. Off to Pellicci's for a bread pudding and a lark; you fill the place, your effervescent self spiralling round your own thermal of tall tales, new exploits and generous helpings of shocking advice. 'Babies! Don't have them! Mewling morons. Can't speak, can't *do* anything!'

And you are sixty-six when you come and stay with me in Ireland. To cheer me up, because I am *down in the dumps* (your expression). It is 1985 and I have lost my first love and am finding it impossible to move on. You hear the gloom in my voice, and that instant you say you're coming over! And I cannot think of anyone I'd rather see. But it won't happen I am sure of it. But it does! And what's more, you will be on your own because Stepmother has a phobia of aeroplanes and will not fly. I collect you from Cork airport in my 2CV. 'Hurraaaah!' we both chime as you load up the back seat with bottles of wine and bars of chocolate. Four whole days! We set off delightedly on our sixty-mile journey to Skibbereen. But only make twenty of them because I have forgotten to fill up with oil (no man, no car maintenance). In a 2CV, no oil is a DISASTER — I burn out the something-or-other and we come to a smoky halt. You are roaring with laughter for you are now in your element. A PROBLEM TO SOLVE. Miraculously, and in typical Irish fashion (and with *your* luck), there is a farm up the road with another 2CV parked in view, right outside it. Probably the only other 2CV in the whole of West Cork. And it is from this farm we call the garage down the road, who come, look, poke about a bit, then declare my 2CV a write-off. So the farmer buys my 2CV for spares for his 2CV the tyres alone are worth a fortune, and we shake on seventy Irish punts, and catch the bus to Skibbereen, where we have a pint in Gerald O'Brien's, where Gerald's brother, Tom, just happens to know of a Morris Minor that might be for sale. Tom drives us there, two miles up the road, where a black split-screen Morris Minor is parked half inside a barn and half outside with moss growing along its rain gutters.

'That's a fine car you have there, now, Mrs McCarthy,' you say.

'It is,' says Mrs McCarthy.

'Would you be thinking of selling it, at all?'

'I might.'

And so we have a cup of tea, and discuss other things, and you tell Mrs McCarthy you were born in Dublin, and Mrs McCarthy says, 'Were you now.' And then you say, 'About that car.' And you like her face, and she likes yours. And Mrs McCarthy says we'd have to be paying sixty punts for it. And you say it's a fair price, and then we jump-start it from Tom O'Brien's car, and miraculously it splutters slowly into life, and we count six pink-brown tens into Mrs McCarthy's mug-warmed hand, and drive it away. We are ten punts up so decide to splash out on a new battery and are home by four. Car sold, car bought. 'Only in Ireland!' you cry, tears rolling down your cheeks. I couldn't have arranged the day better. But, yes, I could, for then my best friend, Helen O'Sullivan, arrives at the door bringing us a bowl of Dublin Bay prawns, straight off her husband's fishing boat, and we sit in my tiny front garden in Rineen, overlooking the estuary, in the glorious Irish sun, cracking prawns, sucking out their salty flesh. And then we hear the telephone ringing. And I answer it. And it is Guess Who. And I call you to the phone. And you thunder, 'Hello!' happily and unsuspectingly. But I know.

Her father is dying, you tell me solemnly, after the twenty-minute call.

'Dad, he's been dying for years . . . '

'Darling, I must go home and support her.'

'But you've only just arrived . . . '

★   ★   ★

You change your ticket and fly home the next day. Astonishingly and *thanks be to whoever decides these things*, Stepmother's father survives quite a few more years to die another day.

PART 4

THE DENSE MIXED WHAT?

1

After returning from France, Dad and some of the other British Jeds joined Force 136 — the cover name for SOE's clandestine operations in the Far East. Scarcely with time to unpack, go on a bender, get married, have a honeymoon (like Dad), or anything else they decided to squeeze in the interim, they were on board the P&O liner, *Otranto*, and slipping out of Liverpool docks in the blackout. It was five weeks before they arrived in Bombay. Dad took two books with him: T. E. Lawrence's *Seven Pillars of Wisdom* (his personal account of guerrilla warfare with the Arabs against the Turks in the First World War), and *The Rubaiyat of Omar Khayyam* ('Ah, make the most of what we yet may spend, / Before we too into the Dust descend'), and read both, twice, cover to cover. One of the Jeds remembered a sergeant pacing the deck with a remarkably loud voice bellowing, 'Asia for the Asiatics; turn the boat around!' From Bombay the officers were flown to Ceylon (sergeants caught the train), and from the capital Colombo it was another forty miles south by truck to Force 136's base camp, code-named ME25, hidden in the middle of a coconut and rubber plantation.

It was an idyllic location with huts of interwoven palm leaves in amongst the coconut trees; yoked oxen pulled painted carts; women in brightly coloured saris sold tropical fruit;

195

Buddhist monks in saffron robes walked along the nearby Bentota beach where the men could swim in the warm Indian Ocean and watch the fishermen haul their nets. 'I will make you envious when I tell you that I have eaten half a pineapple and five bananas,' Dad wrote home, adding that an officer had just 'sent a boy up a tree to get some coconuts'. The nearest jungle was fifty miles away, so as a training camp for jungle guerrilla warfare it was hardly ideal, yet barely a fortnight after arriving, Dad was briefed on his first mission and given orders to be ready to go. He was a major now and would be leading the first Jedburgh team to be parachuted into Japanese-occupied Burma.

Dad's team, Camel, would be dropped during the next moon phase, into the strip of land along the western coast of northern Burma where mountainous jungle ranges and impenetrable bamboo forests plunge into rain-drenched river valleys, which in turn spill into deltas and waterways called *chaungs*, that thread their way through a feverish coastal mangrove swamp: the vast and largely uncharted territory of Arakan. The three British in the team have next to no jungle training, a lecture in Burmese politics, and a kilo of opium for currency. Dad has just turned twenty-five.

By this time Burma had been under Japanese occupation for more than two years. Before that, since 1824, it had been occupied by us. Which made everything more complicated. For although the British and Burmese shared the same immediate agenda, to oust the Japanese, it was not for

the same outcome. The Burmese wanted independence from *all* imperial powers. And the British
wanted their colony back.

Before the Japanese invasion in 1942, Burma
had been regarded by many as the real jewel in
Britain's crown. A country of jungle-covered
mountains, deep river valleys, alluvial deltas, bamboo
forests, with a central fertile plain drained by
four giant rivers running north to south; the
greatest of all, the Irrawaddy, with its large river
boats, was in some places up to three miles wide.
'This is Burma,' wrote Rudyard Kipling, 'unlike
any land you know about.' Golden spires of Buddhist temples rose from the jungle canopy; tigers
roamed in good numbers; there were crocodiles,
river dolphins, rhinos and bears; thirty-two species of turtle; ninety-two species of bat; myriad
tropical birds and over 1,000 different butterflies.
The hot wet climate supported a paradise of
exotic flora: flame trees, moon flowers, tropical
orchids, 'eyeball' trees bearing fruits like lychees
and elephant grass that could grow ten feet high.
Gardens overflowed with frangipani, bougainvil-
laea and hibiscus, and the heady scents of juniper,
jasmine, ginger, sandalwood and queen of the
night. It was an isolated country. Only tracks
connected it to India and Siam, and the only
road to China was often impassable in the rainy
season. Its 17 million people from a multitude of
ethnic tribes spoke as many as 126 languages.
The plan to govern it as a province of India had
failed, and by 1937 Burma was being run as an
autonomous colony. Here the British enjoyed
their emerald-green golf courses, their cocktail

verandahs and shooting parties. Elephants pulled teak out of the forests and the British got richer as Burma fast became one of the world's largest exporters of rice, oil, minerals, rubies, jade and sapphires.

It was hardly surprising, then, that young, politicised, educated Burmese wanted their country (and resources) back. And one of the places they looked to for inspiration was Ireland, where the Irish Free State had so recently — in 1937 — become a full independent republic.

The most politicised of these student groups called themselves Thakins. The word *thakin* means 'master'. The name simultaneously poked fun at the English colonial structure, and claimed for the Burmese the right to be the true masters of their own country. Before the war in Europe the Thakins had been busy making nationalist speeches and stirring up political conscience. The British authorities in Burma detested the Thakins, regarding them as 'student rickshaw rabble-rousers', and gave orders for their demonstrations to be disbanded by police wielding long metal-tipped batons called *lathis*, a weapon capable of inflicting terrible injury, if not death. By 1940 the British had declared the Thakin Party an illegal organisation.

The most vocal of these Thakins was a graduate in law from Rangoon University called Aung San. In 1938 Aung San was travelling the country making increasingly radical speeches when the British administration issued a warrant for his arrest with a five-rupee reward, an amount that Aung San wryly observed was the

198

price of a fair-sized chicken. Aung San and twenty-nine fellow Burmese nationalists (who would become known as the Thirty Comrades) fled to China. It was here that Japanese intelligence officers made contact and, with promises of Burmese independence, persuaded Aung San and his comrades to go to Japan to receive military training. And so, in 1942 when the Japanese Army invaded Burma from Siam, Aung San was bringing up their rearguard with his small cadre, acting as guides, providing intelligence, and collecting recruits on the way to join what was then called the Burma Independence Army.

Once the British had been swiftly and humiliatingly chased out, it did not take long for the Burmese to see that not only were their new masters more brutal than their predecessors, but also that their promised 'independence' would be a sham. Sickened, they looked on as Japanese soldiers beheaded British officials and 'collaborators', pillaged Burma's forests for timber, stole their cotton mills, made fires in their Buddhist shrines, bathed naked in their streets, ate rice out of chamber-pots, and at the merest irritation slapped the faces of their men, women and children — a Japanese habit deeply offensive to the Burmese. It is hard to see how educated Burmese patriots had believed for a moment the Japanese would further another race's cause with their fascist ideology and imperial track record. Yet, it must have been with heavy hearts that Aung San and the Thakins accepted they had been naive and must rid themselves of their 'liberators' — which would require help, which meant they would have to change sides, which meant they would have to go cap in hand back to the British. What they had yet to agree on was how and when. Some Thakins went underground; others, like Aung San and his brother-in-law, Than Tun, remained in all appearance loyal to the Japanese. In 1943 Than Tun was appointed minister of agriculture in the new puppet government; while Aung San served as war minister and general of his army, the Burma National Army, or BNA.[1] For the next two years Aung San recruited, trained, armed and drilled his men 'to defend Burma from the Allies'. But all the while he was gathering strength and biding his time.

The ousted British colonial government and its governor, Sir Reginald Dorman-Smith, set up home in Simla, the Himalayan summer residence of the British Raj; a town of clubs, cinemas, drinking haunts, gin slings, games of whist, and shops stocked with English marmalade and jam. There they regrouped as a shadow government-in-waiting nursing their bruises, plotting their return to power, making blacklists of Burmese 'traitors', and dreaming of punishment and retribution. To further this cause they added a new military wing to their administration: Civil Affairs Service (Burma), CAS(B). And it was CAS(B) who would become a

---

[1] As Aung San's army's role changed, so did its name: from the Burma Independence Army, to the Burma Defence Army, then the Burma National Army.

whopping great thorn in just about everyone's side.

While the Allies were well on the road to defeating the Nazis in Europe by the end of 1944, military strategists forecast the war against Japan could go on for another six years. Allied attempts to retake Burma in 1942, and again in 1943, had failed disastrously with appalling casualties: the Japanese had been well entrenched while the Allies were both unprepared for the difficult topography and unsupported, with the British-controlled Indian Army tied up in North Africa. In 1943 South East Asia Command (SEAC) was set up as a joint body to take charge of Allied land, sea and air operations with its HQ based in Kandy, Ceylon. The post of Supreme Allied Commander would be British, a forty-three-year-old naval officer with royal connections and matinee-idol looks: Lord Louis Mountbatten.

By July 1944, having at last repelled the Japanese attempt to invade India in the long and terrible battles of Imphal and Kohima, and while the Americans concentrated on the border with China, British land forces began to make headway and were pushing south into the testing terrain of Arakan. Arakan's strategic position was crucial, and most crucial of all was the estuarial island of Akyab, not only for its deep-water port, but for its all-weather airfield which would be needed as the supply base for the invasion's advance into central Burma, and to bring the capital Rangoon into flying range for RAF bombers. This time every stop would be pulled out to ensure success — which included guerrilla resistance on the ground.

Since the Japanese invasion, Force 136 had been trying to get information on the situation inside Burma and contact potential resistance movements, but intelligence was scarce. The breakthrough came when two Thakin envoys, after a perilous journey on foot, managed to cross into India. It took months for them to convince the British they were not spies working for the Japanese, but eventually, a Force 136 officer called Eric Battersby was assigned to liaise with them. The elder, Thein Pe, was code-named Merlin; Tin Shwe, Lancelot; and accordingly the core circle of Thakin leaders would be referred to as the Knights. In December 1943, after some Force 136 training, Tin Shwe was dropped back at a remote spot on the Burmese coast with the mission to make contact with the anti-Japanese Burmese Nationalists. Two months later he returned bringing another Thakin to Force 136, the Arakanese political leader, Nyo Tun.

★ ★ ★

I am back at the National Archives in Kew. My requested files bulk high in my allocated pigeonhole. I loosen binding ties, and wade through the classified reports, letters, and telegrams on thin oniony paper stamped Top Secret in red. I am slowed down by the Burmese names. But I recognise Nyo Tun, because I've already come across him. He is the senior Burmese member of Camel; and Dad and Dr

202

Taylor talk about him on the Burma tapes. He is code-named Galahad. Here he is described as: 'Age 32; height 5ft. 6″; round face, pale complexion, thick lips, educated, speaks English well, sometimes wears dark glasses.' It doesn't make it any easier that the names switch haphazardly from real names to code names to aliases — which they also have. From the complex Who's Who charts, it seems that even Force 136 had trouble working it all out. The communist Thakin Soe, code-named Arthur, has gone underground to lead a resistance group in the Delta region. I scratch away at my desk.

Nyo Tun was important to Force 136 for his knowledge and contacts in Arakan. However, as a close associate of Aung San, he was also high on CAS(B)'s blacklist with a warrant out for his arrest as one of eight leading Thakins to be shot on sight. After two months' training in India he was smuggled back to 'collaborate' with the Japanese, under, dare I mention it, his alias, Hla Maung, but then the Japanese discovered he was working for the British. There are plenty of stories in SOE files, with plenty of exclamation marks, about the exploits of Galahad, aka Nyo Tun, aka Hla Maung, getting into terrible scrapes, being recognised, trying to bribe colonial police, being arrested, escaping, being identified again. After one close shave too many, Force 136 devise an intricate deception plan for news to reach Japanese ears of 'Hla Maung's' death by drowning during a river crossing. The mission succeeded, clearing the way for Nyo Tun to return in August to attend a very secret assembly chaired by Aung San in Rangoon. This was the meeting at which all the different factions in Burma came together and agreed to form an umbrella organisation to represent their common struggle for independence. They named it the Anti-Fascist Organisation, or AFO.

Over the following months AFO volunteers were smuggled out, trained in India, and sent back into clandestine roles in preparation for guerrilla activity against the Japanese. These operations didn't always pan out well. One Burmese radio operator, while under cover as a servant, couldn't understand why he was 'being treated like a servant!' Others were preoccupied about their pay; or their mother, or brother or sister; some would get involved romantically during their mission and have to be diverted from the arms of matrimony. Not many in the British camp had faith in the endeavour:

> certain traits in the Burmese character, particularly amongst the younger politicians with whom we are dealing, such as their vanity, jealousy of each other, lack of discipline, and their inability to organise themselves into well-constituted bands . . . preclude all possibility of their being able to take effective action by themselves on a large scale against the enemy.

The Jedburghs were seen as the solution. The model would be kept close to the one that had succeeded in France: small, discreet, mixed-national teams. Two Jedburgh officers and a radio operator, alongside trained English-speaking native Burmese. But of course this wasn't France. To start with it would be impossible for the Jeds to blend in; and even if they kept themselves hidden, their great big footprints would give them away. They would have to rely far more on their Burmese comrades and the local population for security; furthermore, none had experience of tropical jungle conditions; or knowledge of the terrain; or indeed accurate maps; or more than a few words of the language. And then there was that other matter: once the Japanese had been got rid of, these same Burmese could be setting their sights on the next job in hand, removing their former colonial masters, the British.

2

The regional force, armed and trained by the Japanese to defend Arakan from the Allies, but separate from Aung San's army (BNA), was called the Arakan Defence Force, or ADF.

Force 136 had known for some time the ADF was disillusioned with their Japanese 'saviours'. They had been caching arms for a year and cunningly persuaded the Japanese to set up garrison posts close to the Indian border 'for defence purposes', but which instead enabled the cover for volunteers to be smuggled in and out of India for specialist guerrilla-training with Force 136. Now the plan was to turn the whole ADF — some 3,000 Arakanese-strong — into a carefully timed guerrilla resistance in support of the Allied advance. Their commander was Kra Hla Aung: 'a criminal, a traitor, a murderer, and a common thief and gunmaker', according to CAS(B) reports; and loyal protégé of the even more notorious, wild, speechifying monk (extremely fond, by all accounts, of colourful English words that were not at all monklike), U Panyathiha. As an ardent nationalist, U Panyathiha had helped the Japanese remove the British in 1942, so was also wanted as a traitor and high on CAS(B)'s blacklist. But as far as Force 136 were concerned he was popular and influential, and already covertly engaged in anti-Japanese activity, so would be crucial in bringing his people onside.

In early December, the SOE War Diary reported that 'despite Japanese alertness', useful intelligence was coming out of Arakan with good prospects of resistance; radio contact had been established, stores had been dropped, and 'A JEDBURGH team including GALAHAD would probably be introduced next moon'. The operation was code-named Manual.

This party is a well-balanced team, mutually confident and appreciative of one another, and great hopes are entertained of the Jedburgh team — the first to be used in this theatre, and of Galahad himself, who throughout these difficult months has maintained a staunchness and clearness in out-look which has given us confidence in his ability to bring off a coup in the Arakan.

The Jedburgh team is Camel: Dad; John Cox (his number two); John Sharp (radio operator); Nyo Tun (aka Hla Maung); and four Arakanese, described as 'other ranks'. But the Burmese contingent is not happy. They won't accept that a British officer will be commanding their guerrillas, or that Dad is the leader of the team and not Nyo Tun. Why should they? In the nick of time a semantic solution is found: Nyo Tun is given the title 'Leader of the Arakan Resistance Forces'; Dad becomes 'Head of Military Liaison Mission to Anti-Fascist Organisation Arakan'; with John Cox 'Military assistant to the above'.

Their job is to recruit AFO guerrillas, supply and train them; then try to control them. They are instructed to wire back their arms requirements for a drop on 2 January on a DZ chosen by them, to select targets for attack by guerrilla forces, and to report intelligence of a military nature. Camel's final briefing includes enemy whereabouts: namely that 1,000 Japanese are stationed at a large HQ just south of their designated drop zone.

3. TASKS IN PARTICULAR.

(a) On landing each man will be personally responsible for concealing his own parachute equipment, and for seeing that no incriminating traces are left on the DZ, since it may be necessary to use the same ground again.

(b) HLA MAUNG [Nyo Tun] will immediately get in touch with the leader of the reception committee, and will ascertain what arrangements have been made for the concealment of the whole party for the night. The minimum amount of time however, should be spent on the DZ.

(c) Of the rations dropped, only those that can be carried conveniently should be taken away to the hide-out, the remainder being buried or hidden in the jungle.

(d) Sergt. Sharp should come on the air as soon as possible to report the party's progress.

(e) Identity discs will be issued forth-
with to all those already holding
arms; and Hla Maung will maintain a
register of all those to whom arms are
distributed.

On the day of Camel's departure Dad writes
a letter home chatting about the heat and the
advantages of bush shirts over tropical shirts. He
signs off, 'My letter-writing will lapse considerably during the next month or so as I'll be
rushing all over the place and working rather
hard. From your loving son, Arthur.'

★ ★ ★

It was my good fortune that John Sharp, Dad's
radio operator in Burma, was at the Jedburgh
sixtieth reunion. He still called Dad 'the Colonel', with warmth more than deference. John
could remember Dad fast asleep in the plane on
the flight to Arakan. It completely staggered him.
Aside from the cold, the continual roar, the bumping, swaying and vibrations of the plane, John
said his nerves were so shot he couldn't have
slept 'for love nor money'.

John had brought his 1945 Indian newspaper-
clippings to the reunion. 'There you are, 'the
mad Irishman',' he pointed to the paragraph,
'that was the best way to sum him up.'

'What was Dad like then, John?' I asked when
Dad had gone to bed.

He guffawed.

'Go on,' I urged him.

'He put the bloody wind up me, I'll say.'

'How?' I asked.

'Let's say he was . . . adventurous.'

'What do you mean . . . adventurous?' I was dying to know.

'Nobody wanted to go with him! Going with your father was the short straw!'

'Why?' I was surprised at this, a little taken aback.

'Well. He was brave to the point of . . . ' He didn't want to say it.

'Stupidity?'

'No,' John said firmly, then very slowly, 'he just had no fear at all. He wasn't like any officer I'd met before.'

'In what way?'

'He seemed to be totally fearless. He didn't seem to care about bullets flying around for one thing. He was just physically very, very brave. If I'd known that before, I wouldn't have gone with him.'

I had never thought of Dad in this way; he had always weighed things up carefully, been judicious, shrewd, canny; I did not see him as a risk-taker. He had delusions of immortality, but was definitely not gung-ho.

'I don't think he got on very well with a few of the generals,' I suggested.

John laughed. 'I'm not surprised. We didn't really observe military niceties.'

'Oh, really? What do you mean?'

'You know, saluting in a sloppy manner. We looked a sight too!'

John told me that the day before the drop,

Dad and John Cox had gone on a bender, and that the briefing officer the next morning, a stuffy RAF squadron leader, was not at all amused by their condition.

'I've never seen him drunk in all my life,' I said.

'Haven't you?'

'Never. Drinking, yes, always with a glass of wine in his hand, but never drunk.'

'Ah, but we were young then.'

'Were you together all day?' I asked.

'We were always on the move. I had all the radio equipment to carry. I was busy, I had to code the messages, then I was on air.'

'Did you take any photographs, John?'

'No. Your father had a camera. You know, a spy's camera. For photographing documents and stuff. I don't know what happened to it.'

'He told us he had a brick of opium, for currency, but it was too bloody heavy to carry so he buried it.' I was swearing like them now.

'Did he? I carried the money. Gold blanks.'

It was fortunate they took gold. In France the Jeds had folded and dirtied their newly forged notes, so they copied the same technique in Burma; only to discover the meticulous Burmese kept their money pristine, slipped inside the covers of books, and would only trust crisp clean banknotes in mint condition. Their endless bundles of diligently crumpled rupee notes weren't worth a thing.

★ ★ ★

It is Dad's seventy-fifth birthday and we have been commanded to present ourselves for seating in the dining room of a posh country hotel. I have been placed next to one of Stepmother's friends.

She turns to me and asks, 'Which one are you?'

I tell her.

'Oh,' she says, 'you're the jealous one.'

3

27 December 1944. Eight cumbersome men with their parachutes strapped on hunker down in the belly of a Dakota. No lights below them, just the bright moon reflecting on the sea. They gaze out across the Bay of Bengal. Talking, not talking; the endless drone of the engine; a pitch of turbulence; another cigarette; a pall of smoke ghosts above their heads; John Cox has been chain-smoking all the way from Calcutta. The sickening fear before the jump is always the worst. They have been flying for nearly four hours. Dad is fast asleep. Handy, this trick of his, an ability to shut his eyes, anywhere, anytime, grab what there is. The pilot banks the plane east towards the coast. Below them, a mirror of river opens its mouth into the sea; and beneath their wingtips, as far as they can see into the distance, trees, trees, trees. They drop height. John Sharp shakes Dad's arm to wake him. The navigator checks the co-ordinates: map reference 9528, east of the Kaladan River, south of Kyauktaw.

'Where's the hole?' Dad wants to know.

'There's no hole, there's a door.'

'I've never jumped out of a door!'

'You just walk out,' the dispatcher tells him. The altimeter reads 500 feet. Static lines are hooked up to the roof cable and tugged to test. They check their straps. Wriggle about a bit, adjust their loads. The dispatcher turns out the

lights and pulls up the blackout blinds. Dad
shoves a cushion down the back of his trousers.
He hasn't told anyone but his knees give way so
he never lands on his feet. The dispatch door is
opened and in comes a sudden blast of air.
Quick handshakes all round. 'Action stations.
Number One!' John Sharp moves into position.
Green light: 'Go!' He steps out. Heart in his
mouth.

★ ★ ★

It was a dangerous task for the pilots. No
weather-avoidance radar to detect dangerous
towers of cumulonimbus; no radar altimeters to
give fast and exact readings; no blind-landing
equipment; no fire or crash equipment either.
These aircraft were unpressurised, and without
the power to climb quickly out of trouble. They
had to fly across unmapped mountainous
terrain, often in monsoon rain with terrible
visibility and few distinguishable landmarks to go
on: a river, a patchwork of paddy fields, a hut;
and then pinpoint an almost invisible drop zone
which, for the reception committee's safety, was
often no more than a tiny clearing with a flashing
torch or some candles in a box. The weather was
by far their greatest danger and it could be *very*
frightening. Lightning cracks across the night sky
ricocheting off enormous stacks of cloud,
flashing along the plane's wingtips in violent
torrential rain, lighting up the pilot's white face,
bloodless with the strain of controlling the
bucking of his aircraft. Because of the heat,

turbulence was fierce and sudden, and dense cloud cover on the hills pushed pilots to fly beneath it, increasing the danger of crashing into rising ground. Aerial reconnaissance could not spot all danger signs and agents regularly had to be dropped *blind* without a prepared drop zone or reception committee; they just had to cross their fingers and hope for it. One nasty Japanese trick was to plant out discovered DZs with razor-sharp bamboo to impale the parachutists as they landed; even a tiny wound from *panji* bamboo was likely to turn septic. Trees were a major hazard. The received method of crash-landing into branches was to curl into a tight ball with your hands over your face, knees tucked under your chin, then, theoretically, you climb down. Unless you land in a Kanyin tree, where even from the lowest branch you might be looking at a hundred feet of straight trunk between you and the ground.

★ ★ ★

The wait seems forever to John Sharp, having landed on his own in the dark, in grass taller than him, his eyes straining upwards into the night sky. All he can make out is the plane flying off into the distance. With cold disbelief he realises nobody else has jumped. The plane circles, but still nothing. And no sign of a reception committee.

'I'll never forget it! It's the middle of the night and I'm alone in all this bloody tall grass,' John had told me, puffing out a long breath. 'The

Burmese were supposed to jump after me. I thought something had gone terribly wrong. That the mission had been aborted after I jumped out. I thought they were going to leave me there!' He laughed as if he was still winded. 'The Burmese wouldn't jump, you see. Your old man had to throw 'em out. When the plane came round the next time he just grabbed them and pushed them out the door.'

Dad goes last. He looks up. His parachute is beginning to close down as the shroud lines twist. He grabs them and with all his strength, pulls them apart. Which is exactly what he shouldn't have done, because it sends the twist higher towards the parachute and only makes it worse.

Below, John Sharp, with a flood of relief, picks out seven moonlit parachutes coming down towards him. There is a rustle in the undergrowth. A torch flickers through the grass. The sound of a machete hacking, and voices. One by one, the all-Burmese reception committee, Hound, appears.

Dad lands, with his deflating canopy, very hard. But in one piece, although his shoulder is agony. He must have torn a muscle pulling the ropes apart. He looks around. All he can see is long grass. The grass parts.

John Sharp appears. 'Don't play a bloody trick like that on me again!'

Everyone is down safely and burying their chutes. Nyo Tun is talking rapidly with Hound's leader whose men are collecting the packages. Nyo Tun says their first hideout is a two-mile trek into the hills. Dad, John Cox and John Sharp follow the single-file train of their Burmese guides as the party sets off. The night is warm; their kit is heavy; the track is narrow and steep. They make their way, up and up, into the dense and seemingly never-ending bamboo forest.

The same night, the eight Arakanese 'rumour-mongers' dropped further south are also disappearing quickly. They have hidden the Midget Gestetner printers (for producing propaganda leaflets), and are making their way to the huts of their friends, eager with news: 'Of course, Nyo Tun is not dead! Last week he was staying with the governor of Burma.' 'Haven't you heard? The Japanese are running out of ammunition.' 'When they closed Pagoda Hill, the pagoda fell on them! Many are wounded.' 'Yes, it is true! Japanese officers are stealing our clothes to escape into the hills!'

The truth was that although British West African troops had made inroads into Arakan before the monsoon in May, the Japanese had pushed them back up the Kaladan Valley to higher ground. There the Allies had held the line, avoiding the malarial conditions of the lowlands, waiting for the rains to end. But now the advance had resumed, the army needed intelligence.

John Sharp wires back to HQ in Calcutta that Japanese troops are numerous in the area and 'passing uncomfortably close'. Very quickly it becomes evident the area is 'too heavily infested' to set up a guerrilla camp. The Jeds split up. Dad and Nyo Tun head south to reconnoitre another drop zone and headquarters. Unencumbered they move fast. For the rest of the party — Sharp, Cox, twenty armed Arakanese and fifty coolies carrying the radio equipment and stores — progress is slow: the heavy equipment, the vertiginous hills, the bamboo so thick in some places it would be hard to get a finger between; but there is no choice because the Japanese are using both roads.

30 December. Dad and Nyo Tun have travelled forty miles south and set up camp. Nyo Tun sends a message to Kra Hla Aung, commander of the ADF, who arrives at night with an entourage. He is tall and formidable, handsome with a rugged air of savagery emphasised by a long flowing mane of dishevelled hair. Kra Hla Aung is followed by U Panyathiha, who strides into the camp with his minders, his saffron robe slung over his right shoulder and thrust under his left arm. Dad plays his Irish card. A subtle nationalist nod. The monk smiles, a black-toothed, betel-chewing, ruby-red saliva smile. And there is an immediate rapport.

On 1 January 1945, under Kra Hla Aung's orders, the ADF rise up, kill their Japanese instructors, and join Camel's resistance. The same day Camel radios back to HQ the position of 800 Japanese troops. The following day Sharp radios again: the troops have increased in number and are preparing to cross the Kaladan River. That afternoon, 4.30 p.m. to be precise, the ominous purr of thirty Thunderbolt fighters grows louder and louder, until over the treetops the dark silhouettes of the planes themselves appear. For forty minutes they strafe the Japanese battalion, circling again and again. Camel is in business. This show of British strength brings a stream of recruits. Camel's first supply drop lands right place, right time, all intact. That night they sabotage two boats of Japanese troops. Camel's guerrilla army begins to take shape.

Dad is up at first light. To birdsong he cannot identify, or maybe it's a frog. He nods to a sentry and leaves the camp. He makes his way to a small rise of higher ground above the bend in the river. A low white mist hangs over the surface as if tethered by strands of invisible silk. He wants a minute to himself; he squints through the mist to the inimical horizon, judges it safe enough to light his pipe. From his breast pocket he fishes out his packet of baccy. Hovers his nose over the sweet odour of the soft brown leaves. He pulls out a few strands, packs them lightly into his pipe's bowl. Then flicks the lid of his lighter and spins the wheel. A blue flame sways as the smell of lighter fuel momentarily overpowers the sweetness of the tobacco. He fills his cheeks with the pungent smoke. Crouched on his haunches, he watches tails of vapour rise and disappear. A warm easterly stipples the surface of the river. A noise from behind him makes his heart skip a beat as two large wings soar over him, like sails, *woosh, woosh*, slow and beautiful. Reminding him there is still another world. He watches the bird until it melts into the trees on the horizon. For one brief moment, he is wholly astonished at who and where he is.

4

Dad's pockets are full of notes. I find thoughts and messages to himself jumbled up with the notes we have written for him: 'Tom is 85.' 'You have £60.' 'Keggie is walking the dogs.' Anything in coloured biro is him. Ever since I can remember he switches colour as he goes along:

> <u>My Bath Thoughts</u> *I do not go into the bath to clean, I go to think. I realise what the 'o' was I eat every day. I will list every word that has disappeared as the orange has.*
> <u>Age 85 lost memory</u>. *Now I must tolerate and compensate.*

He does learn to compensate.
'Who am I, Tom?' Sarah, my sister-in-law, asks teasingly.
We wait, eyes flashing sideways to each other, knowing he doesn't have a clue.
He picks up both her hands and looks into her face.
'You're . . . Lovely' he says, trumping us again.

★　★　★

Burma marks him. Dad is a new man even to himself. More alert. More focused. More animal. An ability to sense something moving beyond vision, eyes hovering on a distant target, blurred

220

scanning then a pinpoint bolt of sharp focus. He has tuned into an arcane force. The hunter *and* the hunted. Nose to the air. Edging to cover. Time is only right now. Fear is only physical — cold electricity, beads of sudden sweat. He doesn't even notice that his stammer has completely gone.

I try and imagine what it was like for Dad, but it is not Dad of course, for he is nowhere near a dad. He is young, male (obviously), super-trained, super-fit (no stomach to stick out for us to use as a punchbag), and he has been given his head. Which sounds like an understatement if I think about the situation, the place, the time, the conditions, the responsibility, the decision-making, and being 1,000 miles from blooming anywhere and yet right in the thick of it. He is his own boss (and everyone else's, which he likes far more than he cares to admit). He is his own man who has found his element. Away from English constraints and literally let loose in the jungle. He is different from the British officers the Burmese have known. For one, he genuinely likes them; and they like him back He is Irish, and enjoys the benefits of what the Burmese see as a shared history and innate understanding.[1] He has a reputation, for courage, for being 'the mad Irishman', and he is really enjoying himself. He believes in the Arakanese. They believe in him. Their respect feeds him, it must do. If

---

[1] He is technically British, born in Dublin in 1919 before Irish independence, but identified himself as Irish.

France was his pupation, Burma is his imago, breaking out to realise his full potential; no longer does he have to clown for attention, he has to think fast on his feet and trust his instincts, and he is perfectly suited to it. Everything that was a hindrance before is coming into its own: his upside-down thinking, his recalcitrant impulse, his going it alone. Now it is these traits that will make the difference. In outwitting the enemy. For survival.

By 4 January he has sixty men under arms; by 5 January, 150. Things move quickly in guerrilla land. Morale rises, recruits come in every hour. Supplies are dropped in at night. The camp needs to be bigger so Dad threads a necklace of cordite through the trees and fires a machine gun at the detonator. Instant result! His energy is infectious. Word has got out, something special is going on; he trains up each cadre of young men, teaches them magic with primers, detonators, nitroglycerine and adhesive tape. He learns the Burmese words for 'Terrific!' and 'Now!' and 'Like this!' and 'Blow up!' and 'Wait!' and 'Grenade!' and 'Good work!' and 'Silence!' He bows his head and holds his hands together, fingers pointing to his chin. He trains instructors to train for him. The guerrilla network expands, 500, 600 men. Squads go out at night to lay traps for the enemy. Information of enemy positions pours in. John Sharp sits under a tree coding, decoding, sending transmissions.

From the tight bamboo forests they move into a watery-lacework world. They travel at night or under the dawn cover of mist when the horizon melts into the sky and every shape is smudged by the vapoury air. They cross the Kaladan River, floating silently with the current on dugout canoes in the dark. They thread their way through paddy fields and mangrove swamps. Each bend in the river could be mined or patrolled by enemy sniper. They ambush another boat of Japanese troops. Crocodiles are getting fat in the *chaungs* of Arakan.[1]

★ ★ ★

On 8 January the island of Akyab is back in British hands. The Japanese have pulled their troops out and moved south. Camel splits again. Nyo Tun stays to recruit while Dad and the main guerrilla body travel south-east into the thick of the enemy They move quickly and quietly in league with the jungle, through vast curtains of trailing vines, behind deafening insect cacophonies at dusk, with the flickering camouflage of light cascading through the canopy like silver coins. A scout reports the 'imminent danger of tiger'. They set up another training camp. Fugitive existence becomes normal. There is a rustle in the forest behind them. They watch, they listen, they wait. Exhaustion buzzing in their ears. A branch comes slewing down. Each man's breath cuts the air. There is a sudden commotion. Japanese soldiers crashing through the bamboo turn out to be a band of monkeys.

---

[1] An estimated 900 Japanese trying to escape are killed by crocodiles.

Twice a day John Sharp wires back to Calcutta: the position of 2,000 Japanese; four guns and twenty boats at Thangedaw; the co-ordinates of the Japanese General Sakurai's HQ; where he is during the day; where he is at night. On 13 January the RAF strafe Thangedaw at midday.

Kra Hla Aung, Nyo Tun and U Panyathiha rally their people to liaise with Dad to co-ordinate attacks. Camel guerrillas are dispersed over an area of about twenty square miles covering all likely routes and rivers of enemy retreat. Like parasites you cannot see them but you know they're there. Patrols and ambush parties are out day and night. Any rumour of Japanese presence and a squad is dispatched to investigate. Dad's mind-files must stay sharp, who is who and what is what and where. These supplies, those arms, how many men/miles, information stacking up, compartmentalised. He is a good delegator. He trusts people. And this is repaid again and again.

Seven hundred Japanese reported in twelve boats, a platoon is sent to take them out. Further down the road a Japanese colonel is swiftly dispatched alongside fifty of his men. As Camel's network spreads out, Force 136 brief the next Jedburgh team, Mouse.

★ ★ ★

I check names, dates, places; I read dry military data; my head is swimming with generals, battalions, armies, corps, divisions, troops, platoons. I pester my neighbour James Holland with questions: what is the difference between a division and a corps? (A division: around 15,000 men; a corps: two or more divisions.) Again I am drowning in acronyms: CAS(B), the ADF, the AFO, the BIA, the BNA; there's the 14th Army, the XV Corps, the 81st Division; troops advancing, troops retreating; there are maps and arrows and dates. Yet slowly Dad's anecdotes begin to attach themselves to history for the first time. And slowly I am getting a picture. Trees that ascend to sixty, seventy, a hundred feet before they start branching. A canopy that scatters the searing sun into shadows and flickering shafts. Once strange, now familiar to him: the evening churrings of a nightjar; the sudden eruption of monkeys screeching; the creaking noise of bamboos rubbing against each other in the wind. A dry stick cracking under the foot of a deer — or a Japanese patrol. I learn the rains begin in April with the monsoon proper coming down in May. There are large elephant-ear lilies and exotic bewigged caterpillars. Jungle grass can grow up to twelve feet. I look at satellite maps of Arakan; zoom over the western coast of Burma into the dense green cauliflower, its river trails like the veins of a complicated leaf. At dusk a pewter sky flips into beaten copper. A quarter moon doubles on the windless skin of the silver-pink river. And rats, beetles, red ants, mud, leeches, bedbugs, fleas. Sores and wounds that never heal; mosquitoes and malaria, dysentery. There are times they cannot hear aircraft approach just for the shrilling of mosquitoes in

their ears. I trawl through black-and-white photographs of the Burma campaign: smoke-trails of
bomb blasts; dead Japanese soldiers face down in
ditches; the bloated bellies of dead horses, legs
sticking up like fence posts; pack mules, buffalo
and trunk lines of elephants. A tired elephant will
lean against a tree and just cross its legs.

The village medicine-men cured ulcers with
compresses of leaves. Dad found this far more
effective than sulphanilamide. The purpose of
the leaves, he concluded, was to seal off the
wound from the air and allow it to fester: 'It
would heal itself and have clean skin under the
pus — it always worked but was too simple for
the medics.' Patrick says Dad told him if they
took a prisoner the method was to put chillies up
his arse to make him talk.

Then, just as everything is going so well,
disturbing reports come in. As the army gains
ground, some of the British forward troops — a
West African division — have begun to shoot at
Camel guerrillas.

Force 136 London newsletter:
the West Africans are notoriously
'trigger happy' and it is a difficult
matter to reverse their normal practice of shooting first and having a
look at the body afterwards.

Not only are Dad's guerrillas being fired on,
CAS(B) officers attached to the British advance
are arresting them as enemy collaborators and
putting them on trial. U Ni has been tried for

fifty-two criminal offences and sentenced to forty-two years in prison; U Inga has been condemned to death by hanging five times, plus forty-two years in prison. If that isn't enough, V Force (mostly Indian Muslim groups who had remained in Burma collecting intelligence after the Japanese occupation) are threatening to shoot their old enemies, the ADF, on sight, including U Panyathiha and Kra Hla Aung. It is a menacing situation which compromises not just the Jeds' safety but the whole mission.

Dad hotfoots it to the front line to protest. He is confronted by irate CAS(B) officers who suspect he is improperly in league with Nyo Tun who is wanted as a traitor. It is an awkward situation because Force 136 — already disapproved of as a law unto themselves and nothing but a blasted nuisance with their shadowy operations and powers to side-step the normal chain of command — have purposefully kept CAS(B) in the dark about the whole operation because they know CAS(B) would *never* have sanctioned arming the Arakanese. CAS(B) are incandescent. These criminal ruffians are anti-British traitors and cannot be seen as victors, it is unthinkable! The heated exchange escalates. Dad insists his request for an amnesty for his guerrillas goes over CAS(B)'s heads and stands his ground until it ends up in the lap of General Christison, commander of the British and Indian troops (XV Corps) fighting in Arakan. After a lengthy discussion with Christison, Dad gets a handwritten memorandum from the head of CAS(B), Major General Charles Frederick Byrde Pearce. A trade-off has been struck; Dad gets his amnesty if he can keep his guerrillas under control and make them, when requested, return all their arms. Pearce is a man resolutely anti 'treacherous' patriots, so having to write this directive must have stuck very deeply in his craw.[1]

```
To: Major T. A. Carew
With reference to the Arakanese now
working under you, you are authorised
to inform them that provided they
continue to serve to your satisfac-
tion until discharged and then surrender
their arms, they will not be brought
before a Court of the Military Admin-
istration on a charge of crimes against
the state or of assisting the King's
enemies. As regards other serious crimes
such as murder of British Subjects,
you are authorised to tell these men
that if brought to trial and con-
victed, a sentence of death will not
in any circumstances be carried out,
and assistance to the allied cause on
their [illegible] will be given the
fullest weight and consideration.
```

But the fight between CAS(B), the army and Force 136 is not finished here. On the contrary,

---

[1] Some months later, Pearce orders the collection of land revenue from the local war-ravaged population, despite them being starving and dressed in rags.

it is mushrooming into an almighty row that will reach London, and drag in the Supreme Allied Commander, Mountbatten.

5

Spring 1993, Nicky was 'down in the dumps' as Dad put it. He decided he wanted to give her a holiday and so he hired a small sailing boat to take her sailing on the Broads. Stepmother didn't want to go because she had a phobia of sailing boats, especially if it meant you had to sleep on them, in bunks. So Dad invited Jonathan and me instead. This resulted in a small miracle: four whole days with Dad on our own.

None of us had been to the Broads, except for Dad (according to Granddad's 1951 diary: *gone sailing with Terence*). And so the four of us set off to happily drift and gloop along the emerald-green waterways. In less than a day Dad had gone native. His sarong was back on, tied at the hip, he didn't shave or brush his hair, and on the second day he whopped his head coming up from the cabin producing an alarming amount of blood which he left where it was to dry on his forehead: a ruby tributary from his scalp to the bridge of his nose with a congealed lump of gunk lodged at point of injury in his white mop. He remained like that, wounded, unwashed, undressed and unshaven for the whole four days, brandishing a long stick which he found on the towpath. It would be disingenuous not to admit that much of the delight we took in Dad's wild-man appearance was knowing how much Stepmother would detest it.

The second evening, at his command, we stopped by a bridge and moored up as he strode confidently off through a cornfield informing us we were going to the pub. We trotted after him, sceptical and questioning: were we just going to stumble upon one, or what? At the time it seemed a long shot that he could possibly know his way, without checking a map, without a moment's hesitation, to a pub he could not have walked across the fields to, from the waterway like this, for over forty years. We walked on, and on, doubting him, until we crossed the last field and came out through some trees onto a footpath that led into a lane, to behold the riverside pub! Now, of course, I know better; considering the type of training he'd had he could have probably got us there with his eyes shut. But at the time we had to accept that the smug chuckle was all the explanation we were going to get.

What we were all looking forward to, was getting the photos back — three rolls of film of our disreputable sarong-wearing, beard-toting, stick-wielding, blood-tattooed captain. Nicky dropped them off at the chemist's in Battle, just up the road from Dad's.

'Are they back yet?' I kept on enquiring. But for some reason, they were not. How could it take so long? It never took this long. It was ridiculous. I was dying to see them. Alas. Nicky had dropped them off, but Stepmother had decided, snapping heels, clip, clip up the pavement, to pick them up.

'What do you mean she says they're not

there?!?' my voice high, squealing down the phone to my sister.

'She says they're not there. The factory has lost them.' Nicky's voice was flat, resigned.

'What do you mean the factory has lost them? They *never* lose them.'

I wouldn't drop it. I asked Stepmother, but Stepmother didn't want to discuss it. They've been lost, she told me curtly, so that was that.

'Well, we'll instigate a search,' I said to Nicky. 'We'll get the factory to trace back. They *have* to be somewhere.'

Silence. Followed by a long sigh. 'To instigate a search you need a docket,' Nicky said wearily.

'And?' For even then it hadn't occurred to me.

Of course. The same mysterious fate that befell the photographs, had also occurred . . . to the docket.

★ ★ ★

Courtesy of General Christison, Dad is flown back from the front line to his jungle HQ in a Sea Otter with two Spitfires as escort. Which must have been *very* exciting *except* that the Spitfires draw the attention of the Japanese two miles away who send a patrol out to investigate. That, surely, was a stupid mistake. Now the Japanese are after him and Dad has become a wanted man. Patrick and I remember Dad describing having to hide in the open rafters of a hut as a Japanese patrol combed through the village searching for him. A soldier came into the hut swinging a loaded gun, the family huddled together into a corner, the baby started crying, the Japanese soldier searched everywhere, helped himself to rice from a cooking pot, but miraculously never looked up. The fine splinter of time between existing and not existing. Dad. Patrick. Me.

The Jedburghs had methods to evade Japanese tracking: walking backwards up the muddy bank of a stream to give the impression of going in the opposite direction; walking on blankets. In a taped interview in the Imperial War Museum sound archives, Dad explains his favourite technique:

People of my height are two a penny now, but going back a lot of years they were not, and when I walked through the paddy fields my footprints were enormous, so I used to have somebody walking behind me treading them in. But my real trick . . . [he laughs] . . . I got teams of small boys, and they formed a screen which went in front of me, and I said, 'When you see a Japanese, get a piece of mud and sling it at him and show your arse at him, and then run back and tell me where they are.' So this screen went out and I was able to progress through Burma . . . I used to have one lot at the back, I put another screen out front and of course it was marvellous. I didn't believe, you see, in carrying a rifle and things. I had a pistol. That was all I carried because I thought that if I got to that stage I was finished anyway. The thing was not to get caught.

233

John Sharp said Dad's so-called pistol was more like a sawn-off shotgun. Most of the Jeds very quickly went native, grew beards and discarded their army fatigues for a Burmese *longyi* (Dad never wore pyjamas again, always preferring his chequered cotton sarong). They slept rough, often sitting up against a tree, or dossed down on the slatted bamboo of a village-hut floor. They ate rice, sometimes with chilli, buffalo milk, an egg, the occasional chicken if they could get it. And chewed tablets of Benzedrine. One Jed reckoned they saved his life: 'They were very addictive. You could walk along and you'd walk on air. It was tremendous.' Dad agreed, 'We chewed these pills, and you could just go on and on.' Benzedrine, cordite, a phial of morphine, a sharp *kukri* knife in a leather sheath, gold, opium and a Colt .45. John Sharp's Colt came in handy getting a railway ticket from Cox's Bazaar to Calcutta after they'd been overrun by the army, 'Give me a bloody ticket or I'll blow your fucking head off,' he told the over-officious Indian ticket-seller. John, in his smart blazer, fond of gardening and bowls, didn't moderate his language when he told me this. I hope my face didn't give away my surprise.

'We got on very well with the Burmese,' John told me. 'They would do anything for your father.' He mentioned this a number of times, how much the Burmese loved Dad. In the attic trunks I found a note in Dad's hand with the carefully spelled name 'Kra Hla Aung', next to which he'd written 'Jungle chum, *dacoit,*

234

Arakan'. It was on the strength of these friendships that when the time came to follow through on the terms of Pearce's amnesty, Dad and his Arakanese comrades were able to put their heads together and bring about an extraordinary surrender of arms — described here by Robert Taylor:

When, after the Japanese had been driven from Arakan, the new CAS(B) administration made it clear that it would not deal with the Arakanese Patriotic Front [ADF], Carew arranged with the political monk, U Panyathiha and other leaders, that they surrender their arms in exchange for negotiations with CAS(B). At the appointed time on the Akyab (Sittwe) quayside, Carew met with the Arakanese leaders. There he found not only a stack of arms equalling the number Force 136 had issued, but another identical pile as well.

We knew this story. Dad had explained to us, roaring with laughter, the implicit message of the duplicate pile of weapons: 'There you are, you buggers, you see we are twice as strong as you thought we were, and if we're giving up this many, you can be sure, we have twice the number again!'

Dad was very moved the guerrillas showed their loyalty to him by making this grand gesture, and fulfilling his promise to Christison. But this return of arms had more important ramifications for resistance in the rest of Burma.

The future alliance between the Burmese and Force 136 depended on it.

★ ★ ★

Tim is looking after Dad for the weekend, staying with him at his home in Battle. There is a festival on at Battle Abbey a few doors up the street. An anniversary of the Battle of Hastings or something . . . Dad's garden backs onto the battle site behind the abbey. Spitfires are flying in formation overhead. They splay out into a fan, roll, come together again. Zoom vertically upwards, twist, then dive. They bank away and loop and flip. Then turn in formation to fly overhead again with contrails of red and yellow smoke.

Tim notices Dad standing in the middle of the garden, looking up at the sky, watching the Spitfires with his hands on his hips. So he joins him.

Dad turns to Tim and says disparagingly, 'Well, they're not going to get anywhere if they carry on flying about like that!'

6

The Japanese are being driven south out of Arakan; Akyab airfield is back in Allied use; and Dad is back in Ceylon at ME25 base camp having a rest and feeling pretty pleased with himself. Force 136 in Calcutta are *extremely* pleased because they needed vindication for their existence; only a few months before they had to quash talk of being swallowed up by the American intelligence services. In co-operation with the ADF, Camel guerrillas account for 4,200 of enemy killed, with 248 prisoners, while Camel's tally of fatal casualties is, astonishingly, one man.

For the very first time in his life, Dad is on the receiving end of a stream of back-patting, so who can blame him, at twenty-five, if he is cock-a-hoop about that? Behind the scenes it is even better for him than he could imagine, because in all the paperwork whizzing back and forth from Force 136 to Mountbatten's SEAC HQ, the success of the enterprise is being attributed to 'the personal courage, coolness and resourcefulness of Major Carew', with recommendations to the Supreme Allied Commander he get a DSO for it.

In a letter to his parents Dad allows himself a blast on his own trumpet.

ME25 SEAC

My Dear Mother and Father

237

I can now account for my not writing for some time — I've been playing my old game — I was given the job of trying it out, out here. The whole story of it is more romantic than a Rafael Sabatini novel and unbelievably successful — I shall tell you all about it one day. When I left I was told it couldn't be done and now Generals and Governors are commending me and asking me how it was done. The Carew stock is very high out here. France was not a patch on this.

This sort of job is just what I love — I am completely independent — and do everything my own way — no one watching over me and no one to tell me how to do it. I even wear a beard and get away with it — in fact it's an asset. I'll send you a photo. I got your letters — the first since I got off the boat sent to me by parachute — most romantic. Your airgraph was rather sarcastic and cutting — I could not write to you before Chubby as it was forbidden for shipping and convoy security reasons [Dad's half-brother, Chubby, was stationed in India]. Daddy hasn't written to me either and it's over 3 months now. I was looking forward to one after so long. Sit down now, Daddy and put pen to paper . . .

How *could* Granddad not write? How *could* his mother have written *anything* sarcastic or cutting to her son, so far from home, in enemy territory, in the middle of a war? It is inexplicable. Maud just couldn't help herself.

As Dad signs the letter to his parents, Force 136 are drawing up plans for his next mission, Operation Nation. The head of Force 136, the one-legged Colin Mackenzie, known to the men as Moriarty has once again decided not to share the information with CAS(B).[1] A high-risk strategy, considering the heat building up between them, but one Mackenzie is prepared to take. Intelligence networks have been aware for some time that Aung San is planning to turn his Burma National Army (12,000 strong) against the Japanese in a nationwide rebellion, which in turn will be supported across the country by the resistance networks of the AFO. It is imperative to ensure this is strategically planned with the advance of the British Army. The man chosen to liaise with the AFO and Aung San's army and co-ordinate this uprising is — Dad.

It is strongly recommended that Maj CAREW and his team receive the appointment of Controlling Jed, since this team is the only team with Jed experience in this theatre of war and has proved its capabilities both in the political as well as the military sphere.

---

[1] Colin Mackenzie was an inspired civilian appointment — a student of John Maynard Keynes at Cambridge, he had lost a leg in the First World War.

This time his team is code-named after a small silent killing expert: Weasel.

★ ★ ★

Sometimes even Dad thought he'd gone too far. Like the time he earnestly pointed out to Tim, an extremely freckly and very bright six-year-old, that you *never* saw old people with freckles. The moments of silence that followed were almost too much for Dad, but not quite, watching his youngest son compute the meaning of this. That it was true — you didn't see old people with freckles. What happened to them? Tim paled. Did they or their freckles disappear . . . ?

7

We are in the supermarket. I look round and Dad is gone. He has done an about-turn and is halfway back down the aisle. He is standing very close to a lady inspecting a large plastic laundry basket. He is leaning towards her, and she is leaning away from him. I speed down the aisle towards them. The laundry basket is a powder-blue plastic weave in a latticework design, like a trellis. He is still leaning over her shoulder. Very close. I get there just in time to overhear him say, 'They leak, you know.'

All around Dad's house are notices for reminding. Pinned to kitchen cupboards, in pockets, in drawers, in books. Photographs of us now have our names underneath. In the conservatory there is a large chronological chart of Dad's life: 'Born Dublin 1919; Brothers: Desmond & Chubby; Mother: Maud Emily St Clair; Father: Arthur Edward Patrick Carew; Children: Patrick, Keggie, Nicky, Tim; Dogs: Bryn and Oscar.' And so on. Where the photograph of our stepmother used to be, we have reinstated our own mother. Carers come in daily, but Dad is lonely, distracted, confused. I find a notebook in a biscuit tin.

The Time is 12 o'clock [in pencil]

I have just had a resonable chat with Nicky (in London)

The Time is 12 o'clock exactly
This pencil is not easy

I have found this one it is a bit better
The time is exactly 12 o'clock and
Andy [the gardener] has had a very short
chat and gone home

The pencil was awful [blue biro]
hence the pen and it is super
YESTERDAY
I completed my job of changing the main
[illegible] on the wall
I have
My Father and
My four Children [red biro]
are impressive and super [green biro]
Yesterday I cleared the big picture on the
wall and
replaced with my Father and the four
children [blue]
Andy has gone home and had a chat with
me

From now on I will wright more carefully.
The time is exactly 12 15 I have not eaten
yet
But I will Now

1240 Andy has just gone home & we had a
5 minute chat

1244 I must feed myself and I will report

1245 I had a breakfast 2 slices of toast — super

1250 Raining called the dogs to come in They didnt

1255 They did — good old dogs. Pouring rain outside

★ ★ ★

In 1981, at twenty-four years old, I ran off to Ireland with my Egyptian boyfriend, Faris, who was the only son of the chief imam of the Regent's Park mosque. We existed frugally, doing odd jobs, painting, gardening. For the first time in my life I had found a place in which I felt at home. It was as if something in me recognised a connection, the air, the rocks, the fuchsia hedgerows, the happy naughty spirit of the people — or that is what I thought.

We rented a house on a cliff in West Cork. It was in fact the house where Rose Dugdale, the young English rebel debutante, and her IRA boyfriend, Eddie Gallagher, had been arrested seven years before after a tip-off — having made the most basic error of thinking the more remote they were, the less noticed. They used the barn to hide a stolen Vermeer, *Lady Writing a Letter with her Maid*, and eighteen other priceless works by Goya, Rubens and Gainsborough, which they'd been trying to ransom to raise funds for the IRA.

Our view looked over High Island, Low

Island, Adam and Eve, down the coast beyond the Staggs, to where the Fastnet lighthouse blinked at night across the sea in the distance. The house was ramshackle and so were we, with our chickens, a goat (who liked to stand on the roof of the 2CV), our dogs, our cats, in and out with all the mud from our vegetable garden. Both our fathers came to that house. First, Dr Badawi to check up on his wayward son. It was the time of the Iran-Iraq war, and he was under intense diplomatic pressure, and I remember quite pleased to disappear for a few days 'to avoid Saddam'. He brought us both prayer mats, which the dogs disrespectfully lay on. I presumptuously played him at chess, and lost, of course.

Then Dad wrote to say he and Stepmother were going to Dublin to look up some relations and that he would like to drive down to us afterwards, and stay. Stepmother liked hotels, I just couldn't imagine her picking her way through the flotsam of our scruffy life.

Their impending visit meant days and days of cleaning. Sweeping, weeding, scrubbing. Borrowing sheets, pillows, towels. But eventually we got the place shipshape, put some fuchsia in a jam jar, and made up a clean bed in the very musty spare room. And went back to work in the garden, where we found a collapsed seagull.

It was a noisy irascible bird. So we named it 'de Guile'. What could we do, but take it in and look after it? Which was how it came about, when Dad and Stepmother arrived after a long tiring drive, with Stepmother gasping 'to powder her nose', there was a seagull floating in the bath, and fishy green seagull crap splattered all over the windowsill, and the basin, and the floor . . .

★ ★ ★

It's hard to comprehend where Dad comes from. An Irish stew in a Carew line of grain merchants, sailors and fishermen, up and down on their luck. The female side is more nebulous, but poke about a bit and there are worrying patterns here. History has been repeating itself. Crazy mothers. Cold stepmothers. Marriages out of their social class.

The only record of Granddad's mother's name is in Latin on his torn-up baptism certificate from Port Said: 'Ex.legit.conjug: Thomas Carew, et Carlotta Emma Harbourn.' They were living in Egypt at the time because Granddad's father, Thomas, and his brother George (who had both run away to sea at fourteen and fifteen to escape their stepmother), were now the chief pilots of the Suez Canal. The family scandal goes that Granddad's mother, 'Carlotta', had an affair with the Prince of Wales (later Edward VII), the famous royal philanderer. Squeezed in alongside Lillie Langtry, Nellie Clifton, Lady Randolph Churchill (Winston's mother), Sarah Bernhardt, Alice Keppel (Camilla Parker Bowles's great-grandmother) and various others, was, by Carew accounts, Granddad's mum. Which is supposed to explain why she shot her husband, Thomas, in the neck with a silver pistol. He survived but his pride did not, so he packed her off to England never to be heard of or mentioned again.

245

Granddad was baptised Arthur Edward Patrick — a good clutch of family names, but where, I wonder, did the 'Edward' come from? The story of the affair and the shooting became inextricably linked in Dad's mind with his grandfather's Prince of Wales tiepins — a pay-off, Dad liked to think, from the Prince to the cuckolded husband with the prestigious job of chief pilot thrown in. Oddly it is the cuckolded husband, my great-grandfather, Thomas, who looks the dead ringer for Edward himself. Both navy men. Two fat peas in a pod. They even share the same wardrobe. Maybe 'Carlotta' went for a kind or just got them mixed up.

Exit Granddad's mother, forced to leave her three children — Alice, Arthur and Beryl. Enter the dreaded Miss Sykes. The hired help sent over from Yorkshire. Beryl is five, her first memory is standing up in a cot, kissing her mother goodbye, and it is she who carries the story on in an eight-page handwritten chronicle of her life she called 'The Veil of Tears', a catalogue of the tyranny of Miss Eleanor Sykes.

Beryl was packed off to school in England and in eight years returned home to Port Said only once, when, with rumours of war in 1914, her father sent for her, 'and from the first day I arrived my life was doomed', she writes. Her married sister Alice was not on speaking terms with her father 'on account of Miss Sykes', so did not visit. Granddad was not there either, having run away to sea and worked his passage to Australia where he found a job with horses on a ranch. So Beryl was alone and utterly desolate

— as Miss Sykes 'during her period with Father had certainly got full control'. Beryl recounts her systematic humiliation, her thwarted friendships, her daily tears, her lonely life. Each day she walked down to the end of the pier to the great statue of the Suez developer Ferdinand de Lesseps, thinking of throwing herself into the sea, but rejected suicide because 'there were always people there and it would have been a great scandal'.

Her only friend was her beloved dog, but even he, under Miss Sykes's orders, was taken from her and given to a captain of a cargo ship whose Muslim crew beat the dog so badly it had to be shot, she was so cruelly informed. At the end of the war in 1918 she was at last able to leave home so she returned to England where she secured a job at Grants of Croydon selling pins in the haberdashery department. There was one love in Beryl's life but it did not come to anything, and she chides herself for being too shy to encourage her suitor's advances before he left (in the belief she had no feelings for him) for India to work on a tea plantation. In the last paragraph Beryl asks herself:

Am I happy? No, because I have felt so lonely and yet I know people who have been so kind to me. Knowing unkindness at an age when I was reaching womanhood and being humiliated and having at that time no friend, one has the feeling that one is not wanted. I am a great believer in love, and the lack of love and understanding can

mentally affect one, and it has not left
me . . .

Beryl died aged ninety-nine, alone, intestate,
in St George's Drive, Pimlico. 'The Veil of Tears'
was found amongst her things. During the
sixteen years Granddad lived with us, I had
never heard of Beryl, even though she lived less
than a two-hour train journey away. Yet
Granddad had been in contact with her. A year
after Granddad died, Dad received this letter:

28th April, 1975

Dear Thomas,
    Although I am your aunt we have not had
the pleasure of meeting, but I hope you will
forgive me writing but I have not heard
from my brother (your father) for some
considerable time. I am anxious to know
how he is getting on and I would be most
grateful if you could let me know any news
about him. When he last wrote he mentioned something about having to move. I
should be most grateful for any news.
    Yours sincerely,
    Beryl (A. Carew)

Dad wrote to Beryl with the news of
Granddad's death. Some months later she paid
him a visit in London, meeting her nephew for
the very first time in her mid-seventies. My
sister, Nicky, who was there, remembers a prim
lady in a hat, polite, nervous, inscrutable. As
fleetingly as she came into Dad's life, she

disappeared again, and that was that. Until her sister Alice's descendants, the Kings, turned up with 'The Veil of Tears'. They tracked Dad down from the telephone directory to inform him, as Beryl's nephew, he had inherited £1,000.

While Beryl sold pins at Grants, and her brother drove the pony and trap across the bridge at Ballyseedy, Thomas Carew, their father, packed up his house at Port Said and embarked on a peripatetic life moving from one hotel to another, Miss Sykes in tow, for the next twenty-two years, until 1942, when he died aged eighty-four in Vaughan's Hotel on Parnell Square in Dublin. Vaughan's, famed for being the IRA meeting place favoured by freedom fighter Michael Collins in the civil war.

Two years earlier, Desmond, on a visit to the Chutes, had looked up Captain Carew and reported he was staying in 'a real old cattle dealers' hotel with straw up the stairs', and described him 'going great guns with the manageress'. Which could hardly have helped endear Granddad's side of the family to Maud. Dad described his grandfather as the kind of man people parted the way for, and who snored in the cinema. And that his mother did not get on with him and there was a rift in the family. Whatever was behind the tepid blood between Granddad and his sisters, the resentment on Beryl's part flashes out of a note slipped inside her Christmas card of 1972:

Dear Arthur,
   I would have liked to come down for a

249

day to see you but I go to the Agencies every day to see if I can get a job because I am finding it very hard trying to live on my pension and I am determined not to let myself go in appearance and that is why I am so particular about my clothes as one can get so desperate as to lose all morale. As you find it now that life is terribly lonely and when one has no money no one wants to know you. I get very very depressed at times. So now we are both in the same boat!

Much love, Beryl.

I assume Miss Sykes remained Miss Sykes because Captain Carew was still officially married to Granddad's mother. What, in any case, did he need another wife for? The arrangement didn't seem to bother him. Miss Sykes survived Thomas Carew, and to Maud's chagrin, inherited everything that might have come to Granddad: £1,619 1s 11d, to be exact. On Miss Sykes's death in 1946, a letter from her solicitors, George Drevar Fottrell & Sons, Dublin, offered Granddad a silver hairbrush if he would care to collect it. He didn't, because on 13 September 1947, Molly Long — Miss Sykes's nurse for seven years — wrote to Dad in ravishingly fine handwriting, explaining she had deposited the hairbrush in the Munster and Leinster Bank, Liberty Square, Thurles, along with his grandfather's gold cufflinks bearing the initials TC. Someone must have collected the hairbrush at least, for here it is, twenty-five years later: a missile, with a trajectory of malevolent intent:

Granddad's diary, 1972

19 November: *Rain all night. Electric light went off, cold bed. Such a dark miserable day and no electricity for light. Noon: Jane turned off my gas, room got so cold. Then threw TC's silver brushes etc. through the window . . .*

Little joy for Granddad in all his life. Motherless, rudderless, and shipped off from Port Said to Rugby School at the turn of the century. In Australia he rides horses in a cattle station, a momentary escape into freedom before the Great War breaks out barely a handful of days after he turns twenty-one. Proper fellow that he is, he returns to join the navy, to be blown up. Not expected to survive, he does, and a year later is riding through the gates of a grand Kerry castle.

And maybe for a short time he is where he wants to be and good at what he does. Until he meets a widow, higher than his station, ten years older than himself, with two young sons.

When Maud dies, after thirty-nine hapless years of marriage, Granddad leaves Cambridge, never to return. They had lived in the same rented Housing Association accommodation, for thirty-six of them, and in all the years he lived with us in Fareham, no one came to visit him — that any of us can recall. It was as if Granddad was an unwanted accessory to the world. I don't remember a single framed photograph of his family on display — and as a curious nosy child, if they had been there, I think

251

I would have. The only hints of Granddad's other life were rare glimpses of his two stepsons, our uncles, Desmond and Chubby; and horses. To see Granddad with a horse was the one time you got a proper sense of him. He could take the measure of a horse in the blink of an eye. He just *knew* them.

Granddad's diary, 1949
28 December: *Self gave TC one GV tiepin of Grandfather's.*

Dad's two royal tiepins, with the triple feathers of the Prince of Wales in a golden G, were not, it turns out, a sweetener from Edward, but a token from George in 1911 to the pilots of Suez for ferrying the king. Passed down from Dad's grandfather, they were destined for Patrick and Tim. Until they both disappeared the day a man knocked at the front door and Dad took him up to the attic.

'What did you do that for, Dad?' we groaned.

'Oh, he was a *very* nice man. So *interested* in everything.'

The next time we arrived at Dad's house, there was another man on the doorstep selling him a £40 sponge.

8

Deep in Burma fierce battles flare up on new fronts again and again. Japanese armies are being pushed back but prove a stubborn enemy. In the north-east, the Herculean efforts of American and Chinese roadbuilding have opened up the great python that is the Ledo Road with its first convoys bringing the supply route back into Allied control. The British 14th Army, fighting the Japanese on the central front, are inching south across the Chindwin River. Their tough and inspirational commander, Lieutenant General Sir 'Bill' Slim, newly promoted and freshly knighted too, sets his sights on Mandalay, but must first complete the enormous logistical feat of getting all troops, tanks and supplies across the mighty Irrawaddy.

It's the same hurdle further south for 'Punch' Cowan's troops advancing to Meiktila. And when I say troops I should mention they were Gurkhas, Sikhs, Brahmins, Hindus, Madrassis, Tamils, Pathans, Punjabis; more than three times as many Indians as the 100,000 British; another 90,000 Africans; and South Africans, Australians, New Zealanders and Canadians. 750,000 men scattered across an area the size of Poland, who had to be fed, clothed (not forgetting their personal items — replacement spectacles, for instance; you can't have a man in the jungle who can't see), housed, nursed, policed, paid, and transported by road, ship, boat, rail and air. All that and jungle too!' Slim thundered in a lecture he gave later. 'No boats? We'll build 'em! No vegetables, we'll grow 'em! No eggs? Duck farms! Malaria, we'll stop it! Medium guns bursting? Saw three feet off the barrel and go on shooting!' His motto was, 'God helps those who help themselves.'

The engineering feats alone were mind-boggling. The terrain and lack of communication meant roads and bridges all had to be built: 100,000 coolies and labourers from tea estates in India were flown in to hack the jungle by hand. They too had to be fed, clothed, nursed. Enormous jungle farms were created with pigs, goats, chickens and ducks. Supplies had to be trucked and delivered. Every form of transport was commandeered, mules from Africa, India, America; tiny South African donkeys who had such big heads horse bridles did not fit them; oxen, buffalo and elephants. Elephants were used as bridge-builders and earned the reputation of being able to lay a plank with the precision of a carpenter, but also of downing trunks at 6.00 p.m. whatever the weather. Some elephants were quite violent. Bandoola, one of the army's best workers, killed five of her mahouts who, given how quickly they were replaced, were clearly more dispensable than Bandoola herself.

As the campaign progressed, with Akyab's airstrip now in action supplies could be flown into the combat zone. Which had its own challenges: flying in mules could be risky — they were penned into the fuselage in bamboo stalls, hardly robust enough to hold a panicking beast. In that event muleteers were ordered to shoot their mule, but regularly inflicted more damage in the mayhem by riddling the aircraft with bullets. By the time the army had moved into central Burma, American and British pilots were flying five sorties a day with queues building up on the runways, every day, every hour. The turnaround for a Dakota — refuelling and reloading — was down to as little as fifteen minutes.

★　★　★

CAS(B)'s brush with Camel and Dad on the front line in Arakan, and the resulting amnesty, had left the exiled governor Sir Reginald Dorman-Smith and his colonial entourage fuming. They were not happy about pardoning Arakanese patriots one bit. After all, *they* were going back to Burma to run the place. What the hell were Force 136 thinking? These double-dealing brigands, murderers, communist terrorists and anti-British traitors should be hanged. Dad had particularly wound them up; here is what the frothing Brigadier Chettle (chief of police, CAS(B)) wrote from Arakan:

> [Arakanese] leaders have been guilty of acts which fully justify a firing squad. I am not certain how much their co-operation with Force 136 amounted to, but they have been given the most exalted opinion of themselves by the

255

officers of Force 136 who dealt with them and are now as conceited and truculent as only Arakanese youth knows how to be. We have just received a copy of a letter from an official of the National Front to a Township officer telling him in the most insulting tones not to interfere with the orders of 'Bogyi' Kra Hla Aung and Major Carew!

This brouhaha will not go away. The surrender of weapons at Akyab quayside has done nothing to persuade CAS(B) that arming Burmese 'traitors' is a good idea. But collaborating with the Arakanese is a drop in the ocean, compared to the madness of any notion of arming patriots in central Burma (which is what they rightly suspect Force 136 plan to do). And as far as Aung San and his army is concerned, well, any alliance with him or them is out of the question. Determined to stop this nonsense, CAS(B) bends the ear of General Sir Oliver Leese, commander-in-chief of the Allied land forces in South East Asia, and finds an ally.

On 15 February, just as Force 136 are about to launch Operation Nation and parachute Jedburgh teams in to co-ordinate resistance in central Burma, Leese, ignoring previous agreements, bans the issue of all weapons to the Anti-Fascist Organisation. Colin Mackenzie goes straight to Mountbatten. In support of arming the AFO he cites the successful Camel operation, and the return of arms at Akyab. He points out that snubbing the AFO could jeopardise the safety of Force 136 agents and send the Burmese back to the Japanese. He then plays his most powerful hand: if he cannot support local resistance he will be forced to suspend operations and pull Force 136 out. Mountbatten knows it is vital to keep intelligence channels open. He also knows the army can do with all the help it can get, and it certainly doesn't need more enemies, particularly large numbers of guerrilla forces comfortably at home in this difficult terrain. Mountbatten knows the Japanese are far from defeated; the monsoon is coming in May and there is a lot of ground to cover. Once the rains come and the roads dissolve and air supply is cut and health deteriorates, the British could easily face a disastrous withdrawal. Time is not with him: failure to take Rangoon by May, before the monsoon, will allow the Japanese to regroup and dig in. And Burma is only the first step in conquering Japan in South East Asia. The repercussions of lost faith in the British would ripple out into Malaya. And there are other sensitive political considerations. It will not look good if it gets out that Britain has *prevented* the Burmese from resisting the Japanese occupation. Churchill, vociferously, has no intention of losing the empire. Yet the expectations of the Burmese for self-rule are going to be a minefield. The Americans want to abolish imperialism, not risk their lives reinstating the empire for the British — as it is, the American joke goes that SEAC stands for Saving England's Asian Colonies.

Mountbatten sees things more realistically.

Right now there is a formidable enemy to defeat and Force 136 need these alliances, regardless of the politics, to co-ordinate resistance on the ground. And the ground is where the Jeds have loyalties to the Burmese, who have never pretended their goal is anything other than what it is: their independence. The Jeds' view is hardly surprising — they had been selected for their nonconformist nature, to act independently and think for themselves. Mountbatten sides with Mackenzie and Force 136. He countermands Leese.

Leese looks the other way. Completely ignores it. CAS(B) officers in the recovered territory in Arakan start arresting guerrillas again and Leese's arms embargo stays. Mackenzie's frustration reaches breaking point. He cables Mountbatten again. He will have to pull his men out and halt operations. In the signal rooms the language turns electric-blue, as the transmission wires sending and receiving messages from the top brass in SEAC run red-hot. 27 February, Mountbatten to Leese:

You are not repeat not to limit the activities of Force 136. I would be obliged therefore if you would issue immediate instructions to Force 136 to proceed with their planned operations so that the present moon period is not lost.

The Force 136 victory rankles deeply along the corridors of CAS(B). But this is nothing compared to their spitting rage when they find out about Operation Nation, the Force 136 plan to liaise with the two highest-profile Thakin 'collaborators' in the Japanese puppet government: Than Tun, now minister for transport, but in secret, a communist and the acting head of the AFO; and number-one enemy and traitor, General Aung San, with his Burma National Army.

This leak prompts Mackenzie to tighten security to prevent any more intelligence reaching CAS(B), who 'must be considered hostile'. But the cat is out of the bag.

9

The first time I went abroad on my own was in 1975. I was seventeen and had got a job as an au pair in Barcelona. Before I left I met Dad for lunch in London. We were walking up Charing Cross Road, Dad at his usual breakneck pace always a few strides ahead, when on a whim he swooped left into a second-hand bookshop. In a few minutes he was out again with a book in a brown paper bag which he gave me without explanation. It was *The Story of San Michele*, by Axel Munthe, first published in 1929. The story followed Munthe's life as a doctor in Paris and Naples. Its strange reminiscences, as I remember, had by turns a worldly and unworldly quality about them, accentuated by the shadow of the beguiling ruined chapel of San Michele on the island of Capri — where once stood the villa of Tiberius, which obsessed Munthe and which he eventually managed to buy.

I took the book to Spain, to the modern white home of the celebrated plastic surgeon, whose children were in my charge: four boys aged five, seven, nine and eleven. Who tormented me. The house was in Pedralbes, the most expensive suburb of Barcelona. 'The only part I'm not enjoying is the job!' I wrote home to Dad. 'When I'm not teaching English I still have to be with the kids speaking English and playing games — that wouldn't be so bad if I didn't feel like

260

suffocating them the whole time. I never know when I can have a break — and if I do get one I can't relax as I've been told *not to dent the cushions*. Everything is white!'

I can still feel the stab of mortification when, against my entreaties, the boys' chauffeur encouraged them to throw stones at the psychotic polar bear pacing up and down its tiny concrete enclosure in Barcelona Zoo. I complained bitterly in my letters to Dad. 'Yesterday the worst one wanted something out of my bag and when I wouldn't give it to him he started screaming and hitting me — then he grabbed my bag and practically tore it to pieces! I was furious and angrily told him to stop — he wouldn't so I slapped him [I must have if I wrote it]. He started yelling for the maids and now I'm really in the shit.'

My salvation was reading *The Story of San Michele*. I was transfixed by it, and Axel Munthe. A Swedish physician born in 1857, he had rubbed shoulders with Charcot, Pasteur, Henry James, and mixed effortlessly with the poorest peasants of Capri; he had also been Czar Nicholas's first choice of doctor (before Rasputin) to look after his son. I imagined Dad reading the book when he was a young man, and I found it meaningful that it had impressed him enough to spontaneously buy it for me — on *my* first adventure away from home. While I was in Spain, General Franco died, and it was the underlying ethos of independent thought in *The Story of San Michele* that gave me courage to walk out of that house (with full pay) and away

261

from the nauseous spectacle of four young boys in front of the television wailing with tears at the death of their murderous, tyrannical, fascist dictator. I rang some nice Spanish boys I'd met who rode about town on scooters. They picked me up on a street corner and took me to stay with one of their sisters.

The most abiding memory I retain of the book, after all these years, is the encounter the author has with an enormous bear in a forest gorge in Lapland. Munthe is frozen to the spot, but his guide, a young Lapp woman, walks towards the bear, lifts her skirt to show the bear she is a woman, and the bear goes on its way.

★ ★ ★

I am listening to the 1978 Burma tapes. It's good to hear Dad's old voice back. Dr Taylor is asking him how he ended up in Force 136 — in that 'it was a very secretive thing' (Dad laughs), and how some who were in Burma 'saw them as Genghis Khan's hordes swooping down, doing all sorts of nefarious things, messing up the pie and going off again'.

RT: They reckon if it hadn't been for you chaps, Burma might still be in the empire.
TC: [Dad is incredulous.] Do they think that? Who's they?
RT: Oh, ICS [Indian Civil Service] chaps and Burma civil servants, Dorman-Smith, people like that.
TC: Those old boys? They couldn't leave the

gin alone! They were all in Calcutta! The buggers were *so incompetent*! Except for Eric Battersby of course, who was shrewd, cunning, loyal, a perfect support for us[1] . . . They liked to think of themselves as action men; they pretended they were the elephant men who got teak out of the jungle. Men of action! The buggers weren't! Those of us who worked in the Resistance in France were. We really had to live it tough, act tough, be bloody quick . . .

Taylor moves it on to the subject of Burmese resistance.

RT: The British came back with the assistance of the Burmese resistance.
TC: The British would have preferred there *wasn't* assistance.
RT: Of course. You being there made it embarrassing for them to deny the existence of the resistance. That's the political point.
TC: Aaaah . . . but I only realised that afterwards.

Taylor is interested in the political ramifications of SOE's guerrilla war for Burma's

---

[1] Eric Battersby was formerly in the Burma Police; he escaped to India during the Japanese invasion, and joined Force 136, where he became the liaison officer with Thein Pe, and the Jedburgh controller.

independence. It's a frustrating listen, full of interesting threads that get cut off by Guess Who . . .

TC: I felt the wind of change. What I saw was so simple. I saw Southern Ireland. I saw people who had *nothing* to do with the British. It was so obvious it was painful.

SM: When you talk of Southern Ireland, does Bob know what you mean by Southern Ireland?

Yes, she says that. 'He's a historian for Christ's sake,' I shout out loud. Taylor, graciously, says the Burmese were often referred to as the Irish of the East. Dad says something inaudible then, 'Shit.' Stepmother says (presumably turning to Taylor), 'Used to it, don't worry' I groan.

TC: Yes. I had loyalty to Burmans, not to the British in Calcutta. We had to throw out the Japanese; after that they had to throw out the British — when the ICS were against me, rightly so. I saw no role for the British in Burma. The Burmans could run themselves. No way could I see the British had any right to be there at all. I didn't see it as complicated. I saw highly intelligent people. What the hell were the British doing there? Never saw it any other way. They ate with their hands, wore sarongs; they had paddy fields, rice; they had a perfect society; the women, lovely and attractive; they all read. Calm. Idyllic. How

264

could coarse smelly English come in and think they know better?

Taylor tells Dad they still don't have television and that they sit under street lights and read.

'How lovely! You excite me,' Dad says.

Taylor tells him they have rebuilt the old Second World War army trucks and converted them into buses.

'Really?' Dad reminisces, 'Lovely rivers, rice, chickens, never over-bred, beautiful country . . . '

'It still is.'

Then the ecstatic Tom-cry: 'Aaaaaah! I haven't turned up my hands like that for more than thirty years.'

I assume they are sharing a Buddhist prayer gesture. The reverie is momentary. Clink clink, rattle, rattle, Stepmother's voice: 'Caauffeee?'

★   ★   ★

Thirty years after the tapes were recorded in Dad's Kennington flat, I am sitting opposite Robert Taylor in the Travellers Club in Pall Mall. I have managed to track him down through the educational charity, Prospect Burma. We clink glasses of white burgundy by an open window in the Outer Morning Room. The hot summer traffic roars through his sentences pulling me forward, my ear turned towards him as he tells me how he first came across Dad.

After studying in Burma in 1975, Robert Taylor began working on the English translation of a Burmese book, called *Wartime Traveler.*

The book well known and celebrated in Burma, was the personal account of the extraordinary journey undertaken by the Thakin, Thein Pe, and his comrade Tin Shwe in 1942, on foot and undercover, through Japanese-occupied Burma, to India to seek British assistance. The book describes their long walk (in various guises — as fishermen, businessmen, opium traders), up the Arakan coast, along rivers, across swamps, through jungle, past Japanese checkpoints, over several mountains, until they eventually crossed the border and made contact with the British. Thein Pe recounts the months of cross-examination he underwent to convince the British he was not a spy; and how he was eventually passed over to Eric Battersby to become the Thakin advisor, strategist and negotiator in the ensuing alliance between Force 136 and the Burmese, that would see Thein Pe code-named Merlin, Tin Shwe, Lancelot, and Nyo Tun, Galahad.

Robert tells me as he was translating the book he came across a number of references to 'an intriguing character called Major 'Kayu''. Enquiries through a friend in the Foreign Office revealed 'Kayu' to be 'the mad Irishman, rebel SOE officer, Tom Carew'. He tracked Dad down, and on a stopover en route to Burma, interviewed him in London in 1978. Six years later, he published his English translation of *Wartime Traveler* with his own introductory essay: *Marxism and Resistance in Burma 1942–1945*. He gets up to fetch a copy from the club's library, returns a moment later and places it, open, into my hands. Points to a paragraph in the introduction:

> Many have seen and read of the exploits of Merrill's Marauders and Wingate's Chindits, but few will ever know of the adventures of Major Tom Carew or Thakin Tin Shwe . . .

Over large white plates of lemon sole and asparagus spears in the upstairs dining room, Robert Taylor tells me that Thein Pe died just two days before he arrived in Rangoon with the translated manuscript. Robert watched his funeral procession, a long and crowded affair led by a hearse bearing a wreath from the Soviet Union, and followed by a cavalcade of several dozen buses constructed on the chassis of old British Second World War army trucks, packed with hundreds of people, young and old, as the traffic halted in an enormous display of affection.

We talk about Burma today and the military junta; Aung San Suu Kyi; the 1988 riots; Burma's colonial history. Under-read and out of my depth I must have been a poor companion, yet I cannot deny taking pleasure in the low thought of how infuriated my stepmother would be if she could see me now, talking about Dad in this grand place without her to conduct the proceedings. Taylor promises to send me a copy of his book; he is certain he sent Dad one, yet neither I nor my siblings have seen it before and it is puzzling because we find it hard to imagine Dad, given he is in it, would not have mentioned it. I

267

am excited, yet sad at the same time, knowing I won't be able to share it with Dad, because I know when I show it to him, it won't mean a thing.

It is thanks to Robert Taylor's translation that I had the enormous and unexpected pleasure of reading Thein Pe's appraisal of Dad:

The first English liaison officer who dealt with us was Major Carew. I cannot say whether they deliberately chose the best man from among themselves for this first trial, but certainly Major Carew was a rather elegant man and his understanding was acute. He had courage in battle, and in politics he was broad-minded. Therefore, we were well disposed towards him.

Thein Pe was less generous about the British colonial administration — after all, he had been living under it all his life. He knew CAS(B) would cause trouble. When Force 136 sent him to meet with the exiled colonial government in Simla, he wrote:

The government had trod upon the people of Burma, and when the Japanese came, its leaders fled without their trousers so as not to be noticed, but they still wore their spike shoes with which to tread upon the Burmese people. Now at Simla not only had they put on their trousers again but they also wore greatcoats. And they were repairing the iron spikes on their shoes, which had worn off while they were in flight.

As AFO volunteers began to be smuggled into India out of Arakan and other parts of Burma for training by Force 136, a Burmese HQ camp was set up for resistance members at Behala, south of Calcutta. It was at the Behala camp that Thein Pe, who had been diagnosed with spinal TB, convalesced. In a plaster body-cast that would keep him flat on his back for a year, he conducted meetings — in his role as Merlin — with Eric Battersby from his wooden bed. Thein Pe was frustrated. After Camel's success, the British downplayed the role of the Arakanese guerrillas with a news blackout. He knew this was not to do with 'military security', but rather to undermine any political bargaining. More frustrating was the latest CAS(B) hoo-hah stopping arms being supplied to the AFO. 'Why would the English start strife like this now before defeating our primary enemy, the Japanese fascists?' Battersby was also frustrated. He had at last received a long-awaited message from the AFO's acting leader, Than Tun. Not the answers to the microfilmed questionnaire he sent, but an enormous demand for weapons with a long obtuse communist manifesto outlining a consti-tution for Burma. Battersby held up Than Tun's message, muttering that if they were to send as many arms as he asked for, they would need 2,500 aeroplanes!

Than Tun was the Thakin considered to be the brains behind Aung San, but he had a reputation of being difficult to deal with. He had, after all, been imprisoned by the British, and had to wait for the Japanese to come along and let him out.

Force 136 knew Aung San was planning a rebellion with his army but they didn't know when. To co-ordinate it with the advance of Slim's 14th Army, it was crucial they did.

Weasel, meanwhile, was waiting for the moon.

10

Christmas 1968. Tim has the most enormous present which doesn't even fit under the tree. It is so big it's been wrapped in newspaper and string. Dad stands over it with a half-serious look on his face which we know isn't serious at all.

'Now,' he announces, 'Tim has a choice.'

Tim is told his present has not cost more than five pounds — for a seven-year-old in 1968, not an insubstantial sum — he can have the five pounds *or* he can open the PACKAGE! All eyes on Tim. His freckly face, his birdy eyes calculating. Of course he chooses the package. It is bigger than him. His small arms stretch around it. Yet he can pick it up easily for it is preposterously light. He looks worried. We watch him strip the newspaper away. We are *all* amazed. For what Tim has got for Christmas is a mountain of 1ft x 1ft x 1 inch white polystyrene squares — the type used to insulate floors and walls. There is also a tile-cutter which slices through the polystyrene with a heated wire.

Tim remembers playing with it for months, slicing through the polystyrene, leaning intently over his labours, his young lungs breathing in the pungent acrid fumes.

'It was an absolutely brilliant present,' he says.

He made a model of the Hougoumont farmhouse which was pivotal (apparently) in the Battle of Waterloo.

* * *

March 1945 brings tough resistance at Mandalay; attacks, counter-attacks, air and artillery bombardment, shelling, flamethrowers, phosphorous grenades, ammunition dumps exploding. The ancient Royal Palace is burnt to the ground. The smell of cooked flesh hangs acrid in the air. Sherman tank guns are too hot to touch after all the firing. A branch across a road or a pile of brush or straw is inspected carefully — the Japanese have begun to use human anti-tank mines: suicide soldiers dug into camouflaged holes with unexploded aircraft bombs locked between their knees and a stone in their hand hovering over the detonator. Limbs, guts, whole bodies are snagged in great spirals of barbed wire. Most Japanese will blow themselves up for their emperor rather than be taken prisoner. Further south, at Meiktila, the airfield is being shelled as American pilots land and taxi just long enough to allow reinforcements to jump out, who then have to dodge Japanese snipers in the trees each side of the airstrip. There are men with their packs and kit, in the middle of explosions and gunfire, all over the runway. Young men in the British troops have seen too much and something happens to them. A bayonet charge tips into a savage killing frenzy. Soldiers, possessed, hurl themselves at flashing Japanese swords with bared teeth. If Sten guns jam they are used as clubs. Anywhere else they would have been relieved by now, but there is no option of rest in Burma. Rangoon is still 320 miles away and the clock is ticking.

'What else can you remember?' I'm on the telephone to John Sharp.

'About your father? He was the youngest half-colonel in the army. I'm pretty sure about that.'

'Was he?'

Well . . . Maybe. He might have been, at twenty-five, but that is not such a great accolade if you orchestrate the promotion yourself. Which I discover, when I get hold of Dad's classified file from the Kew archives, is exactly what happened — and there was a hell of a stink about it. Dad knew that to gain access to the most important Burmese leaders as part of Nation's plan to 'co-ordinate' Aung San's uprising, he had to go up in rank, because they were not going to talk to any small-fry major. He successfully argued his case in India and was promoted to lieutenant colonel. Colonel Musgrave, the Jedburgh commanding officer in Britain who only a year before had written on Dad's report beside Leadership 'Does not impress', is still not impressed.

The basis for promotion as I understand it, concerns seniority and/or the responsibility of the particular operation. In the case of CAREW he was promoted to major as recently as September 1944 and as far as I can understand from signals from the field he has not been fulfilling the functions of Control Jedburgh team as originally

273

intended. As this officer shows considerable irresponsibility when not in
the field I consider that he should
revert to the rank of major as soon
as his operation is completed.

I'm not sure what 'irresponsibility when not in
the field' means . . . gadding off; doing his own
thing; ignoring convention; girls? He had never
been 'clubbable', didn't shoot, hunt, fish, and
would have preferred anything rather than have
to press the right flesh at the right bar; and as
far as girls are concerned, I keep forgetting, he
is a newly married man. Adulterer so soon? Six
months celibate, so far from home, so young and
shadowed by constant death . . . Maybe. Or
maybe he just got on a train and buggered off for
a bit.

Whatever it was, there is precious little time
for it. Word has reached Force 136 that Than
Tun, while on tour as a minister, has disappeared
into the jungle and gone into hiding. Aung San is
still operating as normal, drilling and parading
his army in Rangoon; although lately he has been
making increasingly daring anti-fascist speeches
. . . The clever thing about Aung San is that he is
not under suspicion, because as far as the
Japanese are concerned it would be *impossible*
and beyond their wildest imagination for Aung
San to ever ally himself with the British.

Further intelligence comes in that Than Tun is
in the Pegu Yoma — a range of hidden valleys
and forested hills 2,000 feet high, 250 miles long
and forty miles wide between the Irrawaddy and

the Rangoon-Mandalay railway — and that he is on his way to the secret communist hideout, just south of Toungoo, 170 miles north of Rangoon. On 16 March Weasel get their operational orders.

★　★　★

Aung San and Than Tun have planned a nationwide uprising of the BNA with all the different resistance groups under the umbrella of the AFO. Which is *not* what the British have in mind. They want a co-ordinated guerrilla strategy. In the right place at the right time. Not a whole load of uncontrolled fireworks going off all over the place. Their plan is for Weasel to base themselves at Than Tun's headquarters and for Dad to liaise on operations with Than Tun. As each Jedburgh team drops into the Nation area they will contact Weasel to settle their positions and activity. And when that's all sorted, Dad will persuade Aung San and his uprising to 'fit in' with the 14th Army's advance. Hah!

The Weasel team is Dad; a new number two, Captain Brown ('Bill Brown, renegade fella, wild character,' according to Dad, 'very tall'); John Sharp, radio operator; Tha Gyaw, a young Burmese officer who had been in Arakan with Dad; and, so civilised, Bayi, a cook! Weasel pack their kit and are driven out through the noisy streets of Calcutta, within the hour they are hurtling down the runway in a Dakota. Five noisy, nervous hours until they reach their target. Then for each man, with a carbine strapped across his chest 'fighting ready', it's out the door.

Granddad's diary, 1945
28 March: *Letter from TC on his job for 2 or 3 months God Spare him.*

11

Weasel, weapons and supplies are down safely, with Terrier, the all-Burmese reception committee, waiting to pick them up. Terrier's leader, Tun Kyaw (who also was in Arakan with Dad), had been sent on ahead to prepare the DZ, and prime Than Tun for Weasel's arrival. Within minutes every trace of the drop is erased and all the containers are bundled, with the Jeds, into the back of buffalo carts under sacks and straw. Beneath the cover of night they begin a bone-shaking journey, along rutted cart tracks, through a forest, over a railway line, a wide berth to Nyaunglebin, through paddy fields, across a river, and on . . . As the first glimmer of morning light begins to creep along the hills, they skirt a village, take the road towards the irrigation farm, and finally arrive at Than Tun's hideout. They wait for the all-clear. The carts are driven to the rear of some agricultural buildings where the Jeds get the first sight of their new quarters.

At the first opportunity Dad slips off for a pipe smoke alone. A pagoda rises above some trees in the distance; he can hear the tinkling of temple bells; the morning sun strikes the dome — if there is a colour of Burma apart from green it must be gold. He is glad to be back.

★   ★   ★

277

Mandalay and Meiktila are back in British hands; as Allied forces begin to advance into central Burma, Japanese troops are retreating with reinforcements and troop trains coming up from the south. And Weasel are in the heart of it.

Dad's first message back reports that the response to their plans is 'terrific', but very quickly he discovers he's in a real bind. Than Tun is *more* than a nightmare to deal with. Anti-Japanese does not mean pro-British, and Irish charm doesn't seem to be working. Nor have Tun Kyaw's explanations or enthusiasm about the successes of the way the guerrillas have worked with the Jeds so far, persuaded this Thakin to co-operate with his old adversaries. With Aung San's uprising imminent Than Tun is suspicious the British will steal their thunder. The response to his request for arms didn't meet expectations; now he doesn't want British help. The talks get more and more tense. Dad sends a withering transmission back to HQ:

```
He has read the 10-odd pages of the
guerrilla warfare propaganda pamphlet
and imagines he knows the subject from
A to Z . . . On enquiry his plans
seemed very phoney and consisted mainly
in attacking police stations.
```

When Than Tun is told his guerrillas can only be armed on the condition their operations are co-ordinated by Dad, he gets 'huffy'. Then he begins to play games. Then he restricts Weasel's movement. Which makes it impossible for them to receive supplies. With no one to receive them, planes have to return to India with full loads still on board. Then Dad gets the cold, uncomfortable, and quite distinct impression his position has become *very* precarious. He has become dispensable.

'A lot of politics, your father got mixed up in it,' John Sharp had told me. 'We didn't know our enemy from our friend. We were living on a knife edge.'

'Than Tun was the bugger who nearly screwed me,' Dad mutters on the Burma tapes. 'Big square head,' he remembers, then laughs. 'I outwitted him. I knew at one point there was a moment when I was expendable and my situation wasn't safe; I was a nuisance to them. So I told him I'd just sent a message back to Calcutta to say if they lost contact with me, to ask Than Tun . . . ' Dad roars again with laughter. 'He had the grace to smile at that. He knew what it meant. Cunning bugger, Than Tun.'

Then on 20 March Weasel transmit a message to HQ to say the date for Aung San's uprising has been set to begin in eight days regardless of Allied strategy.

Subsequent recovery of arms and present management of Resistance depends on your co-operation. This is to be much more comprehensive than briefing. Failure to agree with proposal will mean loss of face of British and intelligence will suffer severely. Failure to agree within 4 days will have far-reaching consequences. Conversely, upon your agreement, co-operation will be very strong. Sorry to put it so straight but that is the position.

The 'proposal' appears to be that the Burmese want to call the tune, and that either Force 136 should arm them, and then they will pull together, or they will go it alone. So, while Robert Taylor writes that 'Carew must have been seen by the Burmese Communist leader as the living embodiment of the new, progressive Britain that Thein Pe had prophesied', I'm not sure Dad or Than Tun would have quite put it like that.

Meanwhile, unnoticed by the Japanese, Aung San's family have gone into hiding. Back in Calcutta the arguments over arming the Burmese guerrillas are still raging. CAS(B) remains rabid in their preoccupations with those Burmese 'guilty of acts against the British', and are only prepared to contemplate their trials and executions; nor does Churchill want 'collaborators' with Japan to be seen as Burma's 'liberators'. 'Surely we should not boost these people so much,' the Foreign Secretary Anthony Eden says to Churchill, who agrees. But Mountbatten has a war to win. And the 14th Army's advance is making slow progress. Slim has come round to supporting an alliance with the Burmese. He needs the intelligence for one thing; for another, he can sense the BNA rebellion is irrepressible and will soon be under way: Aung San is so popular, and the AFO are spreading their influence in the hills and villages. In Slim's opinion the BNA will 'not fail to be a nuisance to the Japanese and give them an uncomfortable feeling on dark nights'. But in return for supplying arms he wants tactical control and the right timing. Mountbatten fears the uprising is set to come too early.

On 27 March Mountbatten calls a meeting at his headquarters in Kandy; first item on the agenda: the rising in Burma. Brigadier Anstey's solution is simple: just delay it by sending a message to Colonel Carew.

But at the very moment they are discussing it — and, cunningly, a couple of days before anyone is expecting it — the uprising is under way, and there isn't a thing that a beardy sarong-wearing twenty-five-year-old, of whatever rank, can do about it. That morning, after a military parade in Rangoon and some smart goose-stepping in front of their Japanese generals, the diminutive and intense Aung San marches his Burma National Army out of the city, 'To Fight the Enemy!' Who even now the Japanese do not realise is themselves.

So begins the Burmese nationwide uprising, still commemorated in Burma, on 27 March, today.

★ ★ ★

Unaware the BNA rebellion has started, Mountbatten telegraphs London laying out his position to support the proposed Burmese revolt. He reasons:

281

when these Burmans become national heroes (as all those who fight the Japanese occupying forces are bound to become) we shall have largely taken the wind out of their sails by having made it possible to be national heroes with the British rather than against them.

To placate London, Mountbatten assures that the Jedburghs will be given clear instructions *not* to promise amnesty for past crimes, although any help given to the Allies would be taken into account. But it is not strong enough for London. Stricter instructions are issued. The Jeds have to make it clear to the Burmese that 'crimes' cannot be forgotten and that they — as the British like to put it — 'will have to work their passage home' (a gullet-sticking phrase for a patriot fighting for independence, if ever there was one). All arms must be surrendered when required and no political discussions on Burma's future can take place. This harsher message might have posed considerable problems for the Jeds . . . if they had taken any notice. Robert Taylor writes:

Carew and many of his fellow Force 136 officers paid scant attention to the niggling revisions required by London of Mountbatten's first instructions on how they were to deal with the Resistance. The belief of many exiled government officials and CAS(B) officers that the Resistance was led by traitors meant nothing to them. As Carew explained thirty-five years later, he could never understand how a Burmese nationalist could be a traitor to Burma.

As Aung San marches his army out of Rangoon, with Japanese planes overhead tipping their wings in salute and the cheers of his Japanese commanders ringing in his ears, his pulse must surely have quickened. He knows in a matter of hours he will be turning their own weapons against them; as it happens, massacring 700 on the first day including a divisional general and a brigadier. Aung San's soldiers fan out into the jungle, into the villages, collecting young men and volunteers along the way. Morale is high; his men are loyal and after three years of Japanese brutality they are itching to go. The revolt quickly gathers momentum. Reports come in of 5,000 armed BNA troops in the region between Pyinmana and Toungoo; more in the Delta; 2,000 more at Pegu. And the British are hundreds of miles away.

After days of frustrating negotiation, Than Tun finally agrees to accept Jedburgh teams into the area. Mountbatten secures London's agreement for five more teams to be parachuted in to support the revolt, or as the SOE War Diary puts it: 'to ensure the rising does not fizzle out into a fiasco'.

```
[Operation] Nation. Jed teams Reindeer,
Pig, Zebra, Jackal have been success-
fully dropped near Weasel in Toungoo
area and Panda to Yak near Pyapon. All
```

are in contact.

1 Jed team with AFO representatives and crew were killed in plane crash after take-off.

<u>Weasel</u> reports that KLT [Than Tun's alias is Kyaung Let The] is with him. KLT reports progress of the rebellion. Shwegyin is in the hands of the AFO. The revolt in the Toungoo area started on 2 April. Students [BNA] have marched out of the Mingaladon Military Academy. Carew is trying to get in contact with them.

12

We are sitting around the kitchen table. Dad has just arrived. We are in the middle of a muddled conversation about where he is, and what he is doing. There is a 'Mr Fix It' badge pinned to his lapel. My sister must have given it to him. But he doesn't know what it means. I grew up, like many children, with a preposterous belief in my father's capabilities — far cleverer than the prime minister — and secure in the knowledge he could give Muhammad Ali a good thrashing if he had to. Because he *did* fix things; impossible things, injustices and insurmountable problems I thought would never go away.

Having been removed from my old school, Rookesbury after Dad fell out with the headmistress *and* the governors over their education methods (I failed an entrance exam/he couldn't pay the fees), I began my new school, St Mary's of the Angels. I was ten and immediately loved the atmosphere of the convent with its drive hidden in billowing rhododendron bushes; there were black nuns and a vegetable garden, and huge pigs, and classes were held in a series of huts around the main house. It felt so different from the scary Rookesbury, where I had been invisible and mute. But then, just as things were going so happily and I had made a friend (quite a naughty friend, called Pola) my new form teacher, Mrs White, took a very strong

285

dislike to me. I was mortified and perplexed. The whole class noticed it. If I answered a question, she would ridicule what I said. If I didn't put my hand up, she would single me out. I dreaded going to school. I couldn't sleep. Whatever I tried to make her like me only antagonised her and made it worse. Her *coup de grâce* was to confiscate my geography textbook, for nervously fiddling with my pencil case, and then to set our homework from it. The next day, she walked slowly down the aisles collecting our exercise books. Her footsteps stopped by my desk, her palm flipped out, waiting. I looked up slowly in disbelief. Could she have forgotten? There was an uncomfortable murmuring around the room.

'But you took my textbook, Mrs White,' I croaked, and got double detention.

I don't know what Dad did, or said, but without my knowing he went in, and fixed it. And Mrs White changed, utterly and completely. Overnight. To my amazement, to *everyone's* amazement, from Mrs White's *enfant terrible*, I became class pet.

I imagine Dad striding in, chatting up the nuns, waiting outside the staffroom, leaping to his feet for Mrs White, getting out his biggest kindest voice, then commiserating with her. Telling her he knew how *foul* I could be; he would be on her side, charm the pants off her, take all the wind away. Then he might share, conspiratorially a suggestion to make her life easier, his own hard-won lesson, that I was 'an obstinate cow' and the only way to get anything out of me, well . . . she might try a little encouragement, and maybe even some praise, if she could bear it, and then, mark his words, I would be eating out of her hand. Beat the living daylights out of my sister (he could easily have over-egged), but I would only ever respond to the carrot. On the other hand, he just might have told her some whopping great lie. Whatever it was, it did the trick, and I was forever grateful. But more than that, and hard to shake off, was the belief that Dad *could* always fix it.

But now it is my turn to fix it. And I can't.

Dad leans towards me. 'I am very ambitious, you know.'

★ ★ ★

Jedburgh teams are parachuted into the Nation area; Pig, Reindeer, Zebra, Jackal, Hare. Elk is parachuted in without a reception committee, lands ten miles off target in the middle of a village festival on a full moon and has to make a run for it.

Reindeer takes two days to reach Weasel's HQ; crosses the Sittang in dugouts under the cover of night, navigates two enemy-patrolled roads, a busy railway, then a six-mile back-breaking journey across switchback jungle foothills loaded down with kit, 'varied by a lot of backchat from all parties and a Burman halting us to say he smelt tiger — we weren't impressed!' After a short rest and a long meeting with Dad and Than Tun, it is decided they would be better positioned west of Toungoo — so another two nights' travel. As they depart, Zebra then Jackal arrive for instructions.

But Than Tun is not making life easy. Dad has his hands full and co-operation could dry up at any moment. It is like dealing with a petulant, but very crafty cat. And there is that slightly sour taste of mutual manipulation. Both know it. But the AFO will only follow the orders of Than Tun, and the BNA will only follow the orders of Aung San. So somehow Dad has to keep finding the way through. He decides once each team is in place, instead of waiting for instructions from him, they know what to do, it would be far better if they just get on with it. So they do.

Manpower appears unlimited. There are as many able men as there are arms. Waves of villagers pour into the Jed training camps; they learn how to set ambushes, clean firearms, and send information on Japanese patrols. Back home to carry on normal life by day, ready to attack targets of opportunity by night. The greatest difficulty is making them wait.

It is stifling pre-monsoon weather. Dawns are ox-blood and the air grows thick as carded wool. The Nation Jedburghs are in the hottest spots of enemy movement. Camps must move positions, squads splinter off. A journey of thirty miles can take three days. Everywhere is crawling with Japanese; every track imprinted with the recognisable zigzag pattern of their rubber-soled footprints with the separate big toe. The Japanese objective is to stop the 14th Army at Toungoo.

Force 136 have launched Operation Character further east into the Karen hills. Walrus, Otter,

Hyena, Ferret and Mongoose are dropped in to arm 7,000 Karens. The Karens have been harshly persecuted by the Japanese for their loyalty to the British. Many villages have been destroyed and family members murdered. They have scores to settle.[1] They have speed in the hills and cunning in the terrain. They can move silently or remain as camouflaged as a toad.

★　★　★

The difference between the Nation and Character areas is appreciable even from the air. With such high enemy concentrations Nation's drop zones are so discreet they are hardly visible. Here reception committees lurk like spiders at the edge ready to snatch parachutes and supplies back into the jungle within minutes of the drop. A Character drop zone is more like a carnival with bonfires blazing, villagers running around, and elephants and buffalo carts lined up. Aside from the weapons and explosives, the blocks of opium and gold, was everything else they needed to survive: medical supplies, special light clothing, boots, mosquito nets, rations, cooking equipment, tents, quinine, fishing hooks, toolkits . . . Where did it all come from? How many radio sets were lined up on shelves in warehouses in

---

[1] The Karens have also been persecuted by the BNA during the Japanese occupation. Although they now share the common enemy, relations between the Burmese and the Karens are, at best, tense.

289

Calcutta? Everything had to be parachuted in — so more parachutes. So more silk. Acres and acres of mulberry trees, the sound of caterpillars munching away . . . somewhere.

★ ★ ★

Thousands of exhausted troops slog through the ruptured landscape. Burnt-out villages, shelled pagodas, unburied corpses, the incongruity of the white doves stamped on rusting Japanese helmets, buddhas on their backs. The 14th Army presses south between the two great rivers, the Irrawaddy and the Sittang, and the heavily forested mountain ranges either side. Three hundred miles to Rangoon. Slim hedges his bet. Some divisions swing west down the Irrawaddy route (shorter, but more waterways and more chances of blown bridges), while his main body of troops take the road that hugs the Sittang and the north-south railway. At the front of Slim's mind is the approaching monsoon that will gain the Japanese respite, but will bog his army down. Where the Japanese supply line is close to their back, in Rangoon, Slim's air supply would be cut off so he would have to rely on a 600-mile road that would soon become inundated and impassable. So. It is a race to Toungoo. Slim needs the Japanese to be stopped from reinforcing Toungoo before his army gets there, or they could halt the British advance. The Japanese troops have taken the parallel eastern route, flanking the Karen hills, which, unknown to them, passes through Jedburgh-controlled guerrilla country.

On 3 April Slim sends a two-word message to Force 136: 'Up Karens!'

From that moment the Japanese run into ambush after ambush; bridges are blown ahead of them; foraging parties are massacred, sentries disappear, staff cars are shot up. The guerrilla attacks are in full spate and intelligence floods in: co-ordinates for Japanese ammunition dumps, river craft, retreating battalions, tanks, trucks, train movements. They are keeping RAF bombers very busy.

> Our Padaung [a tribe in the Karen area] levies claimed to be killing Japanese in large numbers and kept asking for more ammunition. We said they were probably using it to hunt game, or saving it for use after we had gone. The next day they brought along what looked like baskets of cabbages and tipped them on the ground; there were 42 heads.

Force 136 receive the message: 'Japs offering large rewards for information concerning parachutists.' The Japanese forbid movement between villages at night; any movement is immediately fired on. Meanwhile, at Weasel's HQ, a bullock cart arrives with Jedburgh team Pig and their consignment of arms, but one man short — their Burmese officer broke his leg on landing. They've left him in a village and have come for their instructions, but now they'll need an interpreter and a guide, as well as a team of porters. Than

Tun is uncooperative and delays their deployment. The mood is not helped by the news that Jedburgh team Hart have all been killed on the runway in Calcutta in a crash on take-off. On 12 April, Reindeer lends their interpreter and Dad sends Captain Brown to escort Pig to their operational area. The route should have been prepared, but the next night Pig are halted outside a village by a group of armed sentries from the Indian National Army. Brown demands to see the officer in charge and is escorted into the village. But he does not return. Then another twenty-five Indian soldiers appear and surround Pig with rifles and fixed bayonets. The team decide to fight their way out. They open fire with their carbines, kill four of the Indian soldiers, and make a run for it. They are alive, but separated, and have lost their radio, their codes, their money and all their kit. It takes five days for them all to get back to camp. But still no sign of Brown. Then information comes in that he has been kidnapped by a group of rebel Indian soldiers — POWs commandeered to fight for the Japanese — who are no doubt expecting to pass on their valuable prisoner to their new masters for a sizeable reward. Dad is furious. He is fuelled on Benzedrine and has hardly slept more than six hours in the last three days. He takes Brown's capture as a personal affront. Through his Karen network he soon locates the camp where Brown is being held. Dad tells John Sharp to get ready, they are going to get him. It's quite a simple plan: they march straight into the middle of the camp with their carbines and just open fire. In the adrenalin rush John doesn't remember if he hits anyone, only that he gets through quite a few rounds. The Indians run off, and so they are able to rescue an overjoyed Brown. They all know that if he had been handed over to the Japanese, Brown's head might not have stayed on very long.

Dad is becoming accustomed to this *thing*, this life, this power to bring manna from the sky. He walks taller, lighter, almost gliding through the jungle with his scouts and his guerrillas and his band of boys. They all know a split second makes the difference. They know their time will be the time they are not expecting it, so they make sure they expect it every moment of every day. The air is thick with eyes. They watch. They wait. As long as they have to. A sudden crash. Freeze. Every heart. Only one mantra: don't get caught.

★　★　★

Dracula is the SEAC plan to take Rangoon by land, air and sea; a triphibious assault, Churchill calls it. Convoys are planned and routed; minesweepers, troopships and landing craft prepare and wait for orders; bombers and fighters line up; paratroopers' leave is recalled. Vice Admiral 'Hooky' Walker (Mum's uncle, strangely enough) will command the first naval convoy from Ceylon.

The army pushes on. Nine days behind schedule, more than 120 miles to Toungoo, each day hotter, stickier. More mines, more booby traps. At Pyawbwe there is a stronghold of 7,000

Japanese; a British company advances over a crest, a single shot rings out. A British soldier falls. The men go berserk, charging, screaming, hyped up with anger and adrenalin, rapacious for revenge for their mates who have fallen; their commander can't stop them, it is hand-to-hand with bayonets and tommy guns. By the time they enter the town there are 1,100 Japanese dead. Trophy swords are taken but no prisoners. Then all is quiet. And sickening. And so it goes. Inching south. Nation and Character guerrillas mopping up east and west of the battle fronts. Tanks, infantry, trucks, tearing through clouds of thick ochre dust. Tatkon, Shwemyo, Pyinmana. One Indian division has been fighting continuously for three years and three months.

13

It was Jonathan's idea to take Dad to see *The Lion King*. We hoped he would enjoy the spectacle, the razzamatazz, that it might take his mind off his memory lapses. The three of us walked up the red-carpet steps in the theatre foyer when Dad, one step from the top, tripped on something. And fell, and started rolling down the steps. The usherettes froze, the doormen froze, the other theatregoers froze, we all froze. And stared. As an eighty-five-year-old man rolled over and over, bump, bump, bump, all the way down to the bottom. And then sat straight up. Unscathed, unbruised, and perfectly fine. There was a loud sigh of relief from the usherettes. What we had just witnessed was Dad going straight into a parachute roll — arms tucked in and totally relaxed. His Jedburgh training was still second nature to him — it just clicked in. He stood up, dusted down his trousers, enjoying every second of our incredulity.

★   ★   ★

CAS(B) field officers trailing the British forces to administer the towns and population as the Japanese evacuate, find they are in direct competition with AFO and BNA guerrillas also bent on taking on this role. The clashes get nasty. Both groups are determined to take control.

Both want to eliminate the other. CAS(B) methods are harsh, imposing curfews and jailing the Burmese. Which is not only destabilising, it undermines the alliance. Colonial officials keep pushing for Aung San to be arrested and shot as a traitor, but Mountbatten will not be moved. Sir Philip Joubert, CAS(B)'s deputy chief of staff, complains to Mountbatten about his decision not to arrest Aung San and declares he is going to take the matter up with the exiled governor. Mountbatten swats this fast and forbids it. On 20 April, he writes:

Joubert tells me that the news of the Burma Rising is going to be released to the Press on Saturday so you had better see your Civil Affairs chaps keep off Aung San, however much their fingers may itch! ! It would appear that the Jedburgh teams are achieving a certain degree of control . . . Presumably you will treat this as a matter of Priority if the Rising is paying a big dividend.

The rising *is* paying a big dividend. The Japanese division travelling up from the south, entrusted to defend Toungoo, are delayed for two weeks by BNA troops, which leaves Toungoo virtually undefended. On 25 April, at a cost of less than one per cent of the 3,000 lives Mountbatten was prepared for, the British capture Toungoo. It is a surprise for the Japanese too; when the ground forces arrive a Japanese military policeman directing traffic puts up his hand to halt a British tank, which runs straight over him.

★ ★ ★

On 27 April, not far from Than Tun's headquarters, near Pyu, south of Toungoo, up the road from Rangoon, the 141 milestone to be exact, Dad walks out of the jungle in his sarong, a dagger strung from his belt, carrying a pistol and a camera. I have no idea if he knew that President Roosevelt had died, or that Hitler was sweating in his bunker, or that Mussolini had been captured escaping in the back of a truck with his pyjamas on. While the war in Europe was approaching endgame, the war against Japan still had no end in sight. Dad walks out of the jungle and beneath a tree he meets two British generals: 'Punch' Cowan and Sir Robert Mansergh. I know this because long after I thought I'd finished going through files, I tapped a search configuration into Google I hadn't tried before and the Imperial War Museum film archives came up. Specifically, a SEAC film entitled *Meeting of General Mansergh, General Cowan, and Major Carew on the Rangoon Road:*

> Major Generals Mansergh and Cowan (commanding 5th and 17th Indian Divisions) confer with Major Thomas Carew (Special Operations Executive, attached to the Burma National Army) at Milestone 141 on the Rangoon road, Burma . . . Carew

297

wears local dress and is thickly bearded. The generals consult a map.

Notes
Major Carew had been parachuted behind enemy lines to organise the Burma National Army. This Army had a complex history, its roots being in the 'Thirty Comrades', Burmese men trained by the Japanese to agitate for independence . . . As the emptiness of Japanese promises of independence became more apparent, the loyalty of the BNA wavered . . . [1]

The notes end with:

For the sensitivity of this material the dope sheet for this film is marked with the triangular SEAC Field Press Censor's stamp which reads NOT to be published.

Within the week I am in the Imperial War Museum's film section waiting for my four o'clock appointment. I am nervous and don't quite understand why. I am told the film has just arrived in the building and I am escorted upstairs to a small viewing room. An archive assistant sets up the reel and shows me how to use the stop/rewind/and fast-forward on the Steenbeck monitor. She starts the film running.

---

[1] The precis continues, although confuses Force 136 arming the BNA in November 1944, when it was in fact the underground AFO.

The black-and-white celluloid is mustard-tinted with age. There are tracking shots of jeeps and troops crossing a river, some shaky close-ups lingering on the Rangoon signpost. Then there he is. I spot him straight away. Standing sideways under a tree. My twenty-five-year-old father. The two generals and some officers in uniform form a circle around him. The sun shafts through the trees and catches on his wristwatch. His beard and hair are thick and black, he is wearing his sarong with an open shirt, there is a long knife slung from his hip, and he is talking to his very attentive audience in the same way he always talked, same mannerisms, the tilt of the head, the gleam in the eye. And does he look just a tiny bit like the cat who's got the cream? I fancy he does.

★　★　★

I rewind the reel back and forth, again and again. Cowan, with his back to the camera, just a few days previously had received the news that his son Mike, a company commander, had died of his wounds at Mandalay. Dad is explaining something but there is no sound. I look down and touch the watch on my wrist which is the same SOE issue watch he is wearing in the film. In the palm of his hand, behind his back, he is holding something rectangular that also catches the sun and looks like it might be the sheen of the slim Minox spy camera John Sharp mentioned. The cameraman moves round and Dad is facing towards me between the two generals' heads. I have been told I am not

299

allowed to photograph the monitor, but as soon as I am left alone, I do.

At a jungle camp that night Dad gives an intelligence brief to Mansergh and another general, 'Napoleon' Rees. Both, according to Dad, had taken a dislike to him. (Not unreasonably: cocky, unshaven tike in a native skirt given far too much freedom to act as he pleased.) Dad overhears a heated discussion between the generals and their man in charge of signals who can't get an important message through to a nearby post because of the intervening hills. Dad casually offers to send their message for them. The generals want to know how. They have been hauling enormous bits of long-wave radio equipment through the paddy fields and if they can't get through, how could he? Dad promises he will get a reply to their message by the morning. They look at him disbelievingly. What was he going to do, send a boy through the jungle with a stick or something? They want to know *how* exactly. By radio, Dad tells them. By now they are getting furious (he must have been irritating), but Dad is adamant he is unable to explain for 'security reasons'. So he takes their message and comes back in the morning with a reply.

'That really got their goat!' Dad roared with laughter each time he told the story. While it was virtually impossible to transmit across hilly terrain on long-wave, John Sharp was getting through to Calcutta on short-wave twice a day, every day, without fail; but short-wave wouldn't work over short distances. So Dad simply sent

300

the generals' message to Calcutta (who had a direct short-wave line to each Jedburgh outpost) and got them to forward it to the post across the hills, and received the reply the same way, all on short-wave.

'But the generals never thought of it!' Dad loved the simplicity of it. 'Silly sods! They couldn't work it out. Can you credit that?'

14

Now it's a race against the monsoon. With one last hurdle: Pegu, fifty miles north of Rangoon. 'Punch' Cowan attacks, the Japanese counter-attack, all day, all night, then suddenly, the Japanese withdraw. And the monsoon arrives. Two weeks early. A cyclone is sweeping across the Bay of Bengal. And it's 42°C. In the first deluges of rain airstrips become waterlogged, roads become submerged, bridges come down, rivers rise, and Slim's 14th Army is bogged down forty miles up the road on half rations in a hot mud stew.

On 1 May 600 BNA troops who have been fighting and securing villages in the region march into Rangoon to find a ravaged city in flames and the Japanese aready gone. Starving Allied prisoners climb on the jail roof and paint a message for the RAF: JAPS GONE; and on the next roof some RAF slang: EXTRACT DIGIT![1] The following day Dracula invasion forces land south of Rangoon and advance in a blinding downpour across the flooded fields. By nightfall they still have twelve miles to go. The next morning a Mosquito pilot spots the message on the roof, crash-lands on a broken runway and walks into town. He satisfies himself the Japanese have gone, commandeers a *sampan* and sails

---

[1] Pull your finger out!

302

down the river to meet the advancing troops who finally arrive in the city that evening. That the BNA were already there is a symbolic triumph not lost on the Burmese, and Slim certainly doesn't mention them when he reports that Rangoon is back in British hands on 3 May. Amidst the wreckage and the bodies of executed Burmese prisoners are also Japanese dead — lying in their beds in the smouldering ruins of St Philomena's Convent, used as a hospital for wounded soldiers and blown up on Japanese orders before departure. It seems a miracle that the great Shwedagon pagoda still stamps its burnished golden dome against the bruising sky.

A Burman tells Slim that the name Rangoon means 'the end of strife'. But it is not the end. There are 60,000–70,000 very hungry, very desperate Japanese troops on the loose trying to regroup, and get to the Siam border to join the large forces there. If they make it, they will live to fight another day, and in another country: Malaya. The Jeds, who have by now armed 12,000 guerrillas, still have their work cut out. Weasel reports, 'Fireworks are still in progress.'

Granddad's diary, 1945
8 May: *PEACE declared for Europe War. Now for Japs. Please God TC is safe.*

The men fighting in Burma have been cut off from what has been going on in Europe. A newcomer mentions President Truman. 'Who's he?' 'The president of America!' 'What happened to Roosevelt?' 'He's dead. Hitler is dead too.' 'Oh, so the war in Europe will soon be over.' 'It *is* over!' This is how many behind the lines first hear of it. Rare letter drops are a source of huge excitement and disappointment, making them feel empty and homesick. Everyone is exhausted. There is fighting in Malaya, Sumatra, Indochina. And still a lot of killing and dying to be done.

Japanese troops are scattered everywhere — 20,000 in the Pegu Yoma; more than 6,000 in the Shan hills; 25,000 east of the Sittang; another 24,000 further south, and that's not counting hundreds of small groups of stragglers. They kill all the cattle they can find and take all the food. John Sharp sits sheltered under a tarpaulin at Weasel's HQ camp, coding messages in the cloying smell of a kerosene lamp. There has just been a downpour. A large lemon-yellow butterfly rises from the gloom. A hand on John's shoulder: Dad's, with a message to cypher. Some brief words of encouragement, a comment on the rain. More on its way, Dad reckons, as he points to an amphitheatre of plum-dark cumulus stacking up in the sky. That the weight of it can stay up in the first place is a mystery. Where does it all come from? This eternal supply. Each morning it builds, layer upon layer, with its peculiar deafening silence, until it breaks. And trees dissolve into clouds as great ropes of water lash through the canopy. Until it backs off into a loom of fine threads and within half an hour glints of sun will flash like fish through the leaves, and all that remains will be a slow, slow, dripping. Then quiet again. The drops of water making tiny magnifying glasses on leaves where points of light refract in miniature worlds.

★ ★ ★

When I went for tea with John Sharp and his wife Ivy, at their home outside Guildford, John talked a lot about this time. He called it 'the breakout', when the monsoon came and the thousands of Japanese tried to escape to the Thai border. We sat in the garden eating Ivy's cake under the flight path of Gatwick- as my tape of that afternoon's conversation attests. John told me the story he told Sean Rayment some years later for his book, *Tales From the Special Forces Club*:

> we all got malaria and dysentery . . . Once you got ill, you sort of stayed ill. Even the Karens would suffer occasionally. We managed to get the occasional airdrop, but when the weather changed and the monsoon came the drops stopped because the cloud was too low and the aircraft couldn't fly. The risk of crashing or being shot down was too great and so we became increasingly reliant on the Karen tribespeople for food. But the worst part on that mission was being shelled by our own 25-pounders, because we were between the 14th Army and the Japanese. It was terrifying . . . you had no idea how long a barrage would last or where the shells would land . . . The Karen resistance fighters absolutely hated the Japs because of

305

the atrocities they had carried out during their occupation of Burma. If the Karens ever caught a Jap they killed them immediately. They never really took prisoners, they saw it as payback time.

One day towards the end of the war the Karens captured a number of Japanese soldiers. We wondered what they were going to do with them. One by one they marched them towards the edge of a cliff and shot them. I watched as they toppled over the cliff. You could see the look of sheer terror on the Japs' faces. Carew came up to me and said: 'Now look here, John, don't you get involved in any of this.' I was a bit shocked by what I saw. There was no way we were going to try and stop the Karens killing Japs — it was just tough luck. I think we all hated the Japs by that stage, but even so, watching a load of grown men knowing that they were about to die and then seeing them being killed one by one is not a nice experience. I have to say that I aged quite considerably between 1944 and 1945.

★ ★ ★

Dad is receiving reports that BNA officers are being arrested.

15

The 1978 Burma tapes:

TC: I talked to Mountbatten about it and he agreed. The Burmans were Burmans and no *way* could they accuse those chaps that worked for me as traitors. Mountbatten was the only one who agreed . . . None of the others did. Still in their minds, deeply ingrained, was that all those Burmans were traitors . . . And they particularly accused me because I was born in Southern Ireland and obviously an Irishman by nature, they thought I was trying to get freedom for the Burmans from the British like the Irish had. Then, it was a *very* strong accusation . . . The best thing I did was to read *Seven Pillars of Wisdom* on the boat on the way out. I never forgot my lessons from Lawrence.[1] I saw it all happen again. All the buggers sitting back

---

[1] T. E. Lawrence, a British major working with Bedouin warriors and recruiting local people, pioneered a new form of guerrilla warfare. By example he showed how to leave one's own culture and enter another. Lawrence was ahead of his time and had great sympathy for the Arabs in their struggle for independence (wishing them as allies not subjects), and very painfully witnessed their betrayal by broken British promises.

at base playing; not seeing reality on the ground. I liked those Burmans and I didn't like those old boys drinking gin. I couldn't mix in their club. I was always totally unhappy. 'Come on, old boy,' and all those jokes, and sex . . . didn't please me. But I could sit down with the Burmans . . .

Dad tells Taylor that Mountbatten told him Dorman-Smith would be reinstated as governor of Burma over his dead body.

★　★　★

I don't know if Dad read *Burmese Days* by George Orwell — the story of a disillusioned white teak merchant and the expatriate community in a remote part of Burma published in 1935. For me it is the book that transports me to that time and place; that distils a clear picture of what Dad must have experienced of the entrenched British attitudes of colonial rule and the Burmese people themselves. Sixteen years older than Dad, the young Eric Blair (Orwell) left Eton and joined the military police in Burma in 1922 for five life-changing years. He witnessed first-hand the behaviour of the British stationed there — which provided the material for that first novel: the public-school types (of which he was one) who made their living from Burma; the local indigenous hierarchy; the police and repressive colonial administration; everyone trapped by convention in their own bubbles — socially, economically, sexually, politically.

Orwell's gaze ranges across a fragile and putrid human spectrum in luxuriant discomfort; gin-sozzled, wilting in the tropics; a decadent, bigoted imperial existence; the British Club, the debilitating climate, and the corrupt pecking orders of tyrannical rule. The politics in Orwell's subtext exactly mirror (I think) Dad's understanding of the situation at the time, the pompous British unable to accept or comprehend the natural Burmese dignity and will for independence, their arrogance and unquestioning sense of 'right' and ownership; foreigners trying to cling on to an alien land.

Dad had always been innately against authority, but what he also shared with Orwell, all his life, was his acute sense of social injustice and the championing of the ordinary man. Orwell described himself as a democratic socialist. I've heard Dad describe himself as many things, a communist with a small c, a socialist with a small s — like everything and with few qualms he took what he wanted and ignored the rest. To some in Burma, Orwell is known as the Prophet, and there is a joke that he wrote not just one novel about the country, but three, with *Animal Farm* and *Nineteen Eighty-Four* included. When he died in 1950 of pulmonary tuberculosis, he had begun a short novella called *The Smoking Room Story*; it was to have been about how a fresh-faced young British man's life is irrevocably changed after living in the tropical jungles of colonial Burma. I like to think Dad shared many things with Orwell, and from the author photo on the back of my copy of *Burmese Days*, I think he looks a little like him too.

Dad says to Robert Taylor, 'They put Aung San in the slammer,' which brings me to an episode that forces me to part company with the official version of What Happened Next.

In his memoir *Defeat Into Victory*, Slim writes:

> Force 136 through its agents already had channels of communication and, when the revolt of the Burma National Army occurred and it was clear Aung San had burnt his boats, it was time to deal directly with him. With the full approval of Admiral Mountbatten, the agents of Force 136 offered Aung San on the 21st April a safe conduct to my headquarters and my promise that, whether we came to an understanding or not, I would return him unharmed to his own people. He hesitated until the 15th May, but on that day it was reported to me that he and a staff officer had crossed the Irrawaddy at Allanmyo, and were asking to meet me. I sent an aircraft, which flew them to my headquarters at Meiktila the next day.

This, I believe, is when John Sharp described Dad being plucked off the Irrawaddy by a flying boat, like James Bond.

Dad tells Taylor when they arrived at Slim's headquarters, 'They put Aung San in the slammer and told me to fuck off.' But the official record says Aung San wasn't arrested. Dad swears he was; that Aung San's failure to meet Slim on 21 April gave the old guard at CAS(B) an excuse to renege on their agreement — which meant he could face charges of treason and murder, which effectively meant they could try him and execute him. Dad argued passionately for Aung San's release and clashed very badly with various high-ranking officials who saw Aung San purely as a traitor who had defected to the Japanese, and only when the tide turned had come back to the British. Because of Dad's Irish roots and Burmese sympathies, CAS(B) turned on him with threats of a court martial.

'Ludicrous!' Dad exclaims.

'Were you court-martialled?' Taylor asks.

'No! I think I was a bit uncourt-martialable. To have convened a court . . . well, it would have been a bit going against the results.' He laughs uncomfortably with the memory of it.

Dad claims he eventually 'modified Slim's views', and Aung San was released. Whatever did happen, Aung San had his meeting with Slim, and Dad got his fingers badly burnt for getting in the middle of it.

Slim, in his memoir, describes Aung San as a proud, intelligent, but high-handed man, whose only allegiance could be with a provisional Burmese government — which the British, of course, had no intention of recognising. After the veiled threat of reminding Aung San he was a British subject with 'only a verbal promise' that Slim would return him to 'his friends', Slim had the grace (by the time of writing his book) to appreciate Aung San's honesty. When responding to Slim's jibe about only coming to the British side because they were winning, Aung San replied, 'It wouldn't be much good coming to you if you weren't, would it?' Yet, in reality, Aung San had been in contact with the British long before the Japanese retreat. By the end of their discussion, Slim judged Aung San 'a genuine patriot and realist', not the unscrupulous guerrilla leader he had expected. I know Dad (with a raised eyebrow) would have said history and hindsight helped Slim crystallise these views, because at the time they were very definitely not evident to Force 136 men on the ground who had to fight *very* hard in order to stand by their assurances to Aung San. CAS(B) was certainly bent on arresting him and it was not easy for Dad, an off-the-leash Force 136 guy, to persuade Slim otherwise.

Taylor tells Dad he has seen the cable Slim sent Mountbatten.

TC: What did Slim say?

RT: He said, 'I met with Aung San and I can deal with him.'

TC: Well, he did, he put him in the slammer.

RT: Not what he said, either in the book, or in the records.

TC: He did. Aung San was put in the bloody slammer in disgrace and stripped!

RT: That is very interesting.

TC: That I know! I can say that categorically. Slim had him in the slammer and really gave him a runaround. You see, Aung San was *somebody*! . . . I knew at the time he was one potentially very important man. I liked him. Slim put him in the slammer and split us up, and I was told I couldn't communicate with him any more, and to fuck off.

Mountbatten likes Aung San too. He is a liberal and understands the Thakins, he knows inclusiveness will be by far the best path to political reconciliation; and he appreciates the benefits of guerrilla support. On 30 May Mountbatten gives Aung San's army recognition as part of the Allied forces, but under Allied command. But just a week later he circulates this wire:

```
SECRET
Press message just submitted to me
for censorship contains statement that
' . . . patriotic leaders are being
jailed' presumably referring to AUNG
SAN'S party . . . I am having this cut
out, as it cannot be true since this
would be against my orders.
```

Major General Frederick Pearce, head of CAS(B), whose arm was twisted by General Christison to give Dad the amnesty note for his guerrillas in Arakan, has declared the BNA illegal and, ignoring Mountbatten's orders, issued a directive that Aung San must be arrested and tried as a war criminal. Mountbatten is apoplectic. This could provoke a civil war, *not* something he wants to risk right now; and they should be wary — Aung San and his army know the terrain a lot better than they do, and if he wanted to, he could be far more than a thorn in the 14th Army's side! More telegrams whizz back and forth, instructions and counter-instructions, interventions and counter-interventions, from the War Cabinet, from CAS(B), from Mountbatten, from Force 136. Until Mountbatten has had enough. He sacks Pearce.

But it doesn't remove the problem of vengeful colonial officers. As CAS(B) personnel move into the towns and villages, they continue to rub up against Aung San's BNA, their old adversaries. CAS(B) calls them the Burma Traitor Army, and spins tales of thuggery, rape, murder and pillage, then begins to forcibly disarm and arrest them.

> Mountbatten:
> I am anxious not to take up the point of view of the armchair critic, who disagrees with the man on the spot; but the man on the spot has not made any attempt to follow loyally the policy which I got HMG to approve, and which I have repeatedly laid down.

Mountbatten spells out that anyone guilty of a criminal offence will be dealt with by the normal code, and the best way of dealing with any problem is to contact Aung San, 'who mercifully we prevented Major General Pearce from arresting!' He points out:

> once they have accepted food and pay, they are ours, and if they do not turn against us we are surely in a much

better position than merely to declare illegal the very forces which we have been actively using with the approval of HMG.

Meanwhile, Aung San and Dad are back together again. Force 136 report they have arrived in Rangoon with a letter from General Slim stating the terms of employment of Aung San's army.

In one altercation with a CAS(B) officer being officious with a Jedburgh sergeant and a group of Burmese soldiers. Dad is forced to intervene. The CAS(B) officer eventually backs off but threatens discipline. The Jed sergeant blows him a kiss. Dad smirks silently as he turns his back to walk away. Later the same day, Dad receives the news that his friend, Dave Britten, Reindeer's leader, has been killed in a nasty skirmish.

Granddad's diary, 1945
18 May: *Cable from TC all well and now Lieut Col. MC and self so happy now feel tired and able to sleep well.*
19 May: *Heard on the wireless how TC landed behind the Japanese lines with 4 Burmese and raised 400 guerrillas and did well.*
30 May: *MC and self wrote letter to TC framed his photo.*

On 15 June Mountbatten hosts a Victory Parade to celebrate the reoccupation of Rangoon. It pours with rain. Aung San and his army join the procession flying their red flag with its white star, goose-stepping extra high past the fuming CAS officers with their Union Jack.

There is a cocktail party for the press at Government House afterwards. An American journalist strikes a chill note for Mountbatten by taking it for granted the British will return to their bad imperial ways, invoke the usual curfews, political persecutions and censorship, and generally 'screw' the Burmese down.

After the celebrations Mountbatten meets with Aung San and Than Tun privately. The question for him is how to keep the peace and what to do with Aung San's army. The question, as far as the Burmese are concerned, is whether the British will ever transfer power peacefully, or will they have to be forced to do so.

Four days later, on 19 June, Aung San's wife, Khin Kyi, gives birth to a daughter whom they name Suu Kyi.

16

I've been in thrall to Dad too many years. It's been hard to grow out of the need to impress. Be more fearless. Be wilder. Be braver. Be different. Think differently. Surprise! I knew Dad was out of the ordinary and I wanted to be too. He disliked authority and taught me, by default, to distrust it as well. Dad's response to pretty much everything was usually different to everyone else's response. Rules were there not just to be broken but to pit yourself against, to outwit. It was an intellectual exercise for him. He thought nothing of allowing us to duck out of school for a day if there was something better on. He had no respect for anything if it clashed with common sense: his, that is. On one occasion, I must have been about twelve or thirteen, I skived off to go riding. The next day, on the bus into school something (the sly way Dad had licked the envelope?) made me open the sick note he'd written to my teacher. One sentence. It said: 'I am sorry Keggie was not at school yesterday, she had a bad hangover.' Of course I was furious. I suppose the question is, Did he *know* I would open it?

The most memorable bunking-off day involved my friend Jane, whose mother taught us biology. The weather was too good to be at school, so we decided to borrow Dad's rubber dinghy, catch the bus six miles up the road to Meonstoke and float home on the river. It was a glorious English summer's day; we ate our picnic, pumped up the boat, dragged it across the water meadow, pushed it through the reeds and jumped aboard. And so we drifted along, and very quickly found ourselves in a mysterious landscape, field-level, a coot's-eye view through corridors of sedge, and quivering cow parsley. We were pleased with ourselves, glugging back our Tizer and scoffing all our snacks. We trailed our fingertips through the chalk-stream water, clear as rippled glass, stroking the long skeins of emerald river-weed; the earthy smells of water mint, wet twigs and leaf mould in our noses. We floated through fields of cows, into Private Property and No Trespassing, along the banks of large gardens; in and out of willow thickets, having to lie down to scrape beneath the low branches. We watched a moorhen chick actually hatch from its egg in a nest made of crisp packets that had been trapped midstream by a fishing line tangled in an overhead branch. There were sections so shallow we had to get out and haul the boat along and other parts that were deep enough to swim in. I'd estimated a two- to three-hour journey. What I hadn't factored in was the meandering or the overgrown bits, the walking bits and the stuck bits. The pace was slow. The river went on and on. Great loops spooling out then winding back in on itself. And no sight of our destination, the bridge at Wickham by the mill. The hot sun had long since dipped behind the riverbank trees. Our boat had lost its plump taut sides and was now more of a dirigible submarine, with us, bottoms submerged in the cold river, paddling inexorably along. Then it began to get dark. Six road-miles by river had taken us seven hours.

When finally we approached Wickham Bridge in the gloaming, there were thirty faces peering over it, and every one of them vexed, except for Dad's. Jane's mother, my mother, consternated faces I didn't know; the police had even been called. Dad clapped and gave a cheer. But nobody else did. Dad, who had some vague idea of our plan, was 'irresponsible', because it was 'dangerous', and it was Private Property and not allowed, and there were Fishing Rights, and other Rights (and wrongs), and 'WHY weren't they at school?' and 'WHAT on EARTH did they think they were doing???' and 'How could he POSSIBLY have allowed it???' He was in the shit more than we were. But he thought it was a marvellous adventure and couldn't see anything wrong with two thirteen-year-old girls going off down the river in an inflatable boat. Dad, once again, on his own, against the prevailing tide of opinion.

When I think about it now, after all this time, there isn't one school day I can remember, but I can retrieve that idle river-day lucidly. With all its smells and sights and sounds. The moorhen chick: bulging eye, wet head, tiny neck stretching out through the broken shell; the kingcups and trailing brooklime; the electric-blue bolt of a kingfisher as it flashed past; a bramble that had formed its own crimson root ball on the tip of its stem where it dunked in the water. The day remains with me as one of the most beguiling journeys of my life. As I know it does with Jane.

The Americans are intently studying maps of the Pacific while fighting continues in Malaya, Sumatra, Indochina. It's not in the Japanese psyche to surrender. In Burma, the army is using a screen of 5,000 of Aung Sans BNA soldiers to fight a good deal of the forward action. But still Force 136 have to defend their existence; in a rant to Kandy HQ, Ritchie Gardiner, head of Burma Section, accuses the army of 'a depressing lack of initiative', and that with seventy officers in the field with 8,000 guerrillas against 40,000 Japs Force 136 parties are '<u>killing more of the enemy than the whole of 12 Army</u>'. The Karens are returning to base with such large tallies even the Jeds are sceptical, so now they bring home the right ear of each victim wrapped in a little green leaf parcel like a ration of rice.

On 20 June, Dorman-Smith, Burma's pre-war governor, unable to wait, has clambered aboard HMS *Cumberland* and sailed up Rangoon harbour, and although debarred from coming ashore by constitutional propriety, there he rocks, gently on the waves, in full view, holding court with his pre-war lackeys. He distrusts Aung San. And he distrusts Mountbatten's concessions towards him, which now have reached the point of threatening to court-martial any officer who does not, as Mountbatten so Britishly puts it, 'tag along'. But he needs Aung San and Than Tun on board, and has an oily speech prepared: to sell the new policy for Burma to move *towards* Dominion status (self-government within the Commonwealth), but until this *unspecified* time, to remain under direct British rule.[1] He puts a very rosy spin on it. Aung San and Than Tun smile politely, but will not be swayed. They want a sovereign government. As they see it, they already *have* power, and are not about to hand it back.

★ ★ ★

July, the monsoon lies on the landscape like a leaden weight. The rains force airstrips to close so supplies have to travel 900 miles from the Indian town of Dimapur by river or road. In this weather, under the battering, the rough roads are falling apart. Everything is hanging off a thread. It is not just a problem for the army, the whole country is short of food, clothing and basic necessities. Boots are permanently wet, feet rot, wounds turn septic; tropical ulcers swell to the size of dinner plates; leeches, mosquitoes and rats proliferate. The mud is thigh deep. Everyone is sick. No trenches can be dug, nor graves, nor latrines. The wounded simply drown. Starvation creeps through the country. Cholera has become widespread; and beriberi, dengue fever, malaria, and leprosy. Force 136 are receiving requests for serum for bubonic plague. And percolating through the jungles west to east are Japanese soldiers desperate to escape — looting, setting fire to villages, stealing food, stealing anything,

---

[1] HMG White Paper, 17 May 1945. Dorman-Smith initially wanted direct rule for a period of seven years.

killing cattle, killing anything. It is do or die.

The magnet is the Sittang River. Which the enemy must navigate to regroup at Moulmein. There are miles of riverbank out of reach of the army in bog and dense jungle-grass more than six feet high. Three thousand Japanese have managed to cross in the last three weeks. Reindeer guerrillas will cover the west bank, and Chimp the east. Dick Rubinstein, the Jedburgh officer parachuted in to replace Reindeer's Dave Britten, has captured enemy plans for a large 'breakout'. The Japanese have called it X-Day and are preparing for 27,000 men to cross the Sittang at different locations on 20 July. The Jeds are going to make it 'very hot for the Jap'; their guerrillas know the territory; they have scouts, patrols, have set ambushes. If they don't get the Japanese before they reach the river, they will get them on it. They have dug-in positions at hundred-yard intervals for twenty miles along the bank connected by runs and trenches. When it's not raining the sky is mid-element, between water and air.

When the breakout comes it's a massacre. With the forward intelligence the army is able to just sweep the Japanese off the road and blast the escaping enemy through the paddy fields with everything they've got. Even if they are lucky enough to reach the river and find a bamboo-float, the current is now so strong with all the rains they will be swept downstream for two miles before they reach the other side. For the Jedburghs and their guerrillas it's pathetically easy. Any Japanese in reach are pulled in with long bamboos and shot if they don't surrender. Rubinstein's squad covers a moored dugout made from a burnt-out tree. They allow it to fill with Japanese, wait for it to push off before they fire. They empty it out, moor it up, and get back into position. Again and again. Day after day.

John Sharp is on a hillside overlooking the river. The Sittang runs red, he tells me, literally red, with blood. The image prints itself indelibly in his mind. As Japanese try to cross on flimsy rafts, waves of RAF Typhoons strafe them. There are dead bodies and bits of bodies floating everywhere. Escapees submerge themselves beneath floating branches using a bamboo pipe to breathe through, until the Karens cop on and begin to drop shells on suspicious-looking debris. Thirteen thousand Japanese die crossing the Sittang.

From the top pocket of one dead Japanese captain, a guerrilla removes a small book. Its cover is made of delicate thinly sliced bamboo and between each tissue page is a pressed flower and beside each specimen are carefully handwritten notes in spidery Japanese characters.

★　★　★

Dad is being flown around a bit. At a meeting in Kandy with Mountbatten and various dignitaries Dad notices how perplexed Dorman-Smith looks, with everyone now championing the integrity of Aung San. 'Aung San has never really double-crossed us,' Dorman-Smith mockingly points out 'He has *always* in the past been openly against us.'

Kandy. Calcutta. Jessore. Rangoon. Then back to Force 136 HQ in Calcutta again. Calcutta is another world, a vast cohabitation of parallel universes, swirling, colliding, shouting, hooting, bellowing, barking, screeching. The noise! Rickshaws, carts; mahogany legs scissoring, scissoring; a white Brahman cow ambling across the street; a crow wobbling on a line over a gutter. Dad walks past low doorways peering into the tiny dark interiors of tiny stores: 'International Construction Company'; 'Consolidated Indian Steel'; 'World Brass Corporation'; loinclothed figures bang metal in the gloom, sparks flying from the bellows; a man gobs up a crimson splat of betel juice; a wreath of acrid smoke hangs over a dung fire. Dad rounds a corner, holds his breath against the sharp slap of urine. It is hard to adjust; no need for a sixth sense here, but some things have become so ingrained and it's not easy to drop his guard. He crosses the road, up some steps, his eye snags on a brown ankle flickering behind the turquoise sari coming down. The street widens; Dodges, Hudson Super-Sixes and Studebakers jam bumper to bumper outside the Great Eastern Hotel. A Sikh taxi driver leans on his horn. Dad takes a ride north to the suburb of Jorasanko, the taxi pulls up beside the sign for the School of Eastern Interpreters. It is the colonial mansion of the great poet Rabindranath Tagore, commandeered by SOE and now where Force 136 brief, debrief and rest their agents. He nods at the doorman. Behind the portico is an arbour of misty fountains and lawns perfumed by trailing

324

white jasmine. Maybe there will be a party tonight, cocktails and dancing with the FANYs who have been decoding his messages. Will he go? He might. He misses the diamond-studded Burmese sky. Last night his hotel mattress was too soft for him; he is so used to sleeping sitting up with his back against a tree, he had to abandon the bed and lean against the wall.

★ ★ ★

Force 136 are feeling pretty pleased with themselves. Their tally or Game Book,[1] claims 17,600 of the enemy have been killed under the direction of 120 Force 136 officers, and this does not include airstrikes resulting from providing eighty per cent of the targets to the RAF, or casualties inflicted by the BNA. Nation accounts for 4,250 of these, with just thirty-six casualties of their own.

The assistance provided by the Burmese resistance against the Japanese has long been in dispute. Official British history downplayed the role of clandestine forces, even suggesting the BNA delayed the progress of Slim's 14th Army. I might be biased. But. It's hard to swallow that Burmese resistance was 'nugatory'. With Aung San growing and strengthening his army (at

---

[1] The term 'Game Book' was taken from the records of birds dispatched on a Scottish shoot, where hiding in butts waiting for beaters to flush the quarry into the line of fire resonated with Force 136's methods.

Japanese expense); the AFO networks passing on Japanese military information; Nyo Tun and his Arakanese comrades turning against the Japanese to support the reoccupation of Arakan (so crucial for air supply to reach the army in central Burma); and with Thein Pe liaising with Force 136 for more than two years, guerrilla resistance, surely, *had* to have speeded up the process. And every day as the rains approached, was crucial. It would be naive to suggest the BNA wasn't without huge problems — its ethnic battles against the Karens for one. And CAS(B) had a point about arming a potential enemy But if they had got their way the job would have been so much harder: no intelligence, no back-up, no mopping up, with the strong likelihood of civil war thrown in. Their picture was through a lens fuzzed up by empire, their own future exactly as it was before, its power and its perks with its clubs, coolies, gin slings and shooting parties. *They* were the destabilising force with their long memories and old scores to settle, their blacklists, their brutal policing, their cronyism, the thousands of arrests, trials, curfews, price controls and revenue collections. Force 136 guys were easily dismissed with their 'rosy liberal' communist sentiments and 'simple solutions to problems' which they little understood. It's easy to see why: they were a cocksure lot; yet, as it turns out, they did have the clearer, fairer, more progressive view. I concede I am a Burma War Gatecrasher. I'm no specialist. I have not paid my dues. Metaphorically I too am parachuting into a jungle. Yet . . .

★   ★   ★

On 25 July 1945, President Truman writes in his diary: 'We have discovered the most terrible bomb in the history of the world. It may be the fire destruction prophesied in the Euphrates Valley Era, after Noah and his fabulous Ark. Anyway we think we have found the way to cause a disintegration of the atom.' The 'terrible' bomb had just been tested in the New Mexico desert, its explosion visible 200 miles away.

On 26 July, Churchill loses the British election to Labour's Clement Attlee.

Eleven days later, on 6 August 1945, the Americans drop an atomic bomb on Hiroshima. On 9 August they drop another on Nagasaki.

On 15 August 1945, the Second World War officially ends.

In spite of the many leaflet drops, thousands of Japanese remain in the jungles of Asia either unaware, or unable to believe their emperor could ever surrender.

Granddad's diary, 1945
26 July: *Socialist government in. Letter from TC at Ceylon KANDY & met Mountbatten.*
10 August: *Japan asking for peace.*
15 August: *JAPS dirty yellow monkeys signed for PEACE midnight news came in. MC bed all day with excitement.*

17

Dad and Jonathan are watching telly. Jonathan has flicked through the channels and settled on the BBC series *Walking with Dinosaurs*, narrated by Kenneth Branagh. The computer-generated dinosaurs charge across the real-life savannah roaring with rage. A close-up of a scaly reptilian eye. It blinks. Two Torosaurus lock horns in mortal combat; they squeal and growl. Dad is suddenly on the edge of his seat. Riveted. The camera pans across a forest of tall pines to the sound of a distant mewling beast.

'The mating call of the Tyrannosaurus rex continues to echo across the volcanic slopes,' Branagh informs us. 'And it has been heard. A male Tyrannosaurus has brought down a young Triceratops, but it is not just to satisfy his hunger . . . It is a gift. Female Tyrannosaurus rex are larger and more aggressive than the males, and he needs to court her with food to stop her attacking him on sight.'

I am standing in the doorway. Dad's mouth is open, his eyes are popping out. We watch the Tyrannosaurus lift its head from the carcass and roar, stringy red flesh particles swaying from its teeth. Roar, roar. Belch. Roar. A female Tyrannosaurus approaches. Growl, growl.

'My God!' Dad gasps.

He thinks it's a wildlife programme. It looks and sounds like a wildlife programme. Kenneth

Branagh has the perfect convincing voice, and the music sounds just how we expect wildlife soundtracks to sound. And the dinosaurs are so realistic; their eyes are real reptile's eyes. The muscles beneath their scaly skin actually shudder like a cow's skin shudders when it has a fly on its shoulder. Every creature looks astonishingly alive, just like creatures do in wildlife programmes. Which is the point. And Dad is completely taken in.

'She is wary,' Branagh continues. 'The primary weapon of a Tyrannosaurus is its mouth. Its arms are tiny so it can carry its massive jaw and remain balanced on its legs. This jaw can crush bone and tear off up to seventy kilograms of meat with one bite. The male keeps his distance.'

Sunlight streams through the trees, the orchestra's strings pile in, the dinosaur's growling gets louder and more fierce. Dad is transfixed.

'Later that evening they mate,' Branagh explains. 'This is the first of many couplings as the male stays by the female's side while she is receptive, ready to see off any other males that might appear . . . '

'Well, I never!' Dad says.

And I am almost envious. To inhabit a world that has discovered living dinosaurs, and filmed them, and brought them into the comfort of our homes. It is miraculous. And naturally it is just his luck. To witness real baby dinosaurs hatch from a clutch of eggs.

A flock of screeching Pterodactyls clip their wings on the waves of a raging sea. A pack of young Utahraptors are neck-deep in the belly of their kill. Then comes a close-up of a lethal claw. A tongue flicks out.

'Confrontation always ends in violence,' Branagh says.

A beach of horseshoe crabs is grazed upon by sharp-toothed Rhamphorhynchuses, who are themselves preyed upon by a snacking Marshosaurus. And Dad is all aboard. And why should he not be? It is not, after all, as if they could not exist. And their miraculousness is no stranger to the eye than present-day creatures of the deep, or the microscope, or other natural-history revelations.

The credits roll.

Dad looks out the window and says thoughtfully, 'If I left here, I'd only be in another here.'

★   ★   ★

Of paramount importance
Mr G. Appleton
Director, Public Relations Department
Govt of Burma

Mr Appleton!

I heard your most disgusting talk at the East and West Association (Propaganda Association would be better). You think that we Burmans are all 'suckers' Eh!! You are damn well mistaken, Mr Crafty Blooming Appleton. Ho! Ho! Most of us Burmans who heard your slimy, slippery and soft propaganda talk know at once that your 'move' was a 'stoop to conquer' stunt. We

330

know you were 'soft-soaping us' Appleton — Yes! We could see right through your crafty but loose propaganda.

You fancy you're smart and you know plenty about our fine country — that's just it! You know bugger all — perhaps Appleton you'd like to know what's in store for you British imperialists — Hah! Don't wait for it Appleton if you want to save your insipid self from being punctured or badly handled all you can do for the better of our esteemed Burma is get out! Maldom! (i.e., *medium*, understand?) You are seeing what is happening in our poor oriental brother-land Indonesia. Don't be surprised if the same thing happens in Burma — some day — it is not so far off, we Burmans and Indians unitedly will kick out you blood-sucking Britishers and your goddam children the Eurasians — Ho! Ho! Ho!

The eyes of Burma and its growing generation is [sic] opening with speed and certainty. The Pinnacle of British and European superiority is crumbling to dust. Beware, the pent-up strength of all Asiatics is well near bursting point. The struggle for total freedom of all subject peoples is sure to begin in the not distant future. When we triumph, Appleton, don't forget we shall mark you down as one of the war criminals.

Down with fascists, imperialists and their lousy tools.

Long live Aung San, Than Tun and the rest of our cherished freedom lovers.

331

Down with twerps and low-down punks like Appleton — Doh Bumah!!!

This gorgeous letter was sent anonymously to George Appleton at CAS(B) during the post-war administration period in response to Appleton's offer to address an association formed to further East-West relationships. Appleton assumed it was written by a communist in the RAF. I am not so sure. In view of Appleton's previous position as archdeacon of Rangoon, Thein Pe also viewed him wryly: 'Reverend Mr Appleton, having no followers to preach to, was nearly unemployed, so the exiled government appointed him information director. It appeared that he was appointed in the belief that a man skilled in the dissemination of Christianity would be especially good for government propaganda.'

After the expulsion of Japan, CAS(B) men like Appleton were back, bums on seats, in Government House and under the same pre-war illusion that the avuncular British were there to rule and sort the place out. Burma, so long a battlefield, was in tatters. Whole cities had disintegrated under overgrown ruins. There were no crops, no food, no clothes, no transport, no communications, no economy. Tuberculosis, malaria and scabies were rife. Banditry was epidemic. Rotting garbage piled up; open drains clogged with filth; towns were pitched into frequent blackouts. The country was unrecognisable. An upsurge of tense nationalist feeling simmered across Burma, and the British were unnerved.

Attlee's government had promised Burma Dominion status but with no timetable. Dorman-Smith had, over Mountbatten's live body, been rein-stated as governor.[1] Dad was in hospital with a bad bout of malaria. The AFO was now the AFPFL — Anti-Fascist People's Freedom League, with Aung San as its leader. Than Tun, as leader of the Burma Communist Party (BCP), had broken away from Aung San. And as for the councillor for defence, Dorman-Smith had appointed . . . only our nemesis, Frederick Pearce, the sacked former chief of CAS(B). Mountbatten must have choked on his paw-paw.

★ ★ ★

There was to be a new army for Burma, too. However, the majority of BNA troops were deemed 'unfit' for recruitment and discharged. Others refused to apply in protest, not wanting to take part in a British-dominated post-war army, and they took their weapons and left feeling hostile and alienated. For the 15,000 disenfranchised BNA soldiers (and their weapons) Aung San set up a 'welfare organisation'. It was called the People's Volunteer Organisation (PVO). The PVO

---

[1] On 16 October 1945, in brilliant sunshine, Dorman-Smith arrived in Rangoon by motor launch wearing a white topee. The flag was hoisted at Government House to a salute of seventeen guns with Spitfires flying overhead. The next day *The Times* reported the 'war torn' streets were lined with troops but otherwise empty: 'Civilian spectators were little in evidence, and the few who were appeared to be mainly non-Burmese.'

could be misconstrued as an alternative army
. . . As Aung San's popularity (and welfare organisation) grew so did Dorman-Smith's loathing. 'I
would like to do something to that little so-and-
so,' he wrote to a civil servant friend, blaming
Mountbatten for the situation. Dorman-Smith
refused to give Aung San any recognition: 'He's a
queer chap, I don't think he's all there, he was
always a stormy sort of creature, led students'
strikes and that sort of thing, not a big enough
man to lead this country as, say, her first Dominion prime minister.' Nevertheless, he was nervous
at the increase in nationalist feeling and so recalled
his pre-war conservative premier, U Saw, back to
Rangoon from exile.[1] His next move was to dredge
up the old charges of Aung San's wartime past
(killing a village headman) and revive a case of
murder to be brought against him.

Mountbatten saw Aung San as the one man
capable of uniting Burma. Aung San had the
trust of the people, and headed the most important political party, the AFPFL, for which support
was growing daily. Mounbatten feared a rebellion. He was right to. There must have been
50,000 weapons knocking about, buried, hidden,
in the rafters, under beds. Japanese weapons,
British weapons — CAS(B)'s hard line had long
ago put paid to any thought of them being returned.

---

[1] U Saw was arrested for alleged contacts with
the Japanese and spent the war in detention in
Uganda. Because of his leadership of conservative national forces he was a major opponent of
the Marxist Thakins.

18

It's 1966. Dad is buttering bread out of the back of the Dormobile. We are having an impromptu family picnic on a shingle shore by the sea. My friend Katie Dicker and her mother, Molly, have come too. Everyone is hovering around the door, waiting, hungry. Dad shouts out, 'Who wants what? White or brown?'

'White!' shouts Patrick.

'White!' shouts Nicky.

'Brown!' shouts Katie.

'Brown!' I copy Katie.

Cheese sandwiches issue forth at lightning speed, white and brown orders, to each snatching recipient. Katie is sniggering with her mother. I look across. She has flipped her brown sandwich over. The other side is white. I flip mine over. Guess what.

★ ★ ★

It is not until January 1946 that Dad hears about his DSO. For anyone it is a very big gong. He is in Singapore and he is celebrating, staying at Raffles hotel which has become a mess for lieutenant colonels, and he is chuffed at having taken a couple of games off the champion chess player of Singapore and Indochina. Yet, his letters to his parents are full of apprehension. The local command wants to recall him to India:

The catch being that I am wanted by the people here to investigate Jap war crimes, that of course holds no future for me so I am trying to get out of it. If only the army would make up its mind whether they are going to maintain guerrilla warfare or not. If they do I should be able to keep a peacetime majority in it. I very much hope so as I love the work . . . and the difference in pay is enormous.

It is not to be. SOB has trodden on too many toes. It is disbanded and by February 1946 Dad is back in Rangoon en route to a post in Karachi. Delayed by bad weather, waiting for the plane to take off, he is writing to his parents. Personally, I am amazed he hasn't had leave and been home . . . and of course, what about Margot? Married a fortnight then away for more than a year; I assume she will be meeting him in Karachi. He tells his parents he will be demoted down to major again and continues to fret about what he will do.

Whilst I was in Singapore I started writing a book but it wasn't a success so I think I shall leave it for a few years or just write one or two things for magazines. I've had a tentative offer from an agency — but I find it difficult I don't know where to begin nor in what style to write. There are a lot of things I can't write about yet as they are involved with present politics and it is difficult to write about people honestly and as one sees them whilst they are still close at hand. On the whole I think I shall let it drop for a few years and then think about it again. I'm rather anxious about the next year or so for myself in peacetime army. I wasn't very successful before but I think I've learnt to behave myself better since I've left AA[1] and anyway now that I've a DSO people will be more tolerant although I shall make a point of not relying on it. It's a dangerous thing to live in the past . . . I think everyone is very war weary . . .

Before even the first anniversary of 'Resistance Day' in Burma, factions began to split. Thakin leaders were divided on their future and the atmosphere was fraught with uncertainty Public rallies demanded independence. Dorman-Smith banned military training for Aung San's PVO. Then he banned the PVO altogether. Which incited a huge demonstration. The police opened fire. Three people were killed and many more wounded. In August 1946 Aung San called for a general strike which brought Burma to its knees. Attlee intervened — the plan for a murder trial against Aung San was dropped, and Dorman-Smith, who Attlee wrote 'has lost his grip', was put on a boat back to London. His replacement was a friend of Mountbatten's, Sir Hubert Rance, who a year earlier had replaced our friend Pearce as chief of civil affairs. His brief was to

---

[1] Anti-Aircraft artillery when stationed in Norway and Gibraltar before he became a Jedburgh.

immediately defuse the situation and bring the AFPFL into the government. Aung San accepted the post of defence councillor.

By January 1947, Aung San was on a plane to London to negotiate independence from British rule. On a stopover in Delhi, he made a speech stating that the Burmese wanted 'complete independence' not dominion status, and in order to achieve this they had 'no inhibitions of any kind' about contemplating 'a violent or non-violent struggle or both'. He concluded that he hoped for the best but was prepared for the worst.

Not everyone savoured Aung San's visit. Churchill made a scathing attack on granting Burmese independence to 'a traitor rebel leader' of a quisling army. 'I certainly did not expect to see Aung San, whose hands are dyed with British blood and loyal Burmese blood, marching up the steps of Buckingham Palace as the plenipotentiary of the Burmese government.' Nevertheless, a few days after arriving in London, Aung San left with a signed agreement by Clement Attlee guaranteeing Burma's independence within the year.

★ ★ ★

It would not turn out well for Aung San. Six months later, on 19 July, he and six members of his provisional Cabinet were caught in a hail of machine-gun fire by three gunmen who blasted their way into a meeting in the Secretariat building in Rangoon, killing the guard at the door, Aung San and seven others in the room. Aung San was thirty-two years old.

The man charged with Aung San's murder was U Saw, Dorman-Smith's former prime minister, and arch rival of Aung San.

★ ★ ★

In the BBC documentary *Who Really Killed Aung San?* Eric Battersby, Dad's controller at Force 136, was interviewed. Battersby described Dorman-Smith as 'the kind of man who liked subordinate relationships'. He elucidated: 'Anyone who was not his creature was not acceptable to him, U Saw was his creature, and he liked him.'

After the assassination 170 Bren guns and a hundred Sten guns in watertight containers were dredged up from the pond next to U Saw's residence. Enough arms to support a revolt to seize power. U Saw was arrested and the guns were traced back to an armoury in Rangoon where they had been released on 24 June on the authority of forged documents issued by two British officers, Captain Vivian and Captain Young. Vivian was sentenced to five years for selling arms; Young was acquitted on appeal; while U Saw, waiting for his trial in jail, begged repeatedly and rather mysteriously to see 'the tall Englishman'. He wrote several letters to this end fully expecting help, but nobody came. U Saw was tried and convicted of direct involvement in Aung San's assassination and given the death penalty. Dorman-Smith, although now resident in London, kept close contacts in Rangoon and appealed for clemency on his behalf, but U Saw was hanged on 8 May 1948.

According to the documentary, a recently released classified telegram from the Burmese chief of police to the British ambassador at the time cites Dorman-Smith as the suspected architect of the plot, and that the go-between was a man in the British Council in Rangoon called John Stewart Bingley. Bingley was six feet four inches tall. Although he was questioned, he claimed diplomatic immunity and returned immediately to Britain. The Burmese police were consequently restrained in their investigation, and in the fear that their long-awaited independence might be once again postponed, the matter was dropped.

Whatever the truth, the outcome remained the same: the incalculable loss of the one Burman who had broad legitimacy, and six of his colleagues — the most able politicians and ethnic-minority leaders in the country. And with them, the will that had got them together, for Aung San, the father of Burma's independence, was the hope that might have carried everyone through. One by one various fragile and hard-won relationships collapsed. Within two months of independence, Burma was engulfed in civil war.

*   *   *

In the Burma tapes Dad tells a story which explains why he so loved the Burmese. He was sleeping in a village hut on the bamboo floor

340

with a couple of blankets when a young man came in the middle of the night. One of his guerrillas possibly, back from patrol. Without hesitation the man took one blanket off Dad, lay down, covered himself and went to sleep. He didn't ask or expect Dad to complain. The deduction was obvious, Dad had two blankets, he had none. Yet, that simplest of actions, unencumbered by protocol or deference to rank, without fuss, without submission or social convention, spoke volumes of non-English sense and sensibility to Dad. It was something he identified with, almost alien in his own culture, but which was second nature for the Burmese. A way of being with each other we might all aspire to. It was so powerful in its simplicity, he would remember it all his life.

PART 5

THE TALENTED MR RIPLEY

1

Dad meets Mum in Trieste in 1953. He is now divorced from Margot (I will get to that), and in command of the Trieste Security Office in the Intelligence Corps. Mum is a codist in the FANYs.

Trieste, declared an independent state in 1947, the Free Territory of Trieste, isn't free at all; it is a hotbed of unrest and contention between Italy and Yugoslavia, and is still occupied by the Allies. The political situation is explosive with an uneasy truce barely holding between the fascists, the various communist factions, and Tito's supporters who are determined to reclaim the parts of their country which have fallen under Italian rule. It is the McCarthy era, a paranoid time with the Americans on high alert against the *reds under the beds*. The Intelligence Corps is doing the work of Special Branch — sharing information and co-operating with the CIA in their various methods of surveillance and intelligence-gathering.

Trieste is also a ravishingly handsome merchant seaport on the Adriatic with grand piazzas and neoclassical buildings, a glittering blue sea, within easy reach of Venice, and skiing, and touring, and in 1953 life could be described (for some) as *la dolce vita*.

Harry Dixon, serving in the Intelligence Corps, remembers Dad's arrival in 1951 as 'a breath of fresh air. Always encouraging us to get

345

out and have a good time.' Dad cannot think of a better job. He is his own boss again, and for the first time in his life he has his own flat and a maid to cook for him. He draws a plan of it and sends it home. He buys a Plymouth 1939 (two-seater, heater and radio) off an American for sixty quid 'for going to Italy in'.

They cannot sell them to the Italians as the petrol costs them 7/- a gall but we only pay 1/6d. So when an American goes home he has to give his car away for scrap at next to nothing price. My own workshops are going to overhaul it during the next month . . . the best thing about it is that it holds 45 galls in a specially constructed tank and has room for another 30 galls in tins which gives me over 1,000 miles of motoring in Italy before I have to buy the expensive petrol. My pay has been mortgaged to pay for it. It is much easier to pay for it and be broke than to save up and have the savings burning a hole in my pocket.

'Dear Mummy and Daddy' sounds so peculiar after Burma and France and all that guerrilla warfare. When Dad's not juggling with the Balkans, the fascists, the communists, or the Americans, his letters home are full of dinner parties and sailing. Big sprawling words fill up each page, swoosh, like waves over rocks, dump the water, move on, another helping, same again. That hurried simplicity with which we write to our parents, part duty, part child, a bit lazy, not

346

enough time to lay out our thoughts properly — no need to impress, but at the same time the one safe place we can brag a little. 'The cost of a dinner party for six is much less than the cost of taking a girl out to a meal and in addition I get asked back and so save still more.' Hm. I am searching for the first mention of Mum. But before I find her, someone else, completely unexpected, stops my eye. He is describing a dinner he hosted:

> and everything went well until Sybil Kitson a persistent woman insisted on knowing details of my work. Her husband told her to shut up. But that had no effect on her so we all had a good laugh and talked about other things. For the sixth person I had Pat Highsmith, a young American authoress who has had one of her books, *Stranger on the train* [sic], filmed in Hollywood by Hitchcock — no mean honour . . .

I am amazed that in all the subsequent years he never mentioned this, because over the next few months, Dad and Patricia Highsmith become friends.

Highsmith arrived in Trieste soon after her visit to Positano, the fishing village on the Amalfi coast where she had seen the solitary man walking along the shore who would inspire her eponymous protagonist in *The Talented Mr Ripley*. From that moment the seed began to germinate. She thought Trieste, once the home of Freud and Joyce, would be a city to nourish her. But it was not to be Highsmith's happiest time. Her lover, Ellen Hill, was travelling with her, but the affair was a tortured one. The constant fighting left Highsmith depressed, and she attended most social occasions alone. Which is how she met Dad. Dad described her as 'quiet and interesting'; they met at cocktail parties, they were regularly partnered together, and she became his dinner companion. I like to fancy Dad's company took her mind off the toothache that was troubling her and the worsening relationship with Ellen. I think of Inga Miller, the wife of Dad's oldest school friend, Terence, and the way she described Dad to me on the phone, her voice breaking with emotion: 'Thomas was not like other men of that time, he talked to you, he *really* talked to you in a serious way' Women, she meant. Which is why I think Pat Highsmith and Dad would have got on. He would have certainly muttered something irreverent or surprising out of the corner of his mouth about some stuffy pedant bore; and she was unusual, and clever as a cat. And would she not have gleaned some interesting titbits sitting next to Dad? Ripley was a civilised person; he killed reluctantly, only when he had to. Tom Ripley, Tom Carew, both ambidextrous, both sailed small dinghies (a subject on which Dad would have been more than happy to elucidate), and both acquainted with the methods of silent killing (the similarities stop there). Highsmith liked the idea of shifting identities and, as I am to discover, Dad was not averse to a bit of identity-shifting himself.

After flu, toothache and trouble with Ellen, Pat Highsmith leaves Trieste in 1953, which is when the first mention of Mum appears. Amongst the names in his party attending the Coronation Ball on 10 June: 'and two Foreign Office girls who also work in the discreeter side — Elizabeth Woodward and Jane Suckling, who was my partner and has also been my crew when sailing in the races — and other occasions as well'. He tells his parents the ball went on until 5.00 a.m. when they tried to go sailing but the wind had dropped. (He tells them much more than I would ever have told him . . .)

Barely weeks later his exuberance spills over into great ink loops from his pen: 'Jane and I have decided to take the plunge and get married — when — where and how not decided — but in England soon . . . We are so happy here that I don't know what to say — you know that lovely feeling of elation about everything . . . '

Then riots start up in Trieste, things turn nasty, and Mum gets evacuated back home.

2

There are very few photographs of young Mum. She joined the FANYs the moment she could at eighteen, trained in codes and cyphers, and in 1943 was posted to Meerut in India — the youngest in the first group of codists sent out there. Born in Quetta (now Pakistan) she was familiar with the country and the long journey out. On this occasion the voyage down the Clyde and into the Atlantic was during wartime curfew. Her abiding memory of the trip was the glittering lights of Ceuta; after four years of blackout Morocco's neutrality blazed across the sea, holding everyone on deck in wonder. When they got to Colombo five weeks later, Meerut was another sea crossing and five days by train. They slept in huts under mosquito nets; in her photo album an arrow points to Hut S5 at the end of a long wooden budding. Her boss was training French troops to be parachuted into Indochina and she decoded his messages. Yellow jaundice; mosquitoes; the foxtrot; and lime juice, gin and soda, was how she remembered it; the music, Cole Porter, 'Begin the Beguine'. One of 'the chaps' took her on a horse-drawn Tonga (four annas a ride) to the sound of frogs croaking. Later he took a series of nude photographs of her, and when she wouldn't marry him, sent them to her mother in England in an anonymous package. She told me all this when she came to stay with me in Ireland in 1985, as we walked in the mist to the top of Lough Ine.

After the war Mum was back in England with her mother, with whom she didn't get on, helping to feed the calves (a pedigree herd of Jerseys who took up far more space in the Suckling photograph album than any two-legged creatures) on the farm at Roos Hall in Suffolk. Her father had been killed outside Delhi in a light-aeroplane crash four years earlier, in 1941, when Mum was fifteen. He had been a colonel in the Indian Army, stationed in the north of the country, with polo ponies and servants. Mum's parents were the dying breath of the British Raj with all those strange behaviours, like sending your children the moment they are old enough (five, six, seven years old) off to school in England on a ship, 17,000 nautical miles. The word 'posh' is said to originate from those maritime journeys back and forth to India: affluent Britons favoured cabins on the shaded side of the ship away from the heat and sun, so sailing from England, a north-facing port cabin cost more than a south-facing starboard one, with the opposite applying on the way home. Only the wealthy could afford a cabin that was 'port out and starboard home' — which soon became abbreviated to posh. Bombay, Aden, Suez, Port Said, Marseilles, Algiers, Gibraltar; five long weeks until finally docking in Southampton where Raj children disembarked blinking into cloudy skies to be whisked off to some expensive institution. There they remained term-time and through the holidays and sometimes for Christmas as well. School was where Mum lived, with matron and her younger brother, John. If they couldn't remain at school they were sent to their maternal grandparents' house, Highwood, in Romsey ('Rumsey' as Mum insisted we pronounce it), so preposterously posh it is now a public school called Stroud. This was the home of William Frederick Suckling, a line that galloped back to George II's bastard son, William Duke of Cumberland, who knocked up a Scottish soldier's daughter. Their first issue, Flora Wybrew Davey married the first cousin of the famous Nelson, William Suckling, and give suck to Mum's mother's lot.

At Highwood, in 1940, at such close proximity to the south coast, a real war was raging; during Luftwaffe attacks its grounds regularly got pelted, and Mum remembered dashing around during the air raids of the Battle of Britain, in crazed excitement collecting spent shells with her brother. If Highwood couldn't have them, there were more grandparents on their father's side; a little scary in the photograph and dressed to kill: Lieutenant General Sir Harold Bridgewood Walker, KCB, KCMG, DSO, white-gloved, gold-braided, sword-buckling, buttoned and medalled up to the hilt with a dead swan sticking out of his helmet.

Mum's father was Sir Harold's eldest son. When he was killed Mum's mother returned from India distraught, and it was Mum who was sent back to India, at just sixteen, on a ship, on her own, in the middle of the war, to collect her father's possessions. The only thing she was given belonging to her father was his silver cigarette box which has the words 'Hope Deferred' engraved on the lid. I have puzzled over this strange motto. Certainly hope was deferred (indefinitely) when he died. What an inauspicious dictum to pass on.

And so, in the way of those old families, because of the turbulence or poor visibility or engine failure or bird-strike or high-jinx manoeuvre that went badly wrong, or whatever it was that caused James Coulthard Walker's plane to come down, all the Walker inheritance would go to Uncle Harold (the admiral), the younger Walker son. Which was why Mum's mother, Katherine Wybrew Suckling Walker, needed her maiden name back: a prerequisite, by some obscure machination, for retrieving Roos Hall, an Elizabethan manor house. And, by popular account, the most haunted house in Britain.

London Gazette
FRIDAY, 13 MARCH 1942
Whitehall, 2 February 1942.

The KING has been graciously pleased to give and grant unto Katherine Wybrew Suckling Walker, of Highwood, near Romsey in the County of Southampton, widow and relict of James Coulthard Walker, Esquire, Lieutenant Colonel in the Indian Army, His Royal Licence and Authority that she may take and henceforth use the surname of Suckling in lieu of and in substitution for her own surname of Walker, that she may bear the Arms of Suckling and that such surname and Arms may in like manner be taken borne and used by the issue of her marriage with the said James Coulthard Walker. And to Command that the said concession and Declaration be recorded in His Majesty's College of Arms.

Roos Hall fell neatly into Katherine Suckling's lap, but Mum was sent away to a Dorset finishing school for ladies called Harcombe. Mum kept her three exercise books from Harcombe: 'Housewifery & Laundry Notes', 'Cooking Notes' and 'Dietic Notes'. Neat ink handwriting, no doodles. Sensitive souls look away now: 'The Food value of an Egg = <u>White</u>: Water 75%, Protein 12.6%, Vitamin B2, Mineral Matter 0.59%. <u>Yolk</u>: Mineral constituents calcium, phosphorus, iron, water. No roughage, starch or sugar. Vitamins A, B, B7, D. Fat (in state of fine emulsion).' Tick. ✓.

She drew diagrams for mending hinges on a clothes horse, the heating element of an iron, a sectional view of a Louvre window, and a 'Diagrammatic Representation of the Structure of Meat'. There are drawings of fibres too, woollen, cotton, silk, flax. 'Diagrams of Drainage Systems', 'Changing a Tap Washer' (Teacher's comment: *'Correct! Your tap would not fit together!'*). 'Odd Jobs — Mending the China.' There are recipes for starch and wallpaper paste; the suggested contents for '<u>The Linen Cupboard</u>' ('Management of Linen', and 'Uses of

Linen'). I joke not. As I skim her painstaking descriptions of 'Ventilation', 'Lighting', 'Drainage systems', 'Lamps', the 'Advantages of Carpets', and 'Disadvantages', I have to clutch my fist over my heart. There's even a drawing of a Barclay's Bank cheque. I won't continue, although she had to.

At least at Harcombe Mum had her own room with an iron bed, very neatly made; so important it must have been to her that she photographed it and put it in her album. Mum had been brought up on Rudyard Kipling, 'Rikki-Tikki-Tavi', and knowing to check for scorpions in her shoes. She never lost her longing to return to India, sown by the early smells and sounds of her young childhood, and the dislocation of being removed. But then, in Trieste, everything changed for her. Away from her stiff, stuffy, plummy lot: a whirlwind. Port-starboard-out-and-about. She met Dad.

Granddad's diary, 1953

3 August: *Letter from TC all up in the cloud. Engaged to Jane Suckling? Letter from Jane Suckling say how happy she is engaged to TC.*

8 August: *All set to be vetted by Sucklings & co. 3 p.m. Mrs Suckling and son John came stayed for tea. Left 4.45 p.m. Maud and I were so happy and pleased. TC marrying Jane. Age 28.*

3

The latest experiment is the Armpit Shaving Experiment. Dad has heard on the radio that if you shave your body hair it grows back thicker than it was before. *Woman's Hour*, possibly, or maybe he got it from a magazine, a leg-waxing ad. He won't take anyone's word for anything. So he is shaving under one of his arms, to see, when he lets it grow back, if in a few months the hair is thicker than his unshaven armpit.

Miraculously, six months or so later, I remember to enquire.

'Oh, that,' he shrugs. 'Nothing. No difference at all!'

★   ★   ★

In 1953 Tito becomes president of Yugoslavia; Eisenhower becomes president of the United States; Watson and Crick discover DNA; Stalin has a stroke; Edmund Hillary and Tenzing Norgay reach the summit of Everest; Princess Elizabeth is crowned queen of England; there is a general strike in France; sugar rationing ends in England; the Soviet Union begins to return German prisoners of war; and Mum and Dad get married. Dad is thirty-three years old, Mum is twenty-eight. Happiness! Just when Mum thought it might never happen for her. It is her turn. Not a knight, or a landed farmer, or a titled gentleman, but the wild card: an Irish rover, somebody who had actually *done* something, her passport OUT. It is as if all her life she has been waiting for just this moment. And she can be as proud as punch, an exciting SOE officer with a DSO! Everyone knew what that was. Even her mother might be impressed. Yes, happiness! Brimming over with it. The war was won, they were young, and everything was ahead of them . . . 'you know, that lovely feeling of elation about everything'.

A newspaper cutting — 'Married At Lowestoft' — is pasted into Granddad's diary on 10 October 1953. The wedding photographs show Granddad in attendance, but no sign of Maud. Cambridge to Lowestoft is not so far, but obviously MC bed all day with excitement. I search for clues in the wedding album . . . the different family groups arranged in front of the mullioned windows of Roos Hall, the ubiquitous black Labrador. Dad's six-foot appears diminished by both his new mother-in-law and Mum's brother, John. Do I see a flicker of discomfort across Dad's face? The class infiltrator. Will he get found out?

They snatch a few days' honeymoon in Paris, but within a week Dad has been sent back to Trieste 'where it had all blown up', and for the next four months they are parted. Dad in Trieste with the riots, where no spouses are allowed to remain, and Mum back at Roos Hall; lonely, miserable, fighting with her mother, helping with the calves.

Granddad's diary, 1953

12 November: *Long letter from TC very lonely without JC.*

Here the letter is: 'This separation really is bad luck, but perhaps it's best to get it over and done with — rather like playing cards — it's always best to lose at the beginning then later it may be much better.'

In January 1954, Dad is posted to Gibraltar, a cushy number training cadets, and in February, Mum flies out to join him. Real happiness! Dad's letters to his parents are an exhausting trail of dinners that go on till 10.00 a.m.; garden parties, mess parties, sailing adventures; trips to Seville, Tangier, Morocco, Malaga; to the *feria* returning with crates of oranges; swimming, sleeping out, carpet suppers, picnics; 'At the Casino I won £4 and bought a large budgerigar cage with the winnings. Jane won £3.' Mum chips in, 'Carpet suppers are Tom's invention of putting a sheet on the carpet for a dozen indoor picnickers!'

And then there is the excitement of the Coronation parade as the young Queen Elizabeth passes right outside their door and Dad takes Prince Philip sailing — as Dad's note on the back of one photo reveals: 'Duke of Edinburgh and humble self in *Flying Fox*'.

Jane and I are sitting at the table writing letters — I've warned her that it will be one of her duties to write to you once a week to report our doings. She says if she could

358

borrow my pen and write as big as I do it would be no trouble at all . . .

Their accommodation, Lewis Cottage, is a wooden building halfway up the Rock, thirty yards long and five yards wide, 'which the sappers are now converting into a house for us. It is a lovely place with a very large verandah and overlooks the harbour and bay . . . We are having all the fun of building our own house at the expense of the army.' They grow corn so they can throw corn-on-the-cob BBQ parties; they keep chickens to sell the eggs, 'the envy of everyone', Dad boasts, because he lets the chickens forage for themselves on the hillside. In his workshop he devises automatic feeding troughs and drinking fountains.

The nests are about 30 feet below the verandah, so I'm making an aerial line to take down the daily green stuff which I bring back from the dining hall at lunchtime. With all this effort I don't think I've got enough hens — the hut is big enough for a couple of dozen at least and we can always get rid of the eggs at 5 or 6 shillings per dozen.

Chickens are not a patch on sailing. Mum goes too. They sail snipes, and sixteen-foot clinker-built boats, and gunner boats. They don't seem to stop enjoying themselves. 'The only fly in the ointment is that Jane cannot always crew for me as the subalterns have priority over her as the boats are meant for the gunners.' So they buy their own boat, called *Zeta*. 'Jane won the Ladies' Race most convincingly Jane's winning of the Ladies' cup put me under continuous fire for two days, 'Why don't you give *Zeta* a chance and let Jane sail her more often', 'You know you really ought to take up crewing' and so on. Poor Jane she is practically sorry she won it now — It is a most impressively large cup.'

Then, in 1955 Dad writes: 'Jane gets fatter everyday . . . she is convinced the doctors were wrong. Sometime in October is my bet. Her mother is quite excited about it ('excited' for her that is). The gypsies said it would be a girl and then a boy afterwards . . . ' Mid-page, the writing changes to Mum's: 'Good news to cheer you up. I didn't lose my baby after all and shall have it in October . . . ours is bound to be a granddaughter as the gypsies have predicted . . . Can you think of any good girls' names?'

On 12 October 1955, Patrick is born.

March 1957, Dad writes, 'Our household is simply enormous — I and ¾ children, 1 cat, 3 kittens (10 days old), 5 budgerigars, 15 hens, all laying well, one maid, and one temporary dog we are looking after . . . The Chutes [Desmond and his wife, Elspeth] sent Jane another book — again without a note — on how to bring up children much to Jane's displeasure, addressed to Gibraltar, Spain! . . . this is the third 'last' holiday before the baby . . . '

A month later I am born and Dad writes: 'to me she is still an ordinary baby and nothing compared with the awful Patrick who is always amusing me . . . he would become spoilt if we stayed here much longer.'

It is the first hint that Dad is thinking of leaving the army. He is bored. After the excitement of guerrilla warfare, a bit of spying on the Russians in Finland (which I discover later) and the intelligence work in Trieste, he is going stir-crazy. Organising parades, balls, ceremonies, regimental swimming teams, exercises and firing-practices is not his cup of tea, nor is having to kowtow to the bluff of petty rules and regulations that in wartime he managed to circumvent. He likes teaching his cadets, but there is no action. He is being dragged into the guts of the very establishment he has always tried to avoid. He doesn't fit and he knows he never will. By the time I come along Dad's letters home are full of the conundrum of what to do next.

We are all always talking about what we'll do when we leave. We agree on the whole that we must get to England on a home posting before we leave, then we can use the Army's time getting ourselves organised. I think also that we must forget about prestige jobs but instead join a small business such as a grocer's or ironmonger's and then after two years set up business of my own. The problem is quite a big one — some people do not know whether to find a job and then get a house near it or to get a house and then look around for a job. For my part I'm sure the best thing is to decide where to live and then find a job there. All our spare moments are spent discussing the future and how not to make a nonsense of it.

Your loving Arthur and of course Jane (who is listening to classical music as if she enjoys it). [Mum's writing:] I do! Jane.

Dad considers farming (no capital with which to buy anything); living off the land (risks outweigh profit); a grocer's shop (Mum thinks they will make 'quite enough money selling cornflakes and magazines'). Dad knows himself well enough to know he must be his own boss. 'Jane and I are both certain that a small village business is better than going up to London by train every day . . . ' He even begins evening classes: 'Typewriting and bookkeeping — no matter what job I do I'll want to be able to type a letter and keep accounts in the civilian way — for if you can't keep one set of books how can you keep two?'

I stare at the photographs from Gib. Dad's suits, his neat hair, Mum's startling red lips, her white skin. That old-fashioned elegance that is as timeless as it is set in time. Mum, happy, and I imagine exactly where *she* wants to be, secure, with her own home, away from England, independent of her family. So impossibly perfect: sun, friends, a safe job, holidays, picnics, sailing; they could whizz across to Spain for flamenco, afford a nanny (the adored Mercedes), cadge a batman off the army. They had a ginger cat called Tigger, and the budgie cage had grown into a large aviary. For Roland Barthes at the root of every photograph is the 'catastrophe which has already occurred'. The frozen moment: this was, this has been, this is no longer; the ever-presence of death locked in the past, present and future. Barthes' words harness the revenants of celluloid: he is dead and he is going to die. I want to shout from the sidelines, Look behind you! I want to ignite their happiness again. But the dead hold my gaze, the double bluff of premonition, the contradiction of mortality.

After four years in Gibraltar in a spirit of optimism and determination 'not to make a nonsense of it', Dad chucks it all in and retires from the army. They pack up their little house with the verandah, they give their hens away, they sell *Zeta*, they find Mercedes a job with another young family, rehome the budgies, have their last corn-on-the-cob barbecue and say goodbye to all their friends. Dad loads Patrick, Mum and me into an army transport plane with all our kit and waves us off to England. He is going to drive.

★　★　★

It was always exciting when Dad came home. He'd be away three, maybe four days a week, we didn't know where. No sooner had the door slammed we would rush to greet him. Sometimes he brought gifts. Strings of cheap beads, a doormat, a pineapple! On one occasion he burst through the door and underarm-bowled a couple of small round comets at us which flew through the air with long dark tails. I caught one and screamed. Its long black mane was attached to a miniature head!

'Shrunken heads,' Dad told us. 'Pygmies!'

We scoffed of course. But they were alarmingly realistic. The hair was black and lustrous, and its texture — a little thicker but remarkably like our own. The skin was all leathery and you could see the tiny pores. We prodded them gingerly. Ha! ha! We weren't going to be taken in. Dad shrugged at our scoffing, and we scoffed some more. Yet we were fascinated by the sloping head, the sewn-up mouth, the boneless nose, the squishy blind eyes.

I have since seen shrunken heads in museums and my memory of our heads seems scarily similar. Sadly, they have long since disappeared so I have no way of knowing. I assume they were made of animal skin, but now, nothing would surprise me and I am not so sure.

★ ★ ★

On 16 February 1958, Mum, Patrick and I touch down at some windswept army airstrip in a cold, grey, jobless, post-war Britain. We stay at Roos Hall. Dad arrives five days later. *Snow, freezing, blizzards, floods, Granddad records. Arthur telephoned from Roos Hall, Patrick playing up now fun begins the little darlings?* For the next couple of weeks we move around from in-law to in-law to hotel. Then to a rented house in Hayling Island on the south coast. Two months later Mum and Dad buy a small, attached, almost derelict town house — 75 High Street, in Fareham in Hampshire — for £300.

Granddad's diary, 1958

11 April: *Arthur turned up. Came on motor-bike. MC and self so happy to see him and all news about Jane, children and new house.*

On 17 April, Dad's mother Maud dies. And Dad invites Granddad to come and live with us.

PART 6

THE LAST TANGO

1

We are in the health-food shop. The woman knows Dad, everyone knows Dad now. We are buying muesli and yoghurt. I pick up a packet of Puffed Oat Cakes and put them on the counter. Dad is intrigued by the packet's tubular shape. He picks it up. His hand flies up unexpectedly with the weightlessness of it. He shakes it. Looks dumb-founded and frowns, the question on his face.

'It's empty,' he says.

The woman and I laugh.

I genuinely agree with him, 'Yes, it *is* empty.'

I buy it anyway.

He looks at the woman as if I were mad.

TOM CAREW'S Brain is 'switching'
switching away from [green biro]
'Memory' Memory
of people and their names
SO YOU WRITE ME OFF?? [red biro]
not necessarily
I invent — Yes I do — come to my New
Hut [green biro]
Wednesday 28 July — Tom
I can and invent in material things as
effectively as I ever did and in IDEAS too
FOR EXAMPLE [blue biro]
My lovely house, full of everything, cabable
of loking after (crazy expression 'Looking
AFter) and this pen is clumsy SO replace it

369

I will
FOR EXAMPLE [red biro]
My house is far too big for me — [green biro]
what do I do about it?
CREATE a unique 'living in' place for me and my dogs (and cat) behind the house
I should name it?
What name
How about
'TOMS RETREAT' [red biro]
or [back to green]
'DOGS HOME'
I like 'TOMS RETREAT' [black biro]
Goodby — I am off to working on it 'it' is 0930 hrs July 28th 2004 when I finish I will return
          — Tom (hopefully with a better MEMORY losing no
                    'INVENTIVENESS'

★   ★   ★

The span of time in which Dad leaves the army, returns to England, buys a house, buries his mother and asks Granddad to move in with us is a matter of weeks. By the beginning of May, Granddad, aged sixty-five, has left Howes Place, Cambridge, and moved into the dusty front rooms of our house in Fareham. While Dad dives into the boat-building business. He has bought Felthams Boatyard on the Hamble Estuary by borrowing the money from his elder half-brother, Desmond, and using Mum's mother as

370

guarantor. For the next three years, borrowing more and more money to keep it afloat, he and Granddad and Granddad's corgi, Frou Frou, and quite a few others by the look of this photograph, go down to the boatyard to build boats. Sloops. And lovely wooden ketches.

Granddad's diary, 1958
23 May: *75* [High Street] *in awful state, dust rubble etc., Jane and Arthur hands full with children and dust.*
31 May: *JANE working too hard temper frail. Jane not so kind.*
9 August: *Very warm. Things not going too well with Jane and self, it must be I'm always in the wrong?*

Sometimes Granddad drove to the boatyard in his blue Mini with me and my friend Katie Dicker in tow, because right next to the boatyard were a couple of fields, a few scraggy ponies, Gypsy Lou's caravan and Lou herself, which was where Katie and I, under Granddad's critical eye, learnt to ride. Whenever a boat was finished, Dad and Desmond sailed it in the Solent to test it out. The trouble was, not many people bought sailing boats in 1958, or 1959, or 1960, and Dad's boats always cost more to build than Dad had bargained for. The boatyard got into trouble. There was tension over the borrowed money. Desmond's loan ran out and Dad had to borrow more money from Mum's mother. Then Desmond started writing threatening demanding letters.

Granddad's diary, 1961

10 February: *Jane finds me trying and unbearable, everything I do is wrong — suppose she has a cause?*

11 February: *Things will soon flare up with Jane and self she so detests me.*

26 March: *Feeling something in the air. Self will have to go soon too much hatred from J.*

27 March: *Yard all day. TC sad. Self must find my own way re house no more luncheons with J.*

Granddad's diaries record the plummeting fortunes of the boatyard alongside his worsening relationship with Mum. *TC worried over yards accounts; Desmond terrible worried, so all of us; Jane off deep end. 25 August: Arthur and Desmond here till late discussing yard in a hell of a state, losing on all boats. 31 August: Felt so ashamed when Bank Manager refused firm's wages. Overdraft £6,000. By 15 September it is all up: Arthur last day at yard. Rod made Director of the boatyard, and Arthur out.*

Granddad mentions the time Mum loses her wedding ring in the garden — which she takes as a terrible omen — and the day she finds it three years later digging in the same spot. But mostly he documents our money worries. Dad's jobs that don't materialise and his bright ideas that never come to anything, from wreck-diving for treasure in Minorca (I remember the charts all over the kitchen table) to the invention of a new kind of Hoover — a Heath Robinson contraption of tubes, hoses and fans. And Mum's temper: *Jane off deep end; Jane out of sorts; Things not so well; Jane unstable; Pity about Arthur's wife.* By this time there are two more mouths to feed. Nicky, born in 1959, and Tim who arrives in 1961, two weeks before Dad gets booted out of the yard.

Dad's glory days are over. No call for guerrilla agents in Fareham in 1962. He looks for work all over the country, coming back at midnight, gone again early the next day. While Mum gets thinner, tenser, tireder and angrier. I flick through the diaries looking for respite, but it is painful reading. 1963, 1964, 1965, 1966, year after year, day after mundane day, Granddad scratches away: *Arthur came back early no job up north; Arthur came home Cambridge job fell through; TC no job again; Arthur came home late but hopeful; I pray God will give Arthur better luck with his work; Arthur left early for York; Arthur and Jane wishing for change to live in Ireland? Arthur back from Liverpool; Arthur returned late and off to Norwich; Arthur off to Grimsby; took Arthur to Havant station for job in Aberdeen; Jane very depressed without Arthur.* And so it continues, five, six, seven, eight years out of the army, four kids and *still* no proper job. Instead of going to Ireland, and in spite of *no* property boom, Dad borrows more money to buy and do up the wreck of the house next door.

★ ★ ★

373

Money was not something Dad seemed to have the knack for. Even the £25 a year for life left to him in perpetuity by his grandfather (at the time a considerable sum) he signed over to a shyster, to buy a car, the day he turned twenty-one. Money was just around the corner, one more plan, one more venture, one more more. Yet, wealth surrounded them. Roos Hall had been passed on to Mum's elder brother, Bill; her younger brother, John, had the family farm; Desmond had Chute money so he was able to buy a farm with horses and act the country gent; and Chubby had married a rich American heiress. While Dad, by the seat of his pants, negotiated us through a precarious existence of living far beyond our means, surmounting one disaster with another; our letter box spilling an endless stream of small brown envelopes that lay unopened in drifts, until they disappeared.

I went to Roos Hall twice. The first time I was a baby, the second time, according to Granddad's diary, was 1 August 1964, when I was seven. We drove over a bridge and there it appeared, out of the trees. So tall! Four storeys! With a torment-ingly exciting attic window at the top, and strange chimneys and tall turretty things that looked like *Alice in Wonderland* chess pieces. Young as I was, even I could feel the gulf between Us. And. Them. This was a pile, if ever there was one. Of Tudor bricks and oak panelling, and portraits and pedimented windows, and carvings and cor-nices and crests, and stepped gables, and buttresses and busts, and stained-glass windows, and mul-lions and tapestries and treasure! We had arrived in our scruffy Dormobile at the Other World. My mother's family. Whom we hardly ever saw. In a visceral soup of contradictory shame and excruciating shyness we had to navigate our way through. We were *just* as closely related to Granny as our cousins were, I wanted to remind them, but they were on their patch and we were in steerage. But where on earth was Mum? For the first time I looked at her differently. I would not have been able to express it, of course, but I could see she was in no-man's-land — at home, amongst her own, and not at home at all. I am certain no one enjoyed the visit; not Dad, certainly; nor Mum, but her feelings must have been far more complicated. A mixture of expectation, dashed hope, shame and reality, and all those other unspoken tortuous things that come with matters of English class. Nor did I realise then, in regard to both my parents, how powerful were the lives beyond their own, and the influence and pressure they inevitably brought to bear on their story.

Oh, how achingly I wanted to explore. Upstairs, downstairs, in the attics! But no invitation was forthcoming and I was far too timid to ask. Mum said there was a priest's hole at Roos Hall, but we didn't see it. Nor the window which could never be closed that long ago a blacksmith had ironed up, but next morning was open as usual. Nor the print of the Devil's hoof burned into the solid brick on a bedroom wall. Nor Nelson's tree, the ancient oak once a gallows and now haunted by those who were chained to its branches, their shackles slowly enveloped until trapped forever in its wooden heart. And no mention of the headless coachman either, driving a coach through the gates past the arched front door every Christmas Eve, his horses' nostrils flaming with fire. Patrick wanted to see Nelson's sword, but I can only remember kindly Uncle Bill showing us the original Elizabethan fireplace that you could walk, if you were allowed, right into. I followed gingerly, across long intricate carpets, past golden-framed portraits with name plaques, silent and shrivelled in my numbing smallness. Yet, even then I think I felt a sense of inverted superiority, that birthright was just a flip of a coin, no pride could be taken in it, nor sense of achievement, for nothing had been earned, nothing worked for here. We were given tea in a downstairs kitchen somewhere, Dad itching to get away.

We'd seen enough. We weren't interested in any of it. We didn't want to know about William Frederick Suckling Suckling, or Wybrew Jane, or Nelson's mother, or Romsey pronounced Rumsey. Or, for that matter, how many illegitimate nobs had sweated in dark corners sowing their viable seed to harvest a confection of entitlements and favours . . . for the boys. Our eyes glazed over at a string of names that wound through the generations, possibly because our mother had, uniquely, been given only one: Joan. The slights she'd felt had started very young. And as young as I was, even I could see she had all the disadvantages of her class and none of the advantages. Not even an education: 'Housewifery'! For all the acres of heirlooms under her nose, Persian carpets, oak banisters, family portraits, and crested silver, she knew the rules. None would be hers.

Until. Many years later Mum's elder brother, Bill, gave her two Suckling family portraits from 1701, in opulent gold frames. Turbanned Turkish envoys gone native, magnificent and ridiculous, furred, feathered, bejewelled: the soft-skinned Richard Suckling, and his wife, Ann Kybert, with her haughty eye, cramped together side by side on Mum's tiny bungalow wall. There are long memories in rah-rah-land. After fifteen years, the 'gift' turned into a loan. Just a few weeks after Mum died, my aunt called to arrange their return. I have always had a mild aversion to my mother's class. I put down the phone. Ice. Four words, slow and skinned of modulation: Over. My. Dead. Body.

2

By 1965 Dad is up to his neck in mounting debts and the boys' crippling school fees which he cannot afford. I am not thriving at the local school so to add to their troubles they decide to send me to Rookesbury Park as a day girl where all but half a dozen pupils board full-time. The loathsome Rookesbury. On my first day I was put in the wrong class and had to squeeze into a tiny-tots chair, like Gulliver's giant, and got stuck. I remained welded without a word until, mortifyingly we had to stand to attention — me with chair attached to my bottom like scaffolding. How I dreaded every day at that school, alone in a sea of chummy boarders who linked arms when the bell went, scattering away upstairs in a trill of uniform laughter. The only thing I enjoyed at Rookesbury were the nature walks through the primrose woods or down to the tantalising lake covered in lily pads with creamy-pink flowers, and frogs and dragonflies. On my school report ('Age 7 years, 7 months') beside 'SPELLING', I see Dad has written: 'o/o, She kanot spel proply.' Beside NEEDLEWORK: 'Her needle is blunt, she has two left hands and is hopeless.' Beside GYM-NASTICS he has crossed out 'Has worked hard' and written 'is flat-footed'. Where the teacher has written that I am slow, he loyally counters 'She's bored!' As likely I was either paralysed with fear, or day-dreaming, for which I had developed quite a talent. One alluring word was enough to send me off to another world that I would far more happily inhabit. Rookesbury and I did not get on, but more to the point, the unpaid fees were generating a stream of nasty letters from the headmistress, so it was decided I must try the entrance exam for Portsmouth High. Mum tutored me. Interrogations after the exam revealed I did not spell 'cuboard' correctly so I knew I had not done well. My failure was a bitter disappointment to Mum. Dad blamed Rookesbury, which meant he could default on the fees entirely. Which thankfully meant I could leave the place where I had been friendless and force-fed liver at lunch, and go to the convent up the road (St Mary's of the Angels, where the saga with Mrs White took place).

For my brothers, Patrick and Tim, it was a different story. The necessity of Mum's sons going to public school was so deeply ingrained nothing else was ever an option. Two lots of serious school fees had to be found. Which broke the bank, with the boatyard debts, and interest overdue after borrowing from Desmond, and I don't like to think how much my riding habit drained the family purse. Add hoof oil, riding hat, boots, gymkhana entries, saddle soap, pony nuts . . . We all, except my sister Nicky perhaps, chomped away obliviously; a bunch of beavers felling a tree.

Granddad's diary, 1965
21 February: *midnight, Arthur left for Birmingham.*

379

25 April: *At luncheon with the family, being polite to Jane, & offering her the vegetable & what not, was snapped upon, served me right, I'll learn yet to be polite to her.*

16 May: *Arthur returned late and off to Norwich.*

24 June: *Arthur back from Jersey.*

11 July: *Arthur left for Wales 6.30 p.m.*

30 July: *Arthur took Jane, Patrick and Keggie to town went to Tower of London, next day news — Tower still standing.*

19 September: *Arthur left late for the north.*

23 September: *Arthur came home early from Tyneside.*

25 November: *ARTHUR 46. pm went and chat with Jane her stomach bad, worrying of school fees Rookesbury.*

'Arthur,' I call him.

A spark of remembrance. A glint.

'Arthur,' Dad murmurs. 'Who's that?'

'You.'

'Yes. I know' He is thinking hard. 'The army?'

'No. Your mother, your father, all your family called you Arthur.'

'Yes.' He tilts his head like a robin and laughs lightly.

Granddad's diary, 1966

9 January: *At luncheon the subject of West Indian immigrants to this country set Jane in a fury, she knows I am opposed to it. I'm not to have an opinion of my*

own *it won't be long now she will have a crack at me.*

10 January: *How right I was! Jane came in my room like a banderillero and flung her darts at me saying the West Indians had more right to live in this country than me and I was a foreigner and ought to go hack to Ireland. She can be spiteful.*

13 February: *Jane tells me Arthur's job is dicky.*

13 March: *Family seem in doldrums esp. TC.*

24 March: *Arthur back no luck up north.*

5 April: *Arthur came back no job.*

3 May: *Arthur came home job in Dorset not so hot.*

16 May: *Arthur came home after midnight.*

We didn't understand Mum. It was Dad we wanted to be with. Mum was mostly worrying, or cross, or at her 'wits' end'. The moment Dad got home we clambered all over him. We did not realise there had been so much coldness in Mum's life, and now Dad was getting all the warmth. 'My mother always put me down,' she said, not for a moment noticing the irony. Scrambled on the inside by injustice, paralysed on the outside by how one was supposed to behave, Mum developed her own bite. So we could all go down together.

* * *

I have been looking for stamps in Dad's desk and come across a photograph of Stepmother. She looks very young (which surprises me); she is slim and is standing by some railings in a pencil skirt with a beehive hairdo. I have never seen it before. I turn it over. And get a sudden punch in the pit of my stomach. The date written on the back in Dad's handwriting is 1972. The photograph is frozen in my hand as the brain cogs clunk backwards through the years . . . and the sinking realisation is confirmed. And now two letters are in my hand. Which I don't want to read, but I know I will. Both to my stepmother. One stamped June 1972, posted from Fareham; the other, 1973, posted from Spain. Dad tells her how awful the enforced family holiday is going. Tim is twelve; Nicky, fourteen; I am not there, having been dropped off in France on the way to stay with a friend. 'Sunday morning 8 a.m. on the beach — have for the first time escaped close supervision from the family . . . Nicky has sunburn but is cheerful, Tim is the only one with no problems bless him. It all adds up to me being in no mood to write to you — the two worlds are so totally different . . . ' He mentions Kennington Lane where Stepmother lived. We thought when Dad was in London he was living in his van.

I will try to be there as soon as I can — 8 days to go. The only time to myself is out swimming with goggles watching the fish among the rocks — it is beautiful and reminds me of our bird-watching on the

382

Thames . . . sorry to be so mizz — will cheer up when I am back with you.

It's not good, this spying on him, finding him out. But these dates put a whole different spin on things, for Mum, and for us. The holiday Dad suffered through was their last. It was Mum's attempt to start afresh. But there was never a chance of that. Dad cannot even fake it for the photo. His exhausted eyes, ragged as if they'd been left for days on the washing line. Nicky, Tim and Mum trying their best.

★ ★ ★

For me, our holidays in Spain conjure the best memories of Family Past. Every year, from 1964, we headed off to Berria on the Cantabrian coast in the Dormobile, flashing our lights if we saw another GB. It took us four days to get there, so we free-camped en route, and then for almost the whole month of August we pitched camp on the dunes (also for free) in front of a Spanish *pensión* called Hostal Berria. The patron of the *hostal* (in which we could not afford to stay) was called Señor Jaime and he always welcomed us like long-lost friends. His delight at our arrival mystified and thrilled me. He had a Quixote twizzle moustache that mimicked his beaming smile beneath. Mum spoke Spanish and they kissed! And then he kissed Dad too! And we were doubly astonished. I have no idea why the señor did not seem to mind us spreading ourselves *all over the place* right in front of his *hostal* for the whole of August. In the only photograph I can find I am amazed how close we pitched our gypsy camp. Every morning Dad collected driftwood from the beach to attach to the totem pole we were growing, and the days rolled on, one seamlessly into another.

As a treat, once or twice during the holiday, we had lunch in the dining room at the *hostal*. I remember the white Spanish rolls with the hard baked nipples either end that almost cracked your teeth when you bit them off. And the white dough we pulled out to spread with *melacatón*; we could all say *melacatón*. In Mum's bureau I found four tiny pictures stuck on a pink card: Spanish dancer, horse, mouse, house, that I'd painted on a rainy day in that dining room, in 1964, age seven.

Behind the *hostal* was a huge natural sandhill which we ran down hell for leather until our legs flew out from beneath us and we ended up at the bottom like crumpled spiders with a mouthful of sand. If Dad was watching I would run even faster, showing off daredevil to impress in mammoth flying strides, the burning sand thudding against the soles of my bare feet, *Pow, Pow, Pow*, until I couldn't stop and became airborne. I can smell those dunes; the pungent piney-ness of eucalyptus and juniper, the spiky marram grass, the smoky perfumes of wild thyme and lavender, and the tiny yellow flowers that smelt slightly lemony mixed with sand and sun. And I can feel that sand with its intimate smooth warmth pouring through my fingers; the scratchy bushes snagging past my legs. The thistles and sea holly with their blue-green misty sheen, the clumps of wispy grass with heads like baby rabbit tails, and the couch grass which got tangled up in your toes. The exotic colours of grit quartz and amber were unfamiliar to me, but I drank them in; the sound of the crickets, the salt gathering on my eyebrows. If I could go back, it would be there, and it would be then.

Also behind the *hostal* was 'the mountain', which I, Patrick and our half-cousin, Tony, set off to climb and got lost all night. Tony was older, a little wild, and exciting, so I had tagged along to my brother's dismay. We had timed our adventure badly and were only halfway down when it got dark; we tried a shortcut straight down through the thorny bushes and over rocks, but soon we couldn't see at all. I refused to go any further so we crouched where we were into three tight balls. We knew we'd be in deep trouble because it was the night Mum and Dad had booked to go out for a special meal and Mum had been looking forward to it. After a couple of hours two helicopters flew overhead; I said they must be looking for us, Patrick and Tony said, Don't be stupid, you little twit. At dawn, as soon as the sun came up we scrambled through the undergrowth to the bottom of the hill, which ironically wasn't very far. The next thing I remember is Dad walking very quickly along the road towards us flanked either side by the Guardia Civil in their smart uniforms and glossy black hats. I was sure Dad would run towards us, but he didn't, and there was something in his expression I had never seen before which confused me. It was severe and serious. Dad remained stone-faced in front of the Spanish police, yet, miraculously we were not told off. Not even by Mum. Those two things surprised me — Dad's unbending face, and Mum not telling us off. Nicky said they had thought we had fallen off the cliff into the sea.

I loved Spain. I spent hours in the rock pools, staring into their strange worlds, chasing shrimps that darted about, poking along the encrusted rock face for camouflaged fish, burning my shoulders until the tide came in. At low tide we sometimes waded across the river to Ajo to see the thousands of lobsters gnashing about in the dirty concrete sea pools that were built into the pier. There were steps leading down into them and you were supposed to choose which lobster you wanted to eat, and then a man would go down the steps with a long hooked stick and haul it out for the restaurant to boil alive. We never ate them, we just watched as close as we dared as they crawled over each other, each with its trophy blue claw tied up, vainly held above its head. I felt sorry for them. Nevertheless we jostled and elbowed each other at the edge: the idea of falling in!

But best of all was surfing. Dad made the surfboards out of thin ply sanded down to a mirror smoothness then painted sky blue. When the waves were just right, clear and clean and curling over, this was our heaven-sent pursuit. Early in the morning we had the beach to ourselves. We all loved it. Zipping down the same wave as Mum, white foam in our eyes, steering towards and away from her, seeing who could stay on the wave the longest and the farthest up the beach. She was the best. Back and back for more. Again and again, one more, just one more. Tearing along the shallows, then being dumped on hard wet sand as the wave sucked away, dragging our legs apart. Yes, this is the time I would go back to, that moment, right then.

3

Once fastidious about turning out the lights Dad now contributes the equivalent of a small nation-state to global warming. Everything is on. Blow heaters, spinning heaters, convection heaters, every light in the house. There is even a fan heater on in his shed at the bottom of the garden, which has its doors open, and which I realise he hasn't visited for two days. And another thing, very out of character, he's begun to like money. And he is obsessing about it. Having it. Spending it. Getting it from the hole in the wall. His memory is gone but he remembers his PIN number and he tells everyone: 1919, the year of his birth. He is a marked man. Every day he goes up to town for a fleecing. He buys penknives, heaters, torches, and Polaroid film to go in his Polaroid camera. Which he needs a lot of, because he walks around with his finger firmly on the ON button. The camera spews out the Polaroids and they tumble down his chest at a pound a pop. My sister says it's his money, that he can do what he likes with it. I disagree. And this becomes a point of contention. I think the reason he likes shopping is because he's bored, because he's stopped making things, or rather, 'improving' things as he would say; like his trays with the handles on the long sides so that you can walk through doors without getting your knuckles

388

scraped. His last woodwork venture was a production line of bird boxes painted with white targets round the holes (so the bird could find them). Too late we discovered they were stuck together with non-waterproof glue. One box came apart by the rose bush. Tiny blue speckled eggs scattered all over the ground.

* * *

On 26 March 1968, Dad is on the telly: BBC2, 9.00 p.m., *Man Alive*.[1] He is being interviewed by the 1960s current-affairs TV presenter, Malcolm Muggeridge, about the problems demobbed officers face getting back into civilian life. By all accounts he is dynamic and inspired and impressive, but as Granddad drily points out, *nothing comes of it*.

* * *

That same year, 1968, Than Tun, who had once been in the driving seat at every stage of Burma's struggle for independence, came to a sticky end. From deep in the jungles of the Pegu Yoma, he had been leading his Communist Party of Burma (CPB) in a bitter armed struggle against the government for twenty years. As his communist ideology became more crazed and

---

[1] *Man Alive* was the cutting-edge (and hard-hitting) current-affairs programme of the day. Also famed for being the first programme to show a naked female breast on television!

fanatical he began a ruthless purge that mirrored the Chinese Cultural Revolution, executing any opponents in increasingly gruesome orgy-like rituals. According to CIA documents, he sent his soldiers to China for Maoist indoctrination, and marched about his camp shouting himself hoarse with slogans such as: 'DON'T HESITATE TO KILL YOUR PARENTS IF THEY ARE ENEMIES!' His last victim was his party's most popular commander who Than Tun tricked into coming to party HQ, where he had him tortured and killed. But as Than Tun stood alone by the edge of a creek that evening, the commander's loyal escort, who had managed to slip away unnoticed, crept up from behind and shot him dead.

★　★　★

In September 1968, without mentioning anything to Mum, Dad buys a house four miles up the road from Fareham, in Wickham, called Merriles, for £7,000. Surprise!

Oh calamity, calamity, Granddad writes, *and I'm on Jane's side. Wish Arthur would come down to earth and be realistic.* Granddad hates the new house, *the surrounds are awful*, but more to the point, so does Mum.

The first time I saw Merriles I was entranced. It was beyond anything I could have imagined we could ever have. A house by itself, surrounded by its own garden, front, back, and down both sides. Along the roadside were five huge trees. Trees you could stare up into,

390

through great green petticoats, layer upon layer. And there was a gate. A beautiful wooden five-bar gate with the words 'Manners Maketh Man' actually carved into the top bar. And it had an old Aga, and an old-fashioned bell-system for each of the four bedrooms to ring in the kitchen. It wasn't a grand house by any means, but maybe once it had been a small guesthouse, or inn. It was on the edge of Wickham village which had a square and a pub and a mill, and there were fields out the back with rabbits, where I would make a hide to observe them. And next door was a playground with tennis courts you could hire; and in the garden we had an old garage, a shed and a dilapidated fruit cage. It was brilliant. But Mum said she loved her old garden and her asparagus beds, and all the gooseberry bushes she had nurtured and the pears which she had trained into fans against the wall. This new garden was too big. How would she manage it? And that terrible grey pebble-dash. I couldn't understand my mother's inconsolable distress. Except that 'some louts' had defecated in their bedroom wardrobe while the house was empty just before we moved in . . . Why? How? My mind boggled. In my eyes Merriles was bigger and better in every way. And it was just up the road from the stables.

Dad built a flat-roofed granny annexe for Granddad. It's still there. Or was a few years ago when I took a detour with Jonathan and we drove past. At first I could hardly look. I certainly couldn't speak. My stomach somersaulting as we approached. But lo! The gate was still there, 'Manners Maketh Man'. We pulled over. I stared through the car window at the fat-fingered chestnut tree and the pair of beech trees I had embraced, as beautiful as I remembered. I knew exactly where their silver-grey bark folded over itself like the skin of an elephant. I stared silently, thrown back into my teenage self; out at night among those trees, standing in the rain, the droplets shivering through the branches running down my face, breathing in the wet bark smell, my bare feet pressing into the earth, beech-casts embossing their prickles into my soles. I could not bring myself to direct Jonathan down Mayles Lane, further along the road on the left, which used to be called Lunatic Lane, and then Asylum Lane, which led to Knowle Mental Hospital, which used to be the Hampshire County Lunatic Asylum. In our last year at Merriles, Nicky and I cycled up Mayles Lane twice a week to visit Mum.

We were spooked by Knowle long before we had any connection to it. Like most psychiatric hospitals in those days, it was known as The Loony Bin. It had a brooding presence, inscrutable, hidden behind trees, yet fully fleshed out in our mind's eye: padded cells, screaming hysterics, crazed pop-eyed maniacs trying to escape; it filled us with foreboding. Built in the mid-1800s it had once been walled in like a prison, and in a small ivy-strangled copse there were iron crosses marking the graves of patients with only numbers to identify them. In the 1920s there was a block by the water tower known as the Idiot Block which housed young children. Neither my sister nor I wanted to go near the place.

Each push on the pedal of the bike ride up there, that first visit with Nicky, is branded into my brain. Onward and upward, the river on our right, past the once-wood that had been chopped down where I had scratched off the forester's painted crosses, past the pylons, onward, upward and round the bend, where we stopped and laughed nervously; then into the dark shadowless wood of Knowle, under overhanging branches and trailing ivy, along the impenetrable wall of rhododendrons, until we reached the entrance to the drive. We stopped at the iron gates. No laughing now. Leadenly we pressed on until we were face-to-face with the building that had haunted our imaginations.

And then, we were in the residents' sitting room, and framed in one of the chairs around the edge, was our mother. Which utterly-shocked me. For she had turned into one. Like all the others in that appalling place. Her soft nougat skin was now shiny red plastic, it was taut and stretched, drawn away from her mouth and her nose. Her eyes were even popping out. And worse. She was meek. Grateful for our visit. Quiet. Shy. But even worse than that. She was looking forward to coming home.

Knowle was closed down in 1996 and for ten years lay empty for nature to claim it. If I had known I might have gone back there then. By chance I came across some photographs of its dereliction taken by the artist Gill Horn. I am

393

sure I recognise the sitting room and the very spot beneath the very window where my mother sat. Now the developers have it, and Knowle has become Knowle Village, a Berkeley-home estate of luxury apartments, fifty-five new homes, two new village squares, 3,000 square feet of retail and extensive leisure facilities, a cricket green, a football pitch and a protected woodland. One might describe it as going from one soulless red-brick nightmare to another, but there is no mention on the actual Berkeley sales site, that I could see, of Knowle's unpropitious past. There is, however, a stone plaque in the woods, which reads: 'Five and a half thousand people were buried in this woodland between 1852 and 1971.'

4

'I wanted to live with you but I now realise it's ridiculous,' Dad says, hands dangling by his side.

'Yes, Dad,' I say gravely. 'It's not like this all the time. This is holiday.'

'Yes,' he says gravely, 'I could run your operation.'

'You are going to help Jonathan today, Dad.'

'Yes. Tell me what he looks like.'

'Jonathan. My husband.'

Blank look.

'Short hair. That man. The one who was just sitting here.'

I point to Jonathan's empty breakfast bowl. Another blank look.

I ponder, what would happen if we forgot you, Dad?

★ ★ ★

The move to Merriles marked the descending years where the air curdled with anger: anger past, anger present, anger to come. I don't remember anything but discord. Mum's night-long rants; bricks rocketing through windows; china exploding into shrapnel off the wall; chairs, tables, anything close at hand could become airborne. Sometimes we joined in. It took all my strength to hurl the plastic basin from the sink, with the washing-up, water, suds, glass, knives, plates, all over the kitchen floor. Spite and sarcasm reigned, or silence. 'Manners Maketh Man' the gate said, but Merriles became a violent house. Mum even dug up the rose bush in front of Granddad's window in case he derived any pleasure from it. We rarely talked about it between ourselves; Granddad scribbled away in his diary; my brothers escaped back to school; Nicky stayed in her room. I have no idea how Mum got through her day, everyone hating her. The person we all waited for, from late Friday night into the early hours of Saturday morning, clock ticking, ears straining for the sound of the van's wheels spitting out the gravel, was Dad.

Granddad's diary, 1970
30 January: *What's in the wind after torn PC in letterbox by Jane? in a bad mood with us all it seems.*
17 February: *Jane came to tell me, Desmond sent a telegram about his money from Malta, worrying her so much making her ill.*
20 February: *Jane came in to say she had another stinking letter from Desmond.*

To pay for Merriles Dad had to borrow more money off Desmond — who was now so rich he lived in Malta to escape the top income tax level of eighty-three per cent. But Dad couldn't pay the interest on the loan so Desmond began, once more, to send him threatening letters. Which invariably were intercepted and opened by

Mum. On top of these came building-society letters concerning outstanding mortgage arrears, solicitors' letters concerning enforcement action, estate agents' letters concerning contracts (reneged on by Dad) to sell the house, to sell the garden, and more solicitors' bills ('65 letters out; 45 letters in; 15 telephone calls'). Dad's financial situation was worse than dire. I only get a real picture of this from a faxed copy of a letter he sent to Mum's younger brother, John. It concerned the repayment of various loans from John and Mum's mother (amongst others) to prop up our family life. Dad tells John he is negotiating a loan to liquidate all his debts. What shocks me are the sums beneath his signature: total borrowings of £20,800, with a further loan of £22,000 at thirteen per cent to pay them off. Mum's mother = £1,300; Desmond = £9,000; bank = £7,000; John = £3,500. The amount would be equivalent to more than a quarter of a million pounds today but that doesn't account for the enormous disparity of how much things cost. Merriles cost £7,000 in 1968, which illustrates better how very deep in the shit he was. Dad says to John, 'I will also be paying your mother her loan plus interest which has been building up. I hate to pay her the interest officially and see it go to the taxman. If she is too honest to allow me to pay her £100 in fivers see if you can convert her to the idea of receiving a present, or what about all the Sucklings and us going to London for a show and blowing it that way instead of giving it to Mr Wilson . . . '

Apart from the misplaced humour and BAD

idea, I am struck by Dad's total lack of envy of his brother-in-law's far more fortunate position; in his postscript he asks John what he will do with his £3,500, telling him he still thinks property a good investment. While at the sidelines, how galling it must have been for Mum to have her small annual stipend (£120) of Suckling trust money managed by her younger brother, John. 'Trust' was anything but. There was nothing she could do financially without John's signature (although, had it not been so, anything of Mum's would have long been gobbled up by Dad). Mum and her brother eventually fell out, and a few years later he died, in 1980. The rift and resentment remained: in her bureau I found a tiny square of newspaper she had cut out, with the small heading, 'Latest Wills Residue for Charities'. Beside her brother's name, 'Suckling, Mr John Robert', was the figure: '£402,567'.

★ ★ ★

1970. Nixon is president; de Gaulle dies; the war in Vietnam moves into its sixteenth year; Ulrike Meinhof and Andreas Baader form the Red Army Faction; Thor Heyerdahl sets off across the Atlantic on a papyrus boat; Apollo 13 splashes down in the Pacific; the Beatles release their final album, *Let It Be*; Jimi Hendrix dies; and Dad buys Percy Coutts — a letter-writing service for people who are looking for jobs (funny, that) overseas. It cost him £200.

Granddad's world, meanwhile, is *Call My*

Bluff, *Dad's Army*, horse racing, Lester Piggott, Arkle, the Boat Race, *Oh Brother*, and being scared of Mum. He clings to any kindness: *Nicky popped in bless her; Tim came to say goodbye off to school, looked so smart.* Because I am horse mad he comes with me to gymkhanas and I go and sit with him when I clean my tack.

Granddad's diary, 1970

12 April: *Arthur came to say taking me to Swanmore Pony show. Keggie so nervous, irritable etc., Bracken* [the pony] *bored, she boshed the lot.*

5 June: *Keggie was riding a dapple grey in the working-pony jumping and made an awful flop of it, too tensed.*

3 September: *Keggie making jumps for her paddock Heath Robinson style.*

He is less than complimentary: *Keggie came to say she off the diet, so ate nearly all the box of Black Magic; Saw Keggie going to school not so light on her feet; 8 a.m. Nicky off to school looking bright and alert. Keggie half asleep filling her gob; Keggie came to do some sewing, putting some slits to make her trousers bell bottom, to get her big feet through.* Granddad notes when the first swallow arrives, when he hears the first cuckoo, when the leaves begin to fall. He saves a pigeon from the cat, watches a lovely jay on the lawn, watches a squirrel bury nuts. Then towards the end of 1970, Granddad is bewildered because there is a run of Mum being kind to him: *Jane came for a chat, what a change she was so nice to me; Jane and Arthur came in with drink; Jane looked wonderful in new dress; Dear Jane came in for me to see New Year with them; Luncheon with family and Jane so kind to me; Jane took me to Fareham; Jane gave me a lovely bunch of grapes, bless her.* There are luncheons and outings, and chats, and more grapes, *bless her*; and everything is peace and harmony and kindness. And family . . . And this continues — Mum being nice to Granddad right into the New Year, having him to lunch, bringing him grapes, going in for a chat, even, *sharing her worries, bless her.* But trouble is not far away. By May it's back, *Jane came in and shouted and cursed me . . . This means rest of the family will keep clear of me?*

As far as Mum was concerned Granddad represented the moment when things began to go wrong, the beginning of her unhappiness, and so became the focus for all her blame. I really don't know why, at only sixty-five, he had to live with them. Almost from the day they came back to England to start their life together. She loathed his ever-presence and dependence on us; sitting, waiting, waiting for lunch, or a chat, or to be invited in for a drink, the smell of his boiling cabbage, all his talk about horses, his gout, his blood pressure, his wind! And the Chutes! Granddad's stepsons conveniently shirking filial duties even though Granddad had brought them up since they were small boys. And 'that crooked bastard Desmond' screwing them with his menacing letters. Dad not consulting her on

400

anything, his one-tinpot-plan after another; his blasted liberal ideas; the Carews were a weak and useless lot; and her own family who didn't care and looked down on her; and nothing but slaving for four ungrateful children who were rude and beastly and cut her out of everything. It was all horribly true. The dynamo of Mum's anger just kept replenishing itself. Our household lost control. Every day Mum's fury spilt over. From palpable tension into atomic rage. We kept our distance as much as we could, but at night we were trapped in our beds, and that is when she would come in, stand over us, and not stop ranting until dawn. The anger loop. The worse it got, the worse it got. The deeper in, the more we all knew it couldn't be undone. The more she was desperate to be heard, the more we blocked our ears and shrank into ourselves.

By 1972, we had reached level ten. Dad was more and more away. Mum's invective became more and more unhinged. Locking Granddad in; throwing bricks through his window; turning his gas off so the pilot light went out, then turning it on again; chopping down any flowers in his view; pouring water through his letter box; climbing onto his flat roof from her bedroom window and pulling his TV aerial out. His Waterford crystal, smashed; his grandfather clock heaved over; his clothes strewn about the lawn. Granddad was enemy number one and poor Mum tormented him: *Jane off the deep end again, shouting at Arthur, and as usual broke my kitchen window, Wire cut by Jane. No TV; Hear Jane shrieking at Arthur . . . Won't be long before she does something horrible to me; Jane non compos mentis, shrieking, a brick through my bedroom window, so sad for Arthur and the children; Jane outside, off the deep end again, restrained by the children. Keggie returned my hunting crop because Jane wanting to destroy it; Arthur and children next door going through it with Jane by the row . . .*

I am only thankful Granddad's 1973 diary is missing, it was an abominable year. There was civil war in our house and it looked like it, every window, every spindle on the stairs, smashed to smithereens. I was sixteen, no pony to ride any more, and with the end of my riding, horse chats with Granddad ended too.

We all broke occasionally, shouted back, knew what it felt like to strip our vocal cords, push our noses into our mother's face. I smashed my bedside lamp over her head at three in the morning and was disappointed it didn't electrocute her. What one becomes used to. Weeping, wailing, spitting, broken glass. At the back of Granddad's diary is a Samaritan's telephone number: John, 298; and the police: Wickham, 3292. I took to God briefly, because of some kind poetic boys on the bus who played guitar . . . until they began to pray for me, which put a stop to that. I really don't understand how it went on so long without some kind of intervention. Mum's scenes would only end when the doctor arrived with his bag of pills, or the police, or both. That sound of the gravel, rumbling over itself.

★ ★ ★

Good memories: Mum reading us the *Just So Stories* and 'Rikki-Tikki-Tavi' in her jungly voice. All of us watching *Colditz*. And *It's a Knockout*. And *That's Life*. And *The Galloping Gourmet*. Mum reading 'Come away, come away, though I call all day', and 'the highwayman comes riding, riding, riding / The highwayman comes riding up to the old inn door'. Mum reading *Jamaica Inn* and making creaking noises when Uncle Joss creeps up the stairs. Me and Patrick in the bath singing 'Speed bonny boat like a bird on the wing'. Mum leaving the cobwebs, saying, 'Incy wincy spider . . . ' Mum catching a bat that had got trapped in the house and holding it in her hands laughing as she pointed out its sharp teeth and all its fleas. Mum teaching me the names of weeds in her flower bed: groundsel, nettle, bindweed, dandelion. Us all treading elderberries for Dad's home-made wine with our bare feet. Playing L'Attaque! Taking snuff with Granddad — learning how to trail it, just so, along my thumb's drumstick, and then snort: a little rush, the gorgeous sneeze. Sleeping outside with Dad watching the stars, my sleeping bag inside a large plastic bin bag to protect me from the dew. Dad pulling a train of driftwood along Berria beach with a bottle of wine in his hand. Mum's seventh birthday cake for me: a Beatles guitar with the seven candles as tuning keys on the headstock. Dad pushing his stomach out into a hard boxing balloon for us to pummel with our fists. Picking primroses where they grew in their thousands along the railway cutting.

★ ★ ★

Dad's voice:
  'Roll up! Roll up!'
  'PatrickKeggieNickyTim!'
  'Grub up! Come and get it!'
  'Heads I win. Tails you lose.'
  'Dar — *ling*!'
  'You silly chump.'
  'You silly ninny'
  'You *are* a silly chump.'
  'Now. Tell me . . . '

5

1974. The height of the IRA pub bombings; miners go back to work with an offer of improved pay; Lord Lucan disappears; Philippe Petit walks a tightrope between the twin towers in New York; it's the last episode of *Monty Python's Flying Circus*; and for everyone's safety, Dad asks Desmond to have Granddad to stay in Malta until he can get a home sorted out.

Granddad leaves on 19 January, Nicky's fifteenth birthday. Suddenly his diary is full of happenings: cocktails, cards, bridge, the club, sun, sea, and an endless string of dinners with Desmond's tax-exile friends; people with fantabulous names like Jetski Barnes, Stanley Swash, Bunny Steel and Trostram Eve. A far cry from our world in Wickham. Faithfully he records his encounters with sirs and 'onourables, daughters of counts, German princesses, high commissioners, until 2 February, when he writes: *PC from Jane beastly as usual, spoilt my day*. He kept it for some strange reason. A picture of Wickham Square, postmarked 31 January 1974.

Glad you are enjoying the sun. You should stay as long as you can. Nothing to come back for here. Force 9–10 gales, pouring rain, dreary strike threats, no coal — the lot. We all work too hard to give you the good time D & E can give you so you must enjoy

405

it all you can.
PS Douglas Lambert died last week. Poor man, only 57.

Yrs Jane

Granddad writes to Dad:

My dear Arthur,

We don't know how you have stood it for so long with Jane. God knows why you, of all fellows, should have suffered all these best part of your years with misery with a mad woman. Break away now before it's not too late, I have always felt for Nicky, bless her, I know what she has been going through. I enclose £5 for her birthday, didn't know I would be staying out so long. I am outstaying my welcome, have that feeling although Elspeth and Desmond all wonderful kind to me. I do hope somehow I will get a place somewhere and have some peace with you and dear Nicky. Don't worry about Mother's trust money, I want you to have it when I'm gone . . . Elspeth and Desmond are very guilty about you, specially Desmond, I've seen some of the insulting letters Jane wrote to them and the other day she wrote a postcard to me, of course, had to insult Elspeth that's why she wrote on a postcard so they would see it. Elspeth never says a bad word of anybody. Although I've been to several parties and dinners I have not felt at ease because of you and Nicky and staying out here so long.

Doris tells me my flat is in an awful state . . . I do hope you will at last get rid of Jane for all our sakes.

Your loving father

Desmond writes Dad a curt letter. He says he has no wish to interfere in Dad's family affairs but they know Granddad leads a life of terror, this information reaching them 'from various friends in the area'. Desmond 'gathers' Dad plans to move Granddad, in which case, Desmond thinks Dad ought to: 1) give Granddad the £1,000 which Desmond contributed towards building his flat; 2) repay Granddad any other money Dad owes him. Desmond ends grandly, hoping until Granddad gets what is owed him he will be allowed to live in peace.

I feel like digging Desmond up. Granddad writes again to Dad, he worries about where he will stay when he comes back, he says everyone has been so kind to him in Malta, 'but if they only knew the worries I'm having when I leave here . . . My love to dear Nicky. Your loving father'.

I admit to being hurt at being left off the love-list. I was sixteen going on seventeen and any chance I had, I escaped. In my mind I had been close to Granddad, but his problems and loneliness weighed on me, and my visits had become less frequent and briefer. Dad collected Granddad on 9 April from Heathrow and took him to an old people's home he'd found outside Winchester. There are three more entries in

407

Granddad's 1974 diary, and a last letter from him to Desmond and Elspeth.

Dear Desmond and Elspeth,

Thank you both for the joy and kindness you showered on me, thousand times I thank you both again and again, and I miss you so. Arthur met me at Heathrow and brought me here, and has paid for a month, I've offered to pay, he will not have it. He's having a bad time, when in the car he said, Don't tell me what Desmond and Elspeth think, they are mostly right. When he drove me to Heathrow for Malta it was a Saturday, when he arrived back there was Patrick and Keggie in my flat trying to keep their mother from pulling the place down, they couldn't get her out so they sat with her till Arthur arrived back. Next day Arthur and Patrick packed all my clothes in bags etc. on the Sunday. Monday midday they were put in the furniture remover's van and he lost a day from the office — since then the Welfare Officer and police came, he told them what he did and said, I'll bring all the furniture back and anything happens to him and his belongings I will hold you responsible for it, you know my wife is a dangerous, mad woman, I have had the police, the doctors and been to solicitors, and am unable to put her in a home by the law to keep her there. What else can I do, my two eldest children have left because of her and cannot live with her anymore. Patrick left for another job in

Devon, then Keggie told her father that her mother was driving her mad. She ran away, left school and went off to where Patrick is. Arthur got a strong-worded letter from the headmistress, he had to go and see her and explain what had happened. She was sorry and said she wouldn't report to the education authorities yet, but he must get her back soon as possible or she would be sent down and that would ruin her schooling. As for Nicky he is going to take her to London and put her in a tech college or she will be the next to go. Give me time to pay, I'll sign all the money Mother put into trusts so I could have. He is going through hell, and would have left her years ago, only for the children and he said himself she was blackmailing him. He hasn't told her I'm here or Nicky. On Friday he is coming to take me to Fareham to get anything I want from storage . . . This place is a very large Victorian house, large rooms, carpeted, furniture heavy, full of old crocks like myself and we have to give signs which way we are going, something like the Malta roads, first left then left again, right, straight on, reverse and so on. But I am thankful I'm here. The food, well what can I say after your gorgeous meals, dear Elspeth. Arthur said I was looking awfully well, asked after you both but specially about Anthony. I will write soon again. I miss you both. God bless you.

    All my love, Old Arthur

Last entry, Granddad's diary, 1974

11 April: *Rain. Long time from 6 p.m. dinner to 8.30 a.m. coffee and toast. Wrote to Dr Kinnear and Doris. 7 p.m. Nurse BRADFORD came and injected me . . .*

Beside this entry, Granddad has ominously drawn a picture of a hypodermic needle. He died in his chair the next morning, which was Good Friday. His will was less than half a typed page. Mum wrote in her own diary that day, simply, *Granddad died.* Ten days later, on her birthday, she wrote, *Granddad's funeral.* It beggars belief. Could we not have arranged it for another day? It was a miserable cremation in Gosport. On the way home Mum's head whipped round to us in the back seat, 'I don't know what you're all so glum about!' I flick through her diary for the following month, blank pages, dark rings around dates, black stars, exclamation marks; Mum thwarted by everyone, alive and dead, including herself. The doctor and the police kept coming, three or four times a week, until eventually they took her away.

6

While there was precious little understanding in 1974 for those suffering with the stigmatising catch-all phrase 'nervous breakdown', there were an awful lot of drugs. At Knowle, Mum was put on a cocktail of antidepressants, anti-psychotics, mood stabilisers, anxiolytics, uppers, downers and sleeping pills, and they were doing terrible things physically to her. Hers was an existence in limbo, barred windows, empty sky. Mum must surely have wondered how far from Trieste and Gibraltar could she impossibly have come, from their cottage on the Rock with their carpet suppers, and their aviary, and their corn-on-the-cob barbecues. With all that love. From there, to this. Even my sister and I could see, in our self-orbiting teenage years, the combustion of her fury had given way to fear. The place, and the fact that she was in it, had really shaken her. In the drug-haze, in the blank faces of those around her, in the monotonous texture of the ceiling over her bed, she knew there was only one person who would help her. Mum dug deep to find the steel of self-reliance which unwittingly her upbringing had prepared her for: she slipped her medication under her tongue, held it there until everyone had gone, and pill by pill by pill weaned herself off her debilitating medication; she learned the right answers to the same questions and ground herself down into a meek,

411

compliant state, until, a few months later, she was considered safe to come home. My sister and I were appalled, we preferred her being there. We found life far easier living in the house on our own.

Letter from Gibraltar, 1955
One day when sailing in the bay we saw a small 9-ton single-mast gaff-rigged yacht with two girls trying to clean the topsides. I hailed them and they replied they had just come from Ceuta (other side of the straits) (they sounded American) and that the 'boys' had just gone ashore. On the spur of the moment I asked them all up to dinner — much to Jane's dismay as we had nothing in the larder. Up they all came and we gave them baths, food and drink. They turned out to be American students at Paris aged 25–28 who had scraped every penny to buy this sturdy old boat with enough left over to cruise round Europe living frugally. They were a nice lot and well worth looking after . . . The next evening they came up again and one of them brought up his guitar — he sang rather like Burl Ives with a soft voice and amusing eye . . .

The Americans, realising Dad was longing to have a go in their boat, agreed for him to sail it as far as Malaga, while two of them drove his car. Dad, Mum and remaining crew set off with an easterly levanter blowing so they had to beat all the way.

412

A sea running and no wind to keep sails filled — most uncomfortable. The wind improved, then dropped so we arrived by engine at midnight and slept in the harbour. The next day all six of us piled in the car and we drove over the hills up to Granada in the Sierra Nevada mountains — whilst we were there we did the two things everyone must do — visit the Alhambra palace and go to the gypsy caves to see their dancing . . . We went there in high spirits and the gypsies were in good form too — they were so pleased to have us joining in with them and not just gaping that we had a rare old time with much dancing, laughter and jollification . . .

* * *

After Mum left Knowle her diary entries are stark: *Hair appt; Tim's Sports day; Tom not home. Probably staying with* . . . Gradually our family dispersed. Patrick was away at university in Manchester; Tim remained away at boarding school; I was out as much as possible — up the road at the Dunns', not studying for my A levels; only Mum and Nicky were left. On 27 August 1975 Dad and Mum divorced. Dad came home to say goodbye and get his things. I sat on the stairs with him and we cried. On 11 September 1975 Mum wrote, *Last time I saw Tom.*

Mum sold Merriles and moved to a small house eight miles away. In her 1975 diary beneath 'IN CASE OF ACCIDENT PLEASE

413

INFORM' she has written, *Separated from Lt Col T. A. Carew*, and gives Patrick's address, noting that she had infective hepatitis aged twenty, so might be a dangerous donor, but gives her permission. For the next few years the pages are mostly blank: *Hair appt; Tim home; Sold Granny's ring; Sign on Job Centre*; until in 1979 there is a play at Tim's school in the Greek amphitheatre. 1 June: *Prepare picnic*. 2 June: *Open day*. 10.30. *Tom to collect. All 4 & Tom & I together. Oedipus Tyrannus. Bradfield.*

By this time Mum had moved to a studio flat in London and, using her wartime contacts, got herself a job with MI6.

★ ★ ★

I was seventeen when Dad left home. As far as I knew he lived in London in his van. Nicky secretly knew better — she had found an unidentified key. The first time I went to visit him, he met me off the train at Waterloo. I could hardly wait, I had a million things to tell him and had saved them up. But the reunion was immediately uncomfortable. Dad was not Dad. He was awkward and stiff. And impossible. As if he didn't want to be there. So I was awkward and stiff and impossible. And silently cross. We walked around the station. It was Sunday and everywhere was shut. We had a coffee in a closing fast-food place with fluorescent lights and sat on bright orange plastic chairs as a woman with a broom tried to sweep us out. Dad didn't know what to say. He was fidgety and ill at ease and for the first time in his company I didn't know what to say either. Or understand why this was. Everything was suddenly new and uncharted. I didn't know that he had a 'friend', or that he was *not* living in his van. But I did sense that it was suddenly *all* different now. And we had been blown apart. As if only a shared house could keep you together? I was confused. I wanted to talk. I wanted to talk about it. But he didn't want to. *It* was the last thing he wanted to talk about. He didn't want to know *anything* bad. And everything I had saved up congealed into a no-go area. So it was small talk. Which was unfortunate, because we were both bad at it. And I was a teenager with spots and long hair that fell across my face. So he suggested we go to a movie. So we went to Piccadilly Circus. And we looked around to see what was on. And what was on was *Last Tango in Paris*. Astonishing now, to think our road could lead to this. We hadn't seen *Last Tango in Paris*, so we went. We did. We sat in the dark next to each other on the wine-coloured velveteen seats in the Prince Charles cinema in Leicester Square. Dad bought chocolate raisins so we could eat them and not talk and stare straight ahead. Which is what we did. My oily teenage hair a convenient curtain. Yet through it I could still see the dark browns and greys and shadows of Marlon Brando in a big coat, and a girl in a fur jacket. Of course we did not know then how the film grew from Bernardo Bertolucci's fantasy of having sex with a woman he'd seen on the street without knowing who she was; or that Maria Schneider developed an Oedipal fixation with Brando, and that she saw him 'like a daddy'. Schneider said making that film was her life's one regret. It was our regret too. Brando also said he felt raped and humiliated by the film. Luckily Bertolucci cut out the scene showing Brando's genitals, although we didn't know that at the time either. Nor did we understand that Brando, aka Paul, a middle-aged hotel owner, was mourning the suicide of his wife. Which was fortunate, I suppose, because Dad's wife, my mother, had made a few attempts in that direction herself. I slid down further into my seat, my hair growing greasier, my cheeks burning hotter, my neck vertebrae crushing deep back into my spine. Excruciating doesn't seem a big enough word. We had chosen to sit through a portrait of grief and anonymous sex. The cinema was dark but not dark enough to disappear the line of men in raincoats at the back, or quieten their rustlings. We stared straight ahead. I thought we were going to have fun, but instead we were sitting in a dark cinema watching Marlon Brando smear butter over Maria Schneider's arse.

'Do you want to watch this?' Dad eventually turned to me and asked.

We couldn't get out fast enough. Thankfully before he sodomised her. I've blanked out the rest of the evening; I think we went and had Chinese.

PART 7

GROUND CONTROL

1

On 9 January 1975, the *Daily Mail* published a full-page spread: 'In times like these Tom Carew is THE man to know'. Dad's business was finally taking off. The photograph showed him with his left hand raised, each finger in silhouette. Dad was fond of saying he had two successes in his life: the war, and Percy Coutts, and the rest was a disaster. But Percy was what Dad was most proud of. Dad rented a small office in the bowels of Grand Buildings in Trafalgar Square, and grew Percy Coutts into a business that taught people how to win interviews and get jobs. It was the Age of Redundancy, and redundancy was something he knew a bit about. Dad translated all the years of his own frustrations into a clear, offensive strategy with almost guerrilla tactics, to help others in the same boat. He taught them how to break through the secretary barrier, how to find a name from a box number, and how to avoid recruitment consultants like the plague. The answer to the begging question of why he hadn't used these techniques himself, is that his problem — as inveterate Skipper — was finding a job he was able to keep. Now he was the boss again and could do things exactly how he liked. In Britain in 1975, the idea of actually teaching an executive how to get a job was virtually unheard of, but his methods were pioneering, and they worked, and the press was giving him a bit of attention.

419

The *Daily Mail* reporter, John Edwards, followed him doing a session with sixteen redundant executives.

Carew showed them their seats. He put on a fine smile. 'Gentlemen,' he said to them, 'I am here to tell you how to get jobs. If you don't think that's possible then you're thinking a lot of old . . . There's work for all of you and we're going to —ing well see about it.' If you think the Indians caught Custer unawares you should have seen what Tom Carew did to 16 men with that kind of language . . .

As I read, the old Dad comes back: 'Who wants nice people? Do you know what happens to nice people? They get letters from firms after an interview telling them they were second choice . . . Don't ask for an interview. Tell them you're coming. References? If they want them, get them from titled people, even if they're stupid, bumbling nonentities.'

Carew seemed to have done everything in his life. He made colonel, failed as a pencil salesman, got the heave-ho from more places than he has had time to catalogue, but always he's had the knack of getting people going.

'He pumps you up,' one of the participants told Edwards. 'He makes it war. He makes you feel such a bloody fool sitting around waiting for things to happen . . .'

420

Percy Coutts was my first nine-to-five skirt-wearing job. How many hours I spent over the Xerox machine, making tea, licking stamps, answering the telephone, 'Percy Coutts and Company. Can I help you?' What I liked was its sense of mad energy, hearing Dad's joyous roar reverberating down the corridor; Dad back at the helm, the only place he flourished. Each client was a personal challenge and he would stop at nothing to get them back into work. And he didn't give a shit how 'If they ask you, Can you juggle? Say Yes! And make sure you are juggling by Monday!' He empowered people and they loved him. I remember him telling a black man to change his name. 'You want to get to the interview, don't you? African names don't get interviews! Call yourself Richard Mortimer. And then I'll teach you how to change the buggers' minds when their face drops the moment you walk through the door!'

One of Dad's tricks for redundant executives was demonstrated in the seminar tea break. He would load up a large plate with plain biscuits and add one single chocolate one. The men, for they were mostly men, would politely help themselves to a biscuit with their tea, and predictably the chocolate biscuit would remain untouched. If anyone did take it, Dad would clap his hands and loudly cheer his congratulations, then give the rest of the room hell. 'You all wanted it,' he would accuse them, 'no time for manners in business, not when you need a job.

You've got to take what you want.' His best lessons were simple ones. He would lay out a selection of fifty different pens and pencils on a table — felt tips, coloured crayons, biros — and ask the men to choose *one*. They fumbled. Then he repeated the procedure, reducing the choice to a tiny handful. They quickly picked one. 'Don't show me thirty pencils, show me three! Don't overwhelm me, make it easy for me.'

I was a little overzealous in my discipleship; the letter I got back from the BBC after writing to ask for a job, regretted that, considering all my skills, they didn't think their organisation was big enough.

★ ★ ★

He is beside himself with boredom. Little embers dying in his brain. Sometimes I think, *Time's nearly up, Dad*, then I notice the shine in his silver hair and know time isn't up at all. He wants another job. *Give me another job*. His pyjamas are poking out of the bottom of his trouser legs. He has only just finished laying a dozen washed seed trays out on the lawn. We sit in the shed together. The sun streams in and he is asleep. I begin to creep out, his dogs bark, he is awake and up on his feet. 'Right! Give me a job.'

There is a macabre fascination in the waiting-watching game. I catch myself and don't like it. I see Hope jumping around in his head like sandhoppers on a washed-up frond of bladderwrack. He tiptoes on the edge of reality, in out, in out. I suggest we have a cup of tea. 'Oh yes!' he says as if it's the first one he's ever had.

★ ★ ★

Six in the morning he shouts up the stairs, 'What's my job?'

'Dad, we haven't had breakfast yet.'

I make him sit down. He knows something's up.

'When do I go back?' he asks apprehensively.

'Today Dad.'

'Today?' His face is brave, but crestfallen. Then his eyes sag. 'Right,' he says.

It undoes me. In all my life I have never heard him complain.

'But you're coming back, Dad. Soon. This is your holiday place.'

He smiles, wanly. 'Right,' he says again.

He looms around in the garden. Stands lost in the middle of the kitchen. My old parachuting guerrilla agent father, with his once quick-as-a-flash brain, with his once punch-hard-as-you-can stomach, with his once tickling-the-life-out-of-you hands, cries when he has to go home.

★ ★ ★

I can see myself, eighteen years old, sitting stiffly with Dad and Stepmother in their Kennington flat in 1976. Perched on the edge of their large caramel sofa, leaning forward, awkward, trying to please, trying to be someone else, at the same time hating myself for doing so. Dad had failed

423

to mention he'd got married. It came out in a *by-the-way* moment about six months after the event. Now she was legitimate. She knew and she smiled. A dull glint flickering from her granite teeth, a wrinkle in her carapace. We were done for.

The first time I met Stepmother she was standing in front of her kitchen window, daylight behind her, silhouetting the Darth Vader padded shoulders and wispy hair.

'I am not going to be one of those *fawning* stepmothers,' she informed me, her speech prepared.

I had long dreamed a stepmother would be brilliant. Someone to love Dad. Someone to love us! Someone mothery and kind who wore soft woollen jumpers. But after the raging heat of Mum, Dad was drawn to ice. If the character of our stepmother confounded me, her *taste* confounded me more. At Stepmother's flat everything smelt different. Different cooking, different brands of soap, different cleaning fluids, and plastic chemical pomanders, room fresheners, perfumed loo paper, fly spray that got down the back of your throat. *Stomaching it* was more than a visceral expression of what I felt I had to do. We all instinctively knew our own mother would have been appalled. They couldn't have been more poles apart. Stepmother, for instance, had present-buying down to an art that narrowed the whole process to no more than fifteen minutes. Grab bag. Slam door. March up street. Go into first suitable shop. Decide immediately on first thing in price range, anything between £5 and, well, £5. A brooch possibly (like the fake gold owl Nicky got which bent when you did up the clasp making bits of gold flake off). March back. Wrap it up. Done.

Her decisions were always irrevocable. Long before she'd met us Stepmother had decided she wasn't going to 'make an effort with the children'. If we wanted to be friends, we must go to her. For some inexplicable reason, Dad thought this plan was *marvellous*. And that didn't feel like Dad at all.

★ ★ ★

Andrew Marr, in his documentary about Britain, recounted an anecdote about Reagan on the telephone in the White House that I recognised straight away. Reagan, in the midst of a high-level meeting, holds the phone away from his ear. The voice booming into the room is Margaret Thatcher's. Reagan turns the receiver towards his audience and beaming says, 'Isn't she marvellous?' And that is exactly how it was with Dad. Yet what bewildered me was that it was *he* who had encouraged us to have an independent, questioning, not-quite-respectable way of seeing the world in the first place. The trouble was, that didn't knit with what he now required of us. As far as Stepmother was concerned we were the wrong type. It must have been rotten for her. Four incumbents with greasy long hair, army jackets, desert boots, grunge before there was a name for it. Patrick, jobless and flat-less in the summer break from

Manchester University. Me, too young and too old at the same time. A bit lippy a lot shy. Seen too much, done too little. My younger sister, smart alec; my younger brother, brain-box; both still at school. We must have been like four big ugly ducklings, each one of us representing more financial drain.

★ ★ ★

The doomed, excruciating relationship with my stepmother is inescapable, it is fixed forever and casts its shadow over the subsequent damage it wrought, however unspoken, in my relationship with Dad. My role was to be the difficult one. Because I railed against Dad's sudden transition from my pedagogical father to this rationed man.

★ ★ ★

Who walks behind his eyelids now? His mother comes, *Now Arthur*, in his childhood ear; his father jostling him along; Margot maybe; his dogs, one after the other, Worry, his faithful boyhood friend, then Peter comes to him, beloved Peter, one minute bounding towards him in Palestine, the next to be crushed under a tank; and there's Desmond and Chubby, both old enough to rough his hair. *We're going on a spree!* Knees above socks, bikes rattling down Howes Place. A river in spate rusheth more than runneth. The name's Charm, Tom Charm. All the people of himself in the ring at the same time. Boxing. 'Have I ever told you about . . . ?'

Yes! Dad! A million times.

The jostling of ghosts and soon-to-be-ghosts, yourself included. We think about this, you and I, in private and without telling each other. With morbid secrecy I study your old hand with my younger eye, knowing that soon it will be a lifeless one; it rests on the kitchen table, then fiddles with your penknife; your knuckles and finger joints are a collection of small boulders now, almost bursting through the tissue thin, speckled skin. Your whole body has become geological. Stones and flinty bones. Crags. Hills. Furrows. Fissures. Your nails ridged and calciferous. The frosted forest of your mouth. Breath a mist. Skin starting to resemble a dried lake crust. And ebbing slowly as a pebble, molecule by molecule . . . I am now the spy. Spying. Thinking it. And then your hand lies quite still for a moment, and sadness overwhelms me.

Then all at once there is a gleam in your eye, as if you knew what I was thinking and you thought *Bugger that!* and under your breath you swear at yourself for giving way, even for a moment. You are up, off, wanting a job. 'Give me a job.' Snap, snap. The Present! Here and Now. You've *never* been a Past person, or a Future one for that matter. A stream of autumn sunlight through the window confirms it, its buttery band stripes your face. 'Aaaaah,' you luxuriate in its momentary warmth. Nothing is lost on you. The moon still pulls its tides and you will work with what you have. In the world of the possible. In your world that only goes forward in yeses and exclamation marks. And no explanations, Never Explain; and then as suddenly as a flock of starlings might swoop into its roost, you forget where you are, you lose your place. You lose your place and cannot see a world where there is space for you. Which is *inconceivable*. And each day the possibilities are receding into the past, and the probabilities are cramming into the future.

I hate to harbour this, but even at this good age, I'd hoped for more. I blame her. I know I shouldn't but I do. She took one long last draught and drained you all away. Exhausted you. Up, down, fetch, carry, nurse, nurse, to bursting point. 'Tom!' 'Tom!' 'Tom!!!' Little tiny pops of blood in your brain. She wouldn't care. All night, 'Tom! TOM!!!' At eighty-five you were trying to be seventy. You wouldn't let anyone interfere; pop, pop. Nicky found you trying to drag her on a chair across the room with a Heath Robinson-style rope-pulley system.

★　★　★

After the BBC turned me down, I used my Percy Coutts skills to get a job in a film company in Wardour Street. Except that I had no idea how to type. With two weeks to go before I started, I signed up to a crash touch-typing course in Oxford Street where I sat bashing away with a hundred other automaton girls in a hot room, *the lazy brown dog jumped over the fabulous red fox*, or something or other, until I could just about scrape around twenty words a minute.

Which compelled me to arrive at Pacesetter Productions on my first day with my arm in a sling, in the hope it would give me enough time to speed up a bit before I got rumbled. I'm sure they knew what the score was. But they kindly kept me on, buying fancy cheeses from Camisa & Son for their lunch while they made films about the queen's racehorses.

2

I'm back in my shed. With all this trawling through letters and diaries I am finding a depression setting in. I have become morbid and tense. And obsessed. It has become a drug, an *Alice in Wonderland* project, each letter, each diary entry leads to something else. I am a large girl in a tiny room, my head squashing against the ceiling. The bottle says, Drink me. Yet it is making me wretched and there is nothing I can do. My shed has begun to feel like a mausoleum: Granddad's voice, Mum's voice, wills and divorce settlements, Housewifery and Laundry Notes, Beryl's sad cards, Dad's joyous letters home with happy interjections from Mum. Certificates, citations, cablegrams; Granddad's gun licence, Dad's DSO, signed in ink by George R.I. The dead are haunting me night and day. I feel the subterfuge in the separated piles stacked around my desk, old enemies forced to reconvene, concealing their plots and surprises. With Dad's large magnifying glass I spend ten minutes over a word which turns out to be 'cardigans': *Maud shopping for cardigans*. I am surprised my shed has not combusted with all this stuff in it. It is perverse, to be occupied so. Yet, I cannot let it go. Because I want to understand. To let it go. John Berger wrote, 'Sadness accumulates.' I feel weighed down with the accumulations of sadnesses.

I am listening again to the Burma tapes. Robert Taylor has returned to the political implications of Burmese independence. He explains that a great frustration for a historian in America is that if people become known for being communist, many individuals will deny they ever knew them. 'No!' Dad says incredulously. I wonder, is he playing at this?

TC: When my contemporaries talk about people shoplifting and you ask them, Did you ever pinch from a shop?, none of them ever pinched a thing. I must have been in very strange company when I was younger. I whipped from Boots regularly and all my chums did. What's happened to them all? You won't find them admitting it.

They laugh. Taylor says he is struck by the sudden interest in astrology here. Cue Step-mother.

SM: I think astrology has always been strong here, and belief in astrology, increasing because more people are realising there is er, a sort of, er, strange phenomena . . . [Eerie silence. She continues unabashed] and therefore goes under the heading of astrology. There are a lot of political people and um, er, highly educated people, that in fact go to acceptable astrologists to find out what is happening, er, you know, what is going to happen, and believe it.

Taylor steers the conversation back to the war. Dad tells him about a third, short-lived mission, being parachuted into the jungles of Sumatra where there was trouble with the Japanese at the very end of the war. Something went wrong: there was no reception committee. He walked for days and nearly starved to death. His neck swelled up until he could hardly breathe. Then he went down with a bad case of malaria and was pulled out to convalesce in a grass hut called a *basher*, on the Indian Ocean, where he had the opportunity to stop, think, and contemplate. He tells Taylor without that time he would never have been able to benefit from the experience of Burma, and find out who he was.

So who was he? Stepmother tells Taylor she has seen photographs of Tom when he was in his twenties and knows from his looks she would have thought him 'the most ghastly man'. She wouldn't have given him the time of day at all.

TC: You see, who are you? What are we? The Tom Carew of now has no connection with the Tom Carew you're talking about. No connection. No connection at all. I hope no connection with Tom Carew in five years' time. I hope again to be someone different. Same body. Same name. Possibly same accent. Possibly same basic philosophy, but I hope to change considerably. Developed, or done something different.

Taylor asks Dad if he has thought of going back to Burma. He assures him the Burmese he

432

knew in the war would want to see him again. Dad can't believe that. Stepmother tells him off.

TC: If they did see me they'd think that pathetic old sod. That silly bugger aged ninety-four. Totally different from the one they'd met.

RT: Nyo Tun is not the virile chap you knew thirty years ago either.

TC: He was a very civilised sophisticated chap. I hope I've reached his level — he was certainly much more intelligent and civilised than I was. When I met him I was the boss, the white man, the master race, had coolies, everything else, but he was the more civilised man, blew his nose on his longyi and all the other white people thought he was awful. I knew he wasn't, I knew he was a bloody sight brighter than I was. I was the only one that did know [laughs]. Perhaps that was the only asset I had, I could recognise he was a highly intelligent chap in spite of looking scruffy on the English Raj standards. I hope I've reached him. Possibly now I could talk with him as equal . . . Do they get teak out these days? How do they get it out? Are the elephants still rolling? And are the paddle steamers going up and down?

He sounds vulnerable. Nostalgic.

TC: Small, highly independent, thoroughly badly treated, swamped, beautiful people, the simplicity of their possessions, so clean

433

. . . What have we got all these clocks for? In Burma we didn't even need this roof . . .

Dad's off. But not for long. The voice.

SM: I'm telling you, Bob, I have a terrible time with Tom!

Stepmother begins to talk about her possessions. That she, like so many women, would like 'you know, some itsy-bitsy things around, to collect, ornaments or whatever, but Tom still has this Burmese hang-up . . . To have this here is a major achievement,' she says, pointing to something. 'He won't have anything on the mantelpiece for instance.' She talks at length about a clock. Polite laughter from the historian. In the background I can hear a 1978 Routemaster double-decker bus swoosh past, the windows rattle. Stepmother certainly made up for lack of ornaments in subsequent years. Yet in the aftermath of her death, Dad returned to that 'Burmese hang-up' with a vengeance and he has been hell-bent on getting rid of everything since. Silver spoons line up along the pavement (not for long), books all over the lawn, jackets and shoes flung out of the windows.

TC: I'd be frightened of going back to Burma. When you said, go back to Burma, I found it really quite frightening. I felt suddenly tremendous false pretences, if I went back I'd rather go back *admonitio* and not as if

434

'I'm coming back'. I'd rather say, 'I'm *coming* to Burma', not *going back*. Really, I would be going back to something that would be so small, so tiny and not very great.

RT: Not according to Thein Pe's account.

TC: Whatever he says I know, I know what I did. It wasn't all that great.

SM: You were the youngest DSO ever!

TC: No! I don't know. Well. Not ever.

Robert Taylor politely laughs, tells Dad he's a modest chap. Dad says he's not a modest chap. (True.)

Stepmother goes into a tirade. 'You make me so bloody angry . . . [manoeuvre into a show argument] He belittles himself! He might have influential people round him, and instead of, of . . . playing up . . . you know like any other person would, sort of playing into their hands in order to . . . er . . . I don't know, er . . . '

'Ridiculous!' Dad interrupts, 'Nobody's influential as far as I know. I don't want to play into any bugger's hands.'

Another tirade from Stepmother, 'You belittle yourself!' she shouts.

'I don't belittle myself,' Dad huffs, pleased with himself.

I hit STOP. It was always like this. They occupied parallel universes. Both so totally wrapped up in themselves, neither noticed they were so far apart. They existed side by side on the opposite side of the fence in a state of constant mock combative harmony. A stranger from the sidelines might think they were having an all-out war.

But each non sequitur from Stepmother meant there was a stunned vacuum for Dad to fill, which he usually did with his favourite subject, himself. Yet, as large as his ego was, this massive Self of his was entirely occupied in helping others, and I have never met anyone work so hard at it. From that wellspring came all his joy.

I fast-forward a couple of loops, press PLAY. Dad is defending Machiavelli — '*The Prince* is a simple truism: Don't wound the prince. Kill him or say something nice to him.' Stepmother pipes up, but the only audible phrase is 'and what have you'. Taylor asks what books Dad read before the war.

TC: There were three books in my life: Boswell's *Life of Johnson*; Plato's *Life of Socrates*; and subsequently after the army, Dale Carnegie's *How to Win Friends and Influence People*.

The historian laughs. I laugh. We all got a copy when we were young. He bought that book for everyone. Dad sticks to his guns.

TC: Dale Carnegie prevented me from being a total failure! Before that I was naive. If I thought a man was wrong, I'd tell him he was wrong. From Carnegie I learnt if I want my way and I know I'm right, I've got to go about it another way.

Dad recalls giving the book to someone who joked he hoped no one would see him reading it

436

on the train; he counters forcefully with his own reaction: 'Yes! I'd like to read that book. I'd like to have more friends and I'd like to influence people,' then softens his voice, 'I'm a simple soul' Stepmother delivers another illogical statement on astrology. Taylor deftly moves the thread to Buddhism. Dad thinks you can be rational and Buddhist, but a rational Christian creates a philosophical question.

SM: You have to believe in something bigger than yourself.
TC: No, I don't believe in anything.
SM: Yes, you *do*, darling.
TC: I don't.
SM: You do! I have heard you say many times, 'I thank my lucky stars.'

Eerie silence. I guffaw.

TC: I have been very lucky, I don't *believe* in it.
SM: You *do* believe in it.
TC: I've been bloody lucky.
SM: Then you've believed in something outside yourself.
TC: Mathematical luck! I threw the bloody six for God's sake. I don't have to believe in God for that.
SM: You believe in luck or fate or chance.
TC: I don't believe in any one thing.
SM: *You do*, darling.
TC: I don't believe in any bloody religion, any bloody church, I won't fall in . . .

Here we go. It's theatre now.

I spend the day rewinding and playing the tapes, transcribing, trying to catch every word. Dad's supreme self belief exudes across the thirty years and I don't know why this depresses me, but it does. I just cannot help wondering why, when we were young, for so many years, with everything he had going for him, charisma, resourcefulness, ingenuity, energy, optimism, experience, did he make such an absolute almighty cock of it? Tom fool. Tom cat. A life manqué. His. Mum's. Ours. Everyone's. Nature. Nurture. Luck! Where exactly was the Achilles heel? And is this a mirror I'm looking into?

3

We are having a picnic by the Avon, Dad, me,
Jonathan, and both pairs of dogs, his and ours.
Jonathan and I are swimming, Dad is sitting on a
camp chair watching. We are floating flat,
spreadeagle in the water holding onto the river
weed; the river is fast and if we let go it takes all
our strength to remain swimming in the same
place. We dive down, I open my eyes under water
to see the blur of long horsetails of iridescent
green. And then I look up to see the blurred
shape of Dad at the edge of the bank at a
forty-degree angle. Dad is in his underwear, up
to his calves in mud, trying to get in.

'Dad, no!'

We quickly clamber out.

'Dad! Be careful! The current is too strong.'

'Is it?' he asks crestfallen. He has seen our
pleasure and wants it.

'Yes.'

'Yes,' he repeats after me.

Dad will never lose Yes. Yes, I can. Yes, we will!
Yes, of course I can, you tell me when. Yes! Yes,
and thank you. Thank you, darling. Thank you!
He is the best thank-you sayer in the world. And
predictably it is the next thing he says.

'Thank you.'

★ ★ ★

It is the end of the hot dry summer of 1976. I have flopped my A levels; home life is terrible without Dad; my boyfriend is a year in at Oxford, and I know I am not going to get to university with my lousy grades. I am desperate to get away. I don't just want to leave home, I want to leave the country. So I get a job behind the bar at the Rising Sun in Warsash, pulling pints and playing darts, until I have enough money for a one-way ticket to Toronto. Toronto, because I have an address there and it makes the leap a little less daunting. I catch a train to London to tell Dad. I am apprehensive because he has spent a lot of time writing letters and pulling strings to find me a place at college, any college, and Oxford Polytechnic have eventually offered me a place to study history of art.

He meets me at Waterloo in the Dormobile. We sit on the bench seats opposite each other in the back. 'Right, tell me,' he says. I say I am not going to college, but flying to North America instead. There is a brief computing moment, a flicker across his face, and then he laughs. He roars with laughter. He slots in the table and gets out a box of wine. He says whenever one has a choice, one should always take the most difficult option, because *that* must be the thing you really want to do — or it wouldn't have come up as an option in the first place. Then he hunts around for a sheet of paper and writes down a name, address and telephone number, with a note to go with it, which I am to use when I get to America if I ever need help.

'Who's . . . Bill Colby?' I ask.

He laughs, he already knows I am not going to believe him. 'He's the head of the CIA.'

Of course I interrogate him. He tells me they were friends in the war; Dad says he liked to take his money at poker and thrash him at chess. What he didn't explain was that they trained as Jedburghs together at Milton Hall. I am stunned Dad knows *anyone* in the CIA, let alone its director, but I am also a little chilled by it.

And so off I set on my beginning-to-regret-I'd-ever-mentioned-it adventure with Dad's note and a letter from Colby tucked in my passport, and I almost forgot about it. It was December and bitterly cold. I had met up with my friend Ian, and we decided to hitch south and got as far as Louisville, Kentucky.

Our last ride had dropped us off at the edge of town, so we had to walk into Louisville in our Millets boots under our heavy rucksacks (mine — Dad's 1950s canvas army regulation), looking lost and for somewhere cheap to stay, when a man in a pickup pulled over and asked if we needed help. These friendly Americans. We eagerly explained our predicament. The man said he knew a good budget hotel and offered to drive us there. How kind and helpful we thought. We threw our rucksacks in the back and hopped in. It was disconcerting to turn off the main highway and be heading further and further into a down-and-out neighbourhood, but our new friend was insisting we first go back to his place to meet his folks and have a cup of tea. It was disconcerting, but we didn't want to be impolite, so we sat meekly looking out the window as we drove into no-man's-land, past houses with doors boarded up and the windows broken, and abandoned cars with flat tyres slumped half off the kerb, until we pulled up outside his place, a semi-derelict house in a semi-derelict street. It was disconcerting, but we didn't want to be impolite, so we sat at the crash-site of his kitchen table making small talk, waiting for our cup of tea and his folks . . . for an interminably long time. Until there was nothing left to say and still no sign of tea. Our friend had become nervous and fidgety. Then another man showed up. He didn't look so friendly. There was that sinking feeling when you know you're in the shit. We got up to leave. An arm sprang out to block our passage to the door. They wanted our money. Of course they did.

Ian stood his ground, astonishingly in my view, considering we were in their house behind a locked door, and demanded they let us pass. The two men smiled curiously. I gripped the shoulder straps of my rucksack tightly, then suddenly remembered the note. I told them my dad was a very close friend of the head of the CIA, and I had his name and address in my pocket and if anything happened to me I didn't think he would be too happy about it . . . I waved the letter from Colby to Dad and the two men exchanged glances. An unsure look that flickered back and forth as if there was a faulty light switch. There we stood, by the door in the hall, Ian firmly holding his ground, me holding the letter . . . their predicament teetering in a damp spark in their brains, and then they laughed, said they were only joking and moved aside.

We pushed through, and were back outside in the sun-bright derelict street, but the story doesn't end there . . . No, for even more bizarrely now I look back, than going to tea in the first place, is what happened next. The man who gave us the lift followed us out of the house, blaming every-thing on the other guy, and insisting he drive us to the cheap hotel for the sake of *no bad feeling*. And being so far out of town and in the middle of nowhere with no means of getting anywhere, we let him! We did. As splutteringly incredible as that may sound. And he did drop us off at a cheap hotel. A real dive: rooms with large beds and broken mirrors, swagged in drapes of cheap crim-son velveteen. It was a noisy night of knocking and banging, and people thumping up and down the stairs. The hotel turned out to be a whore-house for paraplegics and one-legged men — which I only understood the next morning when Ian explained *why* there were so many paraplegics and one-legged men in reception at checkout.

I still have the letter from Colby to Dad. 'If your daughter does indeed come this way, please have her look us up as we would be happy to have a renewed contact with the Carew clan.' It seems inconceivable now, not to have taken up an invitation to visit the last of the great spy-masters. At nineteen, friends of one's parents only cramp one's style.

★ ★ ★

Bill Colby's leadership of the CIA began towards the end of Vietnam, and finished in the middle of Watergate. It was a tumultuous tenure during which Colby compiled and released a notorious set of reports known as the Family Jewels. The

443

Family Jewels detailed the controversial activities of the CIA between the 1950s and mid-1970s. Colby called them the skeletons in the CIA closet. These skeletons included the CIA's illegal wiretapping; assassination plots; and the many crazy attempts to kill or discredit Fidel Castro — including exploding cigars, poison pens, a chemical that would make his hair and beard fall off, infecting his diving suit with deadly fungus, and a plan to administer LSD before a public speech. The agency's widespread sabotage in Cuba was manic and endless: sugar contamination, turkeys infected with fatal viruses, pigs infected with swine fever, swarms of *Aedes aegypti* mosquitoes set loose carrying dengue fever, anti-crop warfare, chemicals added to lubricating fluids which caused premature wear on engines (one West German company was even paid to manufacture ball bearings off centre). Added to this litany was the CIA's widespread domestic surveillance and the extremely dubious cases of non-consensual human experimentation. Of these, one of the most sinister was the case of the 'cursed' bread of Pont-Saint-Esprit in southern France. A mass outbreak of hallucinations in 1951 was put down to the presence of a psychedelic ergot mould at the local bakery, but later was revealed to be LSD administered to the unsuspecting town as part of a mind control 'field experiment' by the CIA. One man tried to drown himself screaming his belly was being eaten by snakes; another leapt out of a second-floor window shouting, 'I am a plane!' while an eleven-year-old tried to strangle his grandmother. Five died and dozens of others were taken to the asylum in straitjackets. The code name for this human experimentation programme was MKULTRA. MKULTRA recruited former Nazi scientists prosecuted in Nuremberg with experience in various brainwashing techniques and torture. Hypnosis and personality types susceptible to hypnosis were also studied by the CIA with experiments in anterograde and retrograde amnesia. Derren Brown explored this subject head-on in his TV series *The Experiments* in the episode 'The Assassin' — the one where Brown hypnotises an unwitting (but previously gauged susceptible) member of the public to shoot Stephen Fry (in a packed theatre without knowing his gun was loaded with blanks) to demonstrate the very real possibility of hypnosis having been used to persuade Sirhan Sirhan, a twenty-four-year-old Palestinian refugee (and unlikely assailant), to assassinate Bobby Kennedy on 6 June 1968. Sirhan has been denied parole because he can feel no remorse for something he has no memory of doing. Is Sirhan a real Manchurian Candidate? Derren Brown seems to think he could be. After watching the rigorous step-by-step planning of Brown's terrifying programme, so do I . . .

The commissioning of these shaming reports about the activities of the CIA (that violated its charter) was a response to press reports of CIA involvement in Watergate. Bill Colby testified before congressional committees fifty-six times, giving straight answers when many believed it was his duty to lie. He co-operated with Congress to demonstrate the CIA was accountable to the terms of the Constitution, but also because he'd weighed

445

up the pros and cons and judged the revelations would do the agency no long-term harm. Details of the contents steadily dripped out, but full public access was denied until 25 June 2007, when the papers marked SECRET EYES ONLY were released, albeit heavily redacted.

Colby in many respects was a liberal; he became a supporter of the nuclear freeze and reductions in military spending which, together with his controversial openness policy, caused a major rift within the ranks of the CIA. By the time I was in America on my little jaunt in 1976, he had more enemies than friends, including Gerald Ford and Henry Kissinger. In what was known as the Halloween Massacre, Colby was replaced by George Bush senior; Kissinger was fired as National Security Advisor; and James Schlesinger, the Secretary of Defense, was replaced by Donald Rumsfeld. In a chequered career, with a trolleyload of controversies surrounding him (not least his role in the Vietnam war, in which the CIA was reputedly engaged in the torturing and/or neutralising of 81,000 Viet Cong supporters[1]), the final and most perplexing one was how Bill Colby died.

The scene is Colby's house in Maryland, a turn-of-the-century oysterman's cottage on Rock Point surrounded by water on three sides with a spectacular view across Neale Sound, up the Wicomico River and over to Cobb Island where Colby kept his boat. According to former *Time* journalist Zalin Grant his home was unpretentious, tranquil and anonymous. Which is just how Dad described

[1] The Phoenix Program.

Colby. On 27 April 1996, Bill Colby rang his wife to say he was going home to eat dinner, have a shower then head to bed. The following day his submerged canoe was discovered in the river with a tow rope still attached. Colby had been missing for eight days when his body was discovered forty metres from the canoe. The official autopsy concluded he had had a heart attack or stroke, fallen from his canoe, and died of hypothermia and drowning.

Dad didn't believe it. None of the Jeds believed it. They knew Colby and nothing added up. They weren't the only ones. His neighbours were sceptical he would have gone canoeing that late, the wind was up, the water was choppy, and he was a prudent man. The last person to speak to him was his caretaker at about 7.15 p.m. who said Colby was watering his trees because he was due to return to Washington the next day. The man who found his canoe said it was full of sand, yet it was impossible for only two tides to fill it up to that extent. His shoes were off and there were no paddles or life jackets anywhere to be found. Yet he always took out a life jacket. Back at Colby's unlocked house, the radio and his computer were on. His keys and wallet were on the table. His favourite meal of clams was abandoned half-eaten on his plate, a glass of wine on the counter and a clutter of saucepans in the sink. Yet, Dad said he was a fastidious, meticulous man. He would never have gone out leaving the house open or untidy in such a way. Fellow Jed Dick Rubinstein wrote to Dad: 'Why a canoe trip in fairly rough weather, in the dark and with the computer running and the

447

meal not cleared away?' Why indeed? Why would anyone leave in the middle of dinner and go out in a canoe in darkness? The massive search for him with helicopters, divers, volunteers, sonars and draglines went on for eight days and nights, yet he was recovered from marshes that had been searched numerous times, as if he'd just been tossed in.

There were many conspiracy theories; the *Sun* even ran the headline: 'Dead CIA Chief Was Set to Finally Blow Lid on JFK Assassination'. Whatever/whoever it was, after a long clandestine career that began as a Jedburgh at Milton Hall, in the end it turned out Colby couldn't save his own skin, but I have a strong suspicion he might have saved mine, one nondescript evening in a semi-boarded-up street in Louisville in 1976.

Cable to Bolivia, 5 January 1978, 19.39 GMT: URGENT TO BANCO MERCANTIL LA PAZ FROM APD PALL MALL BRANCH:

```
VERY URGENT
WE UNDERSTAND FROM BOLSA QUITO THAT
THEY INSTRUCTED YOU BY CABLE ON
19.12.77 TO PAY POUNDS 292.64 TO MISS
KATHLEEN CAREW ON APPLICATION AND
IDENTIFICATION. PLEASE CONFIRM TO US
IF PAYMENT HAS BEEN EFFECTED.
IF MISS CAREW HAS NOT YET CALLED ON
YOU TO COLLECT THESE FUNDS PLEASE
REQUEST HER, WHEN SHE DOES TO CONTACT
HER FATHER AS SOON AS POSSIBLE.
MATTER URGENT.
CONFIRM YOUR ACTIONS BY CABLE
```

I was off the radar and Dad was looking for me. I had been gone over a year edging my way further south, four months working illegally with Mexicans in a cotton gin (where raw cotton is processed) at a place called Sweetwater in the heart of Texas (ninety hours a week, $2 an hour, time and a half overtime), then on the road, deeper into the Americas, until my money ran out. By the time Dad was trying to find me I was halfway down South America travelling by local bus. Stapled to Dad's cable is a sheet of graph paper bearing a list of questions in his handwriting (red biro) to Rikki Gilbert Rolfe (Dad's accountant at Percy Coutts); with Rikki's reply in blue, down the right.

Rikki, Can I send her
$700?   *No. £300.*

Can we afford to pay her?   *No.*

Can we send money to her
at American Express with-
out sending cash — you see
she is so footloose we
could not be sure she will
collect — Could A.Express
be credited with the money
but return it if she does
not collect?   *See notes.*

Can we commission her to
do some South American
investigation for us and
so charge the firm?   *If you wish.*

Can we cable her to tell-
her?   *Done*.

Attached behind is another cable addressed to
me, American Express Agents, Avenue Amazo-
nas 399, Quito, Ecuador:

ARRANGING TO SEND MONEY STOP SOME DELAY
ADVISE ADDRESS FOR FOLLOWING SEVEN DAYS
COUTTS LONDON

I never picked this up because I must have
gone on somewhere else. At twenty years old, it
wouldn't have crossed my mind that anyone
(especially Dad) would have been remotely
concerned, let alone worried enough to have
begun searching for me. I was shocked to learn
he'd got all the embassies involved. Of course
there were no emails or mobile phones then; a
phone call had to be booked ahead and cost a
fortune; a letter had to be collected from long
undisciplined queues in chaotic post offices
— where actually extracting a letter felt like
winning the lottery. Eventually, near the end of
1978, I did pick up a letter from Dad at Poste
Restante, La Paz, Bolivia. It said just this: 'Come
in Number 2. Your time is up. Numbers 1, 3, 4
and 5 want you home for Christmas.'
It caught me. I was lonely and tired. After
nearly two years of wandering, I decided it was
time to go home.
What a shock it was, arriving at Heathrow (a
month and one excursion later) on a cold, bleak
January morning. My gift to Dad was an

avocado the size of his head. I had bought it in a Peruvian market the morning of my flight, and cradled it carefully in my hand luggage. The next day I met Dad for lunch and we went to a small bar across the road from his office. He took the avocado with us. But instead of talking to me, he used it as a talking-piece to chat up the waitress, the next table, a man at the bar, *everybody*, while I, in my alpaca jumper, silently fumed. Then he had to rush back for his next appointment.

Back in England I felt isolated and out of place; all my friends had gone to university and had made new friends. I told myself I had been to the University of Life, but from that moment I realised that in the quest for Dad's approval I had put down the foundations, like he had, of (not so cleverly) setting myself apart.

4

We are in the garden centre. Dad likes the tools and gloves and string and bird boxes. I watch him from a few aisles away. I notice he is not looking at the shelves any more. He is looking intently at the people. Every person that walks past him he looks up and down. Then he looks at me. I wave. His face breaks into a smile. He speeds over.

'I'm glad you waved,' he confesses, 'there were quite a few people who could have been you.'

★ ★ ★

'How old am I?' Dad asks again.

'How old am I?' I reply.

'You?'

'Yes. How old do you think I am?'

'I don't know.'

'I'm forty-eight,' I tell him.

'I'm more than three years older than you. How can you be catching me up?'

'I'm not catching you up.'

'You must be.'

'You're ninety-two.'

'I'm not ninety-two, I know that! Ninety-two-year-old men are dreary. I'm not one of those.'

'No, you're not one of those, Dad,' I laugh.

'My dogs don't treat me like that. We sleep together. We go to bed with our heads touching, side by side.'

Dad doesn't understand about Christmas, or why today there are cards all over his mantelpiece. He would like to throw them all out. As he has been doing with everything else in the house: on the street, or in the garden, piles of soggy books all over the lawn.

I read each of the cards out to him.

''Love Ken and Ruth.' You remember Ken, Dad; you sailed together. They lived in the next-door flat in Kennington. You remember.'

He shrugs, puts on a face.

''Happy Xmas to Tom! Love Bar.' She lived in France, you played bridge with her and Grevis. You remember Bar? Deep throaty laugh . . . No?'

He shrugs again.

And then I squawk in disbelief as I read out, ''Tom, Happy Christmas. Love, Francie and Jeremy Clarkson.' Jeremy Clarkson???!'

And, it is *the* Jeremy Clarkson. Dad can't remember, but my sister explains: once upon a time Dad used to employ Jeremy's to-be-wife, Francie. It doesn't surprise me he still receives a Christmas card — everyone who'd ever worked for Dad, especially the girls, loved him. And now I come to think about it, I do remember a man smoking a hundred cigarettes holding court in Dad's conservatory who Nicky said had just got a job on telly talking about cars.

Everyone loved Dad and he loved them in return, but there was a transaction. Dad loved to teach, and the by-product of this was to collect people-he-could-teach. There was always some protégé in the wings. The greater the challenge the better. There was absolutely no filter. Builders who couldn't build; gardeners who didn't garden; managing directors who failed to direct or manage anything. A steady stream of calamities and no-hopers and sometimes people who (as far as we could see) enjoyed his goodwill, let's say, *enormously*. Dad welcomed them all. They became Dad's project. And in later years, they became Dad and Stepmother's project. The worst of all of them, in our eyes — far worse even than young Colin who Dad found hanging out in the bus shelter opposite, who ended up living with them, downloading porn onto their computer, being lavishly funded with bikes, beer and baccy, and bringing his friends round to smoke and drink in Dad's shed — far, far, far worse than Colin was Charlene. And I am thinking of Charlene, because as I resume reading out Dad's Christmas cards, I realise I have been braced for the moment when I pick up the Christmas card with the stomach-turning italicised calligraphy, because that will be Charlene. And yet it doesn't come; I get to the end of the mantelpiece and there is no Christmas card from the cloyingly coy 'adopted daughter', Charlene.

★   ★   ★

Charlene *came into the family* as a young nurse who answered Stepmother's ad to look after her father in the last year of his life. When he died, Dad gave her a job in his company, which was now where Stepmother worked because it was now half her company too. Charlene was everything our stepmother wanted, and everything we were not. Someone she could train up (she *needed* training up apparently): 'I can teach her everything!' Stepmother shrilled with delight. They would go shopping to buy jackets with shoulder pads and gold buttons with anchors on them, and shoes with snaffly bits; Charlene would learn to wear pearls with her collar turned up. She was an excellent pupil. After becoming *one of the family* Charlene graduated to *adopted daughter* even though she had real live parents of her own; and so she thrived, Charlene: cute little nose poking out under Stepmother's wing. But, we all liked her. My sister Nicky *really* liked her. There was even a jokey plan for her to marry Tim. From my point of view, the good thing about Charlene was that she filled a role I didn't want, which took the heat off me. And so it went for a few years, Charlene's meteoric rise up the company and family ladder; curricular and extracurricular activities: cooking, embroidery, calligraphy, and how to be a real tough cookie in the boardroom.

So, when Charlene announced her engagement to a friend of Nicky's, it was accepted Stepmother would be organising the event and Dad would be paying for it. Only a bloody great bells-and-whistles wedding at St James-in-fucking-Piccadilly, with Rolls-Royces plural, and my poor sister head-bridesmaid dressed up as an apricot blancmange. The organisation of this pageant took Stepmother a year. The colour of the ribbon around the bridal bouquet matched the colour of the ribbon on the menu which in turn matched the colour of the ribbon on the invitation. I opted to be an usher in a Moss Bross suit. Yes! I am just so glad I am in *all* her wedding photos, ruining them.

Little things then bigger things began to dawn until, with the cold sweat of the dispossessed, Nicky and I realised that we, in jobspeak, had been made redundant. We smiled stiffly, the two ugly sisters, as Charlene's position and influence grew. And grew. Until Charlene announced she was going to live in Australia. Stepmother was mortified, but hallelujah, Charlene packed all her things — and Stepmother's heirloom gifts — and off she went. All that remained of Charlene were framed photographs in pride of place on the mantelpiece. Peace reigned, but then obliquely she popped into my life again, and it all came to a whopping great head.

I was house-sitting and writing a letter at Dad's desk when I noticed a blue airmail letter with some photographs jutting out. I knew who they were from by the nauseating calligraphy on the envelope. Against my better judgement I eased the photographs out knowing they'd be irksome, but innocent at that point as to how irksome they could possibly be. Good riddance I was thinking as I looked at a fat white Australian cat sitting on an expensive Australian settee. And then I saw it. In the top right-hand corner, almost out of shot. Yet UNMISTAKEABLE. My eyes couldn't stretch open wide enough. Because they were looking at the corner of my lost painting, *The Thames Triptych*. It had been the centrepiece of an exhibition I'd had in 1986, five years before. I had given it to Dad as a present for buying all the wine at the opening. He hung it in his office. And then after his aneurism — which kept him away from work for months — it vanished. All eight feet by four feet of it. Gone. Dad didn't know what happened to it. I asked everyone at Percy. I *thought* I asked Charlene. My sister *thought* she asked Charlene. But nobody seemed to know where it was. It was inexplicable.

I looked at the photograph again. The ochre-yellow glaze, the muddy-water swirl, the rusty prow of a Thames barge. The *incontestable* bespoke wooden frame. And slowly, after the shock, came the Nile-wide grin of satisfaction. I had her. At last I had her. After all these years. Undeniable 'proof'. Surely? Signed; sealed; posted; and delivered. Oh, the sweet, sweet certainty, and the gorgeous warm glow. Of being just about to be proved right. Ha! I would be vindicated.

My sister spluttered on the end of the phone with indignation. 'How on earth did it get there?' I should have been relieved. My painting! But I was frothing. And I wanted an explanation.

I rang Charlene in Australia, delicious righteousness and cold triumph in my voice. I was sure I had my quarry and there was no escape. *Wrong.* She had *rescued* it she said furiously, because no one wanted it! And I should be 'bloody grateful' to her for saving my feelings. She had found it in a skip. She hated the thing. It was just covering up a hole (must have been a bloody big hole) in her sitting-room wall. I said that wasn't my recollection. I said I remembered asking her if she had any idea where it was. I said Nicky remembered asking her. At which point I heard a clunk and the line went dead and I was talking to a satellite.

I called Nicky back. She remembered Charlene staying with her just before she left, with Nicky's house full of Charlene's crates with *Fragile* stickers on them, waiting to be shipped to Australia. Our minds boggled.

I couldn't wait to tell Dad, but when I finally spoke to him on the phone, there was a long silence.

'I'm sure there's been a misunderstanding,' he said.

'What do you mean, a *misunderstanding?!?*'

I explained again, clearly and carefully, that *somehow* the disappeared painting had ended up in Australia and was *covering up a hole* on Charlene's wall. But it was bafflingly clear he didn't want to know. Stepmother certainly didn't want to know. As far as Stepmother was concerned this was a reasonable explanation, and it was just me flying off the handle about Charlene again.

I was indignant. 'But I gave that painting to *you*, Dad,' I passionately exclaimed. 'It was the best painting I've done, it was huge and . . . ' And there I was, sounding thirteen.

'Daaa-arliing,' he said again, 'I'm sure there's been a simple misunderstanding.'

'But you didn't say it was a misunderstanding

when she came back from staying with me in Ireland and told you I was a slob!' I roar. 'Or when she turned Nicky's friends against her with all those stories! Or when — '

'Now! Please! STOP! Darling!'

And there it lay. Never to be spoken of. Ever again (by them). At my own (great) expense I had the painting collected from Charlene's ranch and delivered to a friend in Sydney. And Charlene's photograph remained in the front row, in her upturned lace collar, on the mantelpiece, smiling.

As I double-check Dad's Christmas cards, I am relieved there really is nothing from Charlene. Nicky tells me they stopped coming after Stepmother died.

★ ★ ★

I did try to steer myself through the vagaries of Dad's new life now so far from my understanding, and somehow find a place. But however hard I tried with Stepmother it invariably went wrong. I was late, or misheard the instructions, went to the wrong place, at the wrong time, trod on her cat, left the door open, lost their key, burnt her best pan, broke a glass, found an injured seagull, spilt wine on a cushion, left the tap on and flooded the bathroom. We would never be well matched, yet I knew it was I who had to make the call, because I missed Dad. I *had* to get on with Stepmother, so I did what people often do with people they dislike but are intimidated by: I sucked up. And for a while this was quite successful. Until the scales tipped just too far for me to stomach, and some misdemeanour would trip me up. The biggest setbacks always came when I was least expecting them. The time I left a William Carlos Williams poem on the answering machine, 'This is just to say / I have eaten / the plums / that were in / the icebox . . . '; annoying, I can see, but it was still a shock to hear Stepmother say, 'How bloody ridiculous!' before she slammed down the phone. In the thirty years I knew her, I don't think I ever heard her laugh, not a proper laugh, not a breath-catching, cheek-reddening, tear-streaming, stomach-clutching laugh; only ever hee-hee laughs from the front of her mouth, polite, controlled, fleeting. When I got married and lived in New Zealand, Stepmother for-warded my correspondence, crossing out my name and writing: 'Mrs Jonathan Thomson'. When I explained I was keeping my own name (now her name) and that I wasn't called Jonathan, she wrote straight back: 'I am far too busy to have time for all the long-winded palaver of writing out separate names. So no discussion and NO reply!'

I'm on a roll . . . The time Jonathan and I came back from New Zealand after being away for nearly two years, and were standing outside their front door surrounded by luggage. I could hardly wait to see Dad. I rang the bell preparing to go 'Ta-Ta-Ta-de-Rah!' We had been flying for nearly forty hours, we'd caught the Tube from Heathrow, the train from Waterloo, walked up the hill from Battle station, and finally we were there. They were expecting us. I could hear the dogs bark. The door opened.

'Ta-ta-ah . . . ah . . . ah . . . ah . . . '

No Dad in sight. I looked over Stepmother's shoulder. Maybe he was in the loo, or at the bottom of the garden. We brought our suitcases in, friendly and chatting politely. But still no Dad.

And she didn't mention him either. After five minutes I could stand it no longer and was compelled to ask.

'Oh. He's gone out,' Stepmother said breezily.

'Gone out? Where?'

'To see an architect.'

'To see an architect?' my voice already betraying me.

I tried to digest the information into something palatable, but could not, and there I was again, at the fountainhead of all my teenage rage.

'That is so bloody typical,' I hissed to Jonathan as we put our bags in the spare room. The horrible spare room she had chosen for us, which we hated, which she knew we hated, because it was right on the road, where the trucks thundered past, so you couldn't open the window to get any fresh air; and of course we had the frilly lace bedspread I was bound to stain with a pen or something worse. Not the attic room, of course, where we used to sleep, with the big window opening onto the garden with breeze, and quiet, and birdsong. No, not the attic room, because it was out of bounds now, because it was 'such a palaver'. But my rant to Jonathan was not about the room, it was because

461

I was *so* disappointed. Even though I knew this was playing into her hands. And I was particularly upset this time, and yes, *jealous*, because I knew when bloody Charlene and her husband came back from bloody Australia, Guess Who bloody drove all the way to bloody Heathrow to pick them up. No train and lugging luggage up the hill for them. Not in a godzillion years would Stepmother have allowed Dad to have an architect's appointment if bloody Charlene was coming 'home'. And I bet I bloody know who booked the bloody appointment with the bloody architect in the bloody first place.

By the time Dad got home, more than three hours later, I had fumed myself up into an internal nuclear combustion of seething disappointment and fury. My jaw was rigid from the effort of keeping the poison from escaping. But it was written all over my face. I was incensed and sulking and proving her right again. For I was the difficult one, the jealous one, the confrontational one. I was the pain in the arse.

'Oh, darling! Don't go and spoil it,' Dad said when he saw me.

'But, Dad! Didn't you *know* we were coming home? Didn't you *want* to see us?'

'Of course I *want* to see you! Daaarling!'

And so she won. Again. For thirty years I kept falling into the same trap. And remained confounded. That he could not see. What. She. Was. Like.

PART 8

TO MAJOR TOM

1

At the end of 1988 some news arrives. Dad has received a letter from Aung San Suu Kyi's husband, Michael Aris. Aris has just returned from Burma and has been given the task of tracking Dad down to give him an important letter from Rangoon. The letter, Aris explains, is from 'one of his wife, Suu's, worthy stalwarts', who has been trying to trace Dad for the last ten years. Inside the envelope is a photograph of a young Burmese AFO soldier wearing a black beret and a red armband with a white star. It is Tun Gyaw. Formerly Tha Gyaw, as he explains. Who worked side by side with Dad in Weasel all those years ago. They had been inseparable. 'With great remembrance I am writing you few words. More than forty years we have not seen each other. I hope we may have chance to meet before we die.'

In response to Dad's reply, Tun Gyaw's next letter arrives in immaculate handwriting, dated 27 March 1989, describing how his small group of comrades have held Force 136 get-togethers every year without fail on 27 March, Burma's Resistance Day. One is Mahn Win Maung, president of Burma from 1957 to 1962; another U Tha Kyaw, former ambassador to the UK. Tun Gyaw recounts how in 1949 he went underground to fight against the government with the People's Volunteer Force (originally the PVO — set up by Aung San for his disaffected BNA)

465

but they surrendered in 1958 without achieving any of their demands. For the last twenty years he has been working in a textile factory as a manager. 'I am sure you won't think of me very sentimental just because I send you this letter on the 27th of March.' Paradoxically, 27 March is now Myanmar Armed Forces Day, which marks another occupation, but by their own military junta. It is also Michael Aris's birthday, and it will become the unspeakably sad day he will die of cancer, a decade later, aged fifty-three, having been refused a visa to visit his wife one last time. Suu Kyi, with such strong support from the people as the daughter of Aung San — who is all but sanctified by the Burmese as the father of independence — was unable to leave Burma knowing the military junta would never allow her to return. Like her father, she pays a high personal price for her commitment to her country: unable to say goodbye to her husband, and parted from both her sons.

Dad did not meet Tun Gyaw again. Stepmother did not fly, or go in a lift for that matter, and he would not go (or would not have been allowed to go) without her. I volunteered myself and Jonathan as envoys. Tun Gyaw responded, 'The sure prospect of meeting your daughter and family in a few months will serve as a great solace to us.'

★ ★ ★

By the 1980s, having been run Soviet-style since 1962, Burma was one of the most impoverished countries in the world. Widespread unrest was mounting, fuelled by head of state General Ne Win's disastrous economic strategies. Student demonstrations were growing in size and frustration. Pro-democracy rallies began to spread across the country; monks, farmers and workers joined students, and government buildings were set on fire. The military swiftly retaliated, and blood began to spill on the streets. On 23 July 1988, Ne Win resigned promising a multi-party system; however, Sein Lwin, the man he appointed to head the new government, was known as the Butcher of Rangoon. Demonstrators burned effigies of Ne Win and Sein Lwin in coffins decorated with de-monetised banknotes. On 3 August martial law was imposed, banning gatherings of more than five people from 8 p.m. to 4 a.m. On 8 August 1988, thousands poured onto the streets in a national protest and general strike. It would become known as the 8-8-88 Uprising. Armed troops surrounded the demonstrators with orders that guns were not to shoot upwards. One of the protestors was a teenager called Hla Oo, who some years later wrote a blog of his experience that day.

Hla Oo describes the crowd shouting political slogans and singing the national anthem, when a rumour of more troops arriving sweeps through and the crowd begins to disperse in fear. At this point government agents in the crowd spread news that a State Council meeting has begun, that democracy is near and that the army is going to join the demonstrators. This keeps the huge crowd in front of the Rangoon Town Hall waiting expectantly while the army barricades all the exits to the surrounding streets. Hla Oo finds himself together with an older man and two schoolgirls — the girls are so scared they won't let go of the hem of his shirt. The army cuts off the city's power and everything descends into darkness.

We were all horribly shaking with fears. And the bayonets at the end of their rifles were horribly flashing in the moonlight. The girls asked me what we were going to do if the soldiers started shooting at us. I had not a bloody idea so I just answered them to run to escape. The crowd around us had already accepted the fact that the soldiers were really going to fire soon and some people started crying out aloud while some even sung the anthem louder and louder.

Hla Oo sees a gap between two soldiers so they make a break for it, and get through. Once out of the corral, they climb the barricades, scramble over rows of barbed wire, and eventually get to the backyard of the American Embassy, joining twenty-two others. From there they hear gunfire and the prolonged bursts of automatic machine guns, followed by screaming and the cries of people begging the soldiers not to shoot.

The troops had rapidly tightened their constricting hold of the besieged crowd by shooting anyone on the streets and quickly advancing their attacking lines inward towards the Town Hall where the epicentre of the huge protesting crowd was. Army had even issued hundreds of 12-gauge shotguns to the shooting troops on the front lines to enhance the effectiveness of close-range killings. Conservative estimates put the death toll at 10,000 at least.

Even though we all sat together really close and holding each other's hands tight in the darkness our bodies were shaking with sadness and surprise and fright and anger altogether.

The older man tells Hla Oo to remember the day and time, and never forget it. 'The time was 15 minutes before 12 o'clock on my watch. 11:45 in the night of August 8, 1988.'

The dark screams of the hapless people brutally slaughtered in the dark 8888 night might be like the boiling of hot oil in the cauldrons of the Great Hell we Buddhists believe in. I'd never heard such horrible deep screams ever before in my young life and I still believed I would never hear them again in the future . . . My whole body was uncontrollably shaking as I tried to control my busting anger . . .

After a few hours they hear trucks and the sound of fire engines washing down the streets; then other trucks speeding past the embassy, and the desperate cries for help.

469

As their usual practice to hide the mass slaughter the Army immediately sent in the sand-filled open trucks to remove the dead and dying from the scene. The bodies some of which were still alive were then taken to the sand-filled naval barges waiting at the Rangoon Naval Base and then dumped at the crocodile-infested waters where the Rangoon River meets the sea.

They remain all night in the American Embassy yard, too frightened to leave. At daybreak holding each other's hands they leave the compound. The thoroughly cleaned streets gleam shiny black, and this is the moment Hla Oo begins to comprehend the chilling truth of the brutal nature of the military government.

Two days later soldiers fire into Rangoon General Hospital killing the nurses and doctors tending the wounded. Two more days and Sein Lwin resigns. On 19 August Ne Win's biographer, Dr Maung Maung, is put in charge. The demonstrations resume. On 26 August, one day after Tun Gyaw writes his first letter to Dad, Aung San Suu Kyi addresses a crowd of half a million in front of the Shwedagon pagoda calling for a democratic government. Maung Maung imposes an even fiercer crackdown, and the country is back under military rule. Elections are promised in 1989, yet hundreds of opposition activists are detained, including Aung San Suu Kyi. Reports of torture, beatings and imprisonment filter out. Students flee to the jungle area near the Thai border, only to come under attack by the Burmese Army.

This is the situation as Jonathan and I wait in Bangkok, about to make our way to the Burmese border. In our luggage is an expensive top-of-the-range short-wave radio, the gift Dad has chosen for Tun Gyaw. We linger in our hotel room, not sure what to do. Then we hear that the borders have closed. On 20 July 1989, Suu Kyi is put under house arrest. Party members of Suu Kyi's National League for Democracy are detained and imprisoned. I call Dad. He thinks our presence would be a huge risk and bring dangerous and unwelcome attention to Tun Gyaw. He doesn't think we should go. I feel crestfallen. Somehow cowardly. Added to this, there is no possibility of communicating to Tun Gyaw to tell him we are not coming. It is desperately disappointing. But I know Dad is right.

The awful, awful thing is, we never hear from Tun Gyaw again.

★ ★ ★

In the postponed 1990 election, with Suu Kyi still under house arrest, her NLD party won eighty per cent of the seats. As we know, the military refused to hand over power and she was detained under house arrest in her family home on Inya Lake, Yangon, for nearly fifteen of the following twenty-one years.

I still have the short-wave radio we were unable to deliver; it's our kitchen radio, we listen to it every day and I often think of Tun Gyaw. I wrote a number of times to the address we had in Rangoon; I have tried to trace him or his family through various channels, but have never received a reply. I have asked Robert Taylor to enquire of news of him on his trips to Rangoon, but he has had no success. The closest I have come is an email from Suu Kyi's personal assistant, Dr Tin Mar Aung, acknowledging my letter, but nothing came of it.

Dad stuck Tun Gyaw's photograph to the back of a cornflakes packet; beneath it he wrote:

> When I arrived back with Tun Gyaw off the plane they insisted on separating us even when I explained we had been the closest of colleagues in continued danger and that he had supported me throughout. We could not eat together — because he was Burmese and I was British, unbelievable these days but was imperative in those days . . . I could not stand it. He and I did brilliantly TOGETHER. Forty years later I received a letter saying 'I hope we can meet before we die.' I cried helplessly.

Dad cries a lot. He collapses into his tears. Tears for the loss of a past that cannot be revisited. Tears for the loss of people he will never see again. And he is experiencing another bereavement, tears for the loss of him.

Tears of sadness foment into tears of frustration. Things won't work. People won't come. Water won't boil. And there's nothing for him to do!

'I just want to help someone,' he says, 'all my life I've helped someone.' His voice the merest whisper, dry leaves scraping in the wind.

2

For Dad's seventieth birthday Stepmother bought him a gold tooth-pick from Asprey's. She showed us. It was in an Asprey's gift box with a hinged lid. She brimmed with pride. The toothpick was hall-marked and everything. We looked nonplussed. She explained she bought it because Dad was always cleaning his teeth with banknotes. Which was true, and *every* time he proclaimed the virtue of said banknote as the tooth-cleaning instrument par excellence: strong, malleable, glides through teeth, picks up every morsel on its edge, and usually at hand in his pocket. Tenners were better than fivers, stiffer (apparently), twenties better still.

'What a wonderful idea!' we lied, sniggering snidely behind her back that she did not know him better.

On the day, when he opened it, he hadn't a clue what it was. She explained it to him.

'Aaaaah,' he finally twigged, then tried it out and bent it. It got lost the same day.

Patrick's present was a blue sweatshirt he'd had screen-printed with 'Let Me Percy Coutt You' in bold letters on the front.

★ ★ ★

It was a long way from Roos Hall to our little house in Fareham, but I do remember Mum's mother coming to visit once. Granddad records it on 13 July 1967: *Very warm. Jane's mother arr. about noon, she giving me the impression to make myself scarce?* The photograph says it all. Mum leaning towards her mother, wanting to please, asking what she would like: tea? A cold drink? Was she warm enough? A broken wall behind her and the scruffy lean-to. We look like we are behaving ourselves, thank God. Snow White and Rose Red, my brother and I on wonky deckchairs. I'm reading a Rupert Bear annual. A safe distance away is Granny, shrouded against the sun, or a draught, or us . . . She had probably never sat in the garden of a terraced house in all her life.

The distance and disconnect between Mum and her mother remained. Mum could not have recorded her annual visits more briefly: *Beccles, saw Mother*; or *Saw Mother, no problem*. It was always a whistle-stop, she hated going and couldn't get back quick enough. Except maybe on 8 August 1981: *Left 9.45 a.m. 11.30 train to Norwich. Mother very pleased. Her eyes showed softness and love first time in years altho' old and faded. Poor old soul. She looked so frail and old, it's really v. sad. If only she could let one into her world. Had coffee and snack and straight back.* Then on 15 September 1984, Mum wrote: *Princess of Wales had 2nd son — Prince Harry. Mother died 2 p.m.*

Katherine Wybrew Suckling's last will and testament was her final and unexpected cutting blow. Mum had never questioned the rule of male primogeniture: her elder brother had long since taken on (and sold) Roos Hall. But Mum had always assumed, in the same tradition, that her mother's jewellery, her grandmother's and her great-grandmother's before that, would one day come to her. Yet her mother's will clearly specified: 'To my daughter-in-law, my pearl necklace and earrings and all my other personal jewellery' Mum, her only daughter, was bequeathed a set of china and, rather cruelly in respect of her two-bedroom bungalow, a four-poster bed.

★　★　★

After the family picnic at the amphitheatre at Bradfield in 1979, eight years pass before Dad sees Mum again. It is 10 January 1987, the day I get married at Brixton Registry Office at 9 a.m. It is a high-spirited and spontaneous occasion; I have, after all, only known Jonathan for three weeks. Dad takes everyone to breakfast at a cafe just off Sloane Square for champagne and scrambled eggs. I keep glancing nervously across at Mum and Dad sitting together (Stepmother has not come and I am grateful to her); I am not sure what I expect to happen, but it is Dad who looks awkward, and it is Mum who, twelve years after their divorce, carries off this rare outing together with grace.

Dad sees Mum again at Tim and Emma's wedding, and at Patrick and Sarah's, but it is another ten years before it is thinkable to propose A Family Christmas Together. *Everyone*: Mum, Dad, Stepmother, brothers, sister, in-laws, partners, kids. And the miracle happens. Even though Stepmother is not feeling very well. Everyone comes to our place in Redchurch Street near the top of Brick Lane, and for the very first time in more than twenty years we are all in the same room, and Jonathan cooks, and we eat and play games and pull crackers, and Mum is belle of the ball and twinkles and laughs and wears her paper crown skew-whiff and wins musical chairs, and there is a spark of that indescribable magical something that pings between her and Dad, which everyone notices.

Dad sees Mum one more time. It is another family Christmas, this time at Dad and Stepmother's house; and I am exceedingly anxious because I really didn't want Mum to see their home with the posh polished furniture and antiques, and the fat damask curtains with double lining, and the silver ornaments, the gleaming walnut table, the Brassoed door knocker, and everything I imagine Mum might have wanted once, but never had in her under-heated thin-curtained bungalow. But Mum is bigger than me, for she brims with politeness and smiles with fun and dignified gratitude for being included, which is heartbreaking enough, and then, when we give each other presents she gives Dad the perfectly pitched, not too expensive, four red spotty handkerchieves. And he roars 'Aaaaah!' and then throws them at her, that she remembered! And immediately old sourpuss stands up and announces something to break it up, because she can't let them have even that, and there is not a flicker across Mum's face, for I am watching carefully, and I am thinking that after everything, after everything that has happened, and even through this illness that is raging through her that she knows will carry her away, How On Earth does she manage that? But these are her years, the very few that she has left, and she is filling them with good things for us to remember her by.

★ ★ ★

Mum died just before the Christmas of 2001, at seventy-six, of breast cancer which eventually went into her bones. In her last ten years she gave us back the best thing she possibly could, her real self. What seemed impossible to us all happened, thirty years of bitterness, anger and resentment began to evaporate away, and that seam of fathomless strength of hers rose up and carried her through her illness and all its associated difficulties with selfless courage and a surprising measure of peace. She volunteered for various things, stewarded for the National Trust, went on cultural outings, did the *Telegraph* crossword every day and lived with her naughty cat. We had family picnics, and went for long walks. Her wicked sense of humour came back, her love of books, her passion for travel; it seemed so harsh that no sooner had she dealt with one demon, there was another, more unconquerable one, to face. It was terrible watching it: a bone in her leg reinforced with pins that didn't mend; a weeping boil on her face that never closed so she had to wear a bib; a mouthful of perennial ulcers so painful she had to drink with a straw.

It seemed such a very long journey we'd made. Her little bungalow, home for things that have borne witness: the gluggle jug; the 'Please Remember Don't Forget' still hanging on the bathroom wall; the modesty-tent towels we used in Spain; her Indian pith helmet; the copy of *The World of Pooh* she read to us when we were young with the map of '100 Aker Wood' and 'trap for Heffalumps' and 'Bee Tree' inside the cover; and the *Just So Stories* with its engravings and illuminated first letters of each chapter; her favourite was 'The Cat that Walked by Himself', and most of her life she had to. 'Hear and attend and listen; for this be-fell and be-happened and became and was, O my Best Beloved.'

★ ★ ★

And now she has arrived here. With her eldest daughter in her small sitting room with her small coal fire hardly licking at the cold December air, and we are friends, and in spite of a little mutual awkwardness there is kindness in the room. But she needs to say something. And she points to a small scar, hardly visible, on my forehead and apologises for it. It is so long buried it catches me completely unaware. And at that moment I realise what she has carried all these years. Not just bitterness and anger, but regret too. I had milked that wound, horribly. Got my pound of flesh and more. In a fight at the height of her breakdown she had brought down a flimsy side table over my head. Everything cracked, and the table with it. As the blood poured down my face

I marched to the bus stop brazening out the stares for everyone to see, then got on the bus, and went to Fareham. I stayed at my boyfriend's parents' house, refusing to go home, until my school knew about it, until the whole bloody world knew about it.

Mum says sorry. For something that happened in 1974. And I say sorry too. And I am catapulted into a place I was not prepared for, and my eyes fill with tears; she knows I'm like Dad, I cry easily, but she doesn't, and a look flickers between us and then we look down, because she is made of different stuff and we don't do this, and it embarrasses me, and it is also the edge of a precipice, and I pick up the cat.

* * *

Hardly anyone came to Mum's funeral. She had few friends. None of her extended family were there. Nicky and I were so glad she never knew that her revered first cousin, CBE, Knight of the Realm, respectable diplomat, ex-ambassador to Iraq, her father's brother's son, was too busy to attend: a prior arrangement that couldn't be broken, lunch as it turned out with Mum's niece an hour up the road.

But then nor was Dad there, either.

* * *

Patrick, Nicky, Tim and I sit in Mum's bungalow and begin to sort through her things. We find the

480

box of slides and the Bakelite projector. In her bureau the newspaper cuttings she'd kept; deaths, family marriages, posh yellowing wedding invitations including her own; a letter from her brother beginning 'Frankly your letter is not worth commenting on'; her honeymoon memorabilia; a menu from Trieste; and the newspaper articles about Dad accompanied by a small note in her hand, 'For old times' sake otherwise even the good years will not count for anything.' Then we come across a fat wad of cuttings about Ahmad Shah Massoud. We are perplexed for a moment. Then it dawns. This must be the MI6 work she *never* discussed. Massoud: poet, scholar, guerrilla, leader against the Taliban, the Afghan mujahideen resistance commander who, during the Soviet invasion, defeated the Red Army nine times. Massoud was assassinated by two al-Qaeda suicide bombers two days before the 11 September attacks. He had warned America of a serious Islamic terrorist attack, and his killing was a sign of the magnitude of what was to come. Some suspect it might well even have been the signal to set the plan in motion. The loss of Massoud cut off America's channels in Afghanistan, for as one congressman pointed out, Massoud would have been the man they would have turned to in the crisis. Mum's newspaper cuttings lie side by side, ex-guerrilla Massoud, ex-guerrilla Tom, and caught up amongst them, a stray sprat in the trawl net — a small square photograph on which she had written 'Roos Hall, the Dolomite'. It is the 1939 Dolomite Roadster, a two-door coupé, with a straight six-cylinder engine and triple SU carbs, and one of only 200 made. You can just make out the gorgeous sweep of the automobile's running board scrolling above the wheel, mirroring the curve of the great lawn. This was Mum's strange world before Dad, before Trieste, before Ceylon, but not one she could have been closely attached to, for it had only ever sent her away.

★ ★ ★

Six months after Mum died, I pulled open a drawer and noticed her hanky there, the telltale trim of folded lace. I picked it up. Unfolded it. Her smell rushed up to me; laundered yet full of that inexpressible particular thing, that molecule mix. It shocked me and I wasn't ready for it. I brought her handkerchief to my face. Which was enough to bring me to my knees. And I inhaled. And I inhaled. And I inhaled. Until she was gone.

3

Mum has died; two weeks have passed and still Dad hasn't rung. Nothing. Not a word from him, or Stepmother. My disbelief overflows into a virulent phone call. What *could* he say? Dad wants to know.

'You could say, I'm sorry. You could have a cry with us, Dad. It's our mum.'

'I couldn't have *done* anything.'

'I know you couldn't have *done* anything! Nobody was asking you to *do* anything. You can't always fix everything! Sometimes we just need you to be there. Not to do anything, just to be our dad.'

He passes the phone over. He passes the phone over at the worst possible moment and I am speaking with my stepmother. She says she thought he should have phoned us too. And I bite my tongue for the zillionth time because why hadn't she as the Controller Of Everything suggested it; why hadn't she made him?

Give me a problem, Dad would so often guilelessly invite.

Your wife.

★ ★ ★

I knew Dad was getting old, he had just had his eighty-second birthday; and I knew he was worried about Stepmother, who had been given her own dismal diagnosis. And I had judged him harshly. Later, in his desk, I find pages and pages, and pages, of handwritten false starts: The Letter to The Children after their mother's death — which he never sent. The sentences repeat and repeat, constant rewrites and crossings-out, different ways of putting it; he says he is not sure Mum would have wanted him at her funeral. But I know she would. And I am surprised at what he has written, because I really thought he had forgotten everything. It was Primo Levi who said we forget our essential fragility.

'Dearest Children, I am writing to the four of you with much to say but not knowing how to say it.' He starts again, addressing us each individually. He says he should have tried to explain why he and Mum separated, 'In our early days we loved each other very much, but I was not the brilliant young army colonel with a DSO that she married'; he says he undermined the family security by resigning from the army to start another life, 'from then on I was not the same person that Jane married'.

He says everyone thought he was foolish but he knew he would be a disaster as a peacetime colonel. Then he crosses it all out. He writes that when his mother died he took his father in, and although Granddad was a kind and helpful man it was 'a thoughtless mistake which I continued to make often'. Round and round he goes, trying to explain; Mum, he says, resented our affection for Granddad and the attention it took from her, 'Her main complaint against me was that I isolated her from the family, leaving all the work to her and collecting all the attention myself — which was true but difficult to put right.' He mentions buying the house in Wickham without discussing it with her. Then back to Granddad, then, 'My problem was the difficulty in earning a living once I left the army.'

You children were growing up and I was not making enough money for us to live without getting into trouble. ~~Your mother was being isolated by your father and grandfather.~~ Your mother had the chores and your father and grandfather had most of your attention it was frustrating and unfair, but I was thoughtless of her. She began to realise that we were not making enough money to survive . . . we were never going to pay for schooling and live as we expected . . .

I feel his frustration, the headache of trying to fairly, squarely, coherently, put twenty years of misfortune down, worrying away at it, searching for the right tone he cannot seem to find. He starts again, back to him distracting us away from Mum, back to not enough money, back to all his fault. 'The strain was so much she got some release by putting bricks through your grandfather's window.' He says he began 'living in an old Ford van, job hunting and coming home at weekends, but the tensions built up . . . It was not till later I realised it was my fault.' Dad is not at home in the past, but he manages to get to the end of the page.

In deference to Jane I have never discussed it with you, and I only tell you all this to excuse myself. These confessions help me a bit but not much. My thoughts include you all now and in your childhood which must have been handicapped by our separation. Your mother had such pride and dignity she did not accept help easily. I hope none of you will have her pride and not let me help you. When I am gone cry for both of us.

Your loving father, Tom

4

Tim has reported Dad by letter to the DVLA. Which, to be fair, is overdue, because Dad's driving has become dangerous. He doesn't bother looking in the mirror any more and refuses to stop if he can see the coast is clear. He drives too fast and he drives too slow. Nor does he bother about parking. A few days ago he drove straight through a hedge into a field. 'Lucky!' he exclaimed, roaring with laughter, telling everyone he has Irish luck, his mother always said so. My sister and I glance at each other; he hasn't mentioned his mother for forty years.

The DVLA has written to say he has to take a driving test. He is incensed. 'Ridiculous! Bloody cheek!' Why have they written to him? He has been driving for seventy years! We book him some lessons before the test, but he is unteachable. We test him on the Highway Code.

'What does that mean, Dad?'

He makes a face.

'No entry. And what's that? Come on, Dad.'

'Oh, you know . . . Arrows!' he responds petulantly.

'Give way to oncoming vehicles.'

'Easy for you,' he snorts derisively, 'you've got the book!'

There is truth in that; pages and pages of signs and we don't know half of them. My sister takes him to the test. Because Dad *knows* how to drive, he isn't concerned in the slightest.

'Do you drive on motorways?' the attractive female examiner enquires.

'Oh yes,' Dad says, showing off. He hasn't driven on a motorway for ten years.

'A-roads?' she continues, marking off the last answer on her clip board.

'Oh yes,' he says proudly.

'And local roads?' she asks.

Dad's expression is incredulous. 'Well, you won't get very far if you don't drive on local roads!' he says.

Nicky smiles inwardly for even the examiner has to concede the point.

Then she makes him touch his toes. He doubles over, holding both feet, easy as pie, and stays there.

'Are you all right?' she asks, slightly alarmed.

'Oh yes,' he replies, 'perfectly.'

'You can come up now,' she says.

'Ah, I was enjoying the view,' he replies, tipping his head slightly to pretend to look up her skirt, thinking he was being funny. The test goes badly, he can't identify a single sign, he can't reverse, he doesn't use his indicator; but he is completely happy with it. So when the letter arrives to say his licence has been revoked he is shocked and absolutely devastated. He cannot believe it. 'My car! My lovely little red car!' Then he puts a big felt-tip-pen note on his front door: 'Tom Carew is going back to Ireland.'

★　★　★

488

There is an added pathos to the Jedburgh reunion which takes place in May 2006; with numbers dwindling so quickly, it has been decided this will be the last. But no one anticipated Aubrey Trofimov would expire sitting up at the hotel bar before we'd even begun. 'Trof' had arrived early and was having a drink with his son when he just fell off his chair. I am not sure whether to mention this to Dad, but decide not to because the general consensus, Jedburgh-style, is to carry on. John Sharp is here looking as trim and proper as ever, and Harry Verlander, but Ron Brierley isn't with us any more, nor is Dick Rubinstein. By now Dad's dementia is quite evident, yet not a flicker crosses John Sharp's face when Dad loads up the pockets of his suit with the meat straight from his lunch plate, covered in gravy, to take home to his dogs. After all these years, nothing has changed, John's affection and loyalty to Dad is absolute.

This time the reunion is in Bloomsbury and we are staying at the Bonnington Hotel. It is not ideal: for a start, Dad's room and mine are not together, not even on the same floor and it's a big hotel; but worse, instead of keys we have swipe cards, which is a disaster because I know Dad will never get the hang of it. I check the whereabouts of our rooms. Miles of corridor separate us. Left turns and right turns. I beg Reception to give us two rooms with doors at least in sight of each other, but unbelievably there is nothing they can do.

I know that:
1) He won't take his swipe card when he leaves his room.

2) He won't know how to get back in.
3) He won't be able to explain what has happened.
4) He won't remember what room.
5) If I write it all down for him, he won't remember to take that with him, either.
6) He will DEFINITELY have left his room before I come and get him in the morning, because he gets bored very quickly, and I won't be there to keep reminding him to stay in it.

Not even I can use the swipe card. You don't swipe it in then open the door, you have to swipe it in, then take it out, and then open the door. It takes me ages to work out. Sometimes it unlocks, sometimes it doesn't. We are doomed. I try to explain everything to him carefully. He looks at me, blankly. I give up. We sit on his bed. He eats all the free biscuits on his tray. I make him tea. I make him promise not to leave the room. He promises. I write out a big sign, 'Tom wait here for Keggie.' I kiss him goodnight. He looks confused. I tell him I will come and get him in the morning. I walk down the corridor, half laughing, half shaking my head, I turn right, I turn left, up some stairs, turn right again, down another corridor-mile, until about ten minutes later, I finally find my room.

It's after midnight, I am in bed watching *Later . . . with Jools Holland* and Corinne Bailey Rae is singing 'Put Your Records On'. She is wearing some kind of silky slip and is somewhere between coy and beguiling and I am thinking of

Dad because he would love Corinne Bailey Rae, in the same way he adored Sade. So it takes me a few moments to realise that the voice in my imagination, behind her sweet songbird voice, is a real voice, a breathy incoherent whispery muttering, a voice that sounds an awful lot like Dad's. Suddenly I'm alert, I turn down the TV and tune my ears in. There it is again, the otherworldly murmurings of a very old man, just like Dad, right outside my door. Which is impossible. Because Dad is five corridors, three left turns, four right turns, and a whole floor away. I jump out of bed, open the door, look left. It's Dad! Talking into a corridor phone.

He turns to look at me. 'Oh good,' he says.

'Dad! What are you doing??'

'I can't get into my room and I don't know what they're saying,' he says, pointing to the receiver in his hand.

'I'm sure it's mutual,' I say, picking up the phone. I explain down the telephone to the night porter that everything is all right.

It is an absolute *miracle* in Dad's haphazard wanderings along corridors and up stairs, that the phone he chose to pickup was right outside my door. And that I was awake to hear him. His Irish mother told him he was lucky; she meant it seriously, clairvoyantly. That he had Irish luck. And he has. Dad is used to luck, it is completely normal to him, and he expects it. His favourite motto is 'Luck comes to the prepared mind'. For him, it isn't pure luck that I opened the door and just appeared when he needed me, it is how things are. I walk him back and put him to bed.

I leave a bigger sign on his door, 'DON'T GO OUT! WAIT FOR KEGGIE!' then go back to set my alarm an hour earlier to make sure I am up before he is.

The next day we have lunch at the Special Forces Club in Knightsbridge. The Jeds call it The Club. There is no sign on the door or anything to tell you it's there. It was founded by surviving SOE agents just after the war. Its motto is 'Spirit of Resistance'. Everyone is wearing their Special Forces tie with the Special Forces wings, and we are having drinks and sandwiches in the bar.

All the way up the stairs are photographs of SOE agents, but it is the women who catch my eye: the beautiful face of Noor Inayat Khan, the first female wireless operator sent to France; denounced and caught by the Gestapo, she steadfastly resisted interrogation. She was transported to Germany in 1943 and executed at Dachau on 13 September 1944. And here is Eliane Plewman, radio operator for the Monk circuit in the Jura, denounced, caught, and executed with Noor. Hannah Szenes, caught near the border with Hungary, given away by her SOE transmitter whose code she would not reveal even when they brought her own mother to her cell, threatening her with torture. Hannah was executed by firing squad on 7 November 1944. She kept a diary right until the end. It read, 'In the month of July, I shall be 23. I played a number in a game. The dice have rolled. I have lost . . . I loved the warm sunlight.'

Dad has begun sticking up pictures of semi-naked women all over his sitting-room walls. He cuts them out from magazines and newspapers. Nothing too risqué, bosoms, bums and bikini-clad buxom beauties, oiled thighs and long legs, cleavages presented provocatively, lips pouting, eyes come-hithering. Nothing explicit or vulgar, but girls and lots of them. There is even one pinned to the front door, pavement side.

'What do you want these up for, Dad?'

'Why not?'

I'm stumped for a second. 'Well, maybe all your ladies coming in to look after you won't like it.'

He thinks this is some kind of politically correct feminist disapproval, because next time I come, amongst the pin-up ladies, there are an equal number of pin-up pictures of six-pack men.

'Why on earth do you want these, Dad?' I ask incredulous.

'I don't! Everyone complained about the ladies. So I put up some men.'

I laugh. 'But why do you want all the naked ladies?'

He looks at me in disbelief as though I haven't a single functioning brain cell.

'Because they're beautiful!' he says.

PART 9

BUT, DADDY, THAT'S NOT YOUR NAME

1

In 2000, a book came out called *Jihad!* by Tom Carew. Everyone bought Dad a copy. At the time we thought it just a coincidence. This Tom Carew was ex-SAS and his book was the daredevil account of his activities as an undercover guerrilla agent in Afghanistan, training insurgents against Soviet invaders in the 1980s. Which was another coincidence, being the line of work Dad knew a bit about. Dad began to read it, then threw it away in disgust.

'Bogus!' he pronounced emphatically. 'You would never talk like that if you were really in there, doing it,' he said. 'The man's a fake.'

'Come on. How do you know, Dad?'

'Because you don't do it like that,' he laughed sarcastically. 'And you don't boast.' The blurb on the cover called Carew 'a latter-day Lawrence of Arabia', which would have really got Dad's goat.

Jihad! was serialised in the *Sunday Times* and friends kept sending Dad various Tom Carew articles. It became an international bestseller, Dad pooh-poohing from the word Go. We thought it was sour grapes. On 10 September 2001, the paperback edition came out. The following day, al-Qaeda terrorists trained in Afghanistan hijacked and crashed two passenger jets into the World Trade Center and another into the Pentagon. TV stations needed expert comment and Tom Carew was on hand to give it. There were appearances on CNN and the BBC. Book sales went sky-high. At one point, *Jihad!* (even though it hadn't been published outside the UK) was the second-biggest seller on Amazon in the US.

Tom Carew was eventually outed in November 2001, on Jeremy Paxman's *Newsnight*. Live on air. George Eykyn was the reporter who named and shamed him as Philip Sessarego, hoaxer, fantasist, con man, charlatan. Cornered, with the cameras rolling, Sessarego insisted he was SAS, and boasted he had a team of eleven Albanian bodyguards who would shoot first and ask questions later. Then he punched the cameraman and ran away.

Sessarego had borrowed Dad's name, from we'll never know where (archived SOE files, Second World War Special Forces reports, coincidence?), and invented an identity for himself. Then he hired a ghostwriter and got all the attention he'd ever craved. In *Jihad!* he claimed to be the first British soldier sent into Afghanistan to assess the mujahideen's capabilities and train them, but it turned out he was an SAS wannabe who had failed the selection process, twice. He tried to join the Territorial Army, but failed that selection too, so he did odd jobs for them like pretending to be the enemy in training exercises. Since he was a boy Sessarego had been fascinated by stories of guerrilla warfare, the Special Forces and the SAS, but the closest he got to the action was the mercenary circuit of dangerous jobs for ex-soldiers.

In 1991 he faked his own death in a bomb

explosion in Croatia (purportedly, to avoid child maintenance) but was later found alive and well and living as 'Philip Stevenson', a new identity, he insisted, given to him by British intelligence. As far as Dad was concerned it was his glorifying descriptions of killing Afghan and Soviet soldiers that gave him away: 'The butt of my Kalashnikov was pressed into my shoulder and I let go a long, violent burst at less than two metres' range . . . the weapon bucked and climbed. They had no chance . . . all three were dying as they flopped awkwardly into the dust'; it just took the press a bit longer to discover it.

Meanwhile . . . unsuspecting, and casually watching *Newsnight* that night, at home with her husband, believing that her father had been killed ten years previously in a bomb explosion in Croatia (the body had been too badly damaged for identification, but his papers and belongings had been found close by), was Claire Sessarego, the real daughter of the fake Tom Carew. She saw her father in front of her eyes.

I will never forget the night Ian switched on *Newsnight*. There, looking as well as ever, was my dad. I remember repeating it over and over to Ian: 'That's my dad . . . ' Firstly there was just shock that he was actually alive. Then pure relief flooded through me. All I could think about was how wonderful it was that he had somehow not been blown up in this bomb after all. I watched the programme in tears, with everything I had longed to tell him crowding into my mind.

Then I began wondering what he was doing on TV.

Her emotions slowly changed as she realised what he had done, and thought of the years he had never contacted her. As she watched in disbelief it slowly became clear that the programme was a set-up, exposing him as the fake he was.

Watching my father quite literally rise from the dead in front of me and have his murky past raked up in front of millions was too shocking for words.

After the *Newsnight* fiasco Sessarego disappeared. Until 2008, when a badly decomposed body thought to be his turned up in a garage lock-up in Antwerp. Antwerp, apparently, is the mercenary-recruitment and diamond-smuggling centre of the world. The body had been there a long time. Death from gas poisoning was suspected. Other mercenaries claimed this was exactly the kind of death an assassin would stage to ensure it was declared an accident, while Sessarego's family pointed out he had faked his own death before. His daughter Claire, who never had the satisfaction of confronting her father, who must live with a circling outrage in her head, and who was forced to digest her dad's reincarnation in the guise of Tom Carew, called him a 'twat'.

2

As we grow older and Dad grows younger it is only logical he doesn't recognise us as his children any more. Dad wants to live with me (which Nicky thinks is funny); sleep with his dogs in the shed he always sleeps in when he comes to stay; and wander about in the garden in the sun, fixing things. But I've seen first-hand what having Granddad living with us for all those years did to Mum and I do not rate my chances. Nor could Nicky look after him full-time either, because it is relentless, and mad, and because he is always ranging about the place precariously tying things up, mixing up dog food with Rice Krispies, cutting the cuffs off his shirt or the tongues out of his shoes. Dad's contrail is all destruction, even when he just walks along he is up to no good, head down, hands busy . . . snip, snip, snip. He leaves the front door open, the blow heaters on, the gas hob blazing. Every day it is getting more and more difficult, and more and more stressful.

It doesn't help that Nicky and I have very different ideas about how best to look after him. I want more company for him, to keep him occupied, she wants to give him freedom and let him do what he likes. We are both right in our own ways, but it has begun to result in terrible rows and family divisions. What we do all agree on is that it is time to find a live-in carer . . . If

501

anyone who can manage him exists. Nicky places an advertisement in the *Lady*:

Situations Vacant — Domestic

Carer/Companion, Battle, Sussex, required for fun-loving widower with mid-stage dementia. Good sense of humour and patience advantage, experience with dementia preferred. Duties: caring, cooking, creating fun environment, and some dog walking.

Which is how we find Patricia, who is Irish which is a good thing, and straight-talking which is an excellent thing, and for a while it really goes quite well. She has him painting and cutting out pictures and making things, but she is a strong personality and although Dad is lonely and wants company he doesn't like the intrusion, or being told what he *can't* do. And soon he is fed up to the back teeth with Patricia, and understandably there are times, quite a lot of times, when she is fed up to the back teeth with him.

So she goes and gets herself a puppy. A chihuahua puppy, called Smidgeon. It is a tiny, curious, almost hairless creature with pop-out eyes and wrinkled skin. Patricia carries him everywhere she goes in a little fleecy handbag especially made for the purpose, and she won't let him out of her sight. Not until Dad's two psycho-dogs have got used to him. Smidgeon has all the accessories: a powder-blue lead; a little collar to match with tiny silver studs; and a barrowload of toys. And Dad loves him. And

502

plays with him. And Ooohs and Aaahs all over him. Leads him all around the house, this little dog-thing on its bouncy tiptoes at the end of its thin blue lead. Smidgeon has given both Dad and Patricia a new lease of life. And although both my sister and I rolled our eyes at the thought of a chihuahua in the house, we have been proved wrong. Now with Smidgeon being the centre of attention (instead of Dad), he and Patricia don't fight as much. Smidgeon is a hit with everybody and peace reigns.

Until Boxing Day . . . Jonathan and I have just got home after the three-hour drive from Battle having spent Christmas with Dad. There are twelve messages blinking on the answer-machine. The telephone begins to ring the moment we walk in the door. It's my brother, Tim, ringing from Yorkshire.

'Thank God I've got you,' he gasps, not Happy Christmas or anything.

'Why? What?'

'Oh, disaster!'

'What???'

'Dad's dogs have killed Smidgeon!'

'WHAT???'

'Dad's dogs have killed Smidgeon!'

'No!!! They can't have.'

'YES!!! They have!'

'But we've just come from there.'

'Patricia's beside herself. Hysterical.'

It gets worse, much worse. Tim says Patricia is convinced it was Dad who killed the puppy.

'Why on earth?? That's impossible!'

Tim tells me how Patricia couldn't find

Smidgeon anywhere and was looking for him for hours. She thought Dad had left the front door open and Smidgeon had run out into the road, then she thought someone had stolen him, or that he was hiding, lost and scared. Patricia found some blood on the carpet, and faeces, but no sign of the puppy. She was distraught, she got everyone out searching for him, the neighbours, Marissa (Dad's cleaner), Marissa's husband, everyone was out looking, including Dad. They searched for hours. Then Patricia, looking for Smidgeon's lead, took her bag off the coat hook in the hallway. Tim takes a deep breath. Inside her bag was the dead chihuahua puppy, in bits.

'No!!!'

Tim goes through what he has been able to deduce from the whole garbled story. How Dad must have left the puppy in the sitting room with his two dogs when he went to answer the front door and then forgot about them. His psycho-dogs always go nuts at the sound of the doorbell, barking and whizzing round in circles. Smidgeon must have got in the way, there would have been a fight, and the chihuahua puppy wouldn't have stood a chance. Dad must have wandered back into the sitting room and found Smidgeon savaged and dead on the floor. Knowing Dad he would have tried to fix it, and the only way he could fix this was to remove the fact of it, make it disappear. So he cleared it all away, and the most logical (or comforting) thing for him to do with Smidgeon was to put him back into Patricia's bag. So he did. Then hung it back in the hallway with the coats, which was also logical as that was where it belonged.

I groan.

'And then he would have forgotten all about it,' Tim says.

'Oh God,' I groan again.

'Which is why,' Tim says, 'she thinks Dad killed him.'

'But he'd *never* do anything like that.'

'I know.'

'How is Dad?' I ask.

'Very quiet,' Tim says. 'No one can get anything out of him.'

I ring Patricia. She is still hysterical. She still thinks Dad killed the puppy. I get straight in the car and drive the three hours back to Battle.

And that was the beginning of the end of a live-in carer.

★ ★ ★

After the Smidgeon-killing incident we knew Patricia would leave and no one else could, or would, manage Dad. We were heading for meltdown and we didn't want to look it in the face. We let it drift and each time we tried to discuss it my sister and I ended up in a bitter fight. Meanwhile, every day a new calamity: Dad off in his pyjamas in the middle of the night, the hob left on, the tap running, the door wide open, dog food mixed with ice cream for dessert. Dad ranged around the house like a great beast searching for he-didn't-know-what. He was miserable, frustrated and confused.

The trouble between Nicky and me was that

our assessment of the situation did not coincide. It was a sister thing, a stress thing, an over-sensitised thing, a family history thing; where she thought I was interfering (which I was), and I felt my views were dismissed (. . .); and this grew and grew, until the resentment and arguing and accusations and point-scoring and jealousy and sibling rivalry ended up in a great big sibling spat. I've blocked out how we ever got over it, we just had to. We both wanted the best for Dad, and deep down we both knew we had to find somewhere.

There was one thing we could agree on: neither of us could countenance the idea of Dad without a dog. But perhaps he didn't have to have two of them. With fresh chihuahua blood on their lips they had become unmanageable; after all, they'd been allowed to do whatever they wanted and now they were like a small crazed pack. The task of separating Dad from his dogs felt impossible, physically, emotionally and morally, but split them up we must, and hope to God Dad wouldn't notice. Although we both preferred the larger one, Bryn, it seemed fairer to rehome him and let Dad keep Psycho Dog.

Miraculously — for I didn't believe such a place existed in all the land — I find Dunsfold, just half an hour's drive from Dad's house: a home for Alzheimer's and dementia patients, and they have a ground-floor room available which looks out across a large garden, AND THEY WILL TAKE PSYCHO DOG AS WELL. I don't mention the chihuahua. There are downsides, like not much activity going on, but there is a sense of freedom in the air, of nobody being bossed around or patronised, and the owner, Paul, assures me Dad would be allowed to do what he wants, and his dog would be free to come and go as he pleased. Really? I ask, disbelieving. Really, are you sure? The dog could be the house dog, Paul suggests. And somebody would feed him? For I couldn't imagine Dad would ever remember to feed him. Of course, Paul assures me; we would pay for the food, and whoever was on duty would feed the dog. And he could sleep in Dad's room in bed with him? I venture. Of course, why not? Paul says. I cannot believe it. I just cannot believe it. Kindness and understanding; I am close to tears.

Step 1: Find a home for Bryn. Nicky advertises and finds a local family who immediately fall for him. She doesn't mention the chihuahua. And Dad, with Psycho Dog still around, doesn't notice a thing. Another Irish miracle.

Step 2: We need to slowly make Dad familiar with his new home. This means taking him there for tea. Walking around the garden with the dog and getting them both used to the place. Setting up Dad's room with familiar things. Putting his pictures and photographs on the wall. A painting of a younger me is his mother, Dad tells me. There are photographs of all his family, the crazy paintings he made with Patricia, even Step-mother's embroidery is found a space; and slowly, slowly, Nicky, I and Patricia (who even in the shadow of Smidgeon's demise, finds space in her heart for Dad) bring in his clothes and put them in the wardrobe; and sometimes he lies on his bed and has a nap; and we get a peanut-feeder for the birds which we hang outside his window. For the next month we take him regularly to Dunsfold, leaving him there longer and longer.

As D-Day looms, Nicky and I find the deceit unbearable. The rule for such transitions, when the day finally comes, is to leave the new resident in the home for two whole weeks without any family (or friend) contact; two weeks to bond with the staff and their new surroundings, to transfer all their connections. Paul says if this is not strictly adhered to, if someone visits during those first two weeks, it will disrupt the whole process and make it very hard for Dad to settle.

By fire then. It is dear Nicky who drives Dad away from his home for the last time. Knowing he will never see it again, never shut his gate, never open his door, never walk to the bottom of the garden, never go in his bodger-shed, never sit in his conservatory, never call down the stairs. The treachery of it. The acting and pretending to be jolly so he won't suspect anything, so he won't get upset. He sits meekly in the front seat of her car in his smart jacket waiting to go out for tea. Unsuspecting.

It takes Nicky hours to drive home. She has to keep pulling over to stop, sobbing uncontrollably. She says it feels like the worst thing she has ever done.

No sooner is she home when the phone rings. Dad has escaped. So she has to drive back again. By the time she arrives Dad has been found half a mile down the road stopping the traffic. Nicky sits with him on his bed. He tells her, furtively casting his eyes towards the trees at the end of the garden, that the best plan is to wait until darkness, then go over the fence and find a teacher or priest to help them.

★   ★   ★

Two weeks are up and we are allowed to visit. Nicky goes first with Patricia. Then a couple of weeks later, Jonathan and I and our two dogs turn up in our camper van. 'Oh, hello,' Dad says, because as far as he can see we are acting like we know him. Not even our dogs, whom he's always loved, seem to ring any bells this time, but he is happy to play along so we all sit in the camper van brewing tea and eating chocolate biscuits contentedly. But there is someone looking for him, a voice shouting, 'Tom? Tom?' Dad has got a girlfriend: only the most attractive lady in the place.

3

Fare forward traveller.

Dad died in his ninetieth year on 16 February 2009. Two weeks before, Jonathan and I had taken him out for the day to the sea. On the way we'd stopped to buy him a new jumper and fleece. We walked along the seafront, me one side of him, Jonathan the other, linking an arm through each elbow crook, not quite carrying him along. It was slow progress in small steps with everyone passing us. And then he detached himself and peeled away across the shingle towards a small wooden boat. And there he stood, holding it for a long time. Him and the boat. Looking out to sea. *Between the hither and the farther shore.*

4

A few days after Dad's obituaries in *The Times* and the *Telegraph* appear, I receive a call from the *Telegraph's* obituaries editor, who has received a letter from a Mr David Goodchild. I gasp audibly, whispering back the name 'Goodchild', because Goodchild was the maiden name of Dad's first wife, Margot. He reads me out the letter over the phone. David Goodchild is Margot's younger brother. The editor asks if he can pass my number on.

The next day I answer the telephone to Margot's brother. He tells me he had tried to trace Dad a couple of times over the years, but failed. Now in his eighties, he lives in Paris; he is a lawyer, has a youthful voice, and a remarkable memory for facts. We talk for an hour and a half. Thomas (as David calls Dad) and Margot were childhood sweethearts, both at the Perse School in Cambridge, and married during the war. David remembers having dinner with Margot, Dad and his two Jedburgh teammates, 'a handsome and appealing Frenchman and an American radio operator', at Madame Prunier's in London, just before they were dropped behind enemy lines into France.

Madame Prunier's at no. 72 St James's Street, SW1, was the finest fish restaurant in London and one of the most fashionable places to eat in the first half of the twentieth century. Its famous

511

decor was inspired by Captain Nemo's submarine in Jules Verne's *Twenty Thousand Leagues Under the Sea*, the book that enraptured Simone Prunier as a child. Nemo (Latin for 'no one') hated the British Empire because of its conquest of India, and the *Nautilus* was the submarine he built on a deserted island to cruise the depths of the oceans to battle against oppression and imperialism . . . which was conveniently topical. Madame Prunier's was modelled on the Grand Salon of the *Nautilus* with opulent paintings, oriental sculpture, and collections of corals, pearls and marine wonders.

No expense spared then. A sort of *avant guerre* dinner. A big slap-up spree before you boys leap literally into the unknown. 'This way sir,' a waiter guides you to a round table for six beneath the vaulted ceiling's opulence of another era. You look around admiringly. It's a good choice. Robert Raincourt straightens his tie, he is French and feels proud; John Stoyka lopes down the aisle, spruced up, jaunty, half an eye out for a girl. And you, Dad, are beaming inside. At last you feel you are *somebody*. With everything ahead of you, and exactly where you want to be. And you have really splashed out: in celebration; or the possibility, unspoken still, of danger, that you might not return. *Carpe diem*. If you could have stretched the moment out you would have. There must have been high spirits that night and a good helping of bravado. Maybe you announce your engagement. 'To the happy couple!' 'Hear! hear!' Your disapproving parents — they certainly will not come to the wedding — are pushed to the back of your mind as you explain them away with a shrug, your mother's health ... Fear, love, death, an inch away, and you will keep it there. And everything charging along, heightened with the frisson of the *hush-hush*, the Special Forces, a *secret* operation. But fear is only momentary. Not you. It will never happen to you. You are indestructible.

'*Crabes diablés*,' you pronounce it perfectly, and everyone laughs. A clam bisque, a *potage*, a bouillabaisse, a poached sole, *les fruits de mer*, samphire all the way from Norfolk, maybe even frogs and snails. You have a Frenchman with you, remember. Raincourt (now only known by his alias) attends to the wine list: champagne, a Sauternes, a white burgundy, a young hock. You raise your glasses. '*Salut! Bonne chance.*' French scatters into the conversation, crumbs on the white tablecloth. Dapper young men in uniform toasting each other below a crystal chandelier. '*À Basil!*'

Within twenty-four hours the three of you, Colts in your pockets, poems in your heads, will jump through a hole in an American Liberator, and fall, wind rushing past your ears, through an inky French sky.

★　★　★

After the war David went to stay with Dad and Margot in Quetta, where Dad was stationed in 1946. David says they had horses and dogs, and he remembers Dad wearing corduroys and smoking a pipe. As he talks I recall the line in one of

513

the Indian newspaper cuttings that puzzled me as a child, though I never questioned it, taking for granted the 'wife' mentioned was Mum, and ignoring the 'ATS ack-ack gunner' bit. While Dad was blowing up railway lines in the Jura and running around the jungles of Burma, his young wife Margot was in doodlebug alley where the V-1 rockets were falling in London, in the Auxiliary Territorial Service.[1] Her job was reconnoitring enemy aircraft with spotter telescopes, rangefinders, sound-detectors and radar, and controlling the aim of anti-aircraft fire — although not pulling the trigger. At this time, it was still felt unacceptable for life-givers to be life-takers.

After our conversation, David Goodchild sends me some photographs. It is the first time I have seen a picture of Margot. On the back she had written, 'To darling Daddy, From Thomas, Margot and Ro'.

Dad did not get home from the war until June 1946. Which is when the Maggot entries appear in Granddad's diary. 11 June: *TC arr home. Did not let know own parents until 16th!!*; 20 June: *TC telephoned re rooms. His voice sound glum.* Dad and Margot visit Granddad and Maud but they don't stay: *All 4 acting to be nice. Glad when all over.* Granddad is suspicious of them being on the scrounge, and things do not improve. On 2 August he writes: *DC [Desmond] telephoned to TC. TC never wishes to see his*

---

[1] The forerunner of the British Women's Royal Army Corps. 'Ack-ack' is the slang for anti-aircraft fire.

514

MOTHER or SELF. TC so horrid to his mother. Dad's anger is short-lived, he is being posted to Quetta and he would never want to leave under a cloud. He writes to say he is coming to visit, that he will stay at home, and Margot at her grandmother's. It's hard to believe. The war finally over; Dad has been in the most dangerous situations conceivable; he has been away for more than a year and a half; yet he and his new wife are unwelcome. His behaviour sounds restrained to me. By the end of August 1946 Dad and Margot are sailing for Bombay.

Granddad's diary, 1946

28 August: *TC run off his feet with Margot orders. 8pm, TC telephoned from Southampton on DC's advice I bet.*

Margot and Dad live an army married life in Quetta with their horses and dogs. He never rode a horse when I was young and pony-mad myself, but here he is, in his dutiful letters home, riding all the time. Margot's horse, Flicker, costs them '£7.10 including saddle'. Dad encloses a photograph of Flicker, which (being Margot's) I can't imagine was enjoyed. Happy life in Quetta doesn't last long. By February 1947, Dad is posted without spouse to Palestine. Granddad puts it curtly: *Sunshine freezing. Letter from TC now for Palestine leaving his woman behind.* Dad will be separated from Margot, but not from Peter, his beloved dog and wedding present from Margot, who, after protracted negotiations, goes with him:

I had a hell of a fight to get Peter out with me . . . Since I've been here Peter has been a changed dog, he never leaves me for a second. If I have to go somewhere without him he kicks up a hell of a row and when I come back he won't stop making a fuss of me . . . I hope we never have to be parted as I love him very much, I certainly couldn't ask for a better companion. Margot is still in India waiting to come out . . . I have been trying to get across to Cyprus to lay on accommodation for her there, but I just can't get away.

When Peter is run over by a tank Dad is devastated. I cannot find it in his letters, but the pain of the memory of losing Peter sprang up on him in our garden one day, and left him in floods of tears. The dog had been running towards him; he saw it about to happen and there was nothing he could do.

Dad doesn't find accommodation and has to stay in Palestine until the end of the year, 'A couple of months at the outside and I'd be home. And will I be pleased, Oh boy! Oh boy!' What he doesn't know is that by now Margot is having an affair with Max Robertson, the sports commentator, and later host of BBC's *Going for a Song*. We sometimes watched *Going for a Song* (the equivalent of *Antiques Roadshow*); how strange it must have been for Dad seeing his ex-wife's suitor on the box. But as David Goodchild informs me, Max was married to someone else, and although he got divorced in 1947 it was not Margot he married, but Elizabeth Beresford, creator of *The Wombles*. How long Margot and Max's affair lasted, or exactly when it started I have no idea, but Dad might well have enjoyed a snort at Max Robertson's notorious gaffe during his commentary on a men's doubles match at Wimbledon in 1981. So impressed was he with the play of Peter Fleming and John McEnroe he asked his co-presenter on air, 'Who are they going to play in the final? Do we know yet?' To which his astonished colleague replied, 'This *is* the final!'

Granddad's diary, 1948
14 July: *the more one thinks of TC's life the more pity for the fool.*
15 July: *DC went see MARGOT awful state. DC wrote to TC re his wife.*
20 January [1949]: *Maggot telephoned asking whereabouts TC.*

I ask David what Margot was like. 'Bossy,' he says. I think she looks nice. He also says, 'Margot did not like Thomas's mother.' Which hardly surprises me, but it must have been quite a thing for David to have remembered all these years. He says Margot never married again. She died in a car accident near Guildford 'on the hog's-back' in 1974. I tell David that I remember Dad wept when he heard. He is silent. It touches him.

There was too much against them: the war, the army, enforced separation, youth, Granddad and Maud. In an earlier letter from Karachi Dad tries hard to build a bridge between his parents and his wife:

I've got a bungalow already allotted by the army so that when shipping space is available Margot can come out. I still love her very much and of all the things in the world that I would like best would be for you to ask her down for a weekend before she comes out. You've no idea how much it would mean to me as I do love you both a lot more than perhaps you think I do (in spite of being a bad letter-writter!!)

By 1950 their marriage is officially over. It is David who tells me that after the war Dad was eyed up by MI6, which now explains the curious detail of Dad going to Hull University. We knew he went to Hull, but not why and we never thought to ask. David says he was there to learn Polish with the intention that he become the 'military attaché' at the embassy in Warsaw — in other words, a spy. But somewhere along the line there was a plan-change and he studied Finnish.

There was huge Soviet pressure on the Finns after the Second World War. In February 1948 the communist takeover of Czechoslovakia stoked the fear that the Russians would not honour the peace agreement, and move to occupy Finland. So there was reason to be going to Finland — it was the beginning of the Cold War and British intelligence needed men on the ground close to the borders with Russia. Dad and others with similar experience were seen as an obvious choice. According to David, in 1950 Dad was sent to Helsinki under the guise of setting up an import-export office — trade channels with the West were a way of trying to preserve Finland's independence, so, a credible cover. The real reason was to unravel the mystery of the Italian nuclear physicist, Bruno Pontecorvo, who had just defected to Russia. Dad's job was to discover the safe route Pontecorvo had taken. David remembers Dad saying how all the British, Russian and American spies knew each other because they were always following each other around.

Hunt for Missing Atomic Scientist. The British intelligence service MI5 has been brought into the hunt for the missing atomic scientist Bruno Pontecorvo who has not been seen for about seven weeks. Professor Pontecorvo and his family arrived in Finland at the beginning of September but they have since disappeared. There is speculation the family may have gone to the Soviet Union.

It's hard to say how much spying Dad got up to in Finland; his letters are addressed 'On the move', or simply 'British Attaché', with never a word about his work. He does, however, mention Finnish lessons with a twenty-eight-year-old blonde schoolteacher, Finnish double glazing, and the Finns' fascinating drinking habits. As much as Dad admires Finnish ingenuity, good sense and dignity, Finland is not for him. He misses hot-blooded people who 'fly off the handle' and get things off their chest. He returns to the UK for a course: 'Advanced Intelligence, it's called — I think that's an excellent name for a course — especially for the instructor'; after which he gets his new posting: the Intelligence Corps in Trieste.

5

There is one more surprise for us following Dad's obituaries. A letter from Raymond Bousfield. He is the husband of Barbara Hailstone, known as Babs. Babs. Who Granddad mentioned in his diaries, *Babs for tea, letter from Babs, Babs telephoned*, who even Granddad and Maud approved of, and who was Dad's first love. Now, seventy years later, we learn that Babs had kept her letters from Dad, with his photograph, all her life.

28th February 2009

To the Carew family,

I was very interested to read in *The Times* the other day the obituary of Thomas Carew. You too might be interested to hear that he was my wife's first love. This was not in the sense that word is normally understood, but more like a schoolgirl's infatuation, starting probably at one of those dances we used to go to when she was at Cheltenham Ladies College and he at Woolwich. I used to hear a lot about him in those days, indeed I sometimes was made to feel that he was her number one and I came a long way behind. And her memory of him clearly remained at the back of her mind for the rest of her life. But in her last months of illness when we were together Barbara never failed to say, with a little smile on her still-beautiful face, how much she loved me, so maybe after sixty-four years of marriage I didn't do so badly after all.

On looking through her papers after she died we found an envelope headed 'Desmond Carew'. Well, I remembered who that was and I enclose the photos and his engagement notice to Joan Suckling (your mother?) which were inside and I thought you might like to have. I only met him twice. The first time must have been 1946/7. We were then living in London after being demobbed from the Navy, she as Petty Officer Wren and I as Lieutenant RNVR. She arranged to meet this fellow for lunch at some restaurant. She was then vaguely aware that he had been doing dangerous work in the SOE but this was not the occasion for exchanging wartime experiences and we had a jolly little party and I found that Desmond was indeed a handsome and engaging companion and I could see what she had been on about.

Then there was a big time gap in our acquaintance. Three or four years ago she found that Desmond was living in Battle and she rang him up occasionally. I was never quite sure if he remembered who Barbara was. Then she suggested we go down to see him and maybe take him out to lunch at the pub. We found him with a lady who we gathered was his housekeeper and he was friendly and we had a nice chat but there was no question of a pub lunch. Again I was not sure if he really knew who we were. And we would never know why Barbara called him Desmond and he signed himself that name when he was really Tom. Perhaps you do?

There were a couple of affectionate letters, one dated 1943, I think from his mother's house in Cambridge, the other undated from Karachi must have been just after the end of the war. These are interesting and if you would like to have them I will send them on.

Yours sincerely, Raymond

It is a curious letter; Raymond encloses a photograph of young Dad looking dapper in trilby and coat walking up the street with a girl in a hat.

The photograph is very definitely Tom and not Desmond. It is a duplicate of the same photograph we found amongst Dad's things. They each had kept a copy. On the back of Dad's: 'Tom Carew & Barbara Hailstone (his first love) niece of Bernard Hailstone, Portrait Painter.'[1] But the confusion over the name with that of his brother Desmond, neither Nicky nor I can work out. No theory follows through. It is an impossible thing to get mixed up unintentionally, so we assume it to be some kind of smokescreen, or alibi, or cover-up, but we can make no sense of it. We respond to Raymond eagerly in anticipation of the promised letters to shed some light on the

---

[1] Bernard Hailstone was a royal portrait painter, and in 1974 was a guest on Roy Plomley's *Desert Island Discs*.

mystery. But when the letters from Dad to Babs arrive a few days later, with another photograph, they completely floor us. Raymond's accompanying note remarks, 'It is very odd that he was always Desmond with Bar, whereas he was really Tom, and Desmond was his brother. There must be a story behind this?'

There must be . . . The second photograph Raymond sends is Dad on a horse.

On the back Babs has written, 'Desmond, Cambridge 1939'. The two letters Raymond has sent are unmistakeably in Dad's hand. Affectionate and nostalgic, both incontrovertibly signed 'Desmond'. Desmond's writing could not be further from Dad's, far smaller with fat inky letters that bunch together, and Greek Es and fancy flourishing capital Fs — so there could be no confusion between them. The earlier letter, written in 1943, refers to the first photograph of Dad and Babs in London, not yet twenty years old.

Howes Place, Cambridge
4.3.43

My Dear Babs

I'm sending this photo on to you — I have two of them. Do you remember — London 1938. I was shooting an awful line then. I was a proud man that day. The proudest in London. I have just been searching my kit and have found some photos of you and Christine in Folkestone — 2 of you at Cheltenham. They bring back lots of memories. The more I see of them the more determined I am to come and see you. If I come and see you one weekend I can travel overnight (Friday night) see you Saturday and Sunday and then travel back Monday. OK I can't promise when as I have not the slightest idea what I am doing from hour to hour . . . Have you still got the fringe that you have in the photo. At least your hair cannot change — that always had me stone cold. You don't know how hard it used to hit me. You always knew what colours to wear with it too. I'm telling you how fine you looked and everyone is trying to clear me off the table for supper. I should not accede to them but they are too many for me.

     Bye bye, Desmond
PS It's the same umbrella

The second letter is from Karachi written just after the war, Dad is twenty-six, he has been married to Margot barely a year, and is tired of wandering. Although he mentions his wife, who will soon be joining him, he is still going on about Babs's hair:

If ever you are stationed near some gunners see if I'm around. I shall certainly look out for you in any naval station. I wonder if you've changed much physically you must have — you couldn't still be the lanky schoolgirl I knew. I hope your hair is still the same. It was always very lovely. Give my regards to your sister and your father

— how is Christine? I wish you all the best in the world Babs,

love Desmond.

PS I'm back to Major now the war is over and back in the real army after 2½ years as ½ guerrilla and ½ agent, and I find the army the most difficult of them all.

It appears Granddad did his level best to keep Babs firmly in the picture. Here is what Dad wrote home from Gibraltar, 1942:

I have just this minute had a letter from Babs — she tells me that you had sent her a photo of me some time ago — it is the first time I have heard from her for ages and I don't think I have written for a long time — 9 months or more — I always liked her very much but I'm afraid I saw so little of her that I slowly gave it up. I think I shall write to her again. I always had a good time whenever I went to see her family — they thought I was the 'cat's whiskers' and very clever — nobody has disillusioned them yet and I am not going to. I used to like her family very much as they being artists never had any money and had no 'side' and were very natural . . .

I flick back through Granddad's diaries. August 1939: *TC out with Babs Hailstone red hair; Babs for tea; Babs telephone re TC*; then gradually the disparaging comments about Margot begin. On 15 February 1943: *Babs* telephoned re TC seems sad about TC. By the end of 1943 when Dad is home on short leave it is Margot who is definitely on the scene: *TC out with awful M; TC out all night with bitch; TC out all day with woman looks worn out & old; TC left for town with the awful gang.* But then, on Christmas Eve 1950, and the eve of Dad's divorce, Granddad's diary records: *a telephone call from Babs to TC (8.15 p.m.!).* I am not sure if Granddad has nothing else to record, or if it is telling that he should mention it.

Babs being such a feature in the Carew household in Cambridge in the early war years makes Dad's name-swapping game even more perplexing. She was never a secret from his parents, nor he from hers, and they would never have gone along with calling him Desmond. Nicky and I go through every ramification. Something he started off and couldn't back out of? A code between them? Something to do with Margot? It confounds us. I can hear Dad's laugh ringing in my ears as he decides *not* to tell us the reason. By the time Dad is writing to Babs from Karachi she is also married. And happily to Raymond.

Babs Bousfield née Hailstrom and Dad died within a month of each other. Whatever else this is, it is the thin thread of love that has stretched without breaking across more than seventy years.

★   ★   ★

It is a glorious day at the end of summer. We are in your garden. I have just finished filling your bird-feeders. You are sitting in the new sunlounger I've bought you, on the patio in front of your conservatory. You are luxuriating in the sun's rays. I plump up a cushion and slip it down behind your head. I crouch down, my face beside your face.

'Are you comfy Dad?'

You say nothing.

You just smile and lean your cheek against my kiss.

Granddad's diary, 1970

4 January: *7 p.m. Went and had Arthur's curry supper with the family and what a good one it was, and all so happy.*

Afterwords

I began this book in the present but must finish it in the past. I became submerged in my search to discover who Dad was; what happened. I described it to friends using the analogy of two trains drawing out of the station, going in different directions; as Dad was losing his past with his dementia, I was trying to retrieve it. It took its toll. No man is an island, and it has been a long, and sometimes harrowing, swim through many archipelagoes, for me. 'Thomas was the kind of man you could talk to, really talk to,' Inga Miller said, but that wasn't always the case with his family.

Since Dad died he had been in a Barry's Irish Tea caddy on a shelf in my shed, because I could not bring myself to scatter him away. I didn't think he would like it much, out there in the flower beds on his own. The indisputably constant thing about Dad was his compulsion to dissent from prevailing orthodoxies. Which might help explain the last episode of his story . . . In December 2010, I opened a pop-up shop in Redchurch Street, in the East End of London, for the month. I called it, 'theworldthewayiwantit', and described it as an unconventional shop in reaction to the monotony of the high street; everything would tell a story, I promised. Among the owl-pellet kits and the jam-jar worlds I'd made, on his own table, I gathered together a small homage to Dad. In a tasteful natural box entitled 'Real Spy' was a stapled booklet of extracts from this book (which I had begun to write), his favourite motto about luck, a folio of the 1945 Indian newspaper facsimiles reporting his exploits as 'Lawrence of Burma', the citations for his Croix de Guerre and DSO. His Burmese *Kukri* knife was on the table. His SOE compass. His binoculars in their leather army case. His medals. A kind of reliquary. And under my desk the Barry's tin. At the very least I thought he would appreciate the attention.

One customer to the shop was Nik. He bought the knitted security camera, and in order that I could keep it on display suggested he collect it in January when he returned from his holiday. Naturally I asked where he was going. Burma, he said.

Well, 'Luck comes to the prepared mind', and Nik walking into the shop that day shows how good a motto can be, because it was Dad's luck, and ours, that Nik agreed to take Dad to Burma with him, and scatter his ashes there. 'How often do you walk into a shop, and walk out taking the proprietor's dead dad on holiday with you?' read the shop's blog that night. My brother Patrick arrived the day Nik came to collect Dad, and began to worry how he might fare through Burmese customs carrying the grey powdery ash. An arrest might be good publicity for a shop, but an execution would ruin the holiday, so after Nik thought about it he decided to mix Dad up with a packet of tea.

Nik scattered Dad at Bagan, the ancient city of

temples in the centre of Burma that spreads across an area of sixteen square miles.

It is a beguilingly beautiful place. I don't know if Dad ever went there, but it is very likely he did. In the photographs Nik gave us, you can see the spires, domes, and stepped pyramids of eleventh-century Buddhist temples rise above the treetops through the mist of early morning. I love the picture of Nik with Dad in the packet of tea. He had carried him lovingly all those miles, singing about Major Tom from David Bowie's 'Space Oddity', and after the long journey he told us he had become quite attached. I see Nik is wearing a Burmese sarong, the garment Dad loved and wore all his life.

Glossary

TERMS

ADF — Arakan Defence Force.

AFO — Anti-Fascist Organisation (umbrella organisation for all factions of Burmese resistance against the Japanese).

AFPFL — Anti-Fascist People's Freedom League (formerly AFO).

BDA — Burma Defence Army (Aung San's army during Japanese occupation).

BIA — Burma Independence Army (Aung San's army in 1942 during the Japanese invasion).

Black and Tans — former British servicemen enlisted as auxiliaries to reinforce the RIC.

BNA — Burma National Army (Aung San's army in uprising against Japanese).

CAS(B) — Civil Affairs Service (Burma).

CPB — Communist Party of Burma.

DMR — Délégués Militaires Régionaux. Regional military delegates nominated by the French in London in the national military command structure over the Resistance. DMRs were assigned to each region.

DZ — drop zone.

EMFFI — État-major des Forces Françaises de l'Intérieur — London headquarters of FFI.

FANY — First Aid Nursing Yeomanry.

FFI — Forces Françaises de l'Intérieur.

Force 136 — the arm of SOE in South East Asia.

F Section (SOE) — London-based staff running circuits of French-speaking SOE agents in German-occupied France as distinct from RF (République Française) Section of SOE supporting circuits run by Free French Gaullist staff.

ICS — Indian Civil Service.

IRA — Irish Republican Army.

Irish Free State troops — pro-treaty troops (Anglo-Irish Treaty, December 1921).

Jedburgh — SOE special unit of three-man teams (two officers and a wireless operator) trained at Milton Hall.

ME25 — code name for the Force 136 training camp in Ceylon at Horana.

ME65 — code name for Milton Hall.

NLD — National League for Democracy.

OSS — Office of Strategic Services, the American wartime intelligence agency and precursor to CIA.

PVO — People's Volunteer Organisation.

RC — reception committee.

RIC — Royal Irish Constabulary.

SAS — Special Air Service Brigade (forerunner of present SAS — Special Air Service).

SEAC — South East Asia Command.

SFHQ — Special Forces Headquarters.

SHAEF — Supreme Headquarters Allied Expeditionary Forces.

SOE — Special Operations Executive.

V Force — special force for reconnaissance and intelligence-gathering operating in Arakan and along the border between India and Burma after Japanese invasion (usually in small detachments of native-speakers).

NAMES

'**Albert**' — Alain Jean René Maze-Sencier le Comte de Brouville, also code-named Théodule.

Appleton, Rt Reverend George — Archbishop of Rangoon.

Aris, Michael — husband of Aung San Suu Kyi.

Attlee, Clement Richard — Labour Prime Minister from July 1945.

Aung San — commander of Burma National Army. Leader of the Burmese independence movement. Assassinated in 1947. Father of Aung San Suu Kyi.

Aung San Suu Kyi — daughter of Aung San; leader of the National League for Democracy.

Ba Maw — first Burmese premier under British rule in 1937. Head of the Japanese puppet government during occupation.

Battersby, Eric — former Burma Police. Dad's controller at Force 136 in India.

Chettle, George — CAS(B) Chief of Police until 1945.

Christison, Lieutenant General Sir Philip — commander of British Army XV Corps in Arakan.

Churchill, Winston — Prime Minister and Minister of Defence 1940–5.

Colby, William — American Jedburgh and later director of CIA 1973–6.

Cowan, Major General D. T. 'Punch' — division commander under Slim in Burma, commanding 17th Division.

Dorman-Smith, Sir Reginald — governor of Burma, in exile in India after Japanese occupation.

Eisenhower, General Dwight D. — commander of Allied Forces NW Europe. In 1952 elected president of the United States.

Gardiner, Lieutenant Colonel J. R. 'Ritchie' — head of Burma Section, Force 136.

Gaulle, General Charles de — leader of Free French Forces (soldiers outside France) and the French government in exile against the pro-German Vichy government.

Highsmith, Patricia — American author of *The Talented Mr Ripley*.

Joubert de la Ferté, Air Chief Marshal Sir Philip Bennet — Deputy Chief of Staff (Information and Civil Affairs) HQ SACSEA 1943–5.

Koenig, General Pierre — French commander-in-chief of the FFI.

Kra Hla Aung — commander of the Arakan Defence Force. Arakanese guerrilla and member of the AFO. Disciple of U Panyathiha.

Leese, Lieutenant General Sir Oliver — army commander of SEAC, subordinate to Mountbatten.

MacKenzie, Colin Hercules — head of Force 136 and SOE in South East Asia 1941–5 (a civilian appointment and former student of John Maynard Keynes at Cambridge).

Massoud, Ahmad Shah — Afghan mujahideen resistance commander, assassinated 9 September 2001.

Millar, George — SOE agent Émile in Besançon area (Chancellor circuit). Author of *Maquis*.

Mockler-Ferryman, Brigadier E. F. — director of operations, SOE, NW Europe 1944–5, joint commander of SFHQ.

Mountbatten, Vice Admiral Lord Louis — Supreme Allied Commander of SEAC, 1943–6.

Musgrave, Lieutenant Colonel G. R. — commanding officer of Jedburghs at Milton Hall.

Ne Win — BNA commander. Member of Japanese puppet government in 1943. Member of the AFO. Prime minister from 1958–60. Led a military coup in 1962 and became head of state. President of the Republic until 1981.

Noble, Ronnie — TV cameraman and war reporter.

Nu, U — Thakin leader, formed new government after Aung San's assassination. Prime Minister 1948–56, 1960–2.

Nyo Tun — alias Hla Maung (code name Galahad). Head of Thakin Party in Arakan. Arakan resistance leader. Member of the AFO. Minister for minorities in the 1948 government of Burma. Ambassador to Australia in 1970.

Panyathiha, U — Arakanese Buddhist monk, resistance guerrilla, political leader and member of the AFO.

Park, Daphne (Baroness Park of Monmouth) — cypher instructor at Milton Hall, latterly MI6 controller.

Pearce, Major General Charles Frederick Byrde — chief civil affairs officer, Burma: CCAO(B) 1943–5; then counsellor to governor and minister for defence, Burma, 1946.

Petain, Marshal — leader of the pro-German

Vichy government in France during German occupation.

Rance, Major General Sir Hubert — replacement for Pearce as head of CAS(B); later replacement for Dorman-Smith as governor in August 1946.

Rivière, Robert — alias Robert Raincourt. French officer in Jedburgh team Basil.

Robertson, Max — sports commentator, presenter of *Going for a Song*.

Rubinstein, Dick — fellow Jedburgh; leader of team Reindeer in Burma.

Saw, U — Burmese premier 1940–2. Arrested for having contact with Japanese and exiled to Uganda. Returned to Burma on orders of Dorman-Smith in 1946 as an opponent to Aung San. Tried and found guilty of involvement in the conspiracy to assassinate Aung San, and hanged in 1948.

Sessarego, Philip — author of *Jihad!*, under the name Tom Carew.

Sharp, John — Jedburgh; Dad's wireless operator in Burma (in Camel and Weasel).

Slim, General Sir William 'Bill' — commander of 14th Army in Burma (Field Marshal Viscount Slim).

Soe, Thakin — code name Arthur; leading Thakin and communist. Went underground during Japanese occupation. Split from Than Tun to lead separate communist party in 1946.

Stopford, Lieutenant General Sir Montagu — Commander of XXXIII Corps.

Stoyka, John — American radio operator in Jedburgh team Basil.

Taylor, Dr Robert — professor of Burmese studies.

Than Tun — leading Thakin and founding member of the AFO. Minister of agriculture and later minister of transport in Japanese puppet government. Aung San's brother-in-law. Leader of Communist Party of Burma, 1946. Killed in 1968.

Thein Pe (Myint) — code name Merlin; leading Thakin politician, writer and Burmese Marxist. Travelled to India in 1942 as Thakin envoy with Tin Shwe. Key liaison officer, planner and negotiator between Burmese resistance and Force 136. Author of *Wartime Traveler*.

Tin Shwe — code name Lancelot; Thein Pe's companion on journey to India as Thakin envoy in 1942. Force 136 officer in Burmese resistance and member of AFO.

Tun/Tha Gyaw — member of the AFO. Burmese officer in team Weasel with Dad. Member of Aung San's PVO. Later supporter of Aung San Suu Kyi.

Acknowledgements

Firstly, my deepest thanks to my husband, Jonathan Thomson, who has supported me with love, faith and (almost) endless patience, living with me and this book through thick and thin (quite a bit of thin). Who loved Dad and was so lovely with him.

I am extremely lucky to have a sister and two brothers, Nicky, Patrick and Tim, who without contemplating otherwise, allowed me the freedom to tell a story that so deeply touches their lives. I am grateful to them for raiding their memories and sharpening the details. And I thank Tim for his thoughtful and insightful editorial comments.

Thank you to Claire Paterson Conrad, whirlwind of an agent, for her unwavering belief, passion, energy, wise words, good counsel and terrific humour, and nearly poking my eye out. Thank you to my forensic editor, Becky Hardie, for her searchlight eyes, her steely calmness, her cleverness, kindness, tirelessness, confidence and patience, and being such a huge pleasure to work with. I am grateful to everyone at Chatto who fell in love with Dad. Particular thanks to Suzanne Dean who designed the Chatto & Windus cover, and Charlotte Humphery who helped so tremendously with permissions. I was lucky, again, to have the best copy-editor, in David Milner. Thanks also to Peter McAdie, my proofreader.

A huge thank you to Allison Malecha for her

helpful editorial comments, and Morgan Entrekin at Grove Atlantic who will be publishing *Dadland* in the US. Also to Emma Parry at Janklow & Nesbit, US.

A special thank you to Patrick Harpur, great and diverse writer that he is (*The Savoy Truffle, Daimonic Reality*), for being blunt and rude enough to make me dump my first *Dadland* draft in the bin ('Cut'; 'Cut'; 'Oh, cut'; 'Gibberish!'; 'Eh?'; 'Is this a word?'; 'Oh dear'; 'Your tenses, as you know, tend to be bollocks!'), and subsequently, for his tolerance to periodic pestering, and making me laugh. (There is hope for us all.)

I am indebted to Robert Taylor, for opening up the Burmese side of Burma, for a very nice dinner and for his comments and corrections. To John Sharp, Dad's wireless operator, for hours of patience with my questions, and Ivy Sharp for cups of tea. Glyn Loosmore's manuscript *The Postscript*, on the Jedburghs in Burma, was invaluable. To Arthur Brown for his manuscript, *The Jedburghs*. And to all the Jeds I was privileged to meet at Milton Hall: Fred Bailey Harry Verlander, Dick Rubinstein, Tommy Macpherson, 'Trof' Trofimov, David Stern, Jack Grinham, Os Craster, William Crawshay Bob Kehoe, Ron Brierley Roger Leney, Jack Singlaub, Maurice Roe. It was wonderful to hear from Louise Stoyka White, John Stoyka's daughter, from the States. And to the Jeds I didn't meet, and on Dad's behalf, particularly to the memory of Tun Gyaw.

To Philippe comte de la Rochefoucauld for weeding the FFI memorial at Granges-Maillot at exactly the right moment, and for so kindly walking Jonathan and me to the drop zone where Basil landed seventy years ago. Merci pour votre gentilesse.

Thank you to Terence and Inga Miller, who shared their memories of Dad spanning eighty years back to their Perse schooldays. David Goodchild, for making contact, writing his fascinating letters and sending photographs of Dad and Margot. Raymond Bousfield, for writing so generously and openly to our family and returning Dad's letters to Babs.

My love and thanks to Katie Dicker, for remembering Dad buttering the bread all those years ago; and to Jane Howard and Nicky Dunn, childhood stalwart friends who all loved Dad; and the Dunn family and Mew family whose door was open when times were tough.

The search for a map designer for the Chatto & Windus edition was solved by looking in the least obvious place, right under my nose, there he was: Dad's grandson, my nephew, Laurie; thank you. Thanks also to the artist Gill Horn for her moving photographs of Knowle Hospital in its dilapidation. And to Roy Wort for making me probably the best writing shed on the planet. To Jack McNeill and Charlie Heys for filling it with *Two Fine Days*.

Thank you to the free-spirited Nik Shah, who walked into my pop-up shop and happily agreed to take Dad back to Burma. To Genevieve Clouisot, for knitting the security camera that lured Nik into the shop in the first place. And to Cornelia Parker who took Dad to Buckingham Palace.

To James Holland for his time, expertise and encouragement, corrections, insight and riveting explanations. To Patrick Walsh, for regular interrogation and general hilarity (whose mother, it turns out, was taught Spanish in Venezuela by the spy Garbo, Juan Pujol). To Michael Tillotson for help and suggestions. Also thanks to Hla Oo, Dr Peter Caddick-Adams, Mike Healy, and Harry Dixon at BETFOR.

Neil Belton put Maurice Walsh's *Bitter Freedom* into my hands, and gave me some helpful pointers. Arabella Pike, generous in her words and good advice. To Colin Beavan for his excellent *Operation Jedburgh*.

For kindnesses to Dad, I particularly want to thank Patricia McNamara for looking after him at the most difficult time; to Marissa Padilla; and Paul Hughes at Dunsfold for his great humanity and understanding.

There have been many on this long journey who have made a difference, wittingly and unwittingly: Michele Leggott from Auckland University, and Katharine Weber. Thanks also to Helen Williams, Ian Wilks, Lindsay Brown, Johnny Chute, Clive Bassett, Liz Verlander, Sophie Coste-Mignot, David King, Linda Coggin, Adrian Brewer and Simon Butler. And thank you, Paris Zaki Badawi.

Oh, and a handsome reward for anyone who knows the whereabouts of Dad's grandfather's stolen tiepin.

Back full circle to family, to Sarah Carew and Lekiddo Arbuah, always brilliant with Dad. For family photographs and the many that came from Mum, I thank all. At the end of the line,

Laurie, Jojo, Imogen and Flora, who now can know who their grandfather was.

And of course, to the irreplaceable, irrepressible person without whom it could not have been written, and who has been sitting on my shoulder every day. Any mistakes, I blame Dad entirely.

We do hope that you have enjoyed reading this large print book.

Did you know that all of our titles are available for purchase?

We publish a wide range of high quality large print books including:
Romances, Mysteries, Classics
General Fiction
Non Fiction and Westerns

Special interest titles available in large print are:
The Little Oxford Dictionary
Music Book
Song Book
Hymn Book
Service Book

Also available from us courtesy of Oxford University Press:
Young Readers' Dictionary
(large print edition)
Young Readers' Thesaurus
(large print edition)

For further information or a free brochure, please contact us at:
Ulverscroft Large Print Books Ltd.,
The Green, Bradgate Road, Anstey,
Leicester, LE7 7FU, England.
Tel: (00 44) **0116 236 4325**
Fax: (00 44) **0116 234 0205**

Other titles published by Ulverscroft:

THE DAY THAT WENT MISSING

Richard Beard

On a family summer holiday in Cornwall in 1978, Nicholas and his brother Richard are jumping in the waves. Suddenly, Nicholas is out of his depth, and drowns. Richard and his older brothers don't attend the funeral; incredibly, the family return immediately to the same cottage to complete the holiday. They soon stop speaking of the catastrophe, and Nicky is written out of the family memory. Nearly forty years later, Richard Beard is haunted by the missing grief of his childhood, but doesn't know the date of the accident or the name of the beach. So he sets out on a painstaking investigation to rebuild Nicky's life, and ultimately to recreate the precise events on the day of the accident. Who was Nicky? Why did the family react as they did? And what actually happened?

HORSES, HEIFERS AND HAIRY PIGS

Julian Norton

The star of a television programme about his life as a Yorkshire vet, Julian Norton works at the relocated practice in Thirsk made famous by James Herriot in his *All Creatures Great and Small* books. From his childhood love of animals, through his training and first steps in the profession and the pressures and challenges faced by vets (such as BSE in the 1990s and foot-and-mouth in 2001), and dealing with unexpected exotic pets — and excitable humans too — Julian has seen all sides of the veterinary world. Just as happy calving a cow, treating a dehydrated kitten or tending to a horse trapped in barbed wire, Julian's tales bring to life the world of the working vet and the highs and lows he and his colleagues face on a daily basis.